Perspectives and Implications for the Development of Information Infrastructures

Panos Constantinides
Frederick University, Republic of Cyprus

Information Science
REFERENCE

Managing Director:	Lindsay Johnston
Senior Editorial Director:	Heather A. Probst
Book Production Manager:	Sean Woznicki
Development Manager:	Joel Gamon
Development Editor:	Hannah Abelbeck
Acquisitions Editor:	Erika Gallagher
Cover Design:	Nick Newcomer

Published in the United States of America by
Information Science Reference (an imprint of IGI Global)
701 E. Chocolate Avenue
Hershey PA 17033
Tel: 717-533-8845
Fax: 717-533-8661
E-mail: cust@igi-global.com
Web site: http://www.igi-global.com

Library of Congress Cataloging-in-Publication Data

Constantinides, Panos.
  Perspectives and implications for the development of information infrastructures / by Panos Constantinides.
     p. cm.
  Includes bibliographical references and index.
  Summary: "This book offers fresh new perspectives on information infrastructure development, using and adapting theory that was initially developed to study natural resource common arrangements such as inshore fisheries, forests, irrigation systems, and pastures particularly reviewing complex problems and social dilemmas that often arise in information infrastructures"--Provided by publisher.
  ISBN 978-1-4666-1622-6 (hardcover) -- ISBN 978-1-4666-1623-3 (ebook) -- ISBN 978-1-4666-1624-0 (print & perpetual access) 1. Information technology. 2. Information networks. 3. Information superhighway. I. Title.
  T58.5.C667 2012
  384.3'2--dc23
                        2012003664

British Cataloguing in Publication Data
A Cataloguing in Publication record for this book is available from the British Library.

All work contributed to this book is new, previously-unpublished material. The views expressed in this book are those of the authors, but not necessarily of the publisher.

Table of Contents

Section 2
Case Studies

Section 3
Further Research

Foreword

In the early 1990s, the Clinton-Gore administration in the U.S. famously galvanized a political vision around the concept of information infrastructure (II) as an electronic superhighway. At that time, the IS field recognized the importance of investments in IT infrastructure to support strategic alignment to achieve the firm's objectives and goals. My own work (Barrett & Walsham, 1999) explored the emergence and development of global electronic trading infrastructures and highlighted challenges of social transformation of traditional financial markets associated with their implementation. This work emphasized the importance of time-space relations and risk in processes of modernization (Giddens, 1990, 1991) as central to understanding the implementation of large scale information infrastructure. Hanseth et al (2006) drew on related theories of the risk society and reflexive modernization to challenge notions of control and strategic alignment associated with the development of information infrastructures and instead called for a different language of drift and cultivation (Ciborra et.al., 2001).

Over the last decade, the explosion in the development of numerous types of information infrastructure has frequently made news headlines globally achieving notoriety for their mismanagement and ethical implications. The UK government, well known for privatizing public infrastructures in the 1980s and almost splintering a nation, has been heavily criticized throughout the 2000s for its largely unsuccessful development of a new national health information infrastructure using public-private partnerships. Further developments of global information infrastructures such as the Internet and its many Web 2.0 innovations (e.g. Facebook) raise a number of privacy and security concerns. But, perhaps most dramatically the WikiLeaks information infrastructure, which has been called 'the 9/11 of diplomacy,' raises the biggest stakes and key ethical issues for users and governments alike.

This relatively recent shift in scope and criticality of the information infrastructure landscape requires new and fresh theorizing. In this book, Constantinides adds important new insights which shift our understanding to another level in this fast changing field. He highlights three modes of production, namely state or centralized control toward an integrated infrastructural ideal, private or decentralized involvement; and community-led network-based governance of infrastructures. Following a critical review of traditional and sociotechnical theories of infrastructure development, Constantinides makes the case for a collective action approach. He builds on a commons approach to information infrastructure, put forward by Nobel Laureate Elenor Ostrom who, over the last couple of decades, has successfully applied the theory to natural resource and knowledge-based commons (Ostrom & Hess, 2007). Constantinides carefully applies the commons framework with its focus on the multilevel context, action arena, and outcomes to illuminate our understanding of a regional health II in Greece and the national health II in the UK. A particular emphasis is on the property rights negotiated between key stakeholder groups, as they strive to develop an information infrastructure, and the consequences of the outcomes of these negotiations for Greece and the UK.

While significant in contribution, this is just the first half of the book. Constantinides goes on to tackle the messiness of IT governance, which has largely eluded us as theorists and practitioners but remains of critical importance. Inspired by the commons theory, he proposes a set of general governance principles in an effort to distribute decision-making, monitoring and sanctioning, and conflict resolution across all stakeholders involved with the infrastructure. Constantinides argues that such polycentric governance can only be achieved by building horizontal and vertical linkages across all stakeholders and facilitating multilevel learning processes. In the later chapters, Constantinides widens his scope of examination to what he terms new information infrastructures on the Internet. These online horizontal Web 2.0 networks (e.g. Facebook, FOSS, Mashups) have become a fundamental dimension of everyday life built around user-driven initiatives to participate in processes of social production. Appropriately, he draws on legal and political science scholars such as Benkler (2006) and Lessig (2010) in theorizing their development. Additionally, he draws on Foucault's classic ideas on governmentality in examining ethical issues surrounding information infrastructure such as WikiLeaks, which has consequences for the freedom of individual users.

In concluding the book, Constantinides follows up on this ethical vein by challenging us as researchers of new information infrastructures to adopt a more pragmatic approach (Constantinides et al., 2012). He argues that we should consider much more the consequences and scope of our research choices, and challenges us to reflect on desirable outcomes and long-term impact of our research.

Clearly, this book by Panos Constantinides is timely and of great importance to researchers and practitioners in contemporary economies and societies. It is comprehensive in addressing the wide scope of development of information infrastructures and thoughtfully considers their consequences for individuals, organizations, and governments in the 21st century. Students of multiple disciplines including information systems and philosophy of technology will find this book relevant to their studies at the undergraduate and graduate levels. I have studied the introduction of large scale information infrastructures over the last two decades and have been impressed with the insight and coverage of the issues addressed in this book. The challenges we continue to face in understanding the development and implementation of information infrastructures suggests the ongoing need for scholarship in this area. This book takes an important step in this journey.

Michael Barrett
Professor of Information Systems and Innovation Studies
Judge Business School
University of Cambridge

Michael Barrett *is Professor of Information Systems and Innovation Studies at the Judge Business School, University of Cambridge. He is Co-Editor of a Special Issue of MIS Quarterly on Service Innovation in the Digital Age, Senior Editor of Information & Organization, and Senior Editor of the Journal of the Association of Information Systems. Michael has served as an Associate Editor of MIS Quarterly, Information Systems Research and is a member of the Editorial Board of Organization Science. His research interests include the role of ICT's and knowledge in processes of service innovation in healthcare and financial services across developed and developing economies.*

REFERENCES

Barrett, M., & Walsham, G. (1999). Electronic trading and work transformation in the London Insurance Market. *Information Systems Research, 10*(1), 1–22. doi:10.1287/isre.10.1.1

Benkler, Y. (2006). *The wealth of networks: How social production transforms markets and freedom.* New Haven, CT: Yale University Press.

Ciborra, C. U. (Ed.), & associates. (2001). *From control to drift: The dynamics of corporate information infrastructures.* Oxford, UK: Oxford University Press.

Constantinides, P., Chiasson, M., & Introna, L. (2012). The ends of information systems (IS) research. *Management Information Systems Quarterly, 36*(1), 1–19.

Giddens, A. (1990). *The consequences of modernity.* Cambridge, UK: Polity.

Giddens, A. (1991). *Modernity and self-identity: Self and society in the late modern age.* Cambridge, UK: Polity.

Hanseth, O., Jacucci, E., Grisot, M., & Aanestad, M. (2006). Reflexive standardization: Side effects and complexity in standard making. *Management Information Systems Quarterly, 30,* 563–581.

Lessig, L. (2008). *Remix: Making art and commerce in the hybrid economy.* London, UK: The Penguin Press. doi:10.5040/9781849662505

Ostrom, E., & Hess, C. (2007). A framework for analyzing the knowledge commons . In Hess, C., & Ostrom, E. (Eds.), *Understanding knowledge as a commons: From theory to practice* (pp. 41–81). Cambridge, MA: MIT Press.

Preface

THE NEED FOR A BOOK ON INFORMATION INFRASTRUCTURE DEVELOPMENT

In the same way that infrastructures such as transportation, electricity, sewerage, and water supply are widely assumed to be integrators of urban spaces (Graham & Marvin, 2001), information infrastructures such as national health information networks and online social networks are assumed to be integrators of information spaces.

Interest in information infrastructure development grew with the advent of the Internet and the popularization of computing technologies (Gross, 1986), and was later further promoted through government-led plans towards the creation of national and international information infrastructures (NTIA, 1993; Bangemann et al., 1994).

Information infrastructures have since been conceptualized as pyramidal IT portfolios towards better investments for strategic business-IT alignment (Weill & Broadbent, 1998), open, heterogeneous information systems (Hanseth, 2001), or as ecologies of distributed and often conflicting social and technological systems (Bowker & Star, 1999). Despite this variation of perspectives, most researchers tend to agree that an information infrastructure emerges in time through negotiations between diverse groups and individuals directly involved in its development.

These negotiation processes have been called "the deal-making processes" between stronger and weaker stakeholder groups (Weill & Broadbent, 1998), "involved socio-technical negotiations" (Monteiro, 2001), and "practical politics" (Bowker & Star, 1999). Recent research (Sahay et al., 2009) has highlighted the different sets of actors (both small and large) whose negotiations are significant to understand the how and why of configuring information infrastructures–i.e. their ability to adapt, interconnect, co-evolve, and integrate. In this research, it is argued that actors have little choice but to align their new information systems with the existing institutions' agendas, practices, and routines (also see Braa et al., 2004; Chilundo & Aanestad, 2005).

Despite these developments concerning the importance of negotiations in the development of information infrastructures, it has been argued that further work is needed to better understand "why and how negotiations occur" (Sahay et al., 2009, pp.402). In particular, there is a need to understand how contradictions and contestations around the development of an information infrastructure actually become negotiated.

This need is particularly evident now with the advent of Web 2.0 and new types of information infrastructures, from online social networks such as Facebook, Flickr, and Second Life, to free and open source software (FOSS) development platforms, and blogs, wikis (e.g. WikiLeaks), and smart mobile telephony development platforms (e.g. Android).

These new information infrastructures, like their more conventional predecessors (e.g. enterprise resource planning systems), necessitate a more in-depth understanding of the various rights to access, use, develop, and modify information infrastructure resources, but also of rights to regulate the former, and of rights to own parts of the information infrastructure itself. It is, thus, argued that efforts to understand how contradictions and contestations around the development of an information infrastructure actually become negotiated need to take into consideration the various rights that different stakeholders claim to have on the infrastructure.

This book aims at addressing this need by offering a fresh new perspective on information infrastructure development. It achieves this by drawing and adapting theory that was initially developed to study natural resource commons arrangements such as inshore fisheries, forests, irrigation systems, and pastures–while placing great emphasis on the complex problems and social dilemmas that often arise in the negotiations.

INSPIRATION & INTELLECTUAL ORIGINS

This book was initially inspired by studies in urban planning and infrastructure development toward the binding of scattered geographical time-spaces, while highlighting the complex socio-political and socio-technical entanglements involved (Coutard, 1999; Graham & Marvin, 2001; Hughes, 1983; Sassen, 2001).

In a highly cited book, Thomas Hughes (1983) described the processes of developing large electrical networks in the early 20th century, reflecting and making tangible the power and politics of the spaces within which technologies are developed, implemented, and used. Hughes argued that technology gains "momentum" both by becoming institutionalized in social values, and by the very affordances of its materiality–the possibilities of use it carries in its capabilities. In doing so, technologies "embody, reinforce, and enact social and political power" (Hecht & Allen, 2001, pp.3). Such historical studies of infrastructure later gave way to various sociotechnical approaches to understanding the evolution of large technological systems (Bijker, Hughes, & Pinch, 1987) and laid the foundations for an understanding of technology as "both socially constructed and society shaping" (Hughes, 1987, pp.51).

The field of science and technology studies (STS) has extensively explored the development of information infrastructures (Bowker, 1994; Bowker, Timmermans et al., 1995; Bowker & Star, 1999; Hanseth et al., 1996; Hanseth & Monteiro, 1997; Star, 1999; Star & Ruhleder, 1996). In this field, information infrastructures are thought to support work practices through a vast array of community services and resources (collaboratories and centers, data and code repositories, best practices and standards development, etc.). Two main issues are associated with the development of information infrastructures: first, the tension between efforts to keep the infrastructure open and shared vs. efforts to regulate their use by an expanding community of users (cf. Hanseth 2001; Star & Ruhleder, 1996)–i.e. in the sense of a public or quasi-public good (Bowker et al., 2010)–and second, the challenges involved in controlling the scalability of an information infrastructure vs. acknowledging the processes of "drift" and of unintended consequences (Ciborra, 2001; Hanseth et al., 2006; Sahay et al., 2009).

In seeking ways to better understand these two issues, it became clear that the development of information infrastructures was best approached as a problem of collective action. The term "collective action" refers to joint action by a number of individuals to achieve and distribute some gain through coordination or cooperation (Hardin, 1982). Research in the development of information infrastructures is overflowing with such collective action problems including conflicts between richer and poorer business units engaged in a "deal making process," because of the mismatch between the costs and benefits of receiving different parts of the information infrastructure (Weill & Broadbent, 1998); as well as the politics of deciding the standards and classifications of work supported by an information infrastructure (Bowker & Star, 1999; Hanseth et al., 1996; Hanseth et al., 2006).

Research into collective action problems was initiated with Mancur Olson's (1965) now classic *Logic of Collective Action* and later popularized with Gareth Hardin's (1968) thesis on the "tragedy of the commons." A commons is a set of resources, which are collectively owned or shared between or among a community or a group of communities (Ostrom, 1990). The commons contains public and private property, over which different communities have certain rights (Ostrom, 1990). Potential collective action problems in the use, governance, and sustainability of a commons are thought to lead to social dilemmas such as free-riding and overconsumption (Baland & Platteau, 1996; Ostrom, 1990; Wade, 1994). In turn, recommendations are made where external authorities impose a different set of institutional rules and property rights to manage these dilemmas toward socially optimal actions for the sake of public interest. Some scholars recommend local-based, private property as the most efficient form of ownership, whereas others recommend centralized government ownership and control (see Hess & Ostrom, 2003 for an extensive discussion).

It is this need to define appropriate property rights toward socially optimal actions that eventually led researchers and policy makers to suggest an alternative form of commons development–an approach which could also be relevant and useful for the development of information infrastructures.

Over the last two decades, it has been argued that the logic of collective action is becoming more heterogeneous and multilayered, derived not from a single core structure such as the state, but from networked interdependencies across global markets (Castells, 2010). These networked interdependencies have reconfigured the traditional bureaucratic organization of collective action to a blended action model based on a network of communities of practice that draw on expert as well as local, experience-based knowledge (Snyder & Briggs, 2003; Ostrom, 1999). This shift in the logic of collective action points to processes of "empowered participatory governance"–that is, processes that devolve decision-making power across different stakeholders (Fung & Wright, 2003).

Perhaps the most interesting example of participative, empowered, collective action in recent years has been the open source software movement (Benkler, 2006). Free and open source software is an approach to software development, whereby many individuals contribute to a common project, with a variety of motivations, while sharing their respective contributions without a single person or entity asserting rights to exclude either from the contributed components or from the resulting whole. In order to avoid having the joint product appropriated by any single party, participants usually retain copyrights in their contribution, but license them to others on a model that combines a universal license to use the materials with licensing constraints that make it difficult, if not impossible, for any single contributor or third party to appropriate the project.

At the same time, however, the success of open source software, and other such social production examples, does not mean that collective action entails purely consensual or conflict-free action. Collective action benefits from divergent as well as convergent thinking. There is evidence, for example, that the proliferation of participatory approaches to managing infrastructures for water and other vital resources worldwide has led to many unstructured negotiations, misunderstandings about the meaning of consensus, and a fear of sharing power (Susskind & Hoben, 2004). Creating alternative (i.e. participatory, community-led) processes of infrastructure development that are not only popular, but by definition challenge the status quo in important ways is far more daunting a problem than advancing a particular policy position or winning approval for a particular project. Beyond the structural conflicts over the material properties of an infrastructure and its value, there is a classic "tragedy of the commons": there are varied experiences of the benefits and costs of the infrastructure because of the uneven use of the infrastructure by users of varied wealth, political power, location, and skills (Castells, 2010).

THE SCOPE OF THE BOOK

This book draws on the ideas discussed above to develop a commons perspective and theoretical framework for understanding the development of information infrastructures. It is argued that the commons perspective, with its emphasis on collective action problems as negotiated through different property rights, supports a more detailed analysis of why and how negotiations around information infrastructure development occur.

By placing greater attention to the dynamics of power and resistance in the development of information infrastructures, the commons perspective aims at yielding significant theoretical and practical insights into how attempts at control and regulation are always challenged by those who are subjected to control. Issues of agency, the mutually productive relationship between domination and resistance, and the creation of institutional arrangements can be understood only with greater attention to micro-politics (e.g. definition of property rights and governance structures). Such a shift in focus can also help address the criticism that scholars of information infrastructure development have, for the most part, ignored how users can shape attempts by outside agents such as the state or private companies to intervene into their work practices and modify existing patterns of infrastructure use (see Bowker & Star, 1999). The key point here is to analyze why and when different stakeholders respond in particular and differentiated ways to new strategies of institutionalized power by scrutinizing their historical structural locations and the extent to which they are already privileged or marginalized by new strategies of power.

The contribution of the commons perspective is illustrated in two empirical case studies. The first one focuses on the development of a regional health information infrastructure in Greece during the years 1997-2006. This case study was conducted in joint with Michael Barrett and involved empirical data collection over five field work phases (January 2003, July 2003, January 2004, September 2005, July 2006), each lasting between two and four weeks. During these field trips, a total of 65 interviews were conducted with senior management and engineers at CreteTech[1], the research and development institute behind the development of the infrastructure, healthcare professionals and administrators at nine primary healthcare centers and three hospitals, and senior officers at the Regional Health Authorities of Crete. During these fieldtrips, we also conducted observations of the use of different IT applications at various sites, while contrasting those observations to project reports and white papers in relation to key events in the project timeline. The second case study draws on a secondary analysis of publicly available data on the development of the English National Program for IT (NPfIT). Specifically, this case study draws on publicly available data presented before the Committee of Public Accounts (CPA) assigned to examine the progress made by the English Department of Health in implementing the NPfIT (HC, 2007a, 2007b, 2007c, 2009). The findings from these two case studies are compared and contrasted to findings from other such similar infrastructure projects in the USA, Canada, Australia, Norway, India, and developing countries.

In addition to these empirical case studies, the book provides illustrative examples of information infrastructure development through the commons perspective in other domains, including industry-wide airline reservation systems such as American Airlines SABRE, global FOSS development platforms, online social networks such as Flickr and Second Life, but also global investigative journalist networks such as WikiLeaks.

WHO WAS THIS BOOK WRITTEN FOR?

The discussion around the aforementioned case studies and illustrative examples offers both theoretical insights and practical recommendations for action. Thus, the book is relevant to researchers and policymakers alike.

Researchers will find the comprehensive review of the literature on information infrastructure development of great value (Chapters 1 and 2). They will also value the commons perspective as a fresh new theoretical approach to understanding the negotiations around information infrastructure development and, in particular, how claims to ownership become appropriated and with what implications for different stakeholders and the technology itself (Chapter 3). The book also identifies opportunities for further research, to which the commons perspective can be applied, and which researchers will find stimulating and worth pursuing (Chapters 8 and 9). Finally, researchers will find the questions posed in Chapter 10 around their role in information infrastructure research of great use and relevance, as they pursue new research opportunities.

Policymakers will also enjoy reading the discussion in Chapter 3 around the commons perspective, but they will value the discussions on the two case studies in Chapter 4 and 5 even more. The two case studies provide empirical evidence on the development of information infrastructures in actual practice. These discussions are followed by a synthesis of the key findings, outlining the successes, challenges, and failures observed in the two case studies, that policymakers will find of great value and relevance to their own practical settings (Chapter 6). Finally, Chapter 7 offers a comprehensive discussion of a set of principles for IT governance, derived from the commons perspective and the findings from the two case studies (with links to the information infrastructure literature), that policymakers could apply in other settings.

In addition to the two main readers listed above, this book could also be of use to instructors of undergraduate and postgraduate courses in IT strategy and governance, but also IT project management. Chapters 1 and 2 offer great introductory material to the study of information infrastructures or large-scale systems. Chapters 4 and 5 offer in-depth case material that could be used in class for discussing strategic lessons learned emerging from the two empirical settings. Finally, Chapters 6 and 7 offer material that could be used to explore principles of IT governance and project management.

ORGANIZATION OF THE BOOK

The book is organized into three sections and ten chapters. The book starts with a Section on Theory (Chapters 1-3), where the theory used in the book is explained in detail. This is followed by a Section with Case Studies (Chapters 4-7), where the theory is applied in empirical settings. Finally, the book concludes with a Section on Further Research (Chapters 8-10), where opportunities for further research using the theory and findings in the book are explored. A brief description of each of the chapters follows.

Chapter 1 provides a historical review of studies on infrastructure development and urban planning. This chapter is an introduction to the whole book, as it poses the key questions explored in the rest of chapters, including what is an infrastructure, how infrastructure development has been approached by government agencies and private companies and/or partnerships between the two, and what type of collective action problems have been most critical to infrastructure development.

Chapter 2 offers a critical review of the literature on information infrastructure by tracing the evolution of the concept of infrastructure into the concept of information infrastructure. The key objective is to describe in detail how different researchers have approached the concept from varied perspectives in their efforts to understand information infrastructure and its role in organizational transformation and practice. In particular, Chapter 2 organizes the literature according to two key broad perspectives, namely, the functionalist perspective, which seeks to develop management agendas towards increased strategic business-IT alignment, and the socio-technical perspective, which is not concerned with management prescriptions and more interested in the multilevel context of socio-technical processes of information infrastructure development. This organization of the literature aims at uncovering key themes in past and current research, while at the same time communicating the general positions of this book. Chapter 2 concludes with a summary of some key observations emerging from this critical literature review and identifies implications for the theoretical approach adopted in the rest of this book.

Drawing on the key themes emerging from the critical literature review on information infrastructure research presented in Chapter 2, Chapter 3 discusses a theoretical framework to differentiate and further clarify the nature and type of negotiations that take place between various stakeholders involved in the development of information infrastructures. In particular, Chapter 3 draws on empirical research into commons arrangements such as inshore fisheries, forests, irrigation systems, and pastures with particular emphasis on the complex problems and social dilemmas that often arise in the negotiations. This discussion helps to explain why it is relevant and useful to approach an information infrastructure from a commons perspective. Chapter 3 concludes by highlighting the contribution of a commons perspective to understanding the development of information infrastructures.

Chapters 4 and 5 draw on the theory discussed in Chapter 3, to discuss and analyze empirical data from two case studies, while also developing implications for further research. Specifically, Chapter 4 draws on empirical research carried out during the years 2003-2006 on the development of a regional health information infrastructure in Greece. The chapter starts by looking at the impact that European Information Society programmes have had on related initiatives in Greece and, in particular, the Greek national health sector. Subsequently, using the commons perspective discussed in Chapter 3, Chapter 4 examines the development of a regional health information infrastructure in Crete. Drawing on more recent evidence, the chapter concludes with an analysis of the consequences of the outcomes of the development of the health information infrastructure in Crete, for Greece, and more broadly, for European Information Society programmes.

Chapter 5 draws on publicly available data on the development of the English National Program for IT (NPfIT) during the years 1998-2010. The chapter starts by tracing the historical evolution of policies used to bring the NPfIT into existence by examining broader political discourses in the English national health system toward improving the provision of public sector healthcare services. Then, drawing on the commons perspective discussed in Chapter 3, the following section provides an analysis of publicly available data presented before the Committee of Public Accounts (CPA) assigned to examine the progress made by the English Department of Health in implementing the NPfIT. The chapter concludes with an analysis of the consequences of these negotiations for the English NPfIT and other such national information infrastructure projects.

Chapter 6 synthesizes the findings from the analysis of the two case studies. This synthesis leads to key theoretical implications while establishing stronger links between the literature on information infrastructures and traditional commons arrangements.

Chapter 7 uses the discussion in Chapter 6 as a springboard to explore a set of commons-based principles for governing information infrastructures. Drawing on Ostrom's (1990) original principles for commons arrangements, Chapter 7 discusses and analyzes alternative development strategies for the two case studies presented in Chapters 4 and 5 and analyzed in Chapter 6, by focusing on processes of empowered participation. These principles are also contrasted to current research on IT governance and more recent developments from commons studies. Chapter 7 concludes with implications for further research into IT governance through a commons perspective.

Chapters 8, 9, and 10 explore possibilities of applying the discussions in earlier chapters for further research on new information infrastructures. Specifically, Chapter 8 explores the particular attributes of new and emerging information infrastructures, and why it would be useful to approach those through a commons perspective. The discussion focuses on Free and Open Source Software (FOSS) projects, examining what makes individuals and communities contribute code and ideas towards a FOSS product, but also how they negotiate and eventually agree on a set of institutional rules for structuring their collective action. The chapter also examines the emerging attributes of mash-up projects and the ways that, once again, individuals and communities design and structure their contribution. Chapter 8 concludes with some implications for further research on and around these new information infrastructures.

Chapter 9 builds on parts of the discussion in Chapter 8 by exploring the challenge in governing the consequences of free-willed individual action against collective action and the sustainability of new information infrastructures. In particular, this chapter focuses on the consequences of allowing different users to freely choose–if indeed they are free, i.e. without any external influence–how to interact with others in the Web spaces offered by new information infrastructures. The WikiLeaks information infrastructure is used as an example to set the ground for examining how new information infrastructures generate a number of consequences for the freedom of individual users, and for those seeking to monitor and control infrastructure use. This discussion raises a number of ethical issues which are explored by drawing on Foucault's (1984, 1991) notion of governmentality. The chapter concludes with some implications for further research on the ethical governance of information infrastructure development.

Chapter 10 concludes the book with a critical reflection of the ethical role of researchers in understanding and acting on the consequences of new information infrastructures, as discussed in Chapter 9. Chapter 10 explores the role researchers can and should play in dealing with ethical and other issues emerging from research. In particular, the discussion draws on the notion of "phronesis"–the reflective development of prudent knowledge through ongoing action and reflection that is continuously shaped by and imbued with situated values and interests from a community of inquirers (Flyvbjerg, 2001, 2006). Chapter 10 concludes by proposing a set of practical recommendations that researchers could employ in conducting their own research on new information infrastructures.

Panos Constantinides
Frederick University, Republic of Cyprus

REFERENCES

Balland, J., & Platteau, J. (1996). *Halting degradation of natural resources: Is there a role for rural communities?* Oxford, UK: Clarendon.

Bangemann, M., da Fonseca, E. C., Davis, P., de Benedetti, C., Gyllenhamman, P., & Hunsel, L. ... von Pierer, H. (1994). *Europe and the global information society: recommendations for the European Council.* Brussels, Belgium: European Council.

Benkler, Y. (2006). *The wealth of networks.* New Haven, CT: Yale University Press.

Bijker, W. E., Hughes, T. P., & Pinch, T. (1987). *The social construction of technological systems.* Cambridge, MA: The MIT Press.

Bowker, G., & Star, S. L. (1999). *Sorting things out–Classification and its consequences.* Cambridge, MA: MIT Press.

Bowker, G. C. (1994). *Science on the run: Information management and industrial geophysics at Schlumberger, 1920-1940.* Cambridge, MA: MIT Press.

Bowker, G. C., Baker, K., Millerand, F., & Ribes, D. (2010). Towards information infrastructure studies: Ways of knowing in a networked environment In Hunsinger, J., Allen, M., & Klasrup, S. (Eds.), *International handbook of internet research* (pp. 97–117). New York, NY: Springer Science.

Bowker, G. C., Timmermans, S., & Star, S. L. (1995). Infrastructure and organizational transformation: Classifying nurses' work In Orlikowski, W., Walsham, G., Jones, M. R., & DeGross, J. I. (Eds.), *Information technology and changes in organizational work.* London, UK: Chapman and Hall.

Braa, J., Monteiro, E., & Sahay, S. (2004). Networks of action: Sustainable health information systems across developing countries. *Management Information Systems Quarterly, 28*(3), 337–362.

Castells, M. (2010). *The information age: Economy society and culture I: The rise of the network society* (2nd ed.). Hoboken, NJ: Wiley-Blackwell.

Chilundo, B., & Aanestad, M. (2005). Negotiating multiple rationalities in the process of integrating the information systems of disease-specific health programmes. *Electronic Journal of Information Systems in Developing Countries, 20*(2), 1–28.

Coutard, O. (Ed.). (1999). *The governance of large technical systems.* London, UK: Routledge.

Flyvbjerg, B. (2001). *Making social science matter: Why social inquiry fails and how it can succeed again* (Sampson, S., Trans.). Cambridge, UK: Cambridge University Press.

Flyvbjerg, B. (2006). Making organization research matter: Power, values, and phronesis In Clegg, S. R., Hardy, C., Lawrence, T. B., & Nord, W. R. (Eds.), *The Sage handbook of organization studies* (2nd ed., pp. 370–387). Thousand Oaks, CA: Sage.

Foucault, M. (1984). *Foucault: A reader* (Rabinow, P., Ed.). New York, NY: Pantheon.

Foucault, M. (1991). Governmentality In Burchell, G., Gordon, C., & Miller, P. (Eds.), *The Foucault effect* (pp. 87–104). Chicago, IL: University of Chicago Press.

Fung, A., & Wright, E. O. (2003). Thinking about empowered participatory governance In Fung, A., & Wright, E. O. (Eds.), *Deepening democracy* (pp. 3–42). New York, NY: Verso.

Graham, S., & Marvin, S. (2001). *Splintering urbanism: Networked infrastructures, technological mobilities and the urban condition.* New York, NY: Routledge.

Gross, P. (Ed.). (1986). *Proceedings of the 15-17 October 1986 Joint Meeting of Internet Engineering and Internet Architecture Task Forces. Fourth IETF.* Menlo Park, California: Corporation for National Research Initiatives. Retrieved October 13, 2010, from http://www.ietf.org/old/2009/proceedings/prior29/IETF04.pdf

Hanseth, O. (2001). The economics of standards In Ciborra, C. U. (Ed.), *From control to drift: The dynamics of corporate information infrastructures* (pp. 56–70). Oxford, UK: Oxford University Press.

Hanseth, O., Jacucci, E., Grisot, M., & Aanestad, M. (2006). Reflexive standardization: Side effects and complexity in standard making. *Management Information Systems Quarterly, 30,* 563–581.

Hanseth, O., & Monteiro, E. (1997). Inscribing behaviour in information infrastructure standards. *Accounting Management and Information Technology, 7*(4), 183–211.

Hanseth, O., Monteiro, E., & Hatling, M. (1996). Developing information infrastructure: The tension between standardisation and flexibility. *Science, Technology & Human Values, 21*(4), 407–426.

Hardin, G. (1968). The tragedy of the commons *Science, 162,* 1243–1248.

Hardin, R. (1982). *Collective action.* Baltimore, MD: Johns Hopkins University Press.

Hecht, G., & Allen, M. T. (2001). Introduction: Authority, political machines, and technology's history In Allen, M. T., & Hecht, G. (Eds.), *Technologies of power* (pp. 1–24). Cambridge, MA: MIT Press.

Hughes, T. P. (1983). *Networks of power: Electrification in Western society 1880-1930.* Baltimore, MD: Johns Hopkins.

Hughes, T. P. (1987). The evolution of large technological systems In Bijker, W. E., Hughes, T. P., & Pinch, T. (Eds.), *The social construction of technological systems* (pp. 51–82). Cambridge, MA: The MIT Press.

Monteiro, E. (2001). Actor-network theory and information infrastructure In Ciborra, C. U. (Ed.), *From control to drift: The dynamics of corporate information infrastructures* (pp. 71–83). Oxford, UK: Oxford University Press.

National Telecommunications and Information Administration (NTIA). (1993, September 15). *The national information infrastructure: Agenda for action.* Washington, DC: U.S. Department of Commerce.

Olson, M. (1965). *The logic of collective action: Public goods and the theory of groups.* Cambridge, MA: Harvard University Press.

Ostrom, E. (1990). *Governing the commons: The evolution of institutions for collective action.* Cambridge, MA: Cambridge University Press.

Sahay, S., Monteiro, E., & Aanestad, M. (2009). Configurable politics and asymmetric integration: Health e-infrastructures in India. *Journal of the Association for Information Systems, 10*(5), 399–414.

Sassen, S. (2001). *The global city* (2nd ed.). Princeton, NJ: Princeton University Press.

Snyder, W., & Briggs, X. (2003). *Communities of practice: A new tool for government managers*. Washington, DC: IBM Center for the Business of Government.

Star, S. L. (1999). The ethnography of infrastructure. *The American Behavioral Scientist, 43*(3), 377–391.

Star, S. L., & Ruhleder, K. (1996). Steps toward an ecology of infrastructure: Design and access for large information spaces. *Information Systems Research, 7*(1), 111–134.

Susskind, L., & Hoben, M. (2004). Making regional policy dialogues work: A credo for metro-scale consensus building. *Temple Environmental Law Journal, 22*(2), 123–140.

Wade, R. (1994). *Village republics: Economic conditions for collective action in south India*. Oakland, CA: ICS Press.

Weill, P., & Broadbent, M. (1998). *Leveraging the new infrastructure: How market leaders capitalize on information*. Boston, MA: Harvard Business School Press.

ENDNOTE

[1]   To preserve the confidentiality of the responses, all names in this research have been anonymized.

Acknowledgment

This book is the product of a decade of thinking, conferring, and writing on the topic of information infrastructures. Thus, although this is a single-authored book, many of the ideas draw on collaborative research, as well as discussions and written feedback from other researchers interested in this field.

My interest in the field begun in early 2002 out of discussions with my then Ph.D. supervisor, Michael Barrett, while a Ph.D. student at the Judge Business School, University of Cambridge. Our discussions were motivated by a funded project from the Cambridge-MIT Institute and a joint interest to examine the ways by which information infrastructures supported and enabled the management of critical events in the healthcare value chain. This interest was also motivated by discussions we had with Geoff Walsham, Matthew Jones, Ole Hanseth, Eric Monteiro, Sundeep Sahay, and others who participated in the 2002 Oslo-Cambridge IS workshop on information infrastructures at Oslo University, Norway.

During that time, as serendipity would have it, through a fellow Ph.D. student, Angelina Kouroubali, I had the chance to be introduced to the then president of a research and development institute in Greece who was heading efforts to develop and implement HEALTHnet, a pilot health information infrastructure for the region of Crete. After a series of discussions, and with the help of Angelina, we were eventually given access to study the development and implementation of HEALTHnet, which was initiated in 1997 and came to an end in 2006. This case study (Chapter 4 of this book) offered great empirical material with which to explore a series of theoretical ideas around the development of information infrastructures.

Throughout the years of empirical data collection for the Crete case study, but also later on and up to today, we have presented theoretical ideas to the study of information infrastructures to various audiences, in an effort to fine tune a theoretical framework and make a strong contribution to the field. The commons perspective presented in this book is, thus, a product of collaborative effort between me and Michael Barrett.

While still working with Michael on a possible theoretical framework that would help us understand developments in the Crete case study, I became involved in another infrastructure project. Starting from 2006, the English Department of Health and the National Audit Office begun to release extensive data to the public on the English National Program for IT (NPfIT). This case study (Chapter 5 of this book) offered another possibility to apply the commons perspective, while also offering rich insights for further theoretical development. I am in debt to my ex-colleague Frank Blackler, at Lancaster University's Management School, for his initial contribution and later encouragement for pursuing this project.

Moving beyond the two case studies of what could be called 'conventional' information infrastructures in Crete and the English NPfIT, I began to explore new information infrastructures from a commons perspective. I became particularly interested in the ways that Free and Open Source Software (FOSS) and mashup projects (two new information infrastructures) opened up a new era of information infrastructure development, with significant consequences being generated both for lay users and expert developers. This interest was born after a lecture on the consequences of the use of new social media such as Second Life and Facebook to a group of graduate students at Lancaster University's Management School. This lecture was part of a series of lectures on organizational change, which was developed in partnership with ex-colleagues at the Department of Organization, Work, and Technology from 2006-2008. It was through discussions with my ex-colleagues at Lancaster that I became increasingly interested in understanding the ethical governance of new information infrastructures, which is explored in Chapter 9 of this book.

It is exactly this interest on ethics that pushed me to conclude the book with a discussion on the role of the researcher in information infrastructure research. The key ideas informing Chapter 10 of this book are drawn from a critical reflection on trends in information systems (IS) research and the need for a more pragmatic approach, which was developed in partnership with Mike Chiasson and Lucas Introna, both ex-colleagues at Lancaster University's Management School. The discussion in Chapter 10 is adapted slightly to reflect the broader needs of research on information infrastructures.

In addition, I would also like to thank the publishing team at IGI Global, whose feedback throughout the whole process from inception of the initial idea to final publication has been invaluable. In particular to Jan Travers and Hannah Abelbeck, who assisted in keeping this project on schedule and to the two anonymous reviewers, whose constructive feedback helped to further improve the book.

I would also like to thank Rebecca Koutsoudis for her help in making sure this book was written in clear and sound English.

And last, but not least, a big thank you to my wife, Tina, and, my son, Andreas, for their unfailing love, support, and encouragement throughout the time I was writing this book. I dedicate this book to both of you.

Panos Constantinides
Frederick University, Republic of Cyprus
December 2011

Section 1
Theory

Chapter 1
Introduction:
Historical Review of
Infrastructure Development

ABSTRACT

This first chapter offers a historical review of the development of infrastructures as a prologue to the key themes that will be explored in the rest of the book. This historical review focuses, firstly, on the infrastructural ideal of the early industrialized world toward building integrated cities, and, secondly, on the "splintering" of this infrastructural ideal by disintegrating previously public-held monopolies to private sector involvement. These historical processes of infrastructural development are then further unpacked by approaching them through the problem of collective action. The chapter concludes by summarizing the key learning points from the history on infrastructure development.

INTRODUCTION

The term *infrastructure* has been used since 1927 to refer collectively to the roads, rail lines, electric supply and telecommunication networks, and similar public works that are required for an industrial economy, or a portion of it, to function (Oxford English Dictionary). In this sense, an in-

frastructure is responsible for "rolling out" basic power, water, sewerage, and communications services across geographical territories as public or quasi-public goods using systems of standardized services (Dupuy, 2000). These include: "universal service obligations" in Anglo-Saxon nations, "public service" regimes in France, "services of general interest" in the rest of Europe, and so on (see Offner, 2000). Thus, infrastructures are widely assumed to be integrators of urban spaces

DOI: 10.4018/978-1-4666-1622-6.ch001

and "they are believed to bind cities, regions and nations into functioning geographical and political wholes" (Graham & Marvin, 2001, pp.8).

In this view, infrastructures have become "black boxed" (see Winner, 1980, 1993). That is, they have come to be treated by users as unproblematic and "closed" socio-technical artifacts that could be relied on without much thought or questioning. Once infrastructure services become "domesticated" and "normalized" (Rose, 1995), users rarely consider the huge socio-technical constructions or complex governance arrangements that lie beyond the end-user contact points, such as the light switch and the telephone. As Perry notes (1995, pp.2), when infrastructures "work best, they are noticed least of all".

Infrastructures may "roll out" spaces of increased mobility and interconnection for some; however, they always involve the construction of barriers for others. Star (1999, pp.380) notes:

For the person in the wheelchair, the stairs and door jamb in front of a building are not seamless subtenders of use, but barriers. One person's infrastructure is another's difficulty.

In other words, there is a need to recognize how infrastructures "are inevitably imbued with biased struggles for social, economic, ecological and political power" (Graham & Marvin, 2001, pp.11). These biased struggles often require complex regulatory articulations between markets, national states and increasingly transnational bodies. In fact, broad fears of irresponsible accumulations of either political or economic power have shaped public policies to developing infrastructures. Due to recent increases in the liberalization of markets and investment flows such fears have led to the development of private approaches for infrastructure management in the United States of America (USA), Western Europe, and more recently in Asia (Curwen, 1999; McGowan, 1999). In many cases, public and private monopolies are being replaced by contested, profit-driven markets (Sassen, 2001).

This global wave of infrastructure disintegration through privatization has highlighted the collapse of urban social order simply because contemporary urban life has become increasingly dependent on a huge range of interdependent but, at the same time, contested, and dispersed infrastructures (Pawley, 1997; Suarez-Villa & Walrod, 1999). Such a dependency brings out greater possibilities of failure and disintegration of the infrastructures.

Business organizations are now required to function in an "always-on economy," which depends upon a continuous support by various types of infrastructures, from water supply, electricity, and computer networking, among others. In turn, "for a large business online, the cost of a power interruption can exceed $1 million per minute" (Platt, 2000, pp.116). This shows the systemic qualities of infrastructures, whereby, through interrelated processes of social, political and institutional agency and entrepreneurship, infrastructures evolve to shape the entire technological fabric of society (Hughes, 1983; Summerton, 1994). Infrastructures tend to "warp" the natural and social spaces and times of our daily lives (Latour, 1993).

To begin to comprehend the subtle yet powerful ways in which the development of infrastructures have and still are helping to shape social order and generate (un)intended consequences for different social time-spaces, this chapter will review historical examples of infrastructure development. This historical review will focus, firstly, on the infrastructural ideal of the early industrialized world toward building integrated cities, and, secondly, on the "splintering" of this infrastructural ideal by disintegrating previously public-held monopolies to private sector involvement (Graham & Marvin, 2001). These historical processes of infrastructural development will then be further unpacked by approaching them through the problem of collective action. The chapter will conclude by summarizing some key learning points from the history on infrastructure development.

URBAN PLANNING AND THE INFRASTRUCTURAL IDEAL OF THE INTEGRATED, STANDARDIZED CITY

During the period between 1850 and 1960, the growth of state-regulated network monopolies, particularly in Western cities, supported a transition from the older compact commercial city to the new industrial metropolis with a strong core and a network of residential suburbs (Graham & Marvin, 2001). Across Western cities, small, fragmented islands of infrastructure were integrated towards standardized, regulated networks designed to deliver predictable, dependable services across the metropolis (Tarr & Dupuy, 1988; Cox & Jonas, 1993).

Scientific management, rational organization and the mass production of standardized goods were part of the infrastructural ideal of the integrated, standardized city (Giannopoulos & Gillepsie, 1993). This was a new organizational philosophy based on the principles of throughput, centralized control, coordination and diversification (Preston, 1990 cited in Guy, Graham, & Marvin, 1997). In turn, this required the construction of national, public infrastructures for interconnected highways, rail, communications and energy systems.

Efforts at technological standardization go as back as 1761, with cities like London and Stockholm attempting to regularize the design and paving of street spaces and to systematize the delivery of street lighting and the naming of streets (Ogborn, 1999; Whiteman, 1990). Similar efforts followed in the mid 1850s, with the exemplar of Haussmann's plans for the "regularization" of Paris (Offner, 1999). The laying out of integrated and open street systems provided the physical frameworks for the extension of other infrastructural services and set the legal and territorial boundaries of further urban growth (see Coutard, 1999). Boyer (1994, pp.7) notes that, in North America, for example:

side by side with the creation of a disciplinary order and ceremonial harmony to the American City... improvers[1] gave heed to the creation of an infrastructural framework and regulatory land order.

King (1998, pp.23) adds that these improvers would create rational plans that treated the city

like a machine to be planned as an engineer plans an industrial process, breaking it down into its essential functions (housing, work, recreation and traffic), Taylorizing and standardizing them (in a Master Plan) as a totality.

The city became a space to be ordered, regulated and configured through managing the interplay of territory and infrastructures; "what was discovered at that time was the idea of *society*" (Foucault, 1984, pp.242, emphasis in original).

Although there were substantial national and local variations in the specific technological and social organization of infrastructure providers there were three key features that characterised most cases (Graham & Marvin, 2001, pp.77-81).

Firstly, there was broad consensus that infrastructures through which services were distributed were most effectively managed through "natural monopolies." That is, a single supplier was considered to be more efficient than several suppliers in any particular area. In extension, a publicly regulated monopoly was able to benefit from economies of scale by developing one infrastructure whereas a fragmented industry was likely to lead to duplication of costs. Indeed, Britain's slow economic progress in the 1920s was due to a failure to integrate its 65 electricity suppliers, 49 different power systems, 32 different voltages and 70 different pricing systems (Hughes, 1983). At the same time, the one "natural" supplier that was to be granted a monopoly required significant capital outlay, especially in the early stages of development. In addition, infrastructures represented a form of sunken capital that realistically could not be dismantled or moved. There was, therefore, little scope for infrastructure development to be a contestable activity because of the high sunk costs involved in establishing a competitive, integrated infrastructure. Moreover, despite the efforts of some private companies to develop competing infrastructures in certain areas, from the users' point of view, there were huge physical costs of transferring services without the users physically moving to a new location. Infrastructures, thereby, stood "in a special relation to the State, and need[ed] to be publicly regulated to ensure reasonable charges and adequate services" (Sleeman, 1953, pp.3).

Secondly, infrastructures were largely considered to be public goods, which made them difficult to be distributed within private markets. Public goods are defined by their *non-subtractability*–i.e. that they can be supplied to more than one person without extra costs–and their *non-excludability*– i.e. that once a supply of services has been built no user can be prevented from using the services (see Ostrom & Ostrom, 1977). As public goods, infrastructures were at once under state control.

Thirdly, infrastructures were seen to produce externality effects on the environment and/or particular social groups, such as the positive externality of public health benefits of access to water and sanitation infrastructure, and the negative externality of carbon emissions contributing to global warming and endangering health in parts of a city. Once again, state regulation was needed to manage these externalities to ensure that wider social, economic and environmental objectives were met.

These three key features dominated the infrastructural ideal of the integrated, standardized city and provided the underlying rationale for "a moral and practical social system" (Taylor, 1994, pp.156). Infrastructures became an essential focus of the power, legitimacy, and territorial definition of the modern city (Jessop, 2000).

Despite the aim to integrate and standardize the modern city, however, the bundle of integrated

infrastructures of electricity, telecommunications, road and highway links, and water and sewerage networks enabled social, economic, and cultural participation over greater geographical areas (Fishman, 1990). In other words, more standardization led to more decentralization, especially in European and American cities. For example, in the USA (Rose, 1995, pp.201):

Federal and state government built highway networks that allowed Americans to live far from central cities. Government also financed construction of water and sewer systems extending to distant suburbs, all the while guaranteeing the mortgages of residents. At the same time, electric and gas rates declined; engineers built larger and more efficient plants; regulators kept energy prices low, particularly for natural gas; and lengthy pipelines and electrical interchanges carried that energy throughout the continent.

In the context of such decentralization, the notion of the (sub) urban networked home was re-conceptualized and re-constructed to support the wider dynamics of mass consumption mediated by bundles of integrated infrastructures. Rybczynski (1983, pp.22-3) notes:

The main difference between, say, the house of one hundred years ago and one of today is that the latter contains a great deal of machinery. The contemporary house, as the French architect Le Corbusier remarked, has become a "machine for living," that is, it has become an environment that is conditioned primarily by technology. Electricity, power pumps, motors, furnaces, air conditioners, toasters, and hair dryers. There are technologies for providing hot and cold water, and for getting rid of it. There are telephone systems and cable television systems; unseen waves carry radio and television signals. The house is also full of automated devices–relays and thermostats–which turn these machines on and off, regulate the heat and cold, or simply open the garage door. Remove technologies from the modern home and most would consider it uninhabitable.

The mass diffusion of networked homes and the spinoffs in construction and consumer goods industries supported the economic growth of the 1950s and 1960s by stimulating mass consumption of vast ranges of "specific new products for innovative household electrical products" (Gershuny, 1983, pp.196).

It was only in the 1970s and 1980s, through a wider set of societal and technological shifts that the infrastructural ideal and its associated (un)intended consequences on nations, cities, and individuals began to become problematic. First, the welfare state in Western countries had begun to experience deep financial and legitimacy crises requiring alternative approaches to infrastructural procurement and governance (Leonard, 1997). Second, in the developing world, publicly-financed infrastructures had begun to come under severe stress as many developing countries began to sell off their infrastructural assets to private multinational firms (Harris & Fabricius, 1996). Finally, after Soviet and East European communism collapsed, centralized and often obsolete infrastructures were opened up for bids by multinational firms (Berlage, 1997). In most contexts, politically liberal critiques (e.g. post-colonialist, environmentalist) in conjunction with influential lobbying by private multinational firms against the inefficiencies of centralized public control and ownership fuelled a wave of infrastructural liberalization and privatization (Leonard, 1997). At the same time, "the very idea of controllability, certainty or security collapse[d]" (Beck, 1999, pp.2).

THE SPLINTERING OF INFRASTRUCTURES

The rapid deterioration and physical obsolescence of the infrastructures laid out in the early 20th century gradually led to their disintegration. In one example, Perry (1995, pp.3) found that 40 percent of the U.S.'s 600,000 bridges could be classed as deficient and two thirds of the country's water treatment facilities were substandard. The main problems were a lack of spending on new facilities and a huge backlog in maintenance and rehabilitation caused by the combination of the massively extended infrastructure networks developed during the 19th and early 20th centuries as well as a collapse of the financial capacity to support those networks at local and national levels (Reich, 1992).

Because of these problems, many Western, post-communist and developing nations had, by the 1970s, begun to transfer some or all of their infrastructure assets to private operators (Offner, 2000), with the most extreme example being that of Britain's program of wholesale infrastructural privatization since 1984 (see Martin, 1999).

Graham and Marvin (2001) have called this disintegration the "splintering of infrastructures." This splintering refers to the *vertical, horizontal,* and *virtual* fragmentation of an infrastructure from those parts connected to the consumers or users, the superimposition of new infrastructures in parallel, and the superimposition of new infrastructural services through the use of new information and communication technologies respectively (Graham & Marvin, 2001, pp.141-144).

Three key forces have dominated the splintering of infrastructures: the collapse of state-backed, integrated forms of infrastructure provision; the rising impetus of "glocal" configurations of infrastructures; and the widespread retreat of the idea that infrastructure services are public goods (Graham & Marvin, 2001, pp.96-103).

Firstly, in the 1980s and 1990s, the inefficiencies of state-owned, centralized infrastructures combined with increased financial constraints on governments and influential lobbying by private multinational firms for easing restrictions on entry into previously monopolistic infrastructure markets, enabled entrepreneurial infrastructure companies to begin to attempt to competitively position themselves within dominant and emerging markets (Berlage, 1997; Harris & Fabricius, 1996). These attempts were met by powerful transnational alliances and mergers between infrastructure providers of telecommunications, energy, water, and transport services (see Curwen, 1999; Summerton, 1999). For example, within the electricity industry alone, such mergers and alliances amounted to U.S. $50 billion in 1998 worldwide (Rider, 1999). These mergers and alliances also altered the investment patterns of investors from financial markets as the latter were now reluctant to commit to long-term investments in large-scale, standardized infrastructures and preferred, instead, to engage in "project-by-project assessments ruled by the law of contract" (Clark, 1999, pp. 257). Together, the ease of state restrictions on private entry, the mergers and alliances between infrastructure providers, and short-term, project-by-project financial investments in infrastructure development, led to the splintering of infrastructures of the past (Winsbury, 1997).

Secondly, as a consequence of the above, the development of infrastructures has increasingly become a power struggle of "deterritorialisation" and "reterritorialisation" within a global capitalist system (Thrift, 2000). In other words, the development of infrastructures has aimed at creating links between highly valued local spaces and global networks to support new information flows and interactions between geographically distributed users locked into international divisions of labor (Peck, 1996). "Seamless" global-local–or "glocal" (see Swyngedouw, 1992, 1997)–technological and organizational connection of infrastructures is now the central emphasis geared to the logistical and exchange demands of multinational firms, foreign direct investors, and socioeconomic affluent groups (Castells, 2010). For example, the Priority Pass programme is a fee-based system developed in a joint collaboration between several international airport operators around the world, allowing access to luxury airport lounges to over

200 airports). As Giannopoulos and Gillepsie (1993, pp.51) noted:

Not only is this new industrial and spatial scenario built on the assumption that long-distance, reliable transport and communications networks are implemented, but it rests on the idea that these networks have to be 'integrated networks,' both geographically and technologically.

In turn, there is a general trend "towards the customization of public infrastructure on behalf of private firms" to address corporate needs and meet changing competitive conditions (Peck, 1996, pp. 36).

Thirdly, because of the above, infrastructure services no longer hold the status of public or quasi-public goods to be consumed by all at standardized tariffs. Instead, infrastructure services are restructured within more or less regulated markets between competing private providers (Leonard, 1997). Such a shift is "imposing an ethos of individual choice which belies the role of consumption in the systemic reproduction of capitalism" (Clarke & Bradford, 1998, pp.874). However, the ability to make individual infrastructural choices is usually highly dependent on wealth, location, and skills. Thus, access to various infrastructures will most likely undermine the position of the poor, who often tended to benefit most from universal service obligations found in the infrastructural ideal of the 19th and early 20th centuries (see Castells, 2010, chapters 4 and 6 in particular).

Although, the disintegration of infrastructures has and continues to vary across socio-political and socio-economic contexts, the aforementioned forces have led to distinct yet related processes of splintering (Graham & Marvin, 2001, pp.385):

...from classic new private infrastructures to the sociotechnical reconfiguration of old networks; from classic cases of wholesale privatisation to public 'reregulation' and the changing practices

of continuing monopolies; from the combined secession of interlinked networks and built urban spaces to the 'virtual' construction of infrastructure markets over the single networks that were the legacy of the modern infrastructural ideal.

These processes of splintering have generated new sets of dynamics around the development of infrastructures and are further explored in the next section through an understanding of problems of collective action.

INFRASTRUCTURE DEVELOPMENT AS A PROBLEM OF COLLECTIVE ACTION

The term "collective action" refers to joint action by a number of individuals to achieve and distribute some gain through coordination or cooperation (Hardin, 1982). In turn, all difficulties that arise in the pursuit of collective action goals are called collective action problems.

With the publication of *The Logic of Collective Action* in 1965, Mancur Olson challenged the foundation of modern democratic thought that groups would tend to form and take collective action whenever members jointly benefitted. Instead, Olson (1965, pp.2) offered the provocative assertion that:

unless the number of individuals in a group is quite small, or unless there is coercion or some other special device to make individuals act in their common interest, rational, self-interested individuals will not act to achieve their common or group interests.

This argument has become to be known as the "zero contribution thesis," which kicked off a long and lively debate about the foundation of social order in modern societies (see Hardin, 1982).

On the one hand, some researchers have strived to show that free riding and overconsumption is a potential problem whenever individuals cannot be excluded from receiving the benefits of other's contributions to common outcomes–what has been called "the tragedy of the commons" (e.g. Hardin, 1968; Dawes et al., 1977; Isaac et al., 1984). In turn, extensive field research has shown how participants invest considerable resources to monitor and sanction the actions of each other so as to reduce the probability of free riding and overconsumption (see Baland & Platteau, 1996; Ostrom, 1990; Wade, 1994). On the other hand, other commentators have challenged the assumption that without selective benefits, no individual within a large group will act to achieve their common group interests. This position has been supported by showing how some individuals have formed human rights organizations against dictatorships and sacrificed themselves for the common good (e.g. Loveman, 1998).

Despite the fact that such studies have shown considerable variations in Olson's initial model, the zero contribution thesis has become widely accepted in public policy debates as the foundation for contemporary policies. As a consequence, centrally designed, state-implemented, rule-based incentives have increasingly been accepted as the universal solution for overcoming all types of collective action problems. The state has come to be viewed as a substitute for the shortcomings of individual behavior and the presumed failure of groups (Ostrom, 1999).

As discussed in the previous two sections, the 20th century, up until the 1970s, was characterized by an almost blind faith in the capacity of strong, national governments to solve problems of collective action toward the development of infrastructures. Many national policies were adopted on the presumption that citizens were unable to cope effectively with the governance and management of local infrastructures, turning control over to national bureaucracies charged with the responsibility of devising efficient and effective ways of utilizing common resources.

The state sought to resolve collective action problems by enforcing binding contracts in the form of legal penalties (fines, incarceration), social sanctions (ostracism), social rewards (status and respect), or economic prizes (transfers, assets, or private goods) (Taylor, 1987). According to this line of argumentation, public goods such as a public transportation infrastructure cannot be provided in optimal amounts through a market, due to the fact that free riders will not pay their share of the costs; only authoritative structures and processes make it possible for costs to be efficiently recouped from the users of public goods (Olson, 1965).

Nevertheless, as discussed in the previous section, a state solution is not always necessary, possible, or successful in any case. Since the 1980s, most economic and political processes have involved either a mix of market and hierarchy, or goods having mixed public and private characteristics–as in the cases of infrastructure development discussed earlier. In this context, economic and political processes were implemented to not only construct relatively efficient structures (e.g. contracts) within which to provide public goods and minimize transaction costs in the maintenance of specific assets, but to also manage the overarching system within which both types of goods and assets are produced and exchanged–this system itself constituting a public good (see Williamson, 2002).

Such complex political-economic structures became increasingly popular in the 1990s with the splintering of infrastructures. During this period, many of what constituted public goods (e.g. national-level strategic industries and regulatory and welfare systems) were increasingly integrated into a wider world marketplace. This transformation came through the intensive application of information and communications technologies towards greater performance monitoring (Power, 2007), flexible production systems and organizational structures (Womak, Jones, & Roos, 1991), and market segmentation, deregulation,

and globalization (Crotty, 2009; Robinson, 2001; Sassen, 2000).

In this new context, the logic of collective action is becoming more heterogeneous and multilayered, derived not from a single core structure such as the state, but from networked interdependencies across global markets (Cerny, 1995; also see Castells, 2010, chapter 5). These networked interdependencies have reconfigured the traditional bureaucratic organization of collective action to a blended action model based on a network of communities of practice that draw on expert as well as local, experience-based knowledge (Snyder & Briggs, 2003; Ostrom, 1999). This network of communities of practice is found to engage in cross-sector, inter-organizational cooperation around common problems, such as how to advance "green," environment-friendly technology (Laws et al., 2001).

This shift in the logic of collective action is consistent with the widespread finding that citizens are motivated to actively participate in public affairs, not out of an abstract desire to strengthen democracy, but out of the rational belief that their investment of time, reputation, commitment, and other precious resources should measurably change social conditions (Fung, 2004). The aim is to hold public agencies more accountable and improve results through "empowered participatory governance"–that is, reforms that devolve decision-making power to citizen bodies (Fung & Wright, 2003).

From the standpoint of collective action problem-solving, participation and empowerment are crucial for two main reasons. Firstly, participatory processes, which blend and disseminate different sources of knowledge, can generate better, more actionable ideas than top-down, exclusionary, technocratic planning (Scott, 1998; Williamson & Fung, 2005). Efforts to inform technocratic planning by professional experts through participatory processes must, however, come to terms with some mistaken assumptions: that professional knowledge is superior to other forms of knowledge, including local, indigenous, or "craft" knowledge born of experience (Scott, 1998); that citizens will be persuaded by professional knowledge because technical superiority, according to objective standards of science, makes it more legitimate than other kinds of knowledge (Scott, 1998); and that members of the public share a culture (e.g. norms of communication, decision making, and influence) so that encounters between experts and citizens, or among diverse citizens, will produce learning and trust under rules of fair play (see Briggs, 1998; Healey, 1996; Tauxe, 1995).

These assumptions are rarely true in the real-world and that is why well-structured participation—i.e. under local, community-led rules of participation and use (Ostrom, 1999)—can lead to better decisions that are not merely more popular, but more legitimate across participants which is crucial for joint, common outcomes. Secondly, wider and better structured participation may enable social production: generating knowledge and commitment to drive private, governmental, and non-governmental action, and the blending of actions by these sectors to produce a meaningful impact on common problems (Benkler, 2006).

Perhaps the most interesting example of participative, empowered, collective action in recent years has been the open source software movement (Benkler, 2006). Free and open source software is an approach to software development, whereby many individuals contribute to a common project, with a variety of motivations, while sharing their respective contributions without a single person or entity asserting rights to exclude either from the contributed components or from the resulting whole. In order to avoid having the joint product appropriated by any single party, participants usually retain copyrights in their contribution, but license them to others on a model that combines a universal license to use the materials with licensing constraints that make it difficult, if not impossible, for any single contributor or third party to appropriate the project.

Although the rules of collective action around open source software projects vary according to the size, level of development, and mode of distribution of each project, the development of open source software has had significant success. About 70 percent of Web server software, in particular for critical e-commerce sites, runs on the Apache Web server (an open source software); more than half of all back-office e-mail functions are run by one free software program or another; and companies like IBM and Hewlett Packard, consumer electronics manufacturers, as well as military and other mission-critical government agencies around the world have begun to adopt business and service strategies that rely and extend free software (Benkler, 2006).

At the same time, however, the success of open source software, and other such social production examples, does not mean that collective action entails purely consensual or conflict-free action. Collective action benefits from divergent as well as convergent thinking. There is evidence, for example, that the proliferation of participatory approaches to managing infrastructures for water and other vital resources worldwide has led to many unstructured negotiations, misunderstandings about the meaning of consensus, and a fear of sharing power (Susskind & Hoben, 2004). Creating alternative (i.e. participatory, community-led) processes of infrastructure development that are not only popular, but by definition challenge the status quo in important ways is far more daunting a problem than advancing a particular policy position or winning approval for a particular project. Beyond the structural conflicts over the physical properties of an infrastructure and its value, there is a classic "tragedy of the commons": there are varied experiences of the benefits and costs of the infrastructure because of the uneven use of the infrastructure by users of varied wealth, political power, location, and skills (Castells, 2010).

One example that illustrates this point vividly is the case of infrastructure development in Mumbai. In the early 2000s, Bombay First, a group of corporate, non-governmental organizations (NGOs), and government bodies, in partnership with the international consulting firm McKinsey, worked to produce a high-profile report on Mumbai's future. *Vision Mumbai* pointed at how the city's infrastructure and land use fell far behind those of competitor urban economies, such as Shanghai, and offered recommendations for "transforming Mumbai into a world class city" over a decade of major targeted investments (Bombay First & McKinsey, 2003). However, the fate of the long-range infrastructure plans outlined in the *Vision Mumbai* report are inseparable to prospects for the estimated half of Mumbai's population that lives in slums (Singh, 2006). Slums lie directly in the path of vital upgrading and therefore find themselves in the cross-hairs of the city's makeover (Appadurai, 2001; Bhowmik, 2003). Almost all of Mumbai's metro region's vital commuter railways, as well as many of its major roadways and even the airport were replete with makeshift dwellings, until the government reconsidered a failed policy of sudden evictions and began to work with community groups and NGOs on relocation and resettlement (Patel, D'Cruz, & Burra, 2002). Efficient railways are especially vital to the region's future, since they enable the northward growth that is Mumbai's only physical outlet (Patel, D'Cruz, & Burra, 2002). However, the settlements have made any expansion of rail and other transportation lines a politically contentious, uncertain, and highly expensive task. From the standpoint of its infrastructure, Mumbai has been crushed by its lack of attention to the slums and their "place" in the city, so much so that *Vision Mumbai* has even warned government and business leaders of collapse if the city continues to fall behind competitors (Bombay First & McKinsey, 2003).

Mumbai and such similar cases call for social learning–for deeper changes in the (ethical) models of governance, including a reinvention of planning as an institutional process. Participation and empowerment is not a panacea to collective action problems. Better governance depends on efforts to shift and coordinate both public and private bodies toward broad-based community action with and beyond the aid of the government, at the regional, national, and supranational levels.

CONCLUSION

The aim of this introductory chapter was to stress the importance of infrastructures in binding different geographical time-spaces, while highlighting the complex socio-political and socio-technical arrangements required for their development. The key lessons derived from the long history of infrastructure development across different time periods and parts of the world can be summarized in relation to three modes of production: state (centralized) control toward the integrated infrastructural ideal, private (decentralized) involvement and the splintering of infrastructures, and community-led (network-based) governance through public-private and non-governmental partnerships.

As evident from the historical review, private firms have played an extensive range of roles in the provision of infrastructures as owners, operators, lessees, contractors, and builders of facilities (Graham & Marvin, 2001). Even in places where national governments are the sole owners of their respective infrastructures, portions of many of those have been built by private firms. Decisions concerning infrastructure development, types of public goods demanded, and roles played by private firms have been shaped by the values of politically important actors and the workings of governmental, political, and legal institutions (Sassen, 2000). With respect to the role of private firms specifically, beliefs as to the "publicness" of different goods and services have been of crucial importance in shaping the character of regulatory, franchising, and contracting arrangements (Sassen, 2000). In situations in which a good has been seen as predominantly private, it has been possible for privately owned service providers to be compensated predominantly from user fees, while assigning to them the bulk of decisions as to price, output, and quality of service (Sassen, 2000). By contrast, when goods have been seen as public and subsidized from tax payer revenues or provided entirely free to consumers, many decisions as to price, output, and quality have had to be made by government agencies, regardless of the role played by privately owned service providers (Graham & Marvin, 2001).

Choices as to private and governmental provision of infrastructures have also been shaped by ideas concerning the role of the government in the economy. For example, the far greater role played by private firms in the provision of electric utilities in the USA than in Europe during the early years of these industries, can be greatly attributed to broad differences in beliefs concerning appropriate roles for governments to play in overseeing essential services (Suggs, 1989). On the other hand, however, policymakers seeking ways to improve infrastructure provision in developing countries through increased private sector involvement are unlikely to confront circumstances identical to those in the USA and Europe. Indeed, experiences with different ownership and regulatory arrangements in developed Western countries cannot be assumed to be present in many developing countries (Persaud, 1992). Clearly, attributes of markets and extents to which infrastructures serve public purposes both require close examination when considering whether and how to increase roles played by private firms.

Depending upon circumstances an alternative mode of production may be worthy of consideration. An increasingly emerging mode of production is community-led infrastructure development and governance. By choosing this option, the users of an infrastructure have the authority to make at least some of the rules related to the use and governance of that infrastructure (Andersson & Ostrom, 2008). Thus, they would achieve many of the advantages of utilizing local knowledge as well

as the redundancy and rapidity of a trial-and-error learning process. Most importantly, because this mode of production is community-led, information about what has worked well in one setting can be transmitted to others, who may try it out in their settings. However, the advantage of such an option–that there is no sole dominating central authority–is also potentially a disadvantage since there is no guarantee that the community will find combinations of rules at diverse levels that are optimal for any particular environment. In fact, one should expect that community-led governance will be operating at less than optimal levels, given the immense difficulty of fine-tuning the whole infrastructure bottom-up (Ostrom, 1999).

Advances in information and communication technologies in recent years have increasingly fed into processes of network-based development and the governance of infrastructures (see Benkler, 2006). Examples vary from the early Internet (Abbate, 1999), to the open source software movement (Weber, 2004), and Web 2.0 (Vickery & Wunsch-Vincent, 2007). What is intriguing is that this new information and communication technologies–in joint with the removal of high capital costs found in earlier economies (Castells, 2010)–have enabled the creative splintering of infrastructures through processes of social production. Benkler (2006, pp.111) explains:

The core technologically contingent fact that enables social relations to become a salient modality of production in the networked information economy is that all the inputs necessary to effective productive activity are under the control of individual users.

Online horizontal networks have become a fundamental dimension of everyday life built around user-driven (as opposed to state-or corporate-driven) initiatives, interests, and desires in contributing to social, political, and other forums with global feeding of video, audio, and text (e.g. Facebook, Second Life, WikiLeaks).

The ability of individual users to participate in processes of social production should be understood through a differentiation of the collective action rules for the development of emerging infrastructures. These rules constitute modes of production, and these modes determine the existence of different roles of participation through historical practices. As discussed earlier, in the past, the development of infrastructures has been determined by two predominant modes of production: state control and private involvement. Under state control, the development of infrastructures rested in the hands of the power-holders of the state. Under private involvement, the private ownership of the means of production was based on the control of capital, which determined the basic principle of infrastructure development. In turn, the roles of participation were determined by the orientation of each mode of production. On the one hand, state control marshalled citizens toward economic growth and competitiveness against other national economies, often to the detriment of social protection and public interest regulations. On the other hand, private ownership pushed for increased labor and capital while often being indifferent to national-local interests (Graham & Marvin, 2001; Sassen, 2000).

In the alternative, community-led, IT network-based mode of production the source of productivity lies in the technology of knowledge generation, information processing, and social participation and empowerment (Castells, 2010). Certainly, knowledge and information have always been critical elements in all modes of production. However, what is specific to the IT network-based mode of production is the virtuous circle of interaction between the knowledge sources of technology and the application of technology to improve knowledge generation and information processing. Because knowledge and information are diffused across a network of individual users, there is an especially close connection between distributed norms and interests and social production forces. This third mode of production requires different arrangements at varied levels of implementation and is, thus, more complex than either government control or private ownership. Consequently this third mode of production would require extensive negotiations and compromises.

It should be stressed, though, that none of the three modes of production (state-, private-, or community-led) and their variations (e.g. public-private partnerships) should be viewed as dominant or superior on the others. Trade-offs are unavoidable in all three modes and matters do not always play out exactly as expected. What is clear, however, is that for any evaluation of different choices for the development of infrastructures, local contexts, time, technological changes, and, most importantly, collective action rules must be taken into account.

REFERENCES

Andersson, K. and Ostrom, E. 2008. Analyzing Decentralized Natural Resource Governance from a Polycentric Perspective. *Policy Sciences 41*(1), 1-23.

Appadurai, A. (2001). Deep democracy. *Environment and Urbanization, 13*(2), 23–43. doi:10.1177/095624780101300203

Beck, U. (1999). *World risk society*. Cambridge, UK: Polity.

Berlage, M. (1997). The role of local access networks in regional economic integration in Eastern Europe. In Roche, E., & Bakis, H. (Eds.), *Developments in telecommunications* (pp. 177–193). Aldershot, UK: Ashgate.

Bhowmik, S. (2003). National policy for street vendors. *Economic and Political Weekly, 38*(16), 1543–1546.

Boyer, C. (1994). *The city of collective memory*. Cambridge, MA: MIT Press.

Briggs, X. (1998). Doing democracy up close: Culture, power, and communication in community building. *Journal of Planning Education and Research, 18*, 1–13. doi:10.1177/0739456X9801800101

Castells, M. (2010). *The information age: Economy society and culture I: The rise of the network society* (2nd ed.). Malden, MA: Wiley-Blackwell.

Cerny, P. G. (1995). Globalization and the changing logic of collective action. *International Organization, 49*(4), 595–625. doi:10.1017/S0020818300028459

Clark, G. (1999). The retreat of the state and the rise of the pension fund capitalism. In Martin, R. (Ed.), *Money and the space economy* (pp. 241–260). London, UK: Wiley.

Clarke, D., & Bradford, M. (1998). Public and private consumption and the city. *Urban Studies (Edinburgh, Scotland), 35*(5-6), 865–888. doi:10.1080/0042098984592

Cornes, R., & Sandler, T. (1996). *The theory of externalities, public goods, and club goods*. New York, NY: Cambridge University Press.

Coutard, O. (Ed.). (1999). *The governance of large technical systems*. London, UK: Routledge.

Cox, K., & Jonas, A. (1993). Urban development, collective consumption and the politics of metropolitan fragmentation. *Political Geography, 12*(1), 8–37. doi:10.1016/0962-6298(93)90022-Y

Crotty, J. (2009). Structural causes of the global financial crisis: A critical assessment of the new financial architecture. *Cambridge Journal of Economics, 33*(4), 563–580. doi:10.1093/cje/bep023

Curwen, P. (1999). Survival of the fittest: Formation and development of international alliances in telecommunications. *Info, 1*(2), 141–160.

Dawes, R. M., McTavish, J., & Shaklee, H. (1977). Behavior, communication, and assumptions about other people's behavior in a commons dilemma situation. *Journal of Personality and Social Psychology, 35*(1), 1–11. doi:10.1037/0022-3514.35.1.1

Dupuy, G. (2000). A revised history of network urbanism, *Oase*, 4-29.

Fishman, R. (1990). Metropolis unbound: The new city of the twentieth century. *Flux, 6*(1), 43–55. doi:10.3406/flux.1990.1172

Flyvbjerg, B. (2006). Making organization research matter: Power, values and phronesis. In Clegg, S., Hardy, C., Lawrence, T., & Nord, W. (Eds.), *The Sage handbook of organization studies* (2nd ed., pp. 370–387). Thousand Oaks, CA: Sage.

Foucault, M. (1984). *Foucault: A reader* (Rabinow, P., Ed.). New York, NY: Pantheon.

Fung, A. (2004). *Empowered participation*. Princeton, NJ: Princeton University Press.

Fung, A., & Wright, E. O. (2003). Thinking about empowered participatory governance. In Fung, A., & Wright, E. O. (Eds.), *Deepening democracy* (pp. 3–42). New York, NY: Verso.

Gershuny, J. (1983). *Social innovation and the division of labour*. Oxford, UK: Oxford University Press.

Giannopoulos, G., & Gillepsie, A. (Eds.). (1993). *Transport and communications innovations in Europe*. London, UK: Belhaven.

Graham, S., & Marvin, S. (2001). *Splintering urbanism: Networked infrastructures, technological mobilities and the urban condition*. New York, NY: Routledge. doi:10.4324/9780203452202

Guy, S., Graham, S., & Marvin, S. (1997). Splintering networks: Cities and technical networks in 1990s Britain. *Urban Studies (Edinburgh, Scotland)*, *34*(2), 191–216. doi:10.1080/0042098976140

Hardin, G. (1968). The tragedy of the commons. *Science*, *162*, 1243–1248. doi:10.1126/science.162.3859.1243

Hardin, R. (1982). *Collective action*. Baltimore, MD: Johns Hopkins University Press.

Harris, N., & Fabricius, I. (1996). *Cities and structural adjustment*. London, UK: UCL Press.

Healey, P. (1996). The communicative turn in planning theory and its implications for spatial strategy formation. *Environment and Planning. B, Planning & Design*, *23*(2), 217–234. doi:10.1068/b230217

Hirshleifer, J. (1983). From weakest-link to best-shot: The voluntary provision of public goods. *Public Choice*, *41*, 371–386. doi:10.1007/BF00141070

Hirshleifer, J. (1985). From weakest-link to best-shot. *Public Choice*, *46*, 221–223. doi:10.1007/BF00179743

Holzinger, K. (2008). Treaty formation and strategic constellations: An extension of Sandler. *Illinois Law Review*, *1*, 187–200.

Hughes, T. P. (1983). *Networks of power: electrification in western society 1880-1930*. Baltimore, MD: Johns Hopkins.

Isaac, R. M., Walker, J. M., & Thomas, S. (1984). Divergent evidence on free riding: an experimental examination of some possible explanations. *Public Choice*, *43*, 113–149. doi:10.1007/BF00140829

Jessop, R. (2000). The rise of the national spatio-temporal fix and the tendential ecological dominance of globalising capitalism. *International Journal of Urban and Regional Research*, *24*(2), 333–360. doi:10.1111/1468-2427.00251

King, A. (1998). Writing the transnational city: The distant spaces of the Indian city. In Dandekar, H. (Ed.), *City, space and globalization: An international perspective* (pp. 25–31). Ann Arbor, MI: University of Michigan.

Latour, B. (1993). *We have never been modern*. London, UK: Harvester Wheatsheaf.

Laws, D., Susskind, L., Abrams, J., Anderson, J., Chapman, G., Rubenstein, E., & Vadgama, J. (2001). *Public entrepreneurship networks*. Cambridge, MA: MIT Press.

Leonard, P. (1997). *Postmodern welfare: Reconstructing an emancipatory project*. London, UK: Sage.

Loveman, M. (1998). High-risk collective action: Defending human rights in Chile, Uruguay, and Argentine. *American Journal of Sociology*, *104*, 477–525. doi:10.1086/210045

Martin, R. (1999). Selling off the state: Privatization, the equity market and the geographies of shareholder capitalism. In Martin, R. (Ed.), *Money and the space economy* (pp. 261–283). London, UK: Wiley.

McGowan, F. (1999). The internationalization of large technical systems: Dynamics of change and challenges to regulation in electricity and telecommunications. In Coutard, O. (Ed.), *The governance of large technical systems* (pp. 130–148). London, UK: Routledge.

Offner, J.-M. (1999). Are there such things as small networks? In Coutard, O. (Ed.), *The governance of large technical systems* (pp. 217–238). London, UK: Routledge.

Offner, J.-M. (2000). Territorial deregulation: Local authorities at risk from technical networks. *International Journal of Urban and Regional Research, 24*(1), 165–182. doi:10.1111/1468-2427.00241

Ogborn, M. (1999). *Spaces of modernity: London's geographies 1680-1780.* New York, NY: Guildford.

Olson, M. (1965). *The logic of collective action: Public goods and the theory of groups.* Cambridge, MA: Harvard University Press.

Osborne, D., & Gaebler, T. (1992). *Reinventing government: How the entrepreneurial spirit is transforming the public sector.* Reading, MA: Addision-Wesley.

Ostrom, E. (1990). *Governing the commons: The evolution of institutions for collective action.* Cambridge, UK: Cambridge University Press.

Ostrom, E. (1999). Coping with tragedies of the commons. *Annual Review of Political Science, 2,* 493–535. doi:10.1146/annurev.polisci.2.1.493

Ostrom, V., & Ostrom, E. (1977). Public goods and public choices. In Savas, E. S. (Ed.), *Alternatives for delivering public services: Toward improved performance* (pp. 7–49). Boulder, CO: Westview Press.

Patel, S., d'Cruz, C., & Burra, S. (2002). Beyond evictions in a global city: People-managed resettlement in Mumbai. *Environment and Urbanization, 14*(1), 159–172. doi:10.1177/095624780201400113

Pawley, M. (1997). *Terminal architecture.* London, UK: Reaktion Books.

Peck, F. (1996). Regional development and the production of space: The role of infrastructure in the attraction of new inward investment. *Regional Studies, 28,* 327–339.

Perry, D. (1995). *Building the public city: The politics, governance and finance of public infrastructure.* London, UK: Sage.

Persaud, B. (1992). Foreward. In Christopher, A., Cavendish, W., & Mistry, P. S. (Eds.), *Adjusting privatization: Case studies from developing countries.* London, UK: James Currey.

Platt, C. (2000). Re-energizer. *Wired,* 114-30.

Poundstone, W. (1992). *Prisoner's dilemma.* New York, NY: Doubleday.

Reich, R. (1992). *The work of nations.* New York, NY: Simon & Schuster.

Rider, G. (1999, April 30). Watershed. *Utility Week,* 16-18.

Robinson, W. (2001). Social theory and globalization: The rise of a transnational state. *Theory and Society, 30*(2), 157–200. doi:10.1023/A:1011077330455

Rose, M. (1995). *Cities of lights and heat: Domesticating gas and electricity in urban America.* University Park, PA: University of Pennsylvania Press.

Roth, G. (1987). *The private provision of public services in developing countries.* New York, NY: Oxford University Press.

Rybczynski, W. (1983). *Taming the tiger: The struggle to control technology.* New York, NY: Penguin.

Sandler, T. (2008). Treaties: Strategic considerations. *Illinois Law Review, 1,* 155–180.

Sassen, S. (2000). Spatialities and temporalities of the global: Elements for a theorization. *Public Culture, 12*(1), 215–232. doi:10.1215/08992363-12-1-215

Sassen, S. (2001). *The global city* (2nd ed.). Princeton, NJ: Princeton University Press.

Scott, J. (1998). *Seeing like a state: How certain schemes to improve the human condition have failed*. New Haven, CT: Yale University Press.

Singh, P.D. (2006). Slum population in Mumbai. *ENVIS Bulletin, 3*(1).

Sleeman, J. (1953). *British public utilities*. London, UK: Pitman.

Snyder, W., & Briggs, X. (2003). *Communities of practice: A new tool for government managers*. Washington, DC: IBM Center for the Business of Government.

Star, S.-L. (1999). The ethnography of infrastructure. *The American Behavioral Scientist, 43*(3), 377–391. doi:10.1177/00027649921955326

Suarez-Villa, L., & Walrod, W. (1999). Losses from the Northridge earthquake: Disruptions to high-technology industries in the Los Angeles basin. *Disasters, 21*(1), 19–44. doi:10.1111/1467-7717.00103

Suggs, R. E. (1989). *Minorities and privatization: Economic mobility at risk*. Washington, DC: Joint Center for Political Studies.

Summerton, J. (Ed.). (1994). *Changing large technical systems*. Boulder, CO: Westview Press.

Summerton, J. (1999). Power plays: The politics of interlinking systems. In Coutard, O. (Ed.), *The governance of large technical systems* (pp. 93–113). London, UK: Routledge.

Susskind, L., & Hoben, M. (2004). Making regional policy dialogues work: A credo for metroscale consensus building. *Temple Environmental Law Journal, 22*(2), 123–140.

Swyngedouw, E. (1992). Glocalization, interspatial competition and the monetary order: The construction of new scales. In Dunford, M., & Kafkalas, G. (Eds.), *Cities and regions in the New Europe*. London, UK: Belhaven Press.

Swyngedouw, E. (1997). Neither global nor local: "Glocalisation" and the politics of scale. In K. Cox (Ed.), *Spaces of globalization: Reasserting the power of the local*. New York, NY: Guilford/Longman.

Tarr, J., & Dupuy, G. (Eds.). *Technology and the rise of the networked city in Europe and North America*. Philadelphia, PA: Temple University Press.

Tauxe, C. (1995). Marginalizing public participation in planning. *Journal of the American Planning Association. American Planning Association, 61*(4), 471–482. doi:10.1080/01944369508975658

Taylor, P. (1994). The state as container: Territoriality in the modern world-system. *Progress in Human Geography, 18*(2), 151–162. doi:10.1177/030913259401800202

Taylor, S. (1987). *The possibility of cooperation*. Cambridge, UK: Cambridge University Press.

Thrift, N. (2000). Performing cultures in the new economy. *Annals of the Association of American Geographers. Association of American Geographers, 4*, 674–692. doi:10.1111/0004-5608.00217

Vickery, G., & Wunsch-Vincent, S. (2007). *Participative web and user-created content: Web 2.0, wikis and social networking*. Paris, France: OECD Publishing.

Weber, S. (2004). *The success of open source*. Cambridge, MA: Harvard University Press.

Whiteman, J. (1990). Responding to Fritz: On disarming words and pictures in the telling of teleological stories. In Angeli, M. (Ed.), *On architecture, the city and technology* (pp. 26–32). Washington, DC: Butterworth.

Williamson, A., & Fung, A. (2005). Public deliberation: Where are we? Where can we go? *National Civic Review, 93*(4), 3–15. doi:10.1002/ncr.66

Williamson, O. E. (2002). The theory of the firm as governance structure: From choice to contract. *The Journal of Economic Perspectives, 16*(3), 171–195. doi:10.1257/089533002760278776

Winner, L. (1980). Do artifacts have politics? *Daedalus, 109*(1), 121–136.

Winner, L. (1993). Upon opening the black box and finding it empty: Social constructivism and the philosophy of technology. *Science, Technology & Human Values, 18*(3), 362–378. doi:10.1177/016224399301800306

Winsbury, R. (1997). How grand are the grand alliances? *Intermedia, 25*(3), 26–31.

Womack, J. P., Jones, D. T., & Roos, D. (1991). *The machine that changed the world: The story of lean production.* New York, NY: HarperCollins.

ADDITIONAL READING

Alexander, C. (1979). *A timeless way of building.* New York, NY: Oxford University Press.

Anderson, D. (1981). *Regulatory politics and electric utilities.* Boston, MA: Auburn House.

Brand, S. (1994). *How buildings learn: What happens after they're built.* New York, NY: Viking Press.

Coutard, O., Hanley, R., & Zimmerman, R. (2004). *Sustaining urban networks: The social diffusion of large technical systems.* New York, NY: Routledge.

de Gournay, C. (1988). Telephone networks in France and Great Britain. In Tarr, J. A., & Dupuy, G. (Eds.), *Technology and the rise of the networked city in Europe and America.* Philadelphia, PA: Temple University.

Fischer, C. S. (1992). *America calling: A social history of the telephone to 1940.* Berkeley, CA: University of California Press.

Foucault, M. (1980). *Power/knowledge: Selected interviews and other writings 1972-1977* (Colin, G., Ed.). New York, NY: Pantheon Books.

Foucault, M. (1991). Governmentality. In Burchell, G., Gordon, C., & Miller, P. (Eds.), *The Foucault effect* (pp. 87–104). Chicago, IL: University of Chicago Press.

Friedlander, A. (1995a). *Emerging infrastructure: The growth of railroads.* Reston, VA: Corporation for National Research Initiatives.

Friedlander, A. (1995b). *Natural monopoly and universal service: Telephones and telegraphs in the U.S. communications infrastructure, 1837-194.* Reston, VA: Corporation for National Research Initiatives.

Friedlander, A. (1996). *Power and light: Electricity in the U.S. energy infrastructure, 1870- 1940.* Reston, VA: Corporation for National Research Initiatives.

Helman, J., & Johnson, G. W. (1992). *The politics and economics of privatization: The case of wastewater treatment.* Tuscaloosa, AL: The University of Alabama Press.

Keating, A. D. (1989). *Public private partnerships: Privatization in historical perspective.* Chicago, IL: Public Works Historical Society.

Kern, S. (1986). *The culture of time and space.* Cambridge, MA: Harvard University Press.

Lorrain, D. (1992). The French model of urban services. *West European Politics, 15*(2), 77–92. doi:10.1080/01402389208424907

Meyer, J. R., & Gomez-Ibanez, J. A. (1981). *Autos, transit and cities.* Cambridge, MA: Harvard University Press.

Misa, T. (1998). *A nation of steel: The making of modern America 1865-1925.* Baltimore, MD: Johns Hopkins University Press.

Rosen, C. M. (1986). *The limits of power: Great fires and the process of city growth in America.* New York, NY: Cambridge University. doi:10.1017/CBO9780511471056

Roth, G. (1987). *The private provision of public services in developing countries.* New York, NY: Oxford University Press.

Summerton, J. (Ed.). (1994). *Changing large technical systems.* Boulder, CO: Westview Press.

Summerton, J., & Berner, B. (Eds.). (2002). *Constructing risk and safety in technological practice.* New York, NY: Routledge. doi:10.4324/9780203216774

van der Vleuten, E., & Kaijser, A. (2006). *Networking Europe: Transnational infrastructures and the shaping of Europe, 1850-2000. Sagamore Beach, MA.* USA: Science History Publications.

Vickers, J., & Wright, V. (1989). *The politics of privatisation in Western Europe.* London, UK: Frank Cass.

Weiss, M. A. (1987). *The rise of the community builders: The American real estate industry and urban land planning.* New York, NY: Columbia University Press.

ENDNOTE

1 "Improvers" included urban engineers, politicians, entrepreneurs, and most importantly influential urban utopianists such as Ebenezer Howard, Le Corbusier, and Frank Lloyd Wright (Fishman, 1990).

Chapter 2
Perspectives on Information Infrastructures

ABSTRACT

This chapter builds on the discussion in Chapter 1 by tracing the evolution of the concept of infrastructure into the concept of information infrastructure. The key objective is to describe in detail how different researchers have approached the notion from varied perspectives in their efforts to understand information infrastructure and its role in organizational transformation and practice. The objective is to clarify the distinct aspects of information infrastructures in relation to other information systems, whilst also to identify opportunities for constructing contributions in the existing literature. This chapter concludes with a summary of some key observations emerging from this critical literature review and identifies some implications for the theoretical approach adopted in the rest of this book.

INTRODUCTION

Historians of technology have consistently argued that there is no such thing as autonomous technological progress evolving free from the particularities of the culturally conditioned historical context (Hecht & Allen, 2001). In, *Networks of Power* (1983), Thomas Hughes describes large electrical networks as "evolving cultural artifacts rather than isolated technologies," reflecting and making tangible the power and politics of the spaces within which technologies are developed, implemented, and used. Hughes argues that technology gains "momentum" both by becoming institutionalized in social values, and by the very affordances of its materiality–the possibilities of use it carries in its capabilities. In doing so, technologies "embody, reinforce, and enact social and political power" (Hecht & Allen, 2001, pp.3).

DOI: 10.4018/978-1-4666-1622-6.ch002

Such historical studies of technology later gave way to various sociotechnical approaches to understanding the evolution of large technological systems (Bijker, Hughes, & Pinch, 1987) and laid the foundations for an understanding of technology as "both socially constructed and society shaping" (Hughes, 1987, pp.51). However, the focus of these studies has primarily been on technologies emerging from the industrial revolution including electrical power networks, transportation infrastructures, and telephone networks. A key characteristic of these early technologies is that they were driven by expert communities–scientists, engineers, expert workers, and often the military (Hughes & Hughes, 2000; Noble, 1984). In contrast, the new information and communication technologies emerging in the mid 20th century have given rise to a different style of technological development in which development negotiations include constituents who are not members of the expert community (Abbate, 1999; Benkler, 2006; King, 2006).

The most prominent example is the Internet, which has evolved from a scientific project between a handful of academic and research institutions throughout the United States, to a widely distributed computer network serving millions of users around the globe (Khan, 1994). ARPANET, the predecessor of today's Internet, was originally introduced in the early 1970s, by ARPA[1], the USA's Department of Defense's Advanced Research Projects Agency. The original conceptualization of ARPANET favored military values, such as flexibility and high performance over commercial goals, such as simplicity or consumer appeal. At the same time, however, the group that designed and built ARPA's networks was dominated by academics, who incorporated their own values of decentralization of authority and open exchange of information into the system. Further, as access to the ARPANET and the Internet spread beyond the initial group of computer scientists, non-expert users also exerted some influence on the development of network computing. For

instance, decisions around which applications would become the standard and which would be removed as problematic rested on the spontaneity of the non-expert users, who were continuously improvising innovative ways of using the technology (Abbate, 1999). Electronic mail and the file transfer protocol are examples of informally created applications that became popular, not as the result of 'expert' development and decision-making, but through the spontaneous decisions of thousands of independent communities of users.

The advent of the Internet and the popularization of computing technologies offered great opportunities to drastically re-conceptualize the notion of infrastructure. Specifically, under the auspices of Robert Khan and Vinton Cerf[2] of the Corporation for National Research Initiatives, an organization directly involved with the development of the Internet and the early ARPANET, the notion of *information infrastructure* was born (Gross, 1986). Khan and Cerf (1988, pp.3) first conceptualized information infrastructure as "a Digital Library System based on commonly shared standards and containing information of both local and/or widespread interest". In this sense, information infrastructure referred to possibilities "to augment our ability to search for, correlate, analyze and synthesize available information," situated in geographically distributed sites (Khan & Cerf, 1988, pp.11). This early notion of information infrastructure was, thus, pushing for the development of new distributed working spaces made possible by new and emerging information and communication technologies.

The notion of information infrastructure began to gain some popularity after the extensive announcements of different government-led plans towards the creation of national and international information infrastructures (NTIA, 1993; Bangemann et al., 1994). For example, during the Clinton-Gore administration, the USA envisioned a national information infrastructure–dubbed the "electronic superhighway"–which meant to include more than just the physical facilities used to transmit, store, process, and display voice, data, and images. The "electronic superhighway" was also thought to encompass a wide and ever-expanding range of technical artifacts; the information itself; a wide range of applications and software; the network standards and transmission codes that facilitate interoperability between networks, applications, and software; and the people who create the information, develop applications and services, and train others to tap its potential (NTIA, 1993). Similarly, the European Union envisioned a Pan-European information infrastructure, which would include applications for teleworking, road and air traffic control management, health care networks, and a trans-European public administration network (Bangemann et al., 1994).

These early conceptualizations of information infrastructure were greatly influenced by the corporate infrastructures (the corporate client-server networks) of the 1990s, which provided the basis for the first generation of work on business-IT alignment (e.g. Broadbent, Weill, & St Clair, 1999; Henderson & Venkatraman, 1993; Weill & Broadbent, 1998). In this context, and in contrast to other information systems, *information infrastructures were defined as efforts to integrate other computer-based and social systems, and to regulate and monitor processes that were previously performed in various, isolated settings.* Proponents of this body of research also defined intangible resources such as human knowledge and skills as another dimension of an information infrastructure that has to be integrated or aligned to the business objectives of a given organization (Chung, Rainer, & Lewis, 2003; Duncan, 1995; Weill & Broadbent, 1998). Clear definitions of a firm's "external domain" (i.e. the marketplace in which a firm competes) and "internal domain" (i.e. the strategic logic for (re)designing business processes) are thought to be important in achieving this alignment (Henderson & Venkatraman, 1993).

Recent studies of corporate information infrastructures have called for a need to focus not on the ways by which information infrastructures can be aligned and controlled, but rather on their emergence in practice (e.g. Ciborra & associates, 2001). This research acknowledges that an information infrastructure can never be completely controlled as it constantly grows in complexity and deviates from original intentions. While echoing Hughes' earlier work in *Networks of Power*, it is argued that *information infrastructures have a "'logic of their own'; they possess inertia and momentum; they are embedded in an institutional context"* (Ciborra & Failla, 2001, pp.124).

The importance of context in studies of information infrastructure development was first noted in sociologically-informed research into the ways by which information technology supports cooperative work (Bowker et al., 1997). In one example, Star and Ruhleder (1996) studied the development of an information infrastructure for a geographically dispersed community of geneticists. The authors found that, despite good user prototype feedback and participation in the system development, there were unforeseen, complex challenges to usage. These challenges were born from variations in understanding what is considered to be obvious IT use among users. It was only when the information infrastructure broke down or was completely replaced by something else that different individuals acknowledged each other's distinct IT use (or non-use) and related expectations. In this way, the authors shifted the focus on information infrastructure as a "thing with pre-given attributes frozen in time" (Star & Ruhleder, 1996, pp.112) to a focus on context(s). "Information infrastructure is not a substrate which carries information on it, or in it, in a kind of mind-body dichotomy. The discontinuities are not between system and person, or technology and organization, but rather between contexts" (Star & Ruhleder 1996, pp. 118).

Similar arguments were made in Bowker and Star's (1999) seminal study of the development of the International Classification of Diseases (ICD), a global information infrastructure administered by the World Health Organization (WHO). Their focus was on the historical struggles between different institutions (e.g. the WHO, the U.S. National Library of Medicine), professional healthcare communities (e.g. nurses, general practitioners, etc), and their distinct work classification systems. While conducting a historical analysis, the authors realized that while it was possible to retrieve individual classification systems for reference purposes, in reality none of them stood alone. Classifications were entangled in a kind of ecology of intersecting communities of practice and their technological choices. For this reason, the authors suggested that *information infrastructures are viewed as emergent through temporal negotiations along a trajectory of encounters between people, objects, and classes of action.* Consequently, information infrastructures are only "working infrastructures," constantly being negotiated on the boundaries (Bowker & Star, 1999; Hanseth & Lundberg, 2001; Star & Bowker, 2002; Turner et al., 2006). Each node on the infrastructure is "made up of a different stable configuration of wires, bits and people; but they are all interchangeable" (Star & Bowker, 2002, pp.155).

In summary, depending on the focus on different types of information infrastructures–from publicly available ones such as the Internet, to corporate information infrastructures, and more global, specialized systems such as the ICD–the way these infrastructures become defined and their organizational roles conceptualized varies significantly.

To begin to understand this variation, this chapter will attempt to organize the literature according to two key bodies of research. The first body of research gravitates towards business schools' tendency to employ a positivistic epistemological stance, combined with the functionalist influence of computer engineers, while seeking to develop management agendas of strategic business-IT alignment (e.g. Henderson & Venkatraman, 1993; Weill & Broadbent, 1998). The second body of research is "less immediately concerned with modelling and prescriptions" (Ciborra, 2001, pp. 21)

and more interested in an interpretive understanding of the multilevel context of information infrastructures (e.g. Ciborra & associates, 2001; Star & Ruhleder, 1996). This positioning strategy of the literature aims at uncovering some key themes to (a) theorizing information infrastructures, and (b) exploring the role of information infrastructures in practice, while at the same time communicating the general positions of this book. The differences and similarities between these diverse bodies of research are next discussed in more detail. Table 1 provides a summary of the key characteristics of each of these bodies of research.

THEORISING INFORMATION INFRASTRUCTURES

Functionalist Perspectives

Strategic alignment is perhaps the most widely adopted perspective with which to theorize information infrastructures and refers to the potential of IT as a key domain of strategic choice for an organization (Byrd & Turner, 2000; Chung, Reiner, & Lewis, 2003; Duncan, 1995; Henderson & Venkatraman, 1993; Weill & Broadbent, 1998). Information infrastructures are viewed as the fundamental component in a firm's total "IT portfolio," aiming at providing business value by successfully implementing current strategies, as well as enabling new ones. For example, Weill and Broadbent[3] (1998, pp. 26) suggest that an information infrastructure is best viewed as a pyramidal IT portfolio, which involves, in ascending order, infrastructure technology investments (referring to the underlying component of systems and applications), transactional technology investments (referring to systems supporting the routine transactions of an organization), informational technology investments (referring to systems for automation and control functions), and strategic technology investments (referring to technologies thought to increase the competitive advantage of

Table 1. Key perspectives on information infrastructures

Perspectives	Definition & key aspects of information infrastructures (II)	Key concepts for understanding the role of information infrastructures (II) in organizational transformation & practice
Functionalist (e.g. Henderson and Venkatraman, 1993; Weill and Broad-bent,1998; Weill and Ross, 2004)	*II as the fundamental component of a firm's IT investment portfolio* Key aspects of II: • *Shared (reach & range)* • *Reusable &modular* • *Built on installed base* • *Involving a human infrastructure*	*II have a teleological role to play in meeting an organization's business objectives and can only do so by adopting evolutionary, 'best-fit' maxims* • *Strategic fit*–aligning the external positioning and internal arrangements of an organization • *Functional integration*–aligning business and IT strategies, and organizational and IT processes • *Management-by-maxim*–the means by which business strategy is expressed in actionable terms • *Management-by-deals*–the deal-making process between stronger and weaker stakeholder groups
Sociotechnical (IS group) (e.g. Ciborra et al., 2001; Hanseth and Mon-teiro, 1997; Hanseth et al., 2006)	*II as heterogeneous collages of people, systems, and processes* Key aspects of II: • *Enabling* • *Shared & open* • *Embodied in standards* • *Heterogeneous* • *Built on an installed base*	*II have a combination of roles to play, from building evolutionary paths of technological dependence, to enacting teleological 'envisioned' business agendas, and offering the ground with which to resolve dialectical tensions* • *Translation*–the social process of aligning interests between different people • *Inscription*–the way technical artifacts embody patterns of use • *Irreversibility & Path Dependency*–the way in which 'strong' inscriptions resist competing translations, mediating subsequent actions and interpretations, thus creating path dependencies • *Cultivation & Reflexivity*–the way of "destabilizing current strategy and creating imbalances"; reflecting on original intentions (Ciborra, 2001 pp.21)
Sociotechnical (Sociology group) (e.g. Bowker and Star, 1999; Star and Ruhleder, 1996; Turner et al., 2006)	*II as fundamentally and always a relation* Key aspects of II: • *Embedded in social & other structures* • *Transparent in use* • *Learned as part of membership* • *Linked to conventions of practice* • *With extensive* • *reach or scope* • *Embodied in standards* • *Built on an installed base* • *Fixed in modular increments, not all at once or globally* • *Visible upon breakdown*	*II bring out the information-communication aspects of social order, while generating a number of intended and unintended consequences for the communities involved* • *Community of Practice*–a set of relations between people doing things together including their artifacts and classes of action. • *Membership in a Community of Practice*–the resolution of tensions between encounters with people, artifacts, and classes of action. • *Naturalisation of Artifacts in a Community of Practice* – the way artifacts become part of community routines (taken for granted) • *Boundary Objects*–these objects may have different meanings in different communities but their structure is common enough to more than one community to make them recognizable; a means of translation

organizations). In this sense, the strategic alignment perspective pays particular attention to the business scope of an information infrastructure.

The business scope of any information technology is defined through the variables of *reach* and *range*, first proposed by Keen (1991), and initially adopted towards the conceptualization of information infrastructures by Duncan (1995). Reach refers to the connectivity of IT components, or the number and variety of information systems to which an organization can connect at any point in time, locally or remotely, while range refers to the capacity to share types of IT services, data, and information between different information systems. Reach and range essentially refer to the ability of a given technology to be *shared* by a community of users and other information systems, locally and remotely, inside and outside organizational boundaries (Duncan, 1995, pp.42). A second aspect considered to be highly critical for the design of information infrastructures is the *reusability* or *modularity* of its components.

Modularity translates to an ability to add, modify, and remove IT components with ease and with little or no effect on the technical features and processes of other components (Byrd & Turner, 2000; Duncan, 1995; Chung, Rainer, & Lewis, 2003). Modularity is based on the widely accepted belief that IT applications and data are more manageable when required routines are processed in separate modules. For example, modularized middleware provides interoperability between legacy applications and newer applications (Chung, Rainer, & Lewis, 2003). Furthermore, modularity leads to the sub-principles of decomposition and recombination of IT components, that is, the segregation, integration, and rearrangement of different modules, as well as their re-usability (Duncan, 1995). Therefore, an information infrastructure is understood to be constantly built on different layers, that is, it constantly evolves on the existing installed base (Weill & Broadbent, 1998). Finally, some advocates of the strategic alignment perspective have also included a human aspect to theorizing information infrastructures, which involves a number of intangible resources, such as human values and norms, knowledge and skills, commitments, and competencies (Byrd & Turner, 2000; Chung, Rainer, & Lewis, 2003; Weill & Broadbent, 1998). The constant upgrading and steering of these intangible resources falls in the hands of upper management. Thus, in a sense, the human aspect of information infrastructures is viewed as another dimension of the total IT portfolio.

Sociotechnical Perspectives

Functionalist accounts of information infrastructures are criticized for failing to account for the "'multilevel context' of interesting, complex infrastructures, and the processes of technical, organizational, and economic change within which the infrastructure is a key element" (Ciborra, 2001, pp.25). In this multilevel context, information infrastructures are found to emerge through an interplay of the diverse interests and intentions of participant stakeholder groups and are, thus, partly out of control. Information infrastructures tend to "drift," that is, they deviate from the planned purpose for a variety of reasons often outside the influence of an organization's top management (Ciborra, 2001). As Ciborra and Hanseth (2001, pp.5) argue, in contrast to Weill and Broadbent's (1998) focus on a top-down process towards the measurement and control of resources, "alignment is a long, tortuous, and fragile process whereby multiple actors and resources try to influence each other to constitute a new socio-technical order."

Based on this broad realization, it is suggested that information infrastructures are understood through five key aspects (Hanseth, 2001, pp.56-60)[4]. Firstly, an information infrastructure has a supporting or *enabling* function in the sense that a field of new activities emerge, but not merely to improve or automate something that already exists. This is opposed to it being designed especially to support one way of working within a specific application field. Secondly, an information infrastructure is *shared* by, and *open* to, a large community or collection of users and technological components. This attribute implies that information infrastructures should be approached as irreducible units with unlimited numbers of users and technological components, as well as activities and processes; the removal of any of these elements will have a substantial effect on the functioning and sustainability of the rest of the information infrastructure. Thirdly, the different components of an information infrastructure are *embodied in different standards*, which facilitate the interconnection and interoperation between the different components. However, the requirements and conditions for development are constantly changing because of the shared and open aspect of information infrastructures. Fourthly, information infrastructures are *heterogeneous* in the sense that they are socio-technical networks involving different layers of technological components, humans, organizations, institutions, and so on.

Finally, information infrastructures are never developed from scratch; they *always develop on the existing installed base*. That is, new technologies will always be integrated into or replace part of an existing information infrastructure. This has been the case in the building of more traditional infrastructures, such as transportation and telecommunication infrastructures, as well as more recent information infrastructures, such as the World Wide Web, which was built on the Internet.

In theorizing information infrastructures, Ciborra (2001, pp.23) and Hanseth (2001, pp.56-60) explicitly refer to the work of Star and Ruhleder (1996), who approach information infrastructures as "a delicate balance of language and practice across communities and parts of organizations" (1996, pp.117). To this end, Star and Ruhleder (1996) suggest a move away from the traditional scope of information infrastructure research, which is primarily concerned with a study of work processes and the ways those become mediated by technology. Instead, they suggest a commitment to a study of continuity as opposed to discontinuity (or of an ongoing process vs. a separation of events), plurality as opposed to elitism (or of multiple voices vs. a single 'privileged' voice), work practice as opposed to reified theory (or of empirical vs. formal representations), and relativity as opposed to absolutism (or of context specific vs. 'superior' epistemological positions) (Star, 1995, pp. 15). In this sense, although the approach adopted by Star and her associates (e.g. Star & Ruhleder, 1996; Bowker & Star, 1999; Turner et al., 2006) has strong connections to the work of Hanseth and Monteiro (1997) and Ciborra and associates (2001)–primarily due to that both groups of researchers draw from the broad field of Science and Technology Studies (STS)–the former are informed by a more rooted sociological tradition. Although the differences are subtle and there have not been any prior formal comparisons between these closely related but distinctive groups of researchers, some of the

differences and similarities in their treatment of information infrastructure are discussed below.

Star and Ruhleder (1996, pp.113) suggest that information infrastructures are *embedded* or "sunk into" other structures, social arrangements, and technologies. This aspect may be said to have some resemblance to Hanseth's (2001) (and Hanseth & Monteiro, 1997) conceptualization of information infrastructures as multi-layered entities comprised of technological components, people, and institutional arrangements. Furthermore, Star and Ruhleder (1996, pp.113) suggest that information infrastructures are *transparent in use*, in that, they do not have to be reinvented each time but rather they "invisibly" support different tasks. The closest Hanseth's (2001) definition comes to the notion of transparency is in his suggestion that information infrastructures have an enabling function, i.e., that they are designed to support a wide range of activities (Hanseth, 2001, pp. 56). However, this enabling aspect seems to suggest that information infrastructures are supportive of work tasks by definition, whereas the Star and Ruhleder's (1996) transparency aspect assumes that information infrastructures become supportive in time through community evolution and adoption of IT, "involving new forms and conventions that we cannot yet imagine" (Ruhleder, 1996, pp. 132). These ideas are related to Star and Ruhleder's (1996) third and fourth aspects of information infrastructures, which constitute the key distinction of their approach from others. Specifically, Star and Ruhleder (1996, pp.113) argue that an information infrastructure is *learned as part of membership*. That is, information infrastructures become naturalized through membership in a given community. Moreover, an information infrastructure both *shapes and is shaped by the conventions of a given community* (Star & Ruhleder, 1996, pp. 113). Both these aspects are not addressed by the definition offered by Hanseth (2001), who tends to implicitly focus on 'privileged positions' of key actors (as opposed to plural and communal) (see Bowker & Star, 1999 for a critique) when approaching information infrastructure (but see Rolland & Monteiro, 2002; Sahay et al., 2009, for variations of this aspect).

Hanseth's (2001) definition of information infrastructures seems to have a clear affinity to the fifth, sixth, seventh, and eighth aspects of Star and Ruhleder's (1996) definition. Specifically, in relation to Star and Ruhleder's (1996) point that information infrastructures have *spatial or temporal reach beyond a single event or one-site practice*, Hanseth (2001) argues that information infrastructure is shared and open to a large collection of users and technological components. In relation to Star and Ruhleder's (1996) point that information infrastructures as *embodied into other infrastructures and tools in a standardized fashion* (1996, pp.113), Hanseth (2001, pp.57) argues that "standards are a necessary constituting element" to the collection of information infrastructure connections (also see Monteiro, 1998). In relation to Star and Ruhleder's (1996) point that information infrastructures *build on the "inertia of the installed base"* and inherit strengths and limitations from that base (Star & Ruhleder, 1996, pp.113), Hanseth (2001, pp.60) also states that information infrastructures are never built from scratch but develop on the existing installed base. Further, Star and associates argue that information infrastructure is *fixed in modular increments, not all at once or globally*. This is an aspect added to Star and Ruhleder's (1996) definition by Bowker and Star (1999, pp.35) to refer to the way in which an information infrastructure develops and evolves as an irreducible unit that is never changed from above. Changes take time and negotiation among all participant communities and their associated activities and choice of artifacts. Evidently, this aspect may be said to resemble Hanseth's (2001) notion of information infrastructure as an irreducible unit (also see Hanseth & Monteiro, 1997).

Finally, in the ninth aspect of their definition, Star and Ruhleder (1996) argue that the normally invisible quality of a working information infrastructure *becomes visible when it breaks down* (e.g. the server is down). Similar to the notion of transparency discussed earlier, this aspect is not addressed by Hanseth (2001). However, it can be argued that Ciborra and associates (2001) would most probably agree that the "visibility" of information infrastructure is interlinked with the "breakdown" of information infrastructure, since when viewed as an irreducible unit, an information infrastructure depends on the continuous functioning of all its elements; if an element breaks down the whole information infrastructure becomes visible because it is immediately transformed by the event.

In summary, in contrast to functionalist perspectives that place a great deal of emphasis on prescriptive, upper-management control, sociotechnical perspectives view information infrastructure as an ever-evolving socio-technical network of people, social arrangements, artifacts, and activities. Furthermore, the broad body of sociotechnical research in this topic area can be distinguished between two groups of researchers, who, although exhibit some similarity in their conceptualization of information infrastructures, differ in their methodological directions. Although acknowledging the importance of formal representations of technologies (e.g. technical, scientific, managerial) as Hanseth and Monteiro (1997) and Ciborra and associates, (2001) do in their own work, Star and Ruhleder (1996) and Bowker and Star (1999) distinguish their approach by paying particular attention to the communicative processes and community conventions entangled in the development and use of new technologies, and the ways in which those technologies acquire symbolic representations of work in the practices of those communities. In order to understand this key distinction, as well as to further discuss the differences between the two broad bodies of information infrastructure research, the next section will provide a discussion of the ways in which the different proponents have explored the role of information infrastructure in practice. This examination will be preceded by a brief discussion of concepts concerning organizational change and development, which are central to understanding information infrastructures as involved in historical processes of transformation.

THE ROLE OF INFORMATION INFRASTRUCTURES IN PRACTICE

In a path breaking study towards an understanding of the ways in which organizations change, Van de Ven and Poole (1995) identified four main change-process models: (1) life-cycle, (2) evolutionary, (3) teleology, and (4) dialectical. Firstly, the life-cycle model employs the metaphor of organic growth as "a heuristic device to explain organizational development from its initiation to its termination" (Van de Ven & Poole, 1995, pp.513). In this model, change is linear and imminent much like the birth, evolution, and maturity of natural organisms–each phase of change sets the stage for the next and each contributes a piece to the final outcome. The life-cycle model, as used in organizational research, often explains change and development in terms of institutional rules "that require developmental activities to progress in a prescribed sequence" (Van de Ven & Poole, 1995, pp.515). Similar to the life-cycle model, change in the evolutionary model is prescriptive and natural, in that, each phase is prefigured from the previous one. The difference between the two is that change in the evolutionary model is nonlinear but based on a probabilistic progression of variation (changes created randomly or by chance), selection (environment selects the best competitors), and retention (forces like inertia and persistence that balance variation and selection). The evolutionary model, as used in organizational research, explains change and development in terms of competitive survival and how organizations compete for scarce resources as well as how the environment selects entities that best fit the resource base of an environmental niche (Van de Ven & Poole, 1995).

Unlike the first two models, which are prescriptive in nature, the teleology and dialectic models are constructive in nature. On the one hand, the teleology model explains change and development as a means to achieve a goal or an end state. According to this model, an organization is assumed to be purposeful and adaptive and change is seen as a repetitive sequence of formulation, implementation, evaluation, and modification of goals based on what was learned or intended by the members of a given organization (Van de Ven & Poole, 1995, pp.516). On the other hand, in the dialectical model, stability and change are explained by reference to the balance of power between opposing entities, whether those are individuals or organizations (Van de Ven & Poole, 1995). In this sense, opposition does not necessarily mean conflict, rather it refers to the dialectical process of give and take, of negotiating meaning and synthesizing action. For example, an entity subscribing to thesis A may be challenged by an opposing entity with an antithesis Not-A, and the conclusion of the conflict produces a synthesis of something like Not Not-A. Over time, this synthesis can become the new thesis as the dialectical process continues.

Evidently, there are multiple variations as well as combinations of these four main models to understanding organizational change and development (Van de Ven & Poole, 1995). However, by presenting these models here the aim is to further analyze the similarities and differences between different bodies of understanding the development of information infrastructures. To exemplify this effort, the following paragraphs will first describe the ways in which different proponents have explored information infrastructure in practice and then these approaches will be discussed as to how they relate to the four main models of organizational change and development.

Functionalist Perspectives

Explored through the lens of the functionalist body of research, information infrastructures are seen as being able to facilitate "a number of as-yet-unspecified business strategies to be implemented more rapidly" (Weill & Broadbent, 1998, pp.101). Although highly optimistic in their approach, Weill and Broadbent (1998) acknowledge that complete alignment is usually non-sustainable because of various barriers, such as an organization's fluctuating strategic context (e.g. the adaptability of the human infrastructure's IT knowledge and skills to emerging needs and requirements). In an attempt to overcome these barriers, Weill and Broadbent (1998) identify two approaches to managing strategic alignment: "management-by-maxim" (i.e. firm-wide enforceable statements such as "develop partnerships with customers on a world-wide basis") and "management-by-deals" (i.e. the deal-making process between diverse business units in an organization). The management-by-deals approach essentially refers to political power issues and an uneven development of information infrastructures. As Weill and Broadbent (1998, pp. 159) state, "[t]he deal-making process is the free market of information technology infrastructure formation. The free market often means that powerful, successful, and rich business units are far better served by the information technology infrastructures." The authors acknowledge that there is strong evidence to suggest the deal-making process is present in approximately 50 percent of the cases examined, involving such issues as conflict of interest and benefits gained, political agendas, and economies of scale (Weill & Broadbent, 1998, pp. 158-59). However, as noted by Ciborra (2001, pp.20), apart from making a list of different issues involved in the deal-making process (Weill & Broadbent, 1998, pp.159), the authors barely touch the management-by-deals approach. In fact, in line with a series of normative prescriptions or "maxims" introduced throughout the book, the authors end with the proposal of "Ten Leadership Principles" (Weill & Broadbent, 1998, pp. 244) that promise to achieve up to 40 percent of an organization's strategic alignment objectives.

In this sense, functionalist approaches for exploring the role of information infrastructures in practice can be said to primarily employ a teleological model of organizational change, in that, they tend to approach information infrastructures as a purposeful enactment: an investment to meet the strategic business objectives of an organization (Weill & Broadbent, 1998). Although constructive in principle, the teleological model employed by the strategic alignment perspective tries to prescribe change through different maxims, as if trying to enforce the 'natural selection' of 'best fit' scenarios, tweaking the evolutionary model into a teleological philosophy. Such normative prescriptions (and their bold predictions) are very common in management literature and usually aim at providing guidelines for central coordination and control of IT projects. However, many empirical studies and insightful thinking related to the actual management of IT, point out that information infrastructures evolve in the interplay between multiple and contradictory forces. These include unplanned systems requirements emerging from the lack of IT knowledge and skills of the users (Duncan, 1995), the interplay between the local needs of the users and the global intentions and interests of the larger, distributed community (Rolland & Monteiro, 2002), and the tension between standardization and flexibility (Hanseth, Monteiro, & Hatling, 1996; Hanseth, Jacucci, Grisot, & Aanestad, 2006).

Even in the empirical data presented in Weill and Broadbent's (1998) work, there is evidence of such interplays (i.e. the deal-making processes). In addition, extensive review of top managers' opinions does not seem to lead to any clear-cut answers towards the relationship between strategic alignment and flexibility or adaptability to change (Byrd & Turner, 2000; Chung, Rainer, & Lewis, 2003; Duncan, 1995). In summary, although the strategic alignment perspective has offered some valuable insights towards an understanding of information infrastructures, it lacks analytical depth as to the role of technology in organizational change. For example, the proponents of the strategic alignment perspective develop various "constructs" or "benchmarking instruments" for measuring the flexibility of information infrastructures (Byrd & Turner, 2000; Duncan, 1995), and propose a series of "leadership principles" for managing the emergence of new technologies (Weill & Broadbent, 1998). However, all these proposals take little (if any) note of the interplay between multiple and contradictory forces shaping and being shaped by the use of technology in practice.

Sociotechnical Perspectives

In contrast to functionalist perspectives, sociotechnical perspectives have argued that the development and use of an information infrastructure is "an involved, socio-technical process of negotiation" (Monteiro, 2001, pp.69). To approach the open-ended character of this negotiation process and to enlighten how information infrastructures develop in practice, some researchers employ principles from actor-network theory (ANT) (e.g. Ciborra & Failla, 2001; Hanseth & Monteiro, 1997; Monteiro, 2001). There are two key concepts from ANT that are of particular relevance here: *inscription* (Akrich & Latour, 1992) and *translation* (Callon, 1991; Latour, 1991).

On the one hand, the concept of inscription refers to the way technical artefacts embody patterns of use. For example, information infrastructures in the healthcare sector employ different types of standards (classification and coding schemes, terminologies, etc.), which provide a *shared* pattern of use among different healthcare centres and between different healthcare professionals (Hanseth & Monteiro, 1997). On the other hand, the concept of translation refers to the social process of aligning interests, that is, the ability

to re-interpret, re-present, or appropriate others' interests to one's own (Monteiro, 2001). Translation presupposes a medium or "material into which [translation] is inscribed"; translations are "embodied in texts, machines, [and] bodily skills [which] become their support, their more or less faithful executive" (Callon, 1991, pp.143). In this sense, the development of information infrastructures is considered to be a process of translating the needs, interests, and work tasks of the users and the broader organizational community into inscriptions. Inscriptions include patterns of use or "programs of actions" (Latour, 1991) which define the roles to be played by each participant in the overall network. When a program of action is inscribed in the different components of the information infrastructure, the information infrastructure becomes an actor imposing its inscribed program of action on its users (Monteiro, 2001). However, the inscribed patterns of use may not succeed because the actual use may deviate from it and users may use the system in ways unanticipated by IT developers or they may follow an "anti-program of action" (Latour, 1991).

The strength of inscriptions (i.e. strong/inflexible vs. weak/flexible programs of actions), whether they must be followed or avoided, depends on the "irreversibility" of the actor-network into which they are inscribed. Irreversibility is the way in which existing translations resist assaults from competing translations and the extent to which the actor-network shapes and determines subsequent translations (Callon, 1991). In this way, through early design choices, information infrastructures can become path dependent (Hanseth, 2001).

For example, in a case study on the development of information infrastructure standards in the Norwegian health sector, Hanseth and Monteiro (1997) examine the programs of actions inscribed in the standards and the ways in which these "strong" inscriptions help realize information infrastructure as an irreversible actor-network that can resist competing translations. In another example of research on the development of a customer relationship management (CRM) infrastructure at IBM, Ciborra and Failla (2001, pp.117) argue how by building the main steps of CRM on Lotus Notes, IBM was able to "freeze the CRM discipline in silicon". The growing use of Lotus Notes by IBM employees increased the scope and depth of control of CRM processes by "'enforcing' globally behaviours on how to run the business" (Ciborra & Failla, 2001, pp.118).

Despite these empirical examples, many advocates of the ANT approach have indicated that, an actor-network can never be completely aligned as it constantly grows in complexity bringing about more competing translations and unintended consequences that constantly negotiate the actor-network's once irreversible nature (Ellingsen & Monteiro, 2003; Monteiro, 2001). As argued earlier, alignment is neither straightforward nor controllable in any strict sense (Monteiro, 2001). Thus, even if decision-makers set out to inscribe programs of action in the technology, there is no guarantee that the users will align their activities accordingly. The inscribed programs of action may or may not succeed depending on the strength of the users' anti-programs of action (Latour, 1991).

As Ciborra and Failla (2001, pp.123) note, the implementation of a vision does not solely depend on the inscriptions in the technology, but more importantly on pre-existing capabilities and context. Context refers to the organizational, technological, and social environment in which implementation takes place, including formal and informal arrangements between employees, as well as the existing installed technological base. It is by understanding this context that managers can "cultivate"–i.e. destabilize current strategy and create imbalances with the current level of technology (Ciborra, 2001). That is, managers need to be aware of reflexive processes; they need to appreciate that the intended objective of standardized systems will often lead to alternative and unanticipated outcomes (Hanseth et al 2006). These observations bring out the following implications.

Ciborra and associates can be said to employ a combination of different models of organizational transformation. Firstly, within the premises of actor-network analysis, they can be said to employ some of the concepts of the evolutionary model, in that, each translation and each inscription, is prefigured from the series of translations and inscriptions that precedes them. These are also defined by levels of strength or weaknesses and their ability to resist competing translations. In addition, by employing the theoretical lens of ANT, researchers in this first group can also be said to move from an ecological to a teleological model of organizational transformation, in that, they pay particular attention to an "envisioned enactment"–translating and inscribing the concerns of several actors into an envisioned "obligatory passage point" (Latour, 1991; Law & Callon, 1995). This is not to say that actor networks cease to negotiate change, but rather it points to the ongoing process of translation between the diverse interests and intentions of multiple stakeholders and the heterogeneous resources they employ. Thus, researchers in this tradition can also be said to acknowledge the presence of dialectical change, whereby different actants in a heterogeneous network of people, artifacts, processes, etc., engage in a continuous negotiation process in their attempt to appropriate emergent change.

Despite such a wide ranging appreciation of the role of information infrastructure in organizational change, sociotechnical approaches are criticized for their relaxed decision of where and when to 'cut' the information infrastructure, i.e. what/who is to be included or excluded and when. This is a consequence of the underlying methodology employed by most sociotechnical studies of information infrastructures that requires researchers to "follow the actors," often ethnographically. In following the actors, researchers enter the world they are studying, uncovering strategies, practices, negotiations and outcomes, both intended and unintended. At the same time, however, through this methodological approach, researchers blindly tune-in the strategies of those actors leading the agenda with the risk of losing the bigger picture, as Bowker and Star (1999, pp. 48-49) critically note in the following quote:

... if we just follow the doctors who create the ICD [International Classification of Diseases] at the WHO [World Health Organization] in Geneva, we will not see the variety of representation systems that other cultures have for classifying diseases of the body and spirit; and we will not see the fragile networks these classification systems subtend. Rather, we will see only those who are strong enough, and shaped in such a fashion as to impact allopathic medicine. We will see the blind leading the blind.

What Bowker and Star (1999) are suggesting here is that, although it is important to understand the design choices behind a given technology, it is even more essential to pay attention to the practices that allow for that technology to be used. That is, while it is significant to investigate the intentional plans of inventors, policy-makers, and other strong bodies, it is also important to investigate the practices of those directly involved in the project who may negotiate developments from the bottom up (Bowker & Star, 1999). Such an approach builds on the premises of symbolic interactionism, which (Van House, 2003, pp. 25):

is concerned with patterns of commitments formed by negotiation of alliances and development of conventional procedures and arrangements.

While employing such a methodological direction, Bowker and Star (1999) and their associates, focus on relationships and community conventions and the indefinite number of ways in which entrepreneurs from different participating communities may create alternative strategies in their own world. They argue that these are the kinds of "politics in action" that researchers should be paying attention to (Bowker & Star, 1999).

To study these politics, it is suggested that researchers not only pay close attention to the material and symbolic properties of information infrastructures, i.e. what each element means and how it is applied in practice, but, more importantly, to look at the historical trajectory of arriving at those material and symbolic properties (also see Monteiro & Hepso, 2002). In other words, researchers need to uncover the multi-vocality of the process of arriving at categories and standards, as well as the process of deciding what will be visible or invisible within the information infrastructure (Bowker & Star, 1999, pp.44). On the one hand, arriving at standards is a process of ongoing negotiation and conflict between multiple voices. On the other hand, the process by which visibility is decided is the result of moral biases to personal and community interests since there are always different advantages and disadvantages for different groups of individuals. In this context, it becomes critical to understand how negotiations take place, as well as how a final outcome is reached, for whom, by whom, and with what consequences. Bearing this in mind, Bowker and Star (1999, pp. 320) note:

'Moral' questions arise when the categories of the powerful become taken for granted; when policy decisions are layered into inaccessible technological structures, when one group's visibility comes at the expense of another's suffering.

In this attempt, advocates of this second group of researchers have immersed themselves into comprehending two sets of relationships: between people and membership; and between artifacts and their naturalization by communities of practice (Bowker & Star, 1999). Firstly, individual membership processes are about the resolution of tensions between ambiguous (new, strange) and naturalized (at home, taken-for-granted) encounters with people, artifacts, and classes of action involved in a community of practice. In an ecology of communities of practice (e.g. academic institutions, professional groups, etc.) not only are people members at multiple communities, but membership to any community of practice is constantly being negotiated. This brings the discussion to the second set of relationships: How could people from diverse communities of practice cooperate without necessarily agreeing on their sets of artifacts and classes of action?

In developing models for this question, Star coined the term *boundary objects* to talk about how scientists balance different categories and meanings (Star & Griesemer, 1989; Star, 1989). Boundary objects, whether abstract (concepts) or concrete (artifacts), are those objects that originate and continue to be negotiated in more than one community of practice while satisfying the informational requirements of each of them. They have two important properties: they are loosely structured in common use, and become more tightly bound in particular locations (Bowker & Star, 1999). In this sense, boundary objects have varied meanings in different communities but their structure is common enough to more than one community to make them recognizable. Thus, Bowker and Star (1999, pp. 297) note:

the creation and management of boundary objects is a key process in developing and maintaining coherence across intersecting communities.

In this sense, the second group of researchers within the broader body of sociotechnical approaches can be said to synthesize and extend the models of organizational change and development. Specifically, they suggest researchers deconstruct more traditional views of technology development and use by "disembedding the narratives" contained in the development of information infrastructures and "unearthing" the deeper social structures embedded in the broader organizational context (Star, 2002, pp.110). Details such as the technical specifications and standards of information infrastructures, as well as the work processes in a given organizational context, cannot reveal the

ways in which people interact behind the scenes or how knowledge is constrained, built, and preserved. As Star (2002) notes, the important point is not to reach the realization that social contexts indeed contain multiple values and biases, but rather, after reaching this realization, to try to theorize about the information-communication aspects of social order and understand the consequential outcomes wrought by information technology.

In summary, this section linked the four main models of organizational change and development proposed by Van de Ven and Poole (1995) to the ways in which different researchers have explored the role of information infrastructures in practice, in an attempt to further analyze the similarities and differences between diverse perspectives.

Firstly, functionalist perspectives are found to greatly emphasize the teleological role of technology in introducing organizational change towards business objectives through the influence of a series of normative prescriptions (Weill & Broadbent, 1998). On the other hand, sociotechnical perspectives are found to acknowledge the mediating role of all socio-technical elements in a given context, thus, embracing a combination of models of change and development. Within the broad body of sociotechnical perspectives, one group of researchers seem to move between an ecological and a teleological model of change by exploring the momentum or heterogeneous trajectory of information infrastructures over time, while paying particular attention to those leading developments toward particular outcomes (Ciborra & associates, 2001). In contrast, a separate group of researchers within the broad body of sociotechnical perspectives are found to move beyond traditional views of organizational change and development and towards an understanding of the visible and invisible elements that allow an information infrastructure to emerge in practice (Bowker & Star, 1999). This exploration entails an understanding of the relationship of people with participant communities of practice, as well as an understanding of the ways in which artifacts and material arrangements become naturalized in those communities. Such an understanding aims at allowing for multiple voices to be heard, whilst also opening up possibilities to unearth some of the deep social structures and "silent back stage elements" behind the development of information infrastructures (Star, 2002, pp.115).

Concluding, it should be stressed that, while this exploration of the literature has been comparative, the purpose was not to evaluate these diverse positions, but rather to point to alternative ways of approaching the development of information infrastructures. Some key implications emerging from this literature review will be discussed next.

CONCLUSION: KEY IMPLICATIONS FROM THE LITERATURE REVIEW

As evident from the above discussion, conceptualizing information infrastructures is not as obvious as it first seems. Unlike other information systems, information infrastructures involve a wide variety of computer-based systems, which are typically integrated and embedded in diverse social and technological arrangements. That is, information infrastructures are different from other information systems in the sense that they are all around us, entrenched in taken-for-granted sociotechnical relations between people, artifacts, and practices. For instance, telecommunication networks are 'ready-to-hand,' allowing us to dial-up a number and talk to our friends and colleagues without worrying about the various technologies and practices that work together to enable us to have long-distance communications across different time zones and geographical spaces. Thus, it is suggested that researchers approach information infrastructures as already existing and embedded in an ecology of heterogeneous arrangements and not as things that exist in isolation (Constantinides & Barrett, 2005).

A first implication emerging from this literature review is the need to unearth the *multilevel context*

of sociotechnical relations that contribute to the development of existing information infrastructures. For example, in a study of the development of a customer relationship management (CRM) infrastructure at IBM, Ciborra and Failla (2001, pp.123) illustrate how the resistance of IBM's "well-managed, centralised bureaucracy" to be transformed into a "decentralized" and "teamwork-based" organisation was due to the extant institutional "formative context" found at IBM–i.e. "the set of institutional arrangements," that govern not only the execution of current routines, but also "the enactment of any socio-technical innovation." Moreover, in Star and Ruhleder's (1996) study, the role of actors' personal feelings such as fear and shame in mediating the introduction of new technologies was understood as the communal context of practices and relationships that can also shape new technological innovations. In other studies, this has been called the human dimension of information infrastructure (Chang, Reiner, & Lewis, 2003; Duncan, 1995; Weill & Broadbent, 1998). In addition, context also includes the material characteristics of the information infrastructure in relation to the work practices of the users (Bowker & Star, 1999; Monteiro & Hepso, 2002). For example, in a study of a Lotus Notes-based infrastructure in an international oil company, Monteiro and Hepso (2002) provide a compelling discussion of how the material properties of an information infrastructure helped to constitute a sociotechnical context within which organizational order could be achieved. These studies demonstrate how unearthing the multilevel context of such practices and relationships can help inform our understanding of the negotiations that take place around the development of information infrastructures.

A second implication concerns the way in which an information infrastructure evolves in time through *negotiations* between diverse groups and individuals directly involved in its development. These negotiation processes have been called the deal-making processes between stronger and weaker stakeholder groups (Weill & Broadbent, 1998), involved socio-technical negotiations (Monteiro, 2001), and practical politics (Bowker & Star, 1999). These negotiation processes need to be considered in relation to the underlying context(s) of information infrastructure development in order not to lose sight of the more complex ecology at work (Bowker & Star, 1999). More recently, the importance of acknowledging the role and interplay of political and technical configurations in the development of information infrastructures has also been emphasized (Chilundo & Aanestad, 2005; Sahay et al., 2009). For example, Sahay et al., (2009) highlight the different sets of actors, both small and large, whose negotiations are significant to understand the how and why of configuring information infrastructures–i.e. their ability to adapt, interconnect, co-evolve, and integrate. They found that smaller actors have little choice but to align their new information systems with the existing institutions' agendas, practices, and routines (also see Braa et.al., 2004). Sahay et al., (2009) coin the term "asymmetric integration" to reflect the uneven distribution of power and resources between stakeholders in the negotiation processes. It is, thus, important to understand how such negotiation processes lead to specific outcomes, and with what possible consequences for both the information infrastructures being developed as well as the organizations developing them.

This last point leads to the third and final implication emerging from the literature review, namely, the need to understand the role that information infrastructures play in particular organizational *outcomes*. Research on information infrastructures ranges from viewing technology as having a teleological function to play in organizational practices such as strategic business-IT alignment (Weill & Broadbent, 1998), to acknowledging that technology gains momentum over time and contributes to evolutionary processes of organizational change (Ciborra & associates, 2001), and finally to paying attention to the dialectical tensions embedded in extant sociotechnical inscriptions and associated forms of resistance (Hanseth & Monteiro, 1997). It has also been argued that research in the development of information infrastructures needs to closely examine the intended and unintended consequences of the technology in supporting particular sets of practices while inhibiting others with significant implications for the different parties involved as well as the infrastructure itself (Bowker & Star, 1999; Hanseth et al., 2006).

The next chapter will incorporate these implications into a theoretical basis for studying information infrastructures.

REFERENCES

Abbate, J. (1999). *Inventing the Internet*. Cambridge, MA: MIT Press.

Akrich, M., & Latour, B. (1992). A summary of a convenient vocabulary for the semiotics of human and nonhuman assemblies. In W.E., Bijker, & J. Law (Eds.), *Shaping technology/building society*, (pp. 259-264). Cambridge, MA: MIT Press.

Bangemann, M., da Fonseca, E. C., Davis, P., de Benedetti, C., Gyllenhamman, P., & Hunsel, L. …von Pierer, H. (1994). *Europe and the global information society: Bangemann report recommendations to the European council*. Brussels, Belgium: European Council.

Benkler, Y. (2006). *The wealth of networks*. New Haven, CT: Yale University Press.

Bijker, W. E., Hughes, T. P., & Pinch, T. (1987). *The social construction of technological systems*. Cambridge, MA: The MIT Press.

Bowker, G., Star, L., Turner, W. A., & Gasser, L. (Eds.). (1997). *Social science, technical systems and cooperative work: Beyond the great divide*. Mahwah, NJ: Lawrence Erlbaum Associates.

Bowker, G., & Star, S. L. (1999). *Sorting things out–Classification and its consequences*. Cambridge, MA: MIT Press.

Broadbent, M., Weill, P., & St. Clair, D. (1999). The implications of information technology infrastructure for business process redesign. *Management Information Systems Quarterly, 23*(2), 159–182. doi:10.2307/249750

Byrd, T. A., & Turner, D. E. (2000). Measuring the flexibility of information technology infrastructure: Exploratory analysis of a construct. *Journal of Management Information Systems, 17*(1), 167–208.

Callon, M. (1991). Techno-economic networks and irreversibility. In Law, J. (Ed.), *A sociology of monsters: Essays on power, technology and domination* (pp. 132–161). London, UK: Routledge Press.

Chung, S. H., Rainer, K. R. Jr, & Lewis, B. R. (2003). The impact of information technology infrastructure flexibility on strategic alignment and application implementations. *Communications of the AIS, 11*(11), 191–206.

Ciborra, C. U. (Ed.), & associates. (2001). *From control to drift: The dynamics of corporate information infrastructures*. Oxford, UK: Oxford University Press.

Ciborra, C. U. (2001). A critical review of the literature on the management of corporate information infrastructure. In Ciborra, C. U. (Ed.), *From control to drift: The dynamics of corporate information infrastructures* (pp. 15–40). Oxford, UK: Oxford University Press.

Ciborra, C. U., & Failla, A. (2001). Infrastructure as a process: The case of CRM in IBM. In Ciborra, C. U. (Ed.), *From control to drift: The dynamics of corporate information infrastructures* (pp. 105–124). Oxford, UK: Oxford University Press.

Constantinides, P., & Barrett, M. (2005). Approaching information infrastructure as an ecology of ubiquitous sociotechnical relations. In Sorensen, C., Yoo, Y., Lyytinen, K., & DeGross, J. I. (Eds.), *Designing ubiquitous information environments: Sociotechnical issues and challenges* (pp. 249–260). New York, NY: Springer. doi:10.1007/0-387-28918-6_19

Duncan, N. B. (1995). Capturing flexibility of information technology infrastructure: A study of resource characteristics and their measure. *Journal of Management Information Systems, 12*(2), 37–57.

Ellingsen, G., & Monteiro, E. (2003). A patchwork planet: integration and cooperation in hospitals. *Computer Supported Cooperative Work, 12*(1), 71–95. doi:10.1023/A:1022469522932

Gross, P. (Ed.). (1986). *Proceedings of the 15-17 October 1986 Joint Meeting of Internet Engineering and Internet Architecture Task Forces. Fourth IETF*. Menlo Park, California: Corporation for National Research Initiatives. Retrieved October 13, 2010, from http://www.ietf.org/old/2009/proceedings/prior29/IETF04.pdf

Hanseth, O. (2001). The economics of standards. In Ciborra, C. U. (Ed.), *From control to drift: The dynamics of corporate information infrastructures* (pp. 56–70). Oxford, UK: Oxford University Press.

Hanseth, O., Jacucci, E., Grisot, M., & Aanestad, M. (2006, August). Reflexive standardization: Side effects and complexity in standard making. *Management Information Systems Quarterly, 30*, 563–581.

Hanseth, O., & Lundberg, N. (2001). Designing work oriented infrastructures. *Computer Supported Cooperative Work, 10*(3-4), 347–372. doi:10.1023/A:1012727708439

Hanseth, O., & Monteiro, E. (1997). Inscribing behaviour in information infrastructure standards. *Accounting, Management and Information Technology, 7*(4), 183–211. doi:10.1016/S0959-8022(97)00008-8

Hanseth, O., Monteiro, E., & Hatling, M. (1996). Developing information infrastructure: The tension between standardisation and flexibility. *Science, Technology & Human Values, 21*(4), 407–426. doi:10.1177/016224399602100402

Hecht, G., & Allen, M. T. (2001). Introduction: Authority, political machines, and technology's history. In Allen, M. T., & Hecht, G. (Eds.), *Technologies of power* (pp. 1–24). Cambridge, MA: MIT Press.

Henderson, J. C., & Venkatraman, N. (1993). Strategic alignment: Leveraging information technology for transforming organisations. *IBM Systems Journal, 38*(2-3), 472–484. doi:10.1147/sj.382.0472

Hughes, A., & Hughes, T. P. (2000). *Systems, experts and computers.* Cambridge, MA: MIT Press.

Hughes, T. P. (1983). *Networks of power: Electrification in western society, 1880-1930.* Baltimore, MD: Johns Hopkins University Press.

Hughes, T. P. (1987). The evolution of large technological systems. In Bijker, W. E., Hughes, T. P., & Pinch, T. (Eds.), *The social construction of technological systems* (pp. 51–82). Cambridge, MA: The MIT Press.

Keen, P. G. W. (1991). *Shaping the future: Business design through information technology.* Boston, MA: Harvard Business School Press.

Khan, R. E. (1994). The role of government in the evolution of the Internet. *Communications of the ACM, 37*(8), 15–19. doi:10.1145/179606.179729

Khan, R. E., & Cerf, V. G. (1988). An open architecture for a digital library system and a plan for its development. *The digital library project vol. 1: The world of knowbots.* Reston, VA: Corporation for National Research Initiatives. Retrieved October 13, 2010, from http://www.cnri.reston.va.us/kahn-cerf-88.pdf

Latour, B. (1991). Technology is society made durable. In Law, J. (Ed.), *A sociology of monsters: Essays on power, technology & domination* (pp. 103–131). London, UK: Routledge Press.

Law, J., & Callon, M. (1995). Engineering and sociology in a military aircraft project: A network analysis of technological change. In Star, S. L. (Ed.), *Ecologies of knowledge: Work and politics in science and technology* (pp. 281–301). New York, NY: State University of New York Press. doi:10.1525/sp.1988.35.3.03a00060

Monteiro, E. (1998). Scaling information infrastructure: The case of the next generation IP in Internet. *The Information Society, 14*(3), 229–245. doi:10.1080/019722498128845

Monteiro, E. (2001). Actor-network theory and information infrastructure. In Ciborra, C. U. (Ed.), *From control to drift: The dynamics of corporate information infrastructures* (pp. 71–83). Oxford, UK: Oxford University Press.

Monteiro, E., & Hepsø, V. (2002). Purity and danger of an information infrastructure. *Systemic Practice and Action Research, 15*(2), 145–167. doi:10.1023/A:1015292508667

National Telecommunications and Information Administration (NTIA). (1993). *The national information infrastructure: Agenda for action.* Washington, DC: U.S. Department of Commerce.

Noble, D. W. (1984). *Forces of production: A social history of industrial automation.* New York, NY: Alfred A. Knopf.

Rolland, K. H., & Monteiro, E. (2002). Balancing the local and the global in infrastructural information systems. *The Information Society*, *18*(2), 87–100. doi:10.1080/01972240290075020

Sahay, S., Monteiro, E., & Aanestad, M. (2009). Configurable politics and asymmetric integration: Health e-infrastructures in India. *Journal of the Association for Information Systems*, *10*(5), 399–414.

Star, R. L., & Bowker, G. (2002). How to infrastructure. In Lievrouw, L. A., & Livingstone, S. (Eds.), *Handbook of new media: Social shaping and consequences of ICTs* (pp. 151–162). London, UK: Sage.

Star, S. L. (1995). Introduction. In Star, S. L. (Ed.), *Ecologies of knowledge: Work and politics in science and technology* (pp. 1–35). New York, NY: State University of New York Press.

Star, S. L. (2002). Infrastructure and ethnographic practice: Working on the fringes. *Scandinavian Journal of Information Systems*, *14*(2), 107–122.

Star, S. L., & Griesemer, J. R. (1989). Institutional ecology, 'translations' and boundary objects: Amateurs and professionals in Berkeley's museum of vertebrate zoology, 1907-39. *Social Studies of Science*, *19*(3), 387–420. doi:10.1177/030631289019003001

Star, S. L., & Ruhleder, K. (1996). Steps toward an ecology of infrastructure: Design and access for large information spaces. *Information Systems Research*, *7*(1), 111–134. doi:10.1287/isre.7.1.111

Turner, W., Bowker, G., Gasser, L., & Zackland, M. (2006). Information infrastructures for distributed collective practices. *Computer Supported Cooperative Work*, *15*(2-3), 1–18. doi:10.1007/s10606-006-9014-3

Van House. N. A. (2003). Science and technology studies and information studies. In B. Cronin (Ed.), *Annual review of information science and technology 38,* (pp. 3-86). Medford, NJ: Information Today.

Weill, P., & Broadbent, M. (1998). *Leveraging the new infrastructure: How market leaders capitalize on information.* Boston, MA: Harvard Business School Press.

Weill, P., & Ross, J. (2004). *IT governance: How top performers manage IT decision rights for superior results.* Boston, MA: Harvard Business School Press.

ADDITIONAL READING

Aanestad, M., Monteiro, E., & Nielsen, P. (2007). Information infrastructures and public goods: analytical and practical implications for spatial data infrastructures. *Information Technology for Development*, *13*(1), 7–25. doi:10.1002/itdj.20055

Barrett, M., & Walsham, G. (1999). Electronic trading and work transformation in the London Insurance Market. *Information Systems Research*, *10*(1), 1–22. doi:10.1287/isre.10.1.1

Borgman, C. L. (2000). *From Gutenberg to the global information infrastructure: Access to information in the networked world.* Cambridge, MA: MIT Press.

Borgman, C. L. (2007). *Scholarship in the digital age: Information, infrastructure, and the Internet.* Cambridge, MA: MIT Press.

Bowker, G. (1997). The history of information infrastructures. In Hahn, T. B., & Buckland, M. (Eds.), *Historical Studies in Information Science* (pp. 81–93). Medford, NJ: Information Today.

Bowker, G., & Star, S. L. (2001). Social theoretical issues in the design of collaboratories: Customized software for community support vs. large scale infrastructure. In Olson, G. M., Malone, T. W., & Smith, J. B. (Eds.), *Coordination theory and collaboration technology* (pp. 123–163). Mahwah, N.J: Lawrence Erlbaum Associates.

Chandler, A. D. Jr, & Cortada, J. W. (2003). *A nation transformed by information: How information has shaped the United States from colonial times to the present*. New York, NY: Oxford University Press.

David, P. A., & Bunn, J. A. (1988). The economics of gateway technologies and network evolution: Lessons from electricity supply history. *Information Economics and Policy*, *3*(2), 165–202. doi:10.1016/0167-6245(88)90024-8

Downey, G. (2001). Virtual webs, physical technologies, and hidden workers: The spaces of labor in information internetworks. *Technology and Culture*, *42*(2), 209–235. doi:10.1353/tech.2001.0058

Edwards, P. (1998). Y2K: Millennial reflections on computers as infrastructure. *History and Technology*, *15*(1 & 2), 7–29. doi:10.1080/07341519808581939

Egyedi, T. (2001). Infrastructure flexibility created by standardized gateways: The cases of XML and the ISO container. *Knowledge, Technology & Policy*, *14*(3), 41–54. doi:10.1007/s12130-001-1015-4

Forster, P. W., & King, J. L. (1995). Information infrastructure standards in heterogeneous sectors: Lessons from the worldwide air cargo community. In Kahin, B., & Abbate, J. (Eds.), *Standards policy for information infrastructure* (pp. 148–177). Cambridge, MA: MIT Press.

Hanseth, O., & Ciborra, C. (Eds.). (2007). *Risk, complexity and ICT*. Cheltenham, UK: Edward Elgar.

Hanseth, O., & Lyytinen, K. (2010). Design theory for dynamic complexity in information infrastructures: The case of building internet. *Journal of Information Technology*, *25*(1), 1–19. doi:10.1057/jit.2009.19

Hepsø, V., Monteiro, E., & Rolland, K. (2009). Ecologies of eInfrastructures. *Journal of the AIS*, *10*(5), 430–446.

King, J. (2006). Modern information infrastructure in the support of distributed collective practice in transport. *Computer Supported Cooperative Work*, *15*(2/3), 111–121. doi:10.1007/s10606-006-9015-2

Rochlin, G. (1997). *Trapped in the Net: The unanticipated consequences of computerization*. Princeton, NJ: Princeton University Press.

Sorensen, C., Yoo, Y., Lyytinen, K., & DeGross, J. I. (Eds.). (2005). *Designing ubiquitous information environments: Sociotechnical issues and challenges*. New York, NY: Springer.

Weill, P., Subramani, M., & Broadbent, M. (2002). Building IT infrastructure for strategic agility. *MIT Sloan Management Review*, *44*(1), 57–65.

Weill, P., & Vitale, M. (2001). *Place to space: Migrating to eBusiness models*. Boston, MA: Harvard Business School Press.

ENDNOTES

[1]   ARPA was formed in 1962 in the midst of the cold war between the USA and the then USSR. ARPA's primary objectives were to research and maximise the capability of computers to enable such activities as artificial intelligence, distributed networking, and remote communication and surveillance. See Abbate (1999) for an extensive historical analysis of the origins of ARPANET and the Internet.

2   Parenthetically, Vinton Cerf is now vice president and "chief Internet evangelist" for Google (Google website).

3   This book is the most widely cited work on information infrastructure, as indicated by Ciborra (2001), and is presented here as the main representative of functionalist perspectives to understanding information infrastructure.

4   The aspects discussed by Hanseth (2001) can be said to be representative of the work of Ciborra and associates (2001), as well as other sociotechnical perspectives by Hanseth and Monteiro (1997), Hanseth and Lundberg (2001), Rolland and Monteiro (2002), and Sahay, Monteiro, and Aanestad (2009) among others. It should be mentioned, however, that although largely influenced by Science and Technology Studies, the work by Hanseth, Ciborra, and colleagues also draws on ideas from Anthony Giddens and Ulrich Beck on risk society and reflexive modernization (see in particular Hanseth & Ciborra (Eds.), 2007).

Chapter 3
A Commons Perspective to Understanding the Development of Information Infrastructures

ABSTRACT

The critical review of the literature on information infrastructures has led to an identification of three key areas where future research needs to pay particular attention. These are: the multilevel context of infrastructural development, negotiations around that development, and intended and unintended outcomes emerging out of the implemented technologies. To understand the interdependencies between these three areas, this chapter explores research into other large-scale social systems (beyond information systems) to try to draw out some possible insights for information infrastructure research. In this effort, this chapter draws and adapts the Institutional Analysis and Development (IAD) framework–which was initially developed to study natural resource commons arrangements such as inshore fisheries, forests, irrigation systems, and pastures–while placing great emphasis on the complex problems and social dilemmas that often arise in the negotiations. The chapter concludes by highlighting the contribution of a commons perspective to understanding the development of information infrastructures.

DOI: 10.4018/978-1-4666-1622-6.ch003

INTRODUCTION

One of the oldest areas of research into large-scale social systems with historical accounts dating back to medieval times (see Hanna, Folke, & Mäler, 1996) is research into commons arrangements such as inshore fisheries, forests, irrigation systems, and pastures (e.g. Balland & Platteau, 1996; Ostrom, 1990; Wade, 1994). Although it may be argued that research into traditional commons may not immediately lend itself to information infrastructure research, an increasing number of scholars have found the concept of the commons helpful to conceptualize new dilemmas concerning new information and communication technologies (Rheingold, 1993; Brin, 1995; Huberman & Rajan, 1997; Gupta et al., 1997).

Indeed, information infrastructure research is found to share a common concern with research into commons arrangements in that both are preoccupied with the development of large-scale systems. Such large-scale systems are thought to be openly accessible by a large population of users, but, at the same time, there are efforts to ensure that the exploitation of private and state interests is not inhibited. That is, there are efforts to enforce clear standards and regulations of practice to enable all parties involved to enjoy the benefits emanating from these large-scale systems. At the same time, while seeking to achieve such a balance, the various parties interested in the development of these large-scale systems do not want to lose sight of emerging problems. These include–in the case of information infrastructures–the interplay between the 'local' needs of the users and the 'global' intentions and interests of the larger, distributed community (Rolland & Monteiro, 2002), and the tension between standardization and flexibility (Hanseth, Monteiro, & Hatling, 1996; Hanseth et al., 2006; Monteiro, 1998), among others.

In the next sections, the literature on traditional commons and the links with information infrastructure research are explored in more detail toward a theoretical framework. The discussion starts with a definition of a commons and other types of goods.

WHAT IS A COMMONS?

A commons is a set of resources, which are collectively owned or shared between or among a community or a group of communities (Ostrom, 1990). The commons contains public and private property, over which different communities have certain rights (Ostrom, 1990).

Since the work of Gareth Hardin (1968) and his famous "tragedy of the commons," most studies have examined appropriate property rights structures for commons-based resource systems by starting with the assumption that the resource (e.g. a forest) generates a highly predictable, finite supply of one type of resource unit (e.g. one species of tress) in each relevant time period. According to this view, *anyone* (e.g. farmers) can utilize the resource and appropriate (i.e. harvest) resource units. Appropriators gain property rights only to what they harvest. The harvested resource units are then privately owned and can be sold in an open competitive market (see Feeny et al., 1990).

Potential problems in the use, governance, and sustainability of a commons can lead to social dilemmas such as free-riding and overconsumption. In turn, recommendations are made where external authorities impose a different set of institutional rules and property rights to manage these dilemmas toward socially optimal actions for the sake of public interest. Some scholars recommend private property as the most efficient form of ownership, whereas others recommend government ownership and control (see Hess & Ostrom, 2003 for an extensive discussion).

One way to clarify this distinction is to examine the definition of private vs. public goods. In the classic treatment of public goods, Samuelson (1954, pp. 387-389) classified all the goods that might be used by humans as either pure private or pure public. Samuelson and other economists, including Musgrave (1959), placed great emphasis on *exclusion*. Goods where individuals could be excluded from use were considered private goods; goods where all individuals were included in use were considered public. When economists first dealt with these issues, they focused on the impossibility of exclusion, but they later moved toward a classification based on the high cost of exclusion. Goods were then treated as if there were only one dimension.

It was not until scholars developed a twofold classification of goods that a second attribute of goods was fully acknowledged (Ostrom & Ostrom, 1977). The new schema introduced *subtractability* (sometimes referred to as *rivalry*), where one person's use subtracted from the available goods for others, as an equally important determinant of the nature of a good.

Building on this two-dimensional classification of goods (according to their exclusion and subtractability), more recent discussions have called for the need to identify the varying degrees of exclusion and subtractability of goods (from low to high), as opposed to defining goods as purely public or purely private. On the one hand, exclusion can be defined according to the cost of exclusion from the good, which may be financial, legal, or political (e.g. subscription to services). On the other hand, subtractability can vary from goods that exhibit low rivalry (i.e. they can be shared, but not endlessly such as oceans) to goods that exhibit high rivalry such as privately owned land or a private computer (Blümel, Pethig, & von dem Hagen, 1986; Cornes & Sandler, 1996).

Another concept was introduced that extends the original taxonomy introduced by Ostrom and Ostrom (1977) and that is the concept of network externalities, which is defined as "the utility that a given user derives from a good," depending on "the number of other users who are in the same 'network' as is he or she" (Katz & Shapiro, 1985, pp.424; also see Katz & Shapiro, 1994; Koelliker, 2001; Shapiro & Varian, 1999). Thus, an additional consumer of the good causes a positive network externality, as the other users benefit from that individual's participation in the network without compensating him or her. Classical examples for goods causing technological network externalities are telecommunications systems (e.g. telephone or e-mail). It is obvious that the utility of using e-mail increases as the number of other users of e-mail increases, because the opportunities to communicate with other people via this medium rise. Negative externalities, such as when the marginal individual benefit of participating in a network is less than the marginal social benefit, may lead to a collapse of the good. As a consequence, it may be difficult to reach the critical mass of network members necessary to finance the good. This type of failure refers to the problem of too many and too small networks, a problem that arises as a consequence of inefficient allocation of the resources of the good (see Chapter 1 of this book on the splintering of infrastructures).

In moving away from pure classifications of goods, scholars have begun to recognize the multiple and interdependent dimensions of goods. That is, they begun to approach goods as commons, exhibiting both private and public good properties.

For example, information infrastructures, in their intangible form (i.e. as digitally distributed repositories of information such as the Internet), exhibit low exclusion, since it is difficult to exclude people from accessing and sharing information that is already digitally distributed. In addition, one person's use of information does not subtract from another person's capacity to use it. On the other hand, in their tangible form (i.e. physical networks, hardware, etc.), information infrastructures exhibit high subtractability, since there are clear ownership structures determining their use. Further, there are network externalities impacting the development of an information infrastructure by means of early exposure of the technology to a large number of users and the possibility of the infrastructure becoming a de facto standard (e.g. the case of Microsoft Windows). Early decisions on the design of the technology may also have an impact on subsequent technological solutions and services (e.g. Google's path from a simple search engine to a comprehensive digital content provider). Finally, there are "switching costs" of changing from one information infrastructure to another once users have been "locked-in" the technology (e.g. changing suppliers, compatible applications, financial costs, organizational change implications, etc) (see Hanseth, 2001 for an extensive discussion of network externalities on information infrastructures).

Indeed, information infrastructures, due to their combined private and public good properties and associated network externalities, are always torn between negotiations around the extent to which they remain open and shared by a growing diversity of users (cf. Hanseth, 2001; Star & Ruhleder, 1996) and negotiations around ways of regulating their use. Institutional rules for regulating use may refer to property rights regimes (Benkler, 2006; Lessig, 2001), standards (e.g. Monteiro, 1998), conventions of practice (e.g. Bowker & Star, 1999), or decision-making structures (e.g. Weill & Broadbent, 1998; Weill & Ross, 2004). These institutional rules are negotiated between interested parties towards specific outcomes, both intended–such as, technical integration and returns on investment (Weill & Ross, 2004)–and unintended–such as, asymmetrical integration and political-technical consequences (Sahay et al., 2009).

In the next section, information infrastructures are approached from a commons perspective, which is sensitive to the three key areas identified in the literature review in Chapter 2. These include the multilevel context in which an information infrastructure is developed (i.e. how open this context is and with what implications), the negotiations around regulating access, use, and other decisions on infrastructural resources, and finally the intended and unintended outcomes emerging from the implemented technologies.

INFORMATION INFRASTRUCTURES AS COMMONS

The most widely used framework in commons studies is the Institutional Analysis and Development (IAD) framework, which has been effectively utilized as an analytical tool to understand the conflicts and social dilemmas that arise from negotiating appropriate structures for managing large-scale systems (e.g. Agrawal, 1999; Anderson & Hoskins, 2004; Heikkila & Isett, 2004; Polski, 2003).

More recently, Ostrom and Hess (2007) have adapted the IAD framework for studies of digital or information-based commons, which exhibit closer links to information infrastructures than traditional commons. In their discussion of the IAD framework, Ostrom and Hess identify three broad sets of interconnected elements that are considered to be the underlying factors affecting the development of a commons and which broadly reflect key themes highlighted in the information infrastructure literature.

One set refers to *context*, including the characteristics of the physical and material world (e.g. a forest), the attributes of the community producing and using a resource, and the property rights regimes affecting the decisions and actions of interested parties. Another set refers to *actions*, including how people cooperate or not with each other in various circumstances, and the incentives and control structures they employ to influence each other's actions. A third set refers to *outcomes*, including the conflicts and agreements that arise out of patterns of interaction between diverse parties, and the outcomes that are generated from those patterns.

What differentiates the IAD framework from extant approaches to understanding the development of information infrastructures is the consideration of property rights regimes. As mentioned earlier, previous research on information infrastructure development has placed great emphasis on negotiations around competing interests toward

Figure 1. A Framework for Understanding Information Infrastructure Development. Source: adapted from Ostrom and Hess (2007).

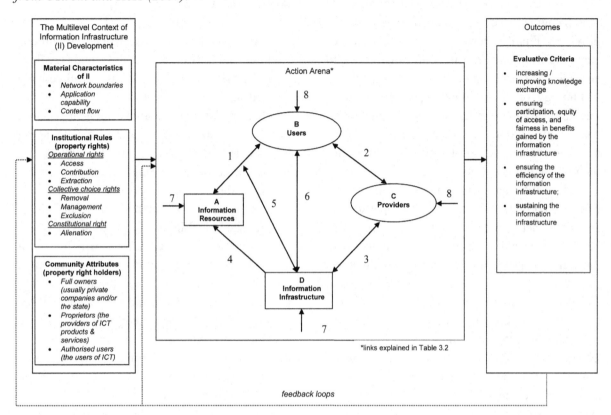

strategic business-IT integration (Henderson & Venkatraman, 1993; Weill and Broadbent, 1998, Weill and Ross, 2004), negotiations around including some participants and excluding others (e.g. Bowker & Star, 1999; Star & Ruhleder, 1996), and negotiations around standardization processes leading to asymmetric integration (Sahay et al., 2009), reflexive side effects (Hanseth et al., 2006), and drift (Ciborra & associates, 2001).

Although each of these studies has presented useful conceptualizations of information infrastructure development, there is little analysis of *why* and *how* negotiations occur (Sahay et al., 2009, pp. 402). Thus, there is a need for further analytical clarity to better understand how contradictions and contestations around the development of an information infrastructure become negotiated in practice. It is argued that a focus on property rights regimes can provide the analytical clarity that is needed.

In the next section, the IAD framework is adapted to information infrastructure research while drawing on well-cited examples in the literature. The adapted framework is summarized in Figure 1.

The Multilevel Context

Past studies have provided extensive discussions of the multilevel context of information infrastructure development. However, there have been few (if any) studies covering all three sets of elements, namely, the material characteristics of information infrastructures, the overarching institutional rules (and especially the role of property rights regimes), and involved community attributes. Drawing on the commons perspective, these elements are broken down for better analytical clarity.

Material Characteristics of Information Infrastructures

First, the material characteristics of an information infrastructure can be broken down to *networks*, *applications*, and *content*, a breakdown which is directly linked to well-established architectural representations of IT infrastructures (e.g. see ISO/IEC, 1995), and recent conceptualizations of information and communication technologies as commons (e.g. Benkler, 2006; Lessig, 2001). Each of these characteristics represents a layer of the information infrastructure, and each is associated with a commons problem. Specifically, these problems entail whether network boundaries are clear and stable or if they are expanding in different directions, whether applications offer competitive capabilities, and whether content flows are managed securely and efficiently will. All of these problems will affect how an information infrastructure becomes adopted in practice.

An example of how these commons problems play out is American Airline's SABRE system–one of the key and most commonly cited infrastructures for airline reservations in the U.S. airline industry in the 1960s-1990s. In this example, the *network boundaries* or reach and range (cf. Keen, 1991) of the SABRE infrastructure can be understood as the number of nodes across travel agents and commercial accounts[1] in the two companies' principal markets; *application capability* can be understood as the capabilities of different applications provided by the infrastructure to meet business objectives; and the *content flow* can be understood as the access and mobility of information regarding flights from different airlines across the network of participants.

In relation to *network boundaries*, initially the SABRE system was installed in a limited number of travel agents and commercial accounts across the U.S. and served as, primarily, an inventory-control system for managing seat availability (Copeland & McKenney, 1988). By 1990, SABRE was operating in more than 14,500 subscriber locations in 45 countries, offering a wide range of travel-related services, including airline, rail, car rental, and hotel bookings (Hopper, 1990). The expansion of these network boundaries produced a number of problems which had implications for the whole airline industry and competing infrastructures for airline reservations (see Copeland & McKenney, 1988).

In relation to *application capability,* early versions of the SABRE system allowed American Airlines to manage inventories of available seats and make reservations across a number of travel agents and commercial accounts (Copeland & McKenney, 1988). However, since not every reservation led to an actual booking, American Airlines realized that their competitive advantage over competing infrastructures such as, United Airline's APOLLO, depended on their capability to combine information about historic booking behavior and available seats from various sources. To this end, they developed the Sales Management and Report Tracking System (SMARTS), a knowledge management system to leverage computerized reservation data from different partners and American Airlines' internal historic data on revenue, bookings, and performance (Christiaanse & Venkatraman, 2002). This is directly related to an earlier application capability of the SABRE infrastructure regarding the way it handled passenger-name records (PNR). PNR capability meant that most transactions required accessing the SABRE control program for seat availability and for passenger information simultaneously. Important innovations in the SABRE control program allowed for a large volume of input-output operations and fast response times (Copeland & McKenney, 1988).

In relation to *content flow*, American Airlines–like other airlines–was faced with the problem of under- and over-bookings. The PNR capability described above gave American Airlines accurate passenger inventories and the opportunity to control under- and over-bookings, thus, optimizing passenger service levels and load factors. Through the PNR capability, American Airlines could use passenger databases to model alternative decision scenarios[2] (Copeland & McKenney, 1988; Hopper, 1990).

As evident from the above examples, the three layers are interconnected and, therefore, commons problems manifest across networks, applications, and content. To begin to understand how these commons problems are initiated and negotiated one needs to understand the institutional rules that define the relationships between key stakeholder groups involved in the development of an information infrastructure.

Institutional Rules (Property Rights)

In traditional commons studies, institutional rules are analyzed at three levels: *operational*, *collective choice*, and *constitutional*. At the operational level, individuals are interacting with each other and the various IT layers of an information infrastructure, making day-to-day decisions. Operational rules affect who may do what, as well as how to perform those actions. Thus, operational rules can be seen as protocols and/or standards for action, while also specifying how technologies are supposed to work. The second level concerns institutional rules (e.g. policies) that determine the collective-choices individuals make to manage the operational level. For an information infrastructure, most collective-choice rules relate to the responsibilities of administrative staff for making policy decisions. The constitutional level includes the rules that define who must, may, or must not participate in making collective choices.

Rules are substantial at every level in the sense that they "rule in" some actions and "rule out" others. In relation to this inclusion/exclusion of action, the IAD framework makes a distinction between "rules-in-form" and "rules-in-use." On the one hand, rules-in-form are "normative instruc-

tions merely written in administrative procedures, legislation or a contract and not known by the participants or enforced by them or others" (Ostrom & Hess, 2007, pp.50). On the other hand, rules-in-use are "generally known and enforced and generate opportunities and constraints for those interacting" (Ostrom & Hess, 2007, pp.50). The IAD framework places sole emphasis on rules-in-use, thus making the assumption that all participants are aware and knowledgeable of what they must, must not, or may do in a particular action situation. However, as past studies of information infrastructure development have shown, such a shared understanding of who is supposed to do what, when and how with the technology is a rare event and requires ongoing negotiations between different stakeholders and the heterogeneous resources they employ (Monteiro, 2001).

Research into commons does, nonetheless, acknowledge that rules-in-use are often out of sync with the capabilities of the technologies and are, hence, rarely the sole structure for determining human action. Even more challenging, however, is the occurrence of "technological inversion," where the capabilities of technology contradict current practices, values, and even constitutional rights. For example, prior to the 1998 Digital Millennium Copyright Act (DMCA), copyright law clarified exceptions in "fair use" for educational purposes. With the DMCA, licensed software that restricts the number of copies that can be used does not contain the flexibility to make exceptions for fair use. This is an example of usage constrained by the technical characteristics of a resource as well as a newer rule (DMCA) contradicting an earlier rule (fair use). Circumventing the software, even for the sake of fair use, is against the law (Lessig, 2001). During the DMCA hearings, none of the congressional witnesses expressed the opinion that the fair-use exemption should be eliminated. Nevertheless, the DMCA has paved the way for increasing digital-rights management (DRM) as a type of institutional governance (Samuelson, 2003; Madison, 2003; Mendelson, 2003).

In recent years, the advent of new information and communication technologies have led to the proposal of a number of policies whereby property rights have become the national and international formal rules as well as informal rules-in-use with which to govern new technologies (David, 2001). In general, property rights define actions that individuals may take in relation to other individuals regarding some "thing" owned (David, 2001). If one individual has a right, someone else has a commensurate duty to observe that right.

Ostrom and Hess (2007, pp.52-53) identify seven major types of property rights that are most relevant to use in regard to the digital knowledge commons that are also relevant to the study of information infrastructures. These can be grouped into two categories, with the first category referring to *operational rights* of access, contribution, and extraction, and the second category referring to *collective choice rights* of removal, management, and exclusion. There is also a seventh type of property right, namely, alienation, which is a *constitutional right* that defines who must, may, or must not participate in making collective choices.

In the first category of operational rights, *access* refers to the right to enter a defined area of the information infrastructure and enjoy non-subtractive benefits. Consider, for example, how access to defined parts of the Internet (i.e. public areas, non-private) is enjoyed by most[3] people without any subtractability. *Contribution* refers to the right to contribute to the content and is closely tied to access, since depending on access levels to different areas, users will have the right to add, revise, or delete content. Consider, for example, how different users of an information infrastructure, depending on access rights, can contribute to content such as, in the case of SABRE, passenger records. *Extraction* refers to the right to obtain resource units such as, information and data from an application with the intention to use it for further work, such as building databases of passenger records.

Individually, each of these operational rights may not be seen to create any serious implications for the development of information infrastructures. However, combinations of these operational rights can shape the dynamics of interaction between different stakeholders. For example, in the late 1970s, in the SABRE case, American Airlines introduced the "co-host concept" whereby other carriers were given preferential treatment in the display of their schedules on SABRE for a fee (Copeland & McKenney, 1988). This was a combination of operational rights (i.e. access to content and extraction of benefits by contributing content and a fee to SABRE) offered by American Airlines to other carriers with the primary intention to increase SABRE's presence in markets that American Airlines did not serve (American, 1978; Hopper, 1986–both cited in Copeland & McKenney, 1988). Thus, by offering this combination of operational rights, American Airlines hoped to change the market dynamics and extend SABRE's reach to markets served by United Airlines (the key competitor at the time), thereby locking-in travel agents and slowing the expansion of United's APOLLO (Copeland & McKenney, 1988).

In the second category of collective choice rights, *removal* refers to the right to remove one's artifacts from the resource if they are found to be infringing on the rights of other right owners. *Management* refers to the right to regulate internal use patterns and transform the resource by making improvements. Individuals who hold rights of management have the authority to determine how, when, and where usage of a resource, such as a database, can take place, and whether and how the structure of a resource may be changed (i.e. changing keys/relations in the database). For instance, a group of general practitioners who built a database of patient accounts for epidemiological research that limits various types of usage to primary health centers only are exercising rights of management for their resource. *Exclusion* refers to the right to determine who will have access, contribution, extraction, and removal rights and how those rights may be transferred. Individuals who hold rights of exclusion have the authority to define the qualifications that individuals must meet in order to access a resource. For instance, American Airlines limited access to their schedules for carriers without a 'co-host' status.

Evidently, collective choice rights have more impact on the development and usage of an information infrastructure. However, once again, it is the combinations of these rights that create possibilities for shaping the dynamic interactions between different stakeholders. For example, in the SABRE case, American Airlines allowed host airlines to add routes in high traffic markets and drop routes with low traffic. Because of the lack of regulatory price controls at the time, this combination of collective-choice rights (i.e. management of reservation patterns by removal of routes and markets), allowed host airlines to significantly increase the variety of fares and the frequency with which they changed them (Celentino, 1987, cited in Copeland & McKenney, 1988). At the same time, as the nature of passenger inquiries changed from simple seat availability to price shopping, real-time access to different carriers' volatile schedules and fares also became a necessity for travel agents. Moreover, some carriers were questioning the cost effectiveness of their city ticket offices and were looking for ways to control the expense of reservations offices, reservations agents, and internal communications. These factors combined to create a strong incentive for the airlines to transfer the burden from their own reservations offices to travel agencies (Levine, 1987).

Finally, *alienation* refers to the right to sell or lease extraction, removal, management, and exclusion rights. It is, thus, a constitutional right, whereby once property rights are alienated, the former rights-holder can no longer exercise these authorities in relation to a resource or a part thereof. This constitutional right is usually instituted at a higher level of authority such as by a board of directors, a government agency, etc., whereas

collective choice rights can be instituted by a community of practitioners, a departmental unit, etc. For example, in the SABRE case, American Airlines were the sole holders of the constitutional right of alienation–a private ownership solution–which, in the end, was met with the strong resistance of different stakeholders (e.g. airline carriers, travel agencies) leading to significant consequences for the whole of the U.S. airline industry and the way computerization reservation systems were later developed and implemented around more flexible market structures.

To understand the distinction between these different property rights one must comprehend which groups of stakeholders come to exercise them in relation to one another and the implications that such arrangements have on the management of the information infrastructure. In other words, instead of focusing solely on definitions of property rights, it is far more useful to understand these property rights in relation to classes of property-rights holders (Schlager & Ostrom, 1992; Ostrom, 2003).

Community Attributes (Property Right Holders)

In the IAD framework, communities are defined by assessing who the *users*, *providers*, and *policymakers* are (Ostrom & Hess, 2007, pp.48). The users are those appropriating the content of the information infrastructure by using the various software applications. The providers are large diverse communities like those making the content available (e.g. could also be users) as well as those making the software, hardware, and overall infrastructure available. The policymakers may be a voluntary and self-governing community of interested parties, such as a government agency, a board of directors, international standardization bodies, the contributors of the Free and Open Source Software (FOSS) movement, etc. Provider and policymaking communities are usually nested in that some of these communities may function

Table 1. Bundles of rights associated with right holders

PROPERTY RIGHTS		RIGHT HOLDERS		
		Full owner	Proprietor	Authorized user
Operational rights	Access	x	x	x
	Conribution	x	x	x
	Extraction	x	x	x
Collective-choice rights	Removal	x	x	
	Manaement	x	x	
	Exclusion	x	x	
Constitutional right	Alienation	x		

Source: adapted from Ostrom (2003)

at various levels of authority, influencing the decisions of both providers and policymakers.

Traditional commons analyses have demonstrated that small, homogeneous communities are more likely to be able to sustain a commons (Baland & Platteau, 1996; Wade, 1994; Ostrom, 1990). If a community of providers and policymakers are unified in concerns to the purpose and goals of the commons, then the community can be said to be homogeneous (National Research Council, 2002). However, as many studies of information infrastructure development have shown, such homogeneity is rare because the values and goals of the various communities involved are complex, fragmented, and often overlapping (see Ciborra & associates, 2001). In fact, it is understood that, often, the same individuals will be members in diverse communities simultaneously (Bowker & Star, 1999).

In thinking of ways to circumvent this problem, some authors have suggested that communities are defined based on the bundles of property rights they hold, as listed in Table 1 (Schlager & Ostrom, 1992; Ostrom, 2003).

To start with, *authorized users* include all those who have access, contribution, and extraction rights to an information infrastructure. The level of contribution and extraction that they can exercise will be defined in corresponding rights, which are determined by those holding collective choice rights of management and exclusion. Authorized users and their operational rights will vary by application type, time constraints, and information and data being accessed. *Proprietors* possess the operational rights of authorized users, in addition to collective choice rights of removal, management, and exclusion of resources. For example, local groups, such as hospitals, who obtain operational rights to national electronic patient records by a governmental agency, frequently have management rights with which to devise policies on removal rights, and limits on extraction rights across all authorized users. Such proprietors also have the right to determine who may access, contribute, extract, and remove resources from an information infrastructure and how those rights may be transferred. Most property systems involve participants who are proprietors and have six of the property rights previously described, but who do not possess the right to sell their management and exclusion rights. This is because proprietors are often found to develop strict rules of exclusion and extraction rights, while monitoring conformance and using sanctions against those who do not conform to their rules (Blomquist, 1992; Agrawal, 1994). To this end, the right of alienation is most often reserved for *full owners*, who possess all seven of the rights previously described.

However, it should be stressed that the rights of full owners are never absolute, in that, even they have responsibilities not to generate particular kinds of harms to other right holders (Demsetz, 1967).

What becomes obvious through this discussion is that the division of property rights to designated property holders is a complex practice requiring extensive negotiations. The complexity rests with the fact that, in the multilevel context of an information infrastructure, there are groups of individuals sharing property rights as opposed to a single entity (e.g. an individual, an organization) exercising full individual ownership. This is so because the resource system and the resource units produced by that system have such great reach and scope (Keen, 1991) that they require bundles of different property rights. Further, because of the reach and scope of an information infrastructure, some property holders may be formally organized and legally recognized as having a corporate or government existence (linked to private and government ownership respectively), whereas other property holders may be less formally organized, but may still exercise property rights in practice, something that may or may not be legally supported if challenged by others. As Bowker and Star (1999) note in their study of the International Classification of Diseases, which formal and informal classifications eventually become implemented, depend on negotiations and compromises over who is supposed to do what and how, with conflicts always present.

The majority of research on traditional commons has strived to show that variations in forms of property rights make a difference in managing the commons by shaping the incentives of right holders. In parallel to this research, there has been a strong body of research scholars, who have aimed to demonstrate that private ownership or government control do not exhaust the range of plausible institutional mechanisms to govern common use (see National Research Council, 2002). These scholars have argued that a community-based or common ownership solution is more natural as it is rooted in the practices of millions of social groups around the world: from social movements and revolutions, voting and other forms of political participation, collusion and cheating, formation of institutions and their maintenance, cooperation, and conflict. In all these situations, participants attempt to solve collective action problems, by focusing on the conditions under which users cooperate to achieve efficient management. Thus, the development and sustainability of a commons should be far removed from the bipolar exercise of control (private vs. government ownership). Instead, the successful development of a commons depends on the ability of local communities to recognize their common interests and to negotiate rights for the prudent use of the commons themselves (see Li 1996).

The next section provides a discussion of the negotiations that take place between different communities (as property holders) in their effort to define common property rights and, by extension, to govern the relationships between them as well as their relationships with an information infrastructure.

The Action Arena

In the IAD framework, negotiations between property holders are placed in the "action arena" where different stakeholders make decisions within different situations affected by the material characteristics of the information infrastructure, the institutional rules, and the community attributes that will then result in varying patterns of interactions. It is understood that these negotiations can occur at the local, regional, or global levels of information infrastructure development, thus, acknowledging the more complex ecology at work (cf. Bowker & Star, 1999).

To begin to explore the negotiations involved in information infrastructure development, it is suggested that researchers consider the following: 1) the cooperation and potential for collective

Table 2. Links & potential problems in information infrastructure development

Link	Importance	Potential Problems
(1) Between information resources and users (e.g. administrators, general practitioners, etc.)	• availability of information at time of need	• too much or too little information at varying time periods (i.e. inefficiency problems)
(2) Between users and providers (e.g. IT providers, service providers such as hospitals, etc.)	• selecting providers • contributing information resources (e.g. from providers to users) • recommending policies of use by providers • monitoring performance of providers by user committees	• lack of participation in provider selection • providing centralized vs. decentralized IT networks, and standardized vs. customized & IT applications to users • contractual agreements on commercial terms of use • lack of information /incomplete information from providers and users
(3) Between providers and the information infrastructure	• building the infrastructure • maintaining & supporting the infrastructure • monitoring & enforcing commercial terms of use	• procurement issues (contractual agreements, etc.) • overcapitalization or undercapitalization (lack of funds or too many funds) • running over estimated cost and time needed to deliver the infrastructure–return on investment issues

(4) Between the information infrastructure and information resources	• impact of the information infrastructure on the resource level	• ineffective impact
		  o poor flow of information
		  o fragmentation of resources
		  o security issues (privacy and confidentiality of data)

(5) Between the information infrastructure and the dynamics of information resources	• impact of the information infrastructure on the feedback structure of the resource– i.e. on usage dynamics	• disruption of temporal and spatial patterns of use • unintended consequences (i.e. trajectories of IT development outside intended objectives)
(6) Between users and the information infrastructure	• Co-production of the information infrastructure	• resistance to the co-production model prescribed by full owners / providers
(7) External forces on information resources and the information infrastructure	• market / government changes • technological developments	• alienation of the information resources and the information infrastructure
(8) External forces on key stakeholders	• major changes in organization structures • regulation by policymakers	• alienation of relationships between key stakeholders

action must be contained within the information infrastructure, 2) an information infrastructure is dynamic, as are the rules that different communities agree amongst themselves, and 3) an information infrastructure can occupy multiple stable states and move rapidly between them.

These considerations have originally been proposed for analyzing social ecological systems– "interdependent systems of social and biological units tending to form cooperative relationships with one another" (Anderies, Janssen, & Ostrom, 2004, pp. 3). These considerations are adopted here as part of the broader framework and placed within the action arena as illustrated in Figure 1. Table 2 (adapted from Anderies et al., 2004) provides a summary description of the links between

different stakeholders, information resources, the information infrastructure, and external forces, as well as the potential problems that may arise as a result of these links.

As illustrated in Figure 1, there are two key stakeholders in the negotiations: the users, who will represent the authorised users in the group of property right holders (B in Figure 1) and the providers, who will represent the proprietors in the group of property right holders (C in Figure 1). Full owners–whether those are private companies and/or the state, only feature in the links between B and C and the information resources (A in Figure 1) and the information infrastructure (D in Figure 1). The reason is that full owners do not usually have a direct negotiating role and rather adopt a policymaking and monitoring role, intervening only when something goes wrong (see Ostrom, 1990). It should be also noted that, there may be a substantial overlap of individuals in B and C, or they may be entirely different individuals, depending on the structure of the social system governing and managing the information infrastructure (e.g. a hospital may be both a 'group' user and a provider of services).

This model focuses on key interactions between different stakeholders, the institutional rules devised to constrain the actions of those stakeholders, and the collective-choice process used to generate the rules. For example, there are a variety of strategic factors that may influence the interaction between users and providers (Link 2) such as, users selecting providers and providers recommending policies of use; providers and actual investment in the infrastructure (Link 3) such as, building and maintaining the infrastructure; users and the usage rate (Link 1) such as, availability of information at time of need; and, potentially, users and the information infrastructure (Link 6) such as the co-production of an information infrastructure by the users. Furthermore, the links between users, information resources and the information infrastructure (Links 1, 4, and 5) are also sources of fluctuations that may challenge the development of the infrastructure at any particular point in time, by impacting the level of information resources as well as usage rate dynamics. Finally, the model considers the impact of external forces on information resources and the information infrastructure (Link 7) such as, market and government changes, as well as on key stakeholders (Link 8) such as, major changes in organizational structures and regulation. These external forces will have an impact on the constitutional level of property rights by alienating information resources and the information infrastructure itself, as well as the relationships between key stakeholders.

It should be noted that this model for understanding negotiations in the development of an information infrastructure is not meant to capture all the aforementioned potential interactions. It is important, however, to understand the broad structure of the entities in the model and the links between them to begin to show how the strategic interactions within and between entities affect the likelihood of the long-term sustainability of the information infrastructure. Thus, the main focus of the model is to identify the key events and situations in the development of the information infrastructure, including the roles and incentives of key actors and communities in negotiating that development. Particular attention is placed on the link between operational level property right holders (users) and collective-choice level property right holders (providers) and how their interactions become monitored and expropriated through the constitutional right of alienation by full owners. The negotiations between these key stakeholders will generate a number of outcomes, which will in turn feed back to the multilevel context of information infrastructure development.

Outcomes

In traditional commons research, the analytical process often begins with the outcomes, especially negative outcomes, such as "why are fisheries close to depletion?" Analysis can also be motivated by confusing and conflicting outcomes, such as "why is one forest depleted while another ten miles away is thriving?" (Ostrom & Hess, 2007, pp. 60). Usually these outcomes are easily spotted and contrasted because they are relatively easy to measure (e.g. forest degradation, depletion, pollution, etc). In the context of information infrastructure development, however, there could be numerous competing outcomes, some of which are hard to immediately measure, quantify, and classify as either negative or positive (e.g. see Bowker & Star, 1999; Ciborra & associates, 2001).

The broad spectrum of possible outcomes that one can observe in information infrastructure development reflect the complexities of information resources, the diversity of technologies that support multiple access, contribution, and extraction of those resources, and the expanding communities of users and providers of those. In fact, because the outcomes are often the result of numerable actions, it is helpful to keep an interdisciplinary frame of mind by acknowledging that changes in the technical characteristics of an information infrastructure will generate implications for transforming the institutional rules governing the patterns of action and negotiation between different stakeholders. Thus, there is a continuous feedback loop that forces different stakeholders and the information infrastructure itself to adapt to diverse outcomes, either with positive or negative consequences.

One way to begin to understand this transformation process is to employ a set of evaluative criteria with which to assess the different outcomes that are being achieved as well as the likely set of outcomes that could be achieved under alternative actions or institutional arrangements.

Evaluating the outcomes of information technology projects has long been a preoccupation of information systems researchers (e.g. Boehm & Bell, 1977; Chandler, 1982; Delone & McLean, 1992). At the core of evaluating information technology outcomes rests user satisfaction and system usage (Baroudi, Olson, & Ives, 1986; Borovits & Galadi, 1993; McKeen, Guimaraes, & Wetherby, 1994). However, while user satisfaction and system usage are undoubtedly essential for system success, they are insufficient in and of themselves and do not serve as measures of effectiveness or payoff. Instead, some researchers have argued that when evaluating information technology outcomes there is a need to recognize that each system is conceived for specific reasons and, thus, the rationale of a systems development and implementation must form the basis for its evaluation (Evans & Costa, 2003). For example, most systems are developed and implemented because of an identified opportunity or problem in existing business processes and service levels. Technology is, thereby, applied to take advantage

of the opportunity or to solve the problem (Evans, 1999).

In information infrastructure research as in traditional commons studies, a large-scale system is developed to solve collective-action problems whilst also allocating the appropriate institutional rules with which to sustain the system. Thus, the criteria of evaluation need to be expanded to encompass broader concerns than user satisfaction and individual problem solving. Although there are many potential evaluative criteria, some of the most frequently used criteria in commons studies are increasing or improving knowledge exchange; ensuring participation and equity in access to, and benefits from, services provided by the commons; ensuring the efficiency of a commons; and sustaining the commons (Ostrom & Hess, 2007). Each of these are directly associated with information infrastructure development and each are discussed next.

Increasing/Improving Knowledge Exchange

One of the core evaluations made concerning information systems projects is whether they lead to an increase and improvement in knowledge exchange processes between involved participants (see Alavi & Leidner, 2001 for an extensive review). Although there are some disagreements as to whether knowledge can be explicitly captured, codified, and exchanged as an object-like entity or whether knowledge is something that is learned in practice through personal experiences (see Tsoukas, 2005; Walsham, 2001), the evaluation of increasing and improving knowledge exchange can be based on the stocks and flows of knowledge available to involved participants (see Doz, Santos, & Williamson, 2001; Brown & Duguid, 2001); and the ability to utilize local knowledge to build knowledge capacities that can then be transferred globally (e.g. see Barrett et al., 2005). An information infrastructure has the ability to act as a delegator of knowledge exchange, by integrating information resources from various sources and making them available in a standardized fashion to all involved participants (Monteiro, 2001).

Ensuring Participation, Equity of Access, and Fairness in Benefits Gained by the Information Infrastructure

As mentioned above, user participation and equity in access to services provided by an information system is considered to be one of the key factors in information systems success (see Mumford, 1995, 2006 on participatory approaches to system design). A popular approach to evaluating user participation and equity is equity theory, which suggests that individuals are concerned about their inputs, outcomes, and the fairness of an innovation or change that is going to be implemented (Adams, 1963). Individuals are also constantly comparing themselves to others in their reference group to assess whether the relative gains are equivalent. If individuals perceive that a new information system will bring them a decline in their net gains, or inequity compared to others, then those individuals will not accept the new system (see Doctor, 1992; Joshi, 1990). On the other hand, if individuals observe an increase in their equity, then they are more likely to welcome the new information system. Thus, equity is assessed on the basis of the equality between individuals' contributions to the development and use of an information infrastructure and the benefits they derive; and on the basis of differential abilities to pay. In turn, two key questions that arise are: 'what will be the financial and temporal implications for allowing all individuals to participate,' and 'how will compensation and financing of related services be allocated'? Participation and equity will have a direct impact on extant property right regimes, not only for governing the information infrastructure, but also for governing intellectual property rights on information resources (see Lessig, 2001; Litman, 2001). Thus, participation will

require tough decisions in and beyond participatory system development approaches.

Ensuring the Efficiency of the Information Infrastructure

Another core evaluation of information systems is efficiency as determined by three dimensions of organizational benefits: strategic, informational, and transactional (e.g. Mirani & Lederer, 1998; Weill, 1992; Weill & Ross, 2004). Strategic benefits are broken down into changes wrought by information technology toward competitive advantages for the organization (Clemons, 1991; Saunders & Jones, 1992); alignment with organizational goals and environmental changes; and enhancing customer relations through improved products or better service (Henderson & Venkatraman, 1993). Informational benefits are broken down into better information access, increased information quality, and information flexibility for decision-making (Mirani & Lederer, 1998). Finally, transactional benefits are also broken down to communications efficiency across organizational units or departments, systems development efficiency, and business efficiency across employees, business processes, and financial resources (Willcocks & Lester, 1999). Thus, evaluating efficiency plays a determining role in estimating the benefits and costs or rates of return to investments, which are often used to verify the impact of an information infrastructure on various organizational aims and objectives.

Sustaining the Information Infrastructure

Finally, a sustainable information infrastructure is one that meets current needs of participants involved in producing, deciding, and using the infrastructure (from users, to providers and policymakers) without compromising the ability of future generations to meet their needs. Thus, when evaluating the sustainability of an information infrastructure, one needs to examine the processes involving interactions among participants and whether they increase the social and technical capital involved or slowly erode that capital (e.g. see Braa et al., 2004). As Braa et al (2004, pp.355) note:

A fundamental point is that sustainable networks are built through ongoing and continuous translations, around both the vertical (local appropriation) and horizontal (diffusion) axes. This perspective helps to go beyond merely recording the movements of technology, as is the case of the diffusion model, to trying to make these changes happen, which requires understanding, explaining, and engaging with the specific dynamics around the uptake, spreading, and sense making involved.

Thus, any evaluations around the sustainability of an information infrastructure will need to factor in changing actors and participants, adaptive information systems, and constantly evolving institutional rules around different property right holders' long-term commitments to the preservation of the information infrastructure.

CONCLUSION: THE CONTRIBUTION OF THE COMMONS PERSPECTIVE

The commons perspective and the adapted framework discussed above helps fill a gap in the literature by supporting a more detailed analysis of why and how negotiations around information infrastructure development occur. In particular, the framework provides an integrated theoretical approach to analyzing (a) the multilevel context of information infrastructure development across the material characteristics of the infrastructure, institutional rules, and community attributes of property right holders; (b) the action links and potential negotiation problems between different stakeholders; and (c) the potential outcomes

and (un)intended consequences emerging out of those negotiations. These multiple analytical entry points enable researchers to dig into problems of infrastructure development and identify why a particular distribution of interactions and outcomes is generated. As such, the framework helps to analyze more clearly the social, political, and technological-resource relationships and reveal how decisions and actions lead to specific outcomes.

As argued here and in the previous chapter, information infrastructures are large-scale sociotechnical systems that require complex institutional rules between diverse stakeholders in order to define and manage the various links generated through the development of the infrastructure. The problem, however, is that definitions of stakeholders are contested, for it is difficult to place clear boundaries on who is affected by the use of the information infrastructures. Thus, politics and power relations occupy center stage in establishing and enforcing institutional rules and property rights regimes to manage the development of an information infrastructure. As evident in the case of airline reservation systems in the U.S., the visibility and strength of different groups shape the structure and participation in stakeholder forums, the content of the debate, and eventual outcomes. The successful development of an information infrastructure will depend on whether the various stakeholders can establish sufficient trust among themselves to enable cooperation and political consensus. Yet heterogeneity of interests among actors may be so extensive that it is impossible to achieve cooperation or collective action even where it was once successful.

The commons perspective and framework bring these issues to the forefront by focusing on the historical evolution of information infrastructures through continuous feedback loops between context, actions, and outcomes. In this effort, it approaches existing institutional rules and property right regimes as the expression of past political alignments. Attention to power and micro-politics within communities is therefore critical in understanding how an information infrastructure comes to be developed, used, and governed. The objective is not just to try to understand politics because their effects on information infrastructure development are mediated through the prism of institutions. Rather, it is also to try to understand how political relationships imbue information infrastructure development even without being mediated by institutional arrangements.

Greater attention to the dynamics of power and resistance will yield significant theoretical and practical insights into understanding how attempts at control and regulation are always challenged by those who are subjected to control. Issues of agency, the mutually productive relationship between domination and resistance, and the creation of institutional arrangements can be understood only with greater attention to micro-politics. Such a shift in focus can also help address the criticism that scholars of information infrastructure development have, for the most part, ignored how users can shape attempts by outside agents such as the state or private companies to intervene into their work practices and modify existing patterns of infrastructure use (see Bowker & Star, 1999). The key point here is to analyze why and when different stakeholders respond in particular and differentiated ways to new strategies of institutionalized power, by scrutinizing their historical structural locations and the extent to which they are already privileged or marginalized by new strategies of power.

The commons perspective and framework will provide the ground for analyzing the development of two information infrastructures by drawing on empirical data from two case studies, as discussed in Chapters 4 and 5.

REFERENCES

Adams, J. S. (1963). Towards an understanding of inequality. *Journal of Abnormal and Normal Social Psychology, 67*, 422–436. doi:10.1037/h0040968

Agrawal, A. (1994). Rules, rule making, and rule breaking: Examining the fit between rule systems and resource use. In Ostrom, E., Gardner, R., & Walker, J. M. (Eds.), *Rules, games, and common-pool resources* (pp. 267–282). Ann Arbor, MI: University of Michigan Press.

Agrawal, A. (1999). *Greener pastures: Politics, markets, and community among a migrant pastoral people*. Durham, NC: Duke University Press.

Agrawal, A. (2008). Sustainable governance of common-pool resources: Context, method, and politics. In Bardhan, P., & Ray, I. (Eds.), *The contested commons: Conversations between economists and anthropologists* (pp. 46–65). Oxford, UK: Blackwell Publishing.

Alavi, M., & Leidner, D. (2001). Review: Knowledge management and knowledge management systems: Conceptual foundations and research issues. *Management Information Systems Quarterly, 25*(1), 107–136. doi:10.2307/3250961

Anderies, J. M., Janssen, M. A., & Ostrom, E. (2004). A framework to analyze the robustness of social-ecological systems from an institutional perspective. *Ecology & Society, 9*(1), 18–34.

Anderson, K. P., & Hoskins, M. W. (2004). Information use and abuse in the local governance of Common-Pool Forest Resources. *Forests, Trees & Livelihoods, 14*, 295–312.

Balland, J., & Platteau, J. (1996). *Halting degradation of natural resources: Is there a role for rural communities?* Oxford, UK: Clarendon.

Baroudi, J. J., Olson, M. H., & Ives, B. (1986). An empirical study of the impact of user involvement on system usage and information satisfaction. *Communications of the ACM, 29*(3), 232–237. doi:10.1145/5666.5669

Barrett, M., Fryatt, B., Walsham, G., & Joshi, S. (2005). Building bridges between local and global knowledge: New ways of working at the World Health Organisation. *Knowledge Management for Development Journal, 1*(2), 31–46.

Benkler, Y. (2006). *The wealth of networks*. New Haven, CT: Yale University Press.

Blomquist, W. (1992). *Dividing the waters: Governing groundwater in southern California.* San Fransisco, CA: Institute for Contemporary Studies Press.

Blümel, W., Pethig, R., & von dem Hagen, O. (1986). The theory of public goods: A survey of recent issues. *Journal of Institutional and Theoretical Economics, 142*(2), 241–309.

Boehm, B., & Bell, T. (1977). Issues in computer performance evaluation: Some consensus, some divergence. *Performance Evaluation Review, 4*(2), 4–40.

Borovits, I., & Giladi, R. (1993). Evaluating cost/utilization of organizations' information systems and users. *Information & Management, 25*(3), 273–280. doi:10.1016/0378-7206(93)90076-6

Bowker, G., & Star, S. L. (1999). *Sorting things out–Classification and its consequences.* Cambridge, MA: MIT Press.

Braa, J., Monteiro, E., & Sahay, S. (2004). Networks of action: Sustainable health information systems across developing countries. *Management Information Systems Quarterly, 28*(3), 337–362.

Brin, D. (1995). The Internet as a commons. *Information Technology and Libraries, 14*(4), 240–242.

Brown, S. J., & Duguid, P. (2001). Knowledge and organization: A social-practice perspective. *Organization Science, 12*(2), 198–213. doi:10.1287/orsc.12.2.198.10116

Chandler, J. (1982). A multiple criteria approach for evaluating information systems. *Management Information Systems Quarterly, 6*(1), 61–74. doi:10.2307/248755

Christiaanse, E., & Venkatraman, N. (2002). Beyond SABRE: an empirical test of expertise exploitation in electronic channels. *Management Information Systems Quarterly, 26*(1), 15–38. doi:10.2307/4132339

Ciborra, C. U. (Ed.), & associates. (2001). *From control to drift: The dynamics of corporate information infrastructures.* Oxford, UK: Oxford University Press.

Clemons, E. K. (1991). Evaluation of strategic investment in information technology. *Communications of the ACM, 34*(1), 22–36. doi:10.1145/99977.99985

Copeland, D., & McKenney, J. (1988, September). Airline reservations systems: Lessons from history. *Management Information Systems Quarterly, 12*(3), 353–370. doi:10.2307/249202

Cornes, R., & Sandler, T. (1996). *The theory of externalities.* New York, NY: Cambridge University Press.

David, P. (2001). Tragedy of the public knowledge 'commons'? Global science, intellectual property and the digital technology boomerang. *MERIT-Infonomics Research Memorandum series 2001-003.*

Delone, W., & McLean, E. (1992). Information systems success: The quest for the dependent variable. *Information Systems Research, 3*(1), 60–95. doi:10.1287/isre.3.1.60

Demsetz, H. (1967). Toward a theory of property rights. *The American Economic Review, 57*(2), 347–359.

Doctor, R. (1992). Social equity and information technologies: Moving toward information democracy. *Annual Review of Information Science & Technology, 27*, 43–96.

Doz, Y., Santos, J., & Williamson, P. (2001). *From global to metanational: How companies win in the knowledge economy.* New York, NY: Harvard Business School Press.

Evans, G. E. (1999). Information systems as interventions: The case for outcomes based evaluation. *Journal of Computer Information Systems, 39*(2), 69–74.

Evans, G. E., & Costa, B. A. (2003). Outcome-based systems evaluation to assess information technology impact using ARIMA methods. *Communications of the Association for Information Systems, 11*, 660–677.

Feeny, D., Berkes, F., McCay, B. J., & Acheson, J. M. (1990). The tragedy of the commons: Twenty-Two years later. *Human Ecology, 18*(1), 1–19. doi:10.1007/BF00889070

Gupta, A., Jukic, B., Parameswaran, M., Stahl, D. O., & Whinston, A. B. (1997). Streamlining the digital economy: How to avert a tragedy of the commons. *IEEE Internet Computing, 1*(6), 38–46. doi:10.1109/4236.643935

Hanna, S., Folke, C., & Mäler, K.-G. (1996). *Rights to nature: Ecological, economic, cultural, and political principles of institutions for the environment.* Washington, DC: Island Press.

Hanseth, O. (2001). The economics of standards. In Ciborra, C. U. (Ed.), *From control to drift: The dynamics of corporate information infrastructures* (pp. 56–70). Oxford, UK: Oxford University Press.

Hanseth, O., Jacucci, E., Grisot, M., & Aanestad, M. (2006). Reflexive standardization: Side effects and complexity in standard making. *Management Information Systems Quarterly, 30*, 563–581.

Hanseth, O., Monteiro, E., & Hatling, M. (1996). Developing information infrastructure: The tension between standardisation and flexibility. *Science, Technology & Human Values, 21*(4), 407–426. doi:10.1177/016224399602100402

Hardin, G. (1968). The tragedy of the commons. *Science, 162*(3859), 1243–1248. doi:10.1126/science.162.3859.1243

Heikkila, T., & Isett, K. R. (2004). Modeling operational decision-making in public organizations: An integration of two institutional theories. *American Review of Public Administration, 34*(1), 3–19. doi:10.1177/0275074003260911

Henderson, J. C., & Venkatraman, N. (1993). Strategic alignment: Leveraging information technology for transforming organisations. *IBM Systems Journal, 38*(2-3), 472–484. doi:10.1147/sj.382.0472

Hess, C., & Ostrom, E. (2003). Ideas, artifacts, and facilities: Information as a common-pool resource. *Law and Contemporary Problems, 66*(1-2), 111–146.

Hopper, M. (1990, May-June). Rattling SABRE–New ways to compete on information. *Harvard Business Review*, 1–9.

Huberman, B. A., & Rajan, M. L. (1997). Social dilemmas and Internet congestion. *Science, 277*(5325), 535–537. doi:10.1126/science.277.5325.535

ISO/IEC. (1995). Open distributed processing-reference model. *Part 3: architecture.* IS 10746-3/ITU-T Recommendation X.903.

Joshi, K. (1990). An investigation of equity as a determinant of user information satisfaction. *Decision Sciences*, *21*(4), 786–807. doi:10.1111/j.1540-5915.1990.tb01250.x

Katz, M. L., & Shapiro, C. (1985). Network externalities, competition, and compatibility. *The American Economic Review*, *75*(3), 424–440.

Katz, M. L., & Shapiro, C. (1994). System competition and network effects. *The Journal of Economic Perspectives*, *8*(2), 93–115. doi:10.1257/jep.8.2.93

Keen, P. G. W. (1991). *Shaping the future: Business design through information technology*. Boston, MA: Harvard Business School Press.

Koelliker, A. (2001). Bringing together or driving apart the union? Towards a theory of differentiated integration. *West European Politics*, *24*(4), 125–151. doi:10.1080/01402380108425468

Lessig, L. (2001). *The future of ideas*. New York, NY: Random House.

Levine, M. E. (1987). Airline competition in deregulated markets: Theory, firm strategy, and public policy. *Yale Journal on Regulation*, *4*(2), 393–494.

Li, T. M. (1996). Images of community: Discourse and strategy in property relations. *Development and Change*, *27*(3), 501–527. doi:10.1111/j.1467-7660.1996.tb00601.x

Litman, J. (2001). *Digital copyright*. Amherst, NY: Prometheus Books.

Madison, M. (2003, Fall). Reconstructing the software license. *Loyola University of Chicago Law Journal. Loyola University of Chicago. School of Law*, *35*(1), 275–340.

McKeen, J. D., Guimaraes, T., & Wetherbe, J. C. (1994). The relationship between user participation and user satisfaction: an investigation of four contingency factors. *Management Information Systems Quarterly*, *18*(4), 427–449. doi:10.2307/249523

Mendelson, L. (2003). Privatizing knowledge: The demise of fair use and the public university. *Albany Law Journal of Science & Technology*, *13*, 593–612.

Mirani, R., & Lederer, A. L. (1998). An instrument for assessing the organizational benefits of IS projects. *Decision Sciences*, *29*(4), 803–838. doi:10.1111/j.1540-5915.1998.tb00878.x

Monteiro, E. (1998). Scaling information infrastructure: The case of the next generation IP in Internet. *The Information Society*, *14*(3), 229–245. doi:10.1080/019722498128845

Monteiro, E. (2001). Actor-network theory and information infrastructure. In Ciborra, C. U. (Ed.), *From control to drift: The dynamics of corporate information infrastructures* (pp. 71–83). Oxford, UK: Oxford University Press.

Mumford, E. (1995). *Effective systems design and requirements analysis: The ETHICS approach*. London, UK: Macmillan.

Mumford, E. (2006). The story of socio-technical design: Reflections on its successes, failures and potential. *Information Systems Journal*, *16*(4), 317–342. doi:10.1111/j.1365-2575.2006.00221.x

Musgrave, R. A. (1959). *The theory of public finance: A study in public economy*. New York, NY: McGraw-Hill.

National Research Council. (2002). *The drama of the commons* (Ostrom, E., Dietz, T., Dolsak, N., Stern, P., Stonich, S., & Weber, E., Eds.). Washington, DC: National Academy Press.

Ostrom, E. (1990). *Governing the commons: The evolution of institutions for collective action.* Cambridge, UK: Cambridge University Press.

Ostrom, E. (2003). How types of goods and property rights jointly affect collective action. *Journal of Theoretical Politics, 15*(3), 239–270. doi:10.1177/0951692803015003002

Ostrom, E., & Ahn, T. K. (Eds.). (2003). *Foundations of social capital.* Cheltenham, UK: Edward Elgar Publishers.

Ostrom, E., Gardner, R., & Walker, J. (1994). *Rules, games, and common-pool resources.* Ann Arbor, MI: University of Michigan Press.

Ostrom, E., & Hess, C. (2001, November). Artifacts, facilities, and content: Information as a common-pool resource. In *Proceedings of the Conference on the Public Domain, Duke Law School, Durham, NC.*

Ostrom, E., & Hess, C. (2007). A framework for analyzing the knowledge commons. In Hess, C., & Ostrom, E. (Eds.), *Understanding knowledge as a commons: From theory to practice* (pp. 41–81). Cambridge, MA: MIT Press.

Ostrom, V., & Ostrom, E. (1977). Public goods and public choices. In Savas, E. S. (Ed.), *Alternatives for delivering public services: Toward improved performance* (pp. 7–49). Boulder, CO: Westview Press.

Polski, M. (2003). *The invisible hands of U.S. commercial banking reform: Private action and public guarantees.* Boston, MA: Kluwer Academic. doi:10.1007/978-1-4615-0441-2

Rheingold, H. (1993). *The virtual community: Homesteading on the electric frontier.* New York, NY: Addison-Wesley.

Rolland, K. H., & Monteiro, E. (2002). Balancing the local and the global in infrastructural information systems. *The Information Society, 18*(2), 87–100. doi:10.1080/01972240290075020

Sahay, S., Monteiro, E., & Aanestad, M. (2009). Configurable politics and asymmetric integration: Health e-infrastructures in India. *Journal of the Association for Information Systems, 10*(5), 399–414.

Samuelson, P. (2003). Digital rights management {and, or, vs.} the law. *Communications of the ACM, 46*(4), 41–55. doi:10.1145/641205.641229

Samuelson, P. A. (1954). The pure theory of public expenditure. *The Review of Economics and Statistics, 36*(4), 387–389. doi:10.2307/1925895

Saunders, C. S., & Jones, J. W. (1992). Measuring performance of the information systems function. *Journal of Management Information Systems, 8*(4), 63–82.

Schlager, E., & Ostrom, E. (1992). Property rights regimes and natural resources: A conceptual analysis. *Land Economics, 68*(3), 249–262. doi:10.2307/3146375

Shapiro, C., & Varian, H. R. (1999). *Information rules: A strategic guide to the network economy.* Boston, MA: Harvard Business School Press.

Star, S. L., & Ruhleder, K. (1996). Steps toward an ecology of infrastructure: Design and access for large information spaces. *Information Systems Research, 7*(1), 111–134. doi:10.1287/isre.7.1.111

Tsoukas, H. (2005). *Complex knowledge: Studies in organizational epistemology.* Oxford, UK: Oxford University Press.

Wade, R. (1994). *Village republics: Economic conditions for collective action in south India.* Oakland, CA: ICS Press.

Walsham, G. (2001). Knowledge management: The benefits and limitations of computer systems. *European Management Journal, 19*(6), 599–608. doi:10.1016/S0263-2373(01)00085-8

Weill, P. (1992). The relationship between investment in information technology and firm performance: A study of the valve manufacturing sector. *Information Systems Research, 3*(4), 307–333. doi:10.1287/isre.3.4.307

Weill, P., & Broadbent, M. (1998). *Leveraging the new infrastructure: How market leaders capitalize on information.* Boston, MA: Harvard Business School Press.

Weill, P., & Ross, J. (2004). *IT governance: How top performers manage IT decision rights for superior results.* Boston, MA: Harvard Business School Press.

Willcocks, L. P., & Lester, S. (1999). *Beyond the IT productivity paradox: Assessment issues.* Chichester, UK: John Wiley & Sons.

ADDITIONAL READING

Angelsen, A., & Kaimowitz, D. (Eds.). (2001). *Agriculture technologies and tropical deforestation.* New York, NY: CABI Publishing. doi:10.1079/9780851994512.0000

Arneborg, J., & Gullov, H. C. (Eds.). (1998). *Man, culture and environment in ancient Greenland.* Copenhagen, Denmark: Danish Polar Center.

Axelrod, R. (1984). *The evolution of cooperation.* New York, NY: Basic Books.

Beresford, Q., Bekle, H., Phillips, H., & Mulcock, J. (2001). *The salinity crisis: Landscapes, communities and politics.* Crawley, Western Australia: University of Western Australia Press.

Clay, J. (2004). *World agriculture and the environment: A commodity-by-commodity guide to impacts and practices.* Washington, DC: Island Press.

Diamond, J. (2005). *Collapse: How societies choose to fail or survive.* London, UK: Penguin Allen Lane.

Dietz, T., Ostrom, E., & Stern, P. (2003). The struggle to govern the commons. *Science, 302*(5652), 1907–1912. doi:10.1126/science.1091015

Dolšak, N., & Ostrom, E. (2003). *The commons in the new millennium: Challenges and adaptations.* Cambridge, MA: MIT Press.

Ehrlich, P., & Ehrlich, A. (2004). *One with Nineveh: Politics, consumption, and the human future.* Washington, DC: Island Press.

Flenley, J., & Bahn, P. (2003). *The enigmas of Easter Island.* New York, NY: Oxford University Press.

Haug, G. (2003). Climate and the collapse of Maya civilization. *Science, 299*(5613), 1731–1735. doi:10.1126/science.1080444

Janssen, M. (2003). Sunk-cost effects and vulnerability to collapse in ancient societies. *Current Anthropology, 44*(5), 722–728. doi:10.1086/379261

Kirch, P. (Ed.). (1986). *Island societies: Archaeological approaches to evolution and transformation.* Cambridge, UK: Cambridge University Press.

Mackay, C. (1993). *Extraordinary popular delusions and the madness of crowds.* New York, NY: Barnes and Noble.

McGovern, T. (1988). Northern islands, human era, and environmental degradation: A view of social and ecological change in the medieval North Atlantic. *Human Ecology, 16*(3), 225–270. doi:10.1007/BF00888447

Platteau, J. P. (1998). Land relations under unbearable stress: Rwanda caught in the Malthusian trap. *Journal of Economic Behavior & Organization, 34*(1), 1–47. doi:10.1016/S0167-2681(97)00045-0

Siy, R. Y. Jr. (1982). *Community resource management: Lessons from the Zanjera.* Quezon City, Philippines: University of Philippines Press.

Tainter, J. (1988). *The collapses of complex societies*. Cambridge, UK: Cambridge University Press.

Terborgh, J. (1989). *Where have all the birds gone?* Princeton, NJ: Princeton University Press.

Webster, D. (2002). *The fall of the ancient Maya*. New York, NY: Thames and Hudson.

Wecker, M. (1999). *Why the cocks fight: Dominicans, Haitians, and the struggle for Hispaniola*. New York, NY: Hill and Wang.

Whitmore, T., & Turner, B. L. II. (1992). Landscapes of cultivation in Mesoamerica on the eve of the conquest. *Annals of the Association of American Geographers. Association of American Geographers*, *82*(3), 402–425. doi:10.1111/j.1467-8306.1992.tb01967.x

Wiebe, K. (Ed.). (2003). *Land quality, agricultural productivity, and food security: Biophysical processes and economic choices at local, regional, and global levels*. Cheltenham, UK: Edward Elgar.

ENDNOTES

[1]   "A commercial account is an in-house travel department in a large business or government organization. Putting a terminal in such a facility attracted business travellers paying first class fares" (Copeland & McKenney, 1988, pp.358).

[2]   In 1963, the year SABRE initially went live, American Airlines handled data related to 85,000 phone calls, 40,000 confirmed reservations, and 20,000 ticket sales. In 1990, SABRE had 45 million fares in the database, with up to 40 million changes entered every month (Hopper, 1990).

[3]   Even though wide access to the Internet and other information and communication technologies is the norm for Western, developed countries, many developing countries have no access whatsoever–a phenomenon which has been called the "digital divide" (see http://www.digitaldivide.org).

Section 2
Case Studies

Chapter 4
The Development of a Regional Health Information Infrastructure in Greece

ABSTRACT

This chapter draws on empirical research carried out during the years 2003-2006 on the development of a regional health information infrastructure in Greece. Using the theoretical framework discussed in Chapter 3, this chapter examines the multilevel context, action arena, and outcomes in the case, placing great emphasis on the property rights put forward and negotiated between key stakeholder groups, as they strive to develop an information infrastructure. Drawing on the more recent outcomes of these negotiations, the chapter concludes with an analysis of the consequences of these outcomes for the region of Greece, and more broadly, for European Information Society programmes.

INTRODUCTION

In 1993, the European Council requested that a report be prepared by "a group of prominent persons" on the specific measures to be taken into consideration by the European Community and the Member States for the development of information infrastructures (Bangemann et al.,

1994, pp.1). The Bangemann Report as it became to be known urged the European Union to put its faith in market mechanisms to enable its Member States to meet its increasing information needs and challenge more technologically advanced countries like the USA and Japan. This did not mean more public money, financial assistance, or protectionism as the report professed. Rather this meant (Bangemann et al., 1994, pp.4):

DOI: 10.4018/978-1-4666-1622-6.ch004

fostering an entrepreneurial mentality to enable the emergence of new dynamic sectors of the economy… [and] developing a common regulatory approach to bring forth a competitive, Europe-wide, market for information services.

In a tone that is reminiscent of the infrastructural ideal of the integrated, standardized city of the 19th and 20th centuries (see Chapter 1 of this book), the Bangemann report noted (1994, pp.5-6):

Given its history, we can be sure that Europe will take the opportunity. It will create the information society. The only question is whether this will be a strategic creation for the whole Union, or a more fragmented and much less effective amalgam of individual initiatives by Member States, with repercussions on every policy area, from the single market to cohesion… The widespread availability of new information tools and services will present fresh opportunities to build a more equal and balanced society and to foster individual accomplishment. The information society has the potential to improve the quality of life of Europe's citizens, the efficiency of our social and economic organisation and to reinforce cohesion. … Fair access to the infrastructure will have to be guaranteed to all, as will provision of universal service, the definition of which must evolve in line with the technology.

The report continued with a number of proposals based on specific initiatives involving partnerships linking public and private sectors. This is where the report began to shift its focus from the infrastructural ideal and to recognize the need for private investment avoiding monopolistic, anticompetitive scenarios–without however recognizing that private investment could also lead to the very splintering of their envisioned information society.

The proposals in the Bangemann Report were followed by the action plan *Europe towards the Information Society*, which contained four ac-

tion lines: a) the adaptation of the regulatory framework for telecommunications to facilitate infrastructure liberalisation; b) the promotion of network, services, and content applications; c) the harnessing of the social and cultural impacts of the information society; and d) concrete actions to promote the information society (European Commission, 1994; Sancho, 2002).

The Lisbon Summit in March 2000 noted the challenges of the transition to the information society by articulating the need to establish a competitive platform that would simultaneously sustain the European social model and maintain social cohesion and cultural diversity (Council of the European Union, 2000). Furthermore, a new open method of inter-state coordination was adopted for the acceleration of the translation of European goals into national policies. This method was supposed to combine European coherence with national diversity. It operated by initially setting European guidelines in each policy domain, then identifying best practices and reference indicators, and, finally, leading to national plans consisting of concrete targets in accordance with each nation's case (Rodrigues, 2002). The purported aim was to develop a knowledge economy with social cohesion and to promote convergence in Europe.

The new open method of coordination has been applied to a number of policy domains, including infrastructural policies in the context of the *An Information Society for All* initiative (European Commission, 1999). This initiative set out ten priority areas for joint action by the Commission, the member states, the industry, and the citizens. After the Lisbon Summit and the informal Ministerial Conference on the Information and Knowledge Society a month later, the eEurope priorities were clustered around three main aims: a) cheaper, faster, and secure Internet; b) investment in people and skills; and c) stimulation of the deployment of the Internet. An action plan was subsequently prepared by the Commission and was endorsed at the Feira Summit in June 2000, placing specific targets to be reached by specific deadlines by governments and the private sector in member states. The subsequent *eEurope 2005* action plan also set out to stimulate Internet services, applications, and content so as to improve the underlying infrastructure through the promotion of broadband and increased awareness of security matters. It also stressed the need to promote information and communication technology skills and opportunities, something that has been termed "e-inclusion" (Eurostat, 2003).

The European Information Society programmes, particularly the eEurope initiatives, have indeed mobilised the formulation and introduction of strategic national programmes in almost all the member states. However, placed under the open method of coordination, the eEurope initiatives have been operating under state consensus. That is, even though member states have placed a high political commitment to implement such initiatives (always in cooperation with other states, the European Parliament, the European Commission and business and societal actors, and according to predetermined schedules), national needs have always been prioritized (Sancho, 2002). Further, the Lisbon agenda left much room for variation across member states, as it placed a significant role to the state to define the structures and institutions that were called upon to carry out the implementation of eEurope initiatives (Mansell &Steinmueller, 2000; Perrons, 2004).

Thus, contrary to the envisioned European information society found in the Bangemann Report, as well as other early European white papers on the subject, the market mechanisms embraced and encouraged by European Information Society programmes have created possibilities for the splintering of that vision (cf. Graham & Marvin 2001).

This chapter will examine the development of a regional healthcare information infrastructure in Greece, while exploring the paradox between efforts to centralize and possibilities for decentralization. The chapter will start by looking at the impact that European Information Society

programmes have had on related initiatives in Greece and, in particular, the Greek national health sector. The discussion will focus on the development of a healthcare information infrastructure in Crete. Using the theoretical framework discussed in Chapter 3, this chapter will examine the multi-level context, action arena, and outcomes in the Crete case, placing great emphasis on the property rights put forward and negotiated between key stakeholder groups as they strived to develop an information infrastructure. The chapter will conclude with an analysis of the consequences of these outcomes for the region of Greece, and more broadly, for European information society programmes.

INFORMATION SOCIETY INITIATIVES IN GREECE

The first policy document regarding information society initiatives in Greece was a white paper entitled *The Greek Strategy for an Information Society: A Tool for Employment, Development and Quality of Life* (Hellenic Republic, 1995), which raised a number of goals to be pursued in the following 10-15 years. These included the goal to limit the gap between Greece and the other European countries in the use of advanced information infrastructures; to ensure that a considerable proportion of Greek firms and households had access to those information infrastructures; and to see that the greatest part of transactions with the state were carried out electronically (Hellenic Republic, 1995). This first document was mainly concerned with the inadequate national infrastructure, which limited electronic transactions and access to new products and services both for firms and for households in comparison with other European countries. Most of its actions were funded by the 2nd European Community Support Framework, including the development of a national infrastructure linking universities, technological institutes and public research institutes and the promotion of an e-commerce environment for business with the establishment of a National Committee on Electronic Commerce (Constantelou, 2001).

The operational programme *Kleisthenis* (1994-2000) run by the Ministry of Interior and Public Administration and with a total budget of 100 billion Greek Drachmas was the main information society initiative of that period. The central aim of the programme was the modernisation of public administration (both in terms of hardware procurement and regarding services and training of employees). The programme adopted an integrated approach to information systems deployment, including the development of infrastructures, and applications and training in the design and implementation of each separate project.

In the 1990s, the main development in Greece was the liberalisation of the telecommunication sector. Until the late 1980s the telecommunication sector in Greece (and in Europe at large), was based on a state monopoly in the provision of telephone and telecommunication services. Following the early European information society policies, a series of laws carried forward the liberalisation of telecommunications, beginning with value-added services and mobile telephony services (Law 1892/90 & 2075/92). After 31 December 2000, all restrictions, including those on the provision of voice telephony and the network infrastructure, have been removed, and full competition has been officially established under the supervision of an independent regulatory authority, the National Telecommunications and Post Commission (OECD, 2001).

In April 1999, a second white paper entitled *Greece in the Information Society: Strategy and Actions* (Hellenic Republic, 1999) was prepared by ten policy experts and advisors to the Prime Minister based on European and international experiences. This white paper emphasised the potential of information and communication technologies for competitiveness and better public services together with the requirement of constructing human skills to take advantage of these opportunities—both principles were already present in broader European policy documents. The imperative of universal access and the prevention of new types of social exclusion were also highlighted.

Following the 1999 white paper and influenced by the eEurope initiative of 1999 and the Feira Summit of June 2000, the Greek government proposed an *Operational Programme for the Information Society* (OPIS) linking it to funds within the structure of the 3rd European Community Support Framework. This was an innovative horizontal programme, involving a number of government departments, and aiming to implement the essential features of the 1999 white paper. For the period 2000-2006, the OPIS set the objectives to provide better services to the citizen and improve the quality of life through the deployment of information and communication technologies in public administration, health and welfare, transport, and the environment; to promote development and build human potential through actions to increase competitiveness and employment; and to consign a suitable educational system (Constantelou, 2001).

Several bodies were set up to manage and implement the OPIS (Law 2860/2000). Firstly, the Management Authority, operating under the Special Secretariat for the Information Society established within the Greek Ministry of National Economy, dealt with the design of action lines for the OPIS, the follow-up and control of their implementation, as well as the writing of annual techno-economic reports and supervision of financial, legal, and logistical aspects. Secondly, the Monitoring Committee comprised of representatives of ministries, public organisations, economic and social partners, and non-governmental organizations, had a supervisory and advisory role. Thirdly, the Information Society, a public not-for-profit organisation operating under the supervision of the Greek Ministry of Interior and Public Administration, was charged with the administration of public calls for tender, while providing assistance and advice to government and other public and private institutions in the implementation of the OPIS. Finally, the Observatory for the Greek IS, aimed at transferring expertise and best practice relevant with information society issues, as well as at providing training tools and supervising benchmarking studies (Constantelou, 2001).

In 2000, when the OPIS was first implemented, Greece was significantly behind the EU-15 average in the use of information infrastructure services (Dutta & Jain, 2005). In fact, together with Spain, Italy, and Portugal, Greece shared the lowest level of IT development among the EU-15 countries (Dutta & Jain, 2005, pp.19). Since 2004, there has been a stable increase, primarily in the private sector. In particular, in 2003, 92 percent of firms with 11-250 employees possessed personal computers (94 percent in the EU), 82 percent were connected to the Internet (83 percent in the EU), while 48 percent also had a website (52 percent in the EU). These changes were reinforced through the *eBusiness* action of the OPIS, resulting in an 87 percent Internet connection in 2004 (90 percent for the EU-15) (EAITY, 2008). Very small enterprises (up to 10 employees) lagged significantly behind the EU average in 2002, but by 2006 had increased their Internet connectivity substantially (72.4 percent) (EAITY, 2008). In the public sector, the diffusion and deployment of information and communication technologies has been limited in almost all areas, which also explains the low use of electronic means of interaction with public authorities. Exceptions have been noted in certain parts of the TAXIS Net project (addressing fiscal procedures), as well as the area of education and training, with the development of the advanced Greek Research and Education Network (GRNET) interconnecting academic and research institutions, as well as primary and secondary schools.

The next sections discuss the impact of Information Society initiatives within the Greek national health sector, starting with a brief de-

scription of the evolution of the Greek national health system.

The Greek National Health System (1983-2000)

Before World War I there was no public provision of health services in Greece, except for a few charitable hospitals in major cities. Various attempts to provide public health care to the population were made, but it was not until 1983 that the Greek National Health System (GNHS) was established with Law 1397/83. It was a major part of the agenda of the Greek socialist party, which first came into power in 1981 (Tountas et al., 2002).

In its first five years of operation (1983-7), the GNHS proved highly popular. According to Ministry of Health data, as a percentage of Gross Domestic product (GDP), health expenditure in Greece increased substantially to a level similar to that in other European countries such as those of Luxembourg and the United Kingdom (Kyriopoulos & Tsalikis, 1993). There was a marked improvement in facilities and staffing with one of the highest doctor-patient ratios among developed countries (Theodorou et al., 1995). There was also some improvement towards decentralization of health facilities, something which contributed significantly to increased access to hospital facilities in remote areas in Greece.

Gradually, however, it became increasingly difficult for the GNHS to meet patients' expectations, and problems began to pile up. By the late 1990s, the level of public dissatisfaction with the health services was the highest in the European Union (EU), primarily due to the poor quality of health services offered and increased corruption (Close, 2002). In 1994, a committee of health experts reported that the scale of under-the-counter bribes to doctors, nurses, and medical suppliers was extraordinarily high by Organization for Economic Co-operation and Development (OECD) standards (Abel-Smith et al., 1994). In a 1995 poll, 46 percent of those interviewed said that they had used personal acquaintance with a doctor, or other contacts, to jump the queue for attention in hospital (Close, 2002). The Abel-Smith committee also concluded that the GNHS suffered from a lack of planning and structure (i.e. management), non-rational financing mechanisms, and extremely weak provision or primary health care.

Furthermore, from the very beginning, the operation of the GNHS was marked by industrial unrest. Most of these conflicts were about doctors' remunerations. Following the establishment of the GNHS, doctors, as well as other hospital staff, became civil servants and, therefore, in accordance with the Greek Constitution, their remuneration had to be lower than that of justices. This cap created conflicts that led to strikes by the doctors, who felt they should be paid more for their work. To avoid constitutional restrictions, successive governments resorted to "creative accounting" (Ballas & Tsoukas, 2004). For example, in the late 1980s, the socialist government agreed to pay doctors fictitious overtime in order to circumvent the constitutional constraint.

Moreover, there have been significant problems in the financial management of hospitals, which lacked clear decision-making guidelines about where money should be spent or how to select suppliers. This was true both in the case of investments in new facilities and medical equipment and, even more so, in the case of consumables. Specifically, there was no formal procedure, or even a budgeting system, for purchasing equipment on the basis of need. Rather, it all depended on idiosyncratic decisions by hospital directors. In addition, towards the end of the fiscal year, each healthcare organisation usually rushed to buy equipment in order to spend as much as possible from funds allocated by the government (Tountas et al., 2002).

The Greek National Health System (2000-2006)

The growing dissatisfaction with the GNHS has led successive governments to take action in the form of legislating changes to the system. The main problems faced by the public healthcare sector at the time included an unstable legal framework that allowed each newly elected government to introduce even more reforms; a strong private sector under loose control; the presence of a black-market economy where patients were forced to offer cash bribes to doctors in order to receive better treatment; low levels of public expenditure (5.4 percent GNP); and a lack of skilled personnel and adequate healthcare services (Tountas et al., 2002). In addition, due to a large number of social insurance funds (39 in total) with a variety of insurance policies, there were numerous financial and political power conflicts between the funds and the public and private healthcare systems (Davaki & Mossialos, 2005).

Despite the good intentions of the Greek government at the time, none of the above problems were successfully addressed. This failure eventually led to a new set of reforms being introduced by the newly elected socialist party in 2000. The most important change introduced in 2000, was the division of the GNHS into 13, autonomous regional healthcare systems and the decentralization of the organizational structure of the GNHS (Sissouras & Souliotis, 2002) as shown in Figure 1.

All regional healthcare services, including primary and secondary healthcare and the social insurance funds, were grouped under the jurisdiction and management of the regional healthcare systems. The management of medical personnel within the regions also fell under the authority of each regional healthcare system, a responsibility that was previously exercised centrally by the Ministry of Health and Welfare (Tountas et al., 2002). The second major change introduced was the creation of the Organization for the Management of Healthcare Resources (OMHR). The

Figure 1. The thirteen regions of the Greek National Health System

OMHR has the ability to buy services for its clients (hospitals and healthcare centres) from the regional healthcare systems and the private healthcare sector by drawing on social insurance funds and state taxes monitored by the Greek government. The creation of the OMHR aimed at establishing a cooperative internal market between the main purchaser (OMHR) and the main provider (GNHS) of healthcare services in Greece.

Despite the strengthening of public healthcare services through these reforms, the GNHS still faces several hurdles including high costs and low quality of services, poor management, and a lack of skilled personnel (Sissouras & Souliotis, 2002). In fact, a 2001 OECD report found the GNHS to be lacking adequate healthcare reforms resulting in poor performance and a slow convergence towards quality levels of other EU countries (OECD, 2001).

Information Society Initiatives in the Greek Public Healthcare Sector

In the midst of this unstable context, most of the efforts towards the introduction of information and communication technologies in the public healthcare sector of Greece have been fragmented and isolated in individual regions, hospitals, or primary health centers.

For example, one of the earliest of these efforts occurred in 1987, when the Department of Social and Family Medicine at the University of Crete and the Health Sciences Centre at the University of Lund in Dalby, Sweden agreed to establish a DOS (Disc Operating System) database to store patient records at the primary health centre (PHC) at Spili, Crete (Isacsson et al., 1992). This patient records database was mainly used as a statistical tool for conducting epidemiological research in primary healthcare, such as finding the percentage of 0-14 year-olds with acute bronchitis (Isacsson et al., 1992). Unfortunately, this first electronic records database at the PHC at Spili depended on a stand-alone server, which at some point crashed and all patient data was lost[1]. However, the experiences gained from this initiative led to yet another initiative at the PHC at Anogia, Crete. There, a general practitioner, with considerable involvement in the first initiative at Spili and relatively advanced computer knowledge, decided to develop his own patient records database using Microsoft Access. By 2003, this system was being licensed to more than 50 PHCs throughout Greece[2].

Similar initiatives had taken place throughout Greece. The main achievement of these efforts was the installation of various administrative and financial information systems, as well as laboratory information systems in various hospitals throughout the country (EAITY, 2001). However, these efforts did not secure any substantial levels of collaboration between involved parties. This outcome was attributed to reasons such as poor coordination, lack of collective incentives, and common strategies (Sotiriou, 1998), as well as lack of adequate training programs to build information and communication technologies knowledge and skills (Skalkidis, 1998). In addition, although Greece benefited from funds provided by European Community Support Frameworks, as mentioned earlier, these funds were usually reduced to a lesser amount than the one originally announced (EAITY, 2001), or were consumed by a few powerful stakeholders (Tountas et al., 2002).

In 2000, after the establishment of the OPIS and the support of the 3rd European Community Framework, the Greek government proceeded to an open call for tender–under the administration of the Information Society of the OPIS–for the development of regional healthcare information infrastructures with which to support healthcare service chain activities (Sissouras & Souliotis, 2002). Overall, the Information Society directed the 13 newly established regional healthcare systems of Greece to evaluate their existing installed technology bases and their utilization for the development of new technological solutions, or their removal if considered obsolete; the utilization of open architectures supporting the integration of heterogeneous and autonomous information systems; the adherence to internationally accepted standards and protocols with which to support the interoperability between different systems; and the creation of integrated, lifelong electronic patient records (EAITY, 2001).

The next section takes a closer look at the impact of the Information Society in the region of Crete.

THE DEVELOPMENT OF HEALTHnet: A PILOT, HEALTH INFORMATION INFRASTRUCTURE IN CRETE (1997-2005)

Since the late 1980's, the regional government in Crete has assigned high priority to becoming a model region for healthcare services in Greece, and was the first to develop and implement HEALTHnet, a pilot, regional health information infrastructure–even before the Information Society. The development of HEALTHnet is largely attributed to CreteTech (a pseudonym) a local private research and development (R&D) institute.

The development of HEALTHnet, the first pilot health information infrastructure in Crete, came about through CreteTech's strategy to integrate all healthcare services in the region, so that they could assess and scale-up their R&D projects. The HEALTHnet pilot was partly financed from the 1st and 2nd European Community Support Frameworks mentioned earlier, and from other R&D projects that CreteTech had secured on a competitive basis.

Figure 2. HEALTHnet: The first pilot health information infrastructure in Crete

In 1997, having secured the necessary funds, CreteTech formed a working group to discuss and begin to develop an integrated electronic health record (I-EHR) module–the core of the HEALTHnet pilot. The working group for the I-EHR module involved a team of software engineers from CreteTech, and a team of three general practitioners. These healthcare professionals were the pioneers in introducing electronic patient records in the region and also held senior positions (two of them were directors of their respective primary healthcare centers). They were selected for their keen interest in new technological developments and their capability to promote the initiative across the 17 primary healthcare centers, eight hospitals, and six community doctor practices in the region as illustrated in Figure 2. The key development phase of the HEALTHnet pilot took place between 1997-2001 with the aid of this working group.

As mentioned in the previous section, in 2001, the year after they won the national elections, the Socialist party decentralized the Greek national health system into 13 autonomous regional healthcare systems. In 2004, the Democratic Party was re-elected appointing new officials in the regional healthcare systems. In the first instance, the Socialist party used this reform as a means to decentralize the provision of public healthcare by

giving more flexibility and control to the regions to individually manage their human, financial, and technical resources. In the second instance, the Democratic Party restored control back to the center, the Ministry of Health & Welfare in Athens. In both cases, however, Crete, like other regions in Greece, obtained a new public health body that redistributed professional roles and intentions around the HEALTHnet pilot, while also influencing the decisions and choices of the users.

In the next section, an in-depth analysis of events that followed the early development of HEALTHnet will be presented, including the political reforms in the broader public sector in Greece. In the first subsection, particular attention will be placed on the development of HEALTHnet during the years 2002-2005, when CreteTech tried to scale-up the pilot to "a real service," as the then director of the institute said in an interview. This discussion will be followed by the developments during the years 2005-2006 when a new contract was signed between the Greek government and CompeTech (a pseudonym) for the introduction of a new regional health information infrastructure in Crete. Table 1 provides a summary of the key themes derived from the analysis of the data.

Table 1. Key themes from the findings

Analytical focus	The HEALTHnet Pilot (2001-5)	A Contract for a New Information Infrastructure (2005-6)
Multilevel Context	Material characteristics of the infrastructure • *Network facilities*: Microsoft & SAP architecture built on open standards • *Applications*: two major applications–hospital wide IS & primary care IS with a focus on integrated, life-long electronic patient records • *Content*: medical data Institutional rules (property rights) No formal agreements were signed between CreteTech and different stakeholders, however the following property right regimes were implied: • *Operational rights* granted to users • *Collective choice rights* granted to directors of primary healthcare centers and hospitals • *Constitutional rights* reserved by CreteTech Communal attributes (right holders) • *Users* (healthcare professionals & administrative/management staff from hospitals and primary healthcare centers in the region). • *IT Providers* (CreteTech and partners, other IT vendors developing separate systems) • *Policymakers* (Greek government)	Material characteristics of the infrastructure • *Network facilities*: Oracle architecture built on open standards • *Applications*: three major applications–hospital wide IS, primary care IS, and Health Authorities IS with a focus on integrated electronic patient records • *Content:* administrative & medical data Institutional rules (property rights) Formal rights regimes specified by the Information Society initiative • *Operational rights* granted to users • *Collective choice rights* granted to the Regional Health Authorities & directors of primary healthcare centers and hospitals • *Constitutional rights* reserved by the Greek government via the Information Society Communal attributes (right holders) • *Users* (Regional Health Authorities; healthcare professionals & administrative/management staff from hospitals and primary healthcare centers in the region). • *IT Providers* (CompeTech and partners) • *Policymakers* (Greek government–Information Society)

Action Arena (also see Figure 4 & Figure 5)	1. Inefficiency problems (i.e. no support for administrative resources by HEALTHnet)
	2.
	   o No contractual agreements on commercial terms of use which led to property rights disputes between senior managers at CreteTech and senior officials at the Regional Health Authorities
	   o Lack of participation in provider selection which led some hospital directors to proceed with the procurement of their independent (self-funded) systems
	3. Lack of funds by CreteTech to scale up pilot
	4. Poor integration of information resources
	5. unintended consequences (i.e. multiple and diverse IT providers and applications)
	6. Resistance by users
	7. Alienation of the information resources and the information infrastructure due to government reforms and technological developments (i.e. the Information Society initiative)
	8. Alienations of relationships between users and CreteTech due to lack of support from the government
		1. Not applicable yet but possible disruptions to existing information resources
		2. Lack of participation in provider selection and resistance to the co-production model prescribed by the Information Society and CompeTech by users (i.e. Regional Health Authorities, healthcare professionals)
		3. Disputes over procurement procedures around choice of winning consortium for the development of a new information infrastructure for the region between CreteTech and the Information Society
		4. Not applicable yet but possible disruptions to existing information resources
		5. Disruption of temporal and spatial patterns of use
		6. Possible unintended consequences (e.g. keep some existing applications)
		7. Possible alienation of the information resources and the new information infrastructure
		8. Alienations of relationships between users and CompeTech

Outcomes	• some increase/improvement in knowledge exchange among some users • disputes around participation in development and fairness in benefits gained by HEALTHnet • confused/unclear efficiency of HEALTHnet due to the various competing technologies deployed in the region • questions around the sustainability of HEALTHnet	• unclear as to whether the new information infrastructure will increase/improve knowledge exchange • concerns about non participation in procurement decision and future implementation plans • unclear as to whether CompeTech would deliver an efficient solution based on required needs • questions around the sustainability of the proposed infrastructure

Multilevel Context

Material Characteristics of the Infrastructure

The main objective of HEALTHnet was to permit the effective integration of distributed, heterogeneous components and data, ensuring support of different functionalities, whilst interacting transparently with users as a "federation of autonomous systems," as one senior engineer said in an interview. To ensure the achievement of this objective, HEALTHnet was built with Microsoft and SAP components based on the conceptual architecture of the Technical Committee for Health Informatics of the European Committee for Standardization (CEN/TC251, 1995) and the Reference Model of Open Distributed Processing (ISO/IEC, 1995). The initial objective was to create an integrated electronic health record (I-EHR) module for primary healthcare centers. The two major applications included a Primary Healthcare Information System (PHIS), and a Hospital Information System (HIS), both of which supported only patient and medical data, such as x-rays, CT scans, biopsies, etc. There were no modules for administrative tasks, however, such as dealing with patient accounts, or any other finance and accounting functions, as illustrated in Figure 3.

Institutional Rules (Property Rights)

During the early development of HEALTHnet, between 1997-2002, CreteTech did not engage in a discussion about any kind of contractual agreements and property rights for the technology. This meant that hardware and software installations as well as training were provided free of charge according to the interest exhibited by healthcare professionals, while CreteTech retained full control of constitutional rights over the pilot. That is, they controlled who could participate in making collective choices around the removal, management, and exclusion of resources offered by HEALTHnet. In turn, despite the fact that no formal agreements existed, it was implied that the users, i.e. healthcare staff and administrators in primary healthcare centers and hospitals, only held operational rights of access, contribution, and extraction of content from various applications offered by HEALTHnet. Collective choice rights of removal, management, and exclusion were implicitly granted to the directors of primary healthcare centers and hospitals (i.e. the healthcare content providers). Finally, during this phase of the pilot project, the Greek government (i.e. the policymakers) had no direct involvement; however, officials at the Regional Health Authorities eventually questioned the legitimacy of HEALTHnet, as discussed below.

Community Attributes (Property Right Holders)

Due to the lack of formal agreements, there were mixed reactions as to the objectives and value of HEALTHnet among the users, where some exhibited high interest and usage patterns and others were entirely removed from participating in the pilot. A great part of the non-participation by users was due to the fact that HEALTHnet was an R&D project initiated by CreteTech that had never received the formal support from the Greek government. In turn, many users did not buy-into the longevity of HEALTHnet, thinking that this was just a passing project and that soon the Greek government would announce a new initiative. This view was influenced by the repeated changes in the Greek government, with the latter playing a key role as a (distant) policymaker in the delivery of information society initiatives in the public healthcare sector.

Most importantly, the user organizations in Crete were characterized by heterogeneity in size, wealth, and dependency on resources. For example, the two regional hospitals in Heraklion, the capital of Crete (see Figure 2), were much larger than the rest of the other 6 hospitals in Crete

Figure 3. The Conceptual Architecture of HEALTHnet

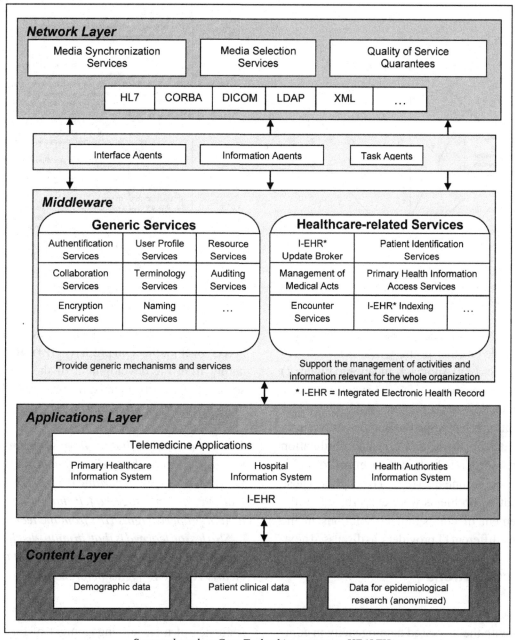

Source: based on CreteTech white papers on HEALTHnet

combined, both in terms of numbers of personnel (3315 vs. 2723), and numbers of work points (688 vs. 400–measured in numbers of computer terminals) (Information Society, 2004). This generally meant that the two regional hospitals in Heraklion had a greater budget to work with, did not depend on resources from other hospitals, and had more bargaining power on decisions made around the procurement of new information systems. Such heterogeneity was also true across the primary healthcare centers with some of them being bigger in size and wealth (e.g Mires, Kastelli, Spili in

Figure 4. Problems during the HEALTHnet Pilot (2001-2005)

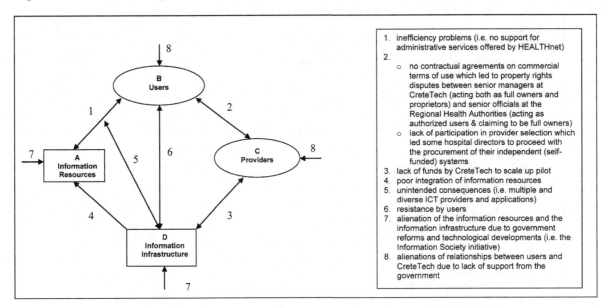

Figure 2), while others were small and dependent on hospitals or other primary healthcare centres for resources (e.g. Anogia, Kandanos in Figure 2) (Information Society, 2004). This heterogeneity had implications on the relationships between user organizations, including the bundles of property rights held by them, and created coordination problems for CreteTech in their effort to mobilize support around the HEALTHnet pilot. These coordination problems were exacerbated by the procurement of competing IT solutions in the region by different IT providers, as discussed next.

The Action Arena

The lack of support by the Greek Government in joint with the increased heterogeneity in community attributes led to a number of negotiation problems as illustrated in Figure 4 and discussed in more detail below.

After the reforms introduced by the Socialist party, one of the general practitioners (who collaborated with the CreteTech team in the initiation of the project) was promoted to vice president of the new Regional Health Authorities. In his new position, this initial participant challenged CreteTech over intellectual property (IP) rights emanating from the development of the I-EHR. A senior applications scientist from CreteTech said in an interview in July 2003:

One of the reasons that we have some problems with a professor at the Medical School, with whom we worked together regarding the I-EHR, was the fact that at some stage he felt that he had intellectual property rights (IP) from the technology. ... So a lesson learned is that, in multi-disciplinary collaborative efforts, it is very important to very clearly resolve IP rights beforehand.

Notably, this IP rights dispute was the consequence of a strong engagement of the initial participants in the development of the I-EHR. The dispute was not entirely surprising, given the lack of contractual agreements. However, none of the parties expected such an outcome when they jointly initiated the project (as can be inferred from the remarks made above).

Despite this dispute, in 2003 some broader European and national developments offered fresh opportunities for CreteTech to scale up their HEALTHnet project. Specifically, the Greek government–drawing on European funds and related Information Society initiatives–directed the newly established Regional Health Authorities to announce competitions for an IT solution while following standard processes toward the definition of functional requirements against contractual agreements. Three of the key requirements imposed by the Information Society initiative were for open architectures, flexible standards, and lifelong integrated electronic health records, all of which had already been introduced by CreteTech in the HEALTHnet project.

In the midst of these developments, CreteTech attempted to mobilize support around HEALTHnet through clearly defined contractual agreements (in late 2003). As a first strategy, they tried to secure the necessary financial support from the government to scale-up a number of telemedicine applications, such as a telecardiology system enabling teleconsultations between a general practitioner at a rural primary healthcare center and two cardiologists at a district hospital (see Constantinides & Barrett, 2006). As a second strategy, they contacted the most avid users of the I-EHR module, offering to upgrade their systems under clearly defined service level agreements (SLAs). CreteTech's first strategy never materialized because the Ministry of Health refused to negotiate any funding due to the upcoming Information Society initiative. CreteTech's second strategy had some success, despite the fact that interested parties had to finance the I-EHR upgrade from their individual budgets. This meant that only those user organizations with healthy budgets were able to acquire the upgrade. The resource constraints imposed on an already heterogeneous user base as a consequence of CreteTech's disagreements with the national and regional authorities created an environment that nurtured competing claims against the adoption of HEALTHnet.

In January 2004, in an interview with the then director of IT services at the Regional Health Authorities, it became evident that a number of hospital directors in the Crete region, having completely lost faith in HEALTHnet and unwilling to wait for the Information Society initiative to materialize, decided to self-fund their own projects. Their efforts were primarily directed toward establishing hospital-wide networks for intra-organizational support of administrative-financial systems for managing patient accounts–a service not offered by HEALTHnet. The consequence of these efforts was that, by 2005, even though parts of the HEALTHnet project were still functional, the region was saturated with multiple inter- and intra-organizational networks (i.e. hospital-wide and hospital-to-hospital networks as opposed to region-wide networks) from diverse vendors. Hence there were also multiple competing claims to property rights around these networks. Essentially, the wealthier user organizations in the region contested CreteTech's constitutional right to control who could or could not participate in making collective choices around the management and exclusion of IT applications within their own hospitals.

These contestations resurfaced after the re-election of the Democratic Party in 2004. Soon after his appointment, the new president of the Regional Health Authorities of Crete questioned the ownership of all the different applications installed in the region's healthcare centers and hospitals. He voiced some key concerns about HEALTHnet in an interview in September 2005:

[CreteTech] has installed some applications to different primary healthcare centers, which enabled the doctors to 'talk' to [CreteTech] and themselves... Each of these doctors had decided to throw away whatever existed and belonged to me [the Regional Health Authorities] and had began using something else, illegal, which does not belong to me. Under whose decision, under what procedures was this decision made?

These concerns raised questions around the legitimacy of the HEALTHnet project and called for a better clarification of the role of each of the various actors in the region.

The new president of the Regional Health Authorities felt that since the various applications installed as part of the HEALTHnet pilot were being used (by different healthcare centers) under the jurisdiction of the Regional Health Authorities, they belonged to that authority. He essentially argued that these applications were resources *de jure* owned by the regional public healthcare sector of Crete. The primary argument centered around whether CreteTech should own data about patients treated in the public sector.

CreteTech held a different opinion. According to a senior engineer from CreteTech, HEALTHnet provided the means by which to standardize health information on different patients while making that information uniformly available across the region. All electronic data were stored both locally at servers situated at each healthcare centre and each hospital, but also globally at a central server located in CreteTech where back-ups were created and traffic on HEALTHnet was monitored. "The main driver for integrated access to clinical information is information sharing through a secure environment," stated a senior engineer from CreteTech. In other words, CreteTech was not interested in owning and controlling collective choice rights around the removal, management, and exclusion of patient data, but in establishing the necessary technical means with which to control the network. Despite these assurances from CreteTech, HEALTHnet, as well as other IT solutions provided in the region, became increasingly rivalrous, as the Regional Health Authorities began to question the distribution of property rights within their jurisdiction.

Outcomes

Despite the aforementioned challenges, the HEALTHnet pilot provided the platform and nec-

essary tools upon which to increase and improve the knowledge about patients and their medical conditions across the regions. A handful of general practitioners reported great satisfaction with the electronic patient records module and contributed to growing databases of patient records.

At the same time, other users questioned the benefits gained by HEALTHnet, since the pilot itself was seen as illegitimate, that is, not under the support of the Greek Ministry of Health.

Consequently, the usage of the various HEALTHnet applications began to significantly drop. For instance, by 2004, the I-EHR system was used by only a handful of general practitioners. An illustrative example of such a decline in use was noted by the head of CreteTech's implementation team in 2004:

Most primary health centers find it very hard to go against the will of the RHA [Regional Health Authorities], because they simply depend on them… A general practitioner who initially used paper records later changed to using electronic records and he was actually one of the most enthusiastic users. …now he has switched back to using paper-based records.

Further, with the change in government, most healthcare professionals in the region were aware that, at any given point in time, the Greek government could intervene and replace HEALTHnet with a completely new information infrastructure. One general practitioner said in July 2003:

CreteTech has installed the system and has done some demonstrations on its use, but now we need the help of the government. We still haven't received any reply from them on this matter.

It became evident that healthcare professionals in the region realized that the HEALTHnet project enclosed them in CreteTech's R&D and later commercial goals, which they did not agree with. In turn, many of those healthcare professionals refused to cooperate and comply to what seemed to them a 'weak resource' (to use a commons theory term). HEALTHnet may be considered to be a weak resource as it failed to provide *commonly* approved ways for supporting the delivery of healthcare by not securing the support of the public healthcare sector and the national policies of the Greek government. Thus, there were negative network externalities making it difficult to reach the critical mass of network members necessary to scale up the HEALTHnet pilot. The repeated disputes between CreteTech's senior management and officials at the Regional Health Authorities of Crete did not help to alleviate this situation.

Beyond issues of non-use, lack of cooperation, and support from the government, the most important outcome was the confused ownership of HEALTHnet and other technologies deployed in the region. The region was saturated with separate systems provided by different IT vendors and it was unclear as to who controlled what and if indeed there was a region-wide network. Questions around the ownership of systems installed in the region of Crete became more important in light of the then upcoming Information Society initiative.

From the public sector's point of view, the key issue remained "to figure out what we have and don't have," (as the president of the Regional Health Authorities stated in an interview in 2005). However, evaluating the now fragmented existing installed base in Crete, in contrast to the various solutions put forward by different consortia for the Information Society competition, proved to be a much more complex process than this quotation suggested. Negotiations now involved competing claims to ownership around the new infrastructure's capacity to account for the property rights of policymakers, providers, and users.

A NEW HEALTH INFORMATION INFRASTRUCTURE IN CRETE (2005-2006)

By late 2005, the competition for the regional health information infrastructure in Crete was completed and the contract went to CompeTech, a consortium of IT vendors that did not include CreteTech or any of the other companies that had previously implemented IT systems in Crete. This development caused a dramatic change in the negotiations by not only bringing new actors onto the stage but also a new information infrastructure.

The Multilevel Context

Material Characteristics of the Infrastructure

The new information infrastructure proposed by CompeTech followed the strict guidelines of the Information Society, which called for distributed architectures, open standards, and integrated electronic healthcare records. Based on these guidelines, CompeTech proposed an Oracle-based system with three key applications: a Primary Healthcare Information System (PHIS), a Hospital Information System (HIS), and an application for the Regional Health Authorities, which would enable the latter to monitor levels of use and manage patient journeys across the region. As in the case of HEALTHnet, at the core of all these applications was the integrated electronic healthcare record, which would be responsible for all data resulting from contact of the patient with a health practitioner (medical history of the patient, prescriptions, and planning for treatment). The difference, though, was that all three of these applications included modules for managing both medical and administrative tasks and data, in contrast to what was offered by HEALTHnet in the past.

Institutional Rules (Property Rights)

Also in contrast to the HEALTHnet pilot, the development of a new information infrastructure was built on clearly formulated contractual agreements and property rights regimes. Under these regimes, the Greek government, via the Information Society initiative, retained full control of constitutional rights over the new information infrastructure. CompeTech was only a contractor IT provider, which would be paid a pre-agreed fee for delivering the hardware and the software. Once these were delivered, CompeTech would have nothing to do with the infrastructure other than to provide maintenance and support, again on a pre-agreed fee. Collective choice rights of removal, management, and exclusion were granted to the Regional Health Authorities and the Directors of primary healthcare centers and hospitals (i.e. the healthcare providers). Finally, the users (i.e. healthcare staff and administrators in primary healthcare centers and hospitals) were granted operational rights of access, contribution, and extraction of content from various applications offered by the new information infrastructure.

Community Attributes (Right Holders)

Despite these formal agreements, there were, once again, mixed reactions as to the objectives and value of the new information infrastructure among the users. The dominant concern was that many healthcare staff and administrators in the region had already invested significant time and effort in learning to use applications introduced during the HEALTHnet pilot, as well as by other independent IT providers. These key users were now worried that their time and effort would be wasted, and that they also risked losing their patient databases, which they had worked hard to build. This view was also shared by the Director of IT Services at the Regional Health Authorities. In addition, CreteTech engineers protested about the procedures for choosing the winning consor-

tium and were critical of CompeTech's proposed solution, which they felt was in fact more rigid.

Thus, likewise to the development of the HEALTHnet pilot, there was great heterogeneity among user organizations and other stakeholders in the region. This heterogeneity had implications on the relationships between these stakeholders, including the bundles of property rights held by them, and created coordination problems for CompeTech.

The Action Arena

The heterogeneous user base generated a number of negotiation problems during this phase. These are illustrated in Figure 5 and discussed in more detail below.

The Director of IT services at the Regional Health Authorities explained that CompeTech was chosen under "a logic of transparency." In particular, each entry to each regional IT competition had to be evaluated by a third party committee against three distinct dimensions: the legal status of bidders (e.g. whether they had declared bankruptcy, etc), the technical specifications of the solutions offered, and the budgets proposed by each entry. CreteTech's consortium was disqualified in the legal dimension of the evaluation due to a legislative policy that required all bidders to name all their share listings to identify possible conflicts between public and private interests. One of the two companies participating in CreteTech's consortium had failed to name all their share listings (apparently because it was impossible for them to categorically name all the investments they had made in the long history of the company) and for this reason their bid was rejected. Two months later, this policy was recalled by the Information Society as it was creating a lot of disruptions and legal disputes against the bids of such companies as Microsoft and Oracle. However, this change was made too late for CreteTech's consortium. Senior managers at CreteTech put this misfortune down to conflicting

Figure 5. Problems during the development of a new information infrastructure for the region of Crete (2005-2006)

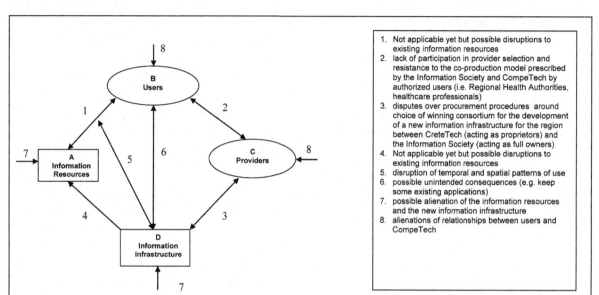

1. Not applicable yet but possible disruptions to existing information resources
2. lack of participation in provider selection and resistance to the co-production model prescribed by the Information Society and CompeTech by authorized users (i.e. Regional Health Authorities, healthcare professionals)
3. disputes over procurement procedures around choice of winning consortium for the development of a new information infrastructure for the region between CreteTech (acting as proprietors) and the Information Society (acting as full owners)
4. Not applicable yet but possible disruptions to existing information resources
5. disruption of temporal and spatial patterns of use
6. possible unintended consequences (e.g. keep some existing applications)
7. possible alienation of the information resources and the new information infrastructure
8. alienations of relationships between users and CompeTech

political agendas, but this claim could not be verified.

Irrespective of the reasons behind CreteTech's failure to win the competition, there were concerns among officials at the Regional Health Authorities of Crete and a number of user organizations that, through the implementation of such "transparent mechanisms" the final selection was made not by those directly involved with the use of the new information infrastructure. The Director of IT services at the Regional Health Authorities explained the situation in an interview in September 2006:

We have reached the point where the users are at least happy with some applications because they enable them to carry on with their work... So we already have an existing base; we already have a bicycle. But we don't know whether we are going to get just a wheel that we will spin around or whether we will get a car... The only thing we know is that they have ticked all the boxes in our list of requirements. And this is true for all the consortia that participated in the competition... If

it's just going to be a wheel then it would be better for us to keep the bicycle that we already have.

This quote makes a number of assumptions about the roles taken and assigned to the various actors involved in the negotiations.

First, the Greek government (via the Information Society) was found to not only retain control of all constitutional rights around the new information infrastructure on behalf of the Regional Health Authorities, but was also the full owner of the infrastructure. This meant that, the competition in Crete–as well as other similar competitions across other regions in Greece–was centrally controlled by the Greek government. Thus, although the "transparent mechanisms" applied by the Information Society may at first be interpreted as a democratic means of selecting the 'best' infrastructural solutions without any political influences, in practice, those mechanisms seemed to exclude interested parties from the decision-making process. The only thing the Regional Health Authorities could do was to negotiate–in the context of a project steering committee, which included two individuals from the Information Society (another transparent mechanism)–whether some of the existing systems could stay.

Through this project steering committee, CompeTech was required to evaluate the existing installed software and keep those components that fitted the original call for tenders. However, from CompeTech's point of view, the more components they kept the more the costs would increase for them and the less likely that their solution would eventually be integrated (i.e. components able to interoperate). CreteTech also had similar concerns, as evident from the following quotation from an interview with a senior engineer in September 2006:

We would have to enter into a discussion around the logic behind making our systems interoperate, which is not the easiest thing in the world... The choice here was to have an Oracle-based system. Our system is Microsoft and SAP-based. You can't really say that you are going to open channels of communication between the two systems... We want to do it but they'll have to secure enough funding for us and also provide guarantees that we will not be risking the rest of our projects. Cause if we were to only see the small picture of Crete and only Crete, then we would be myopic.

CreteTech felt that there were high risks involved for them to negotiate a subcontract with the Information Society and CompeTech as it would have implications for their IP rights over the software code upon which HEALTHnet was built. If CreteTech entered negotiations with the Information Society towards a potential integration of their infrastructural solution with that of CompeTech, they would also have to negotiate a contract around the IP rights emanating from the technology. But entering such a discussion would compromise the security and, thus, the control of their infrastructural solution in other projects which they were running in other regions of Greece. The same was true for other IT providers

who, in the past, had installed systems in Crete. In this context, none of the existing systems installed, including those of CreteTech, could survive the change because of the very clear possibilities of contesting claims to ownership.

In addition, the most avid users of previously installed applications in the region were also concerned that the new proposed infrastructure would not support their data. In an interview in September 2005, one general practitioner, who is also the director of her primary healthcare centre, explained that she had created over 5000 registered patient records in her I-EHR database, originally implemented during the HEALTHnet pilot. She added that she would continue using the database irrespective of whether CreteTech won the regional competition or not. Her biggest concern was not just access to patient data–even though that was imperative–but also familiarity with the interface, which was customized to individual user needs over years of collaboration with CreteTech.

Similar concerns were raised by a hospital director who was interviewed in July 2006. However, from his point of view, "the decision has been made, there is no point of fighting it," thus, reflecting the belief that a closure had been finally reached.

Outcomes

The outcome of the negotiations between CompeTech, the Information Society, and the Regional Health Authorities was an agreement for CompeTech to evaluate the existing installed base with the help of senior management from the Regional Health Authorities. After that, CompeTech would have 15 months to pilot and deliver a new information infrastructure for Crete. In the event that the project collapsed for reasons related to user acceptance, and/or loss of data and application non-interoperability, the Information Society would then intervene and cancel the project. Evidently, as with the "transparent mechanisms" enforced during the evaluation of the tender offers, the implementation approach also followed a number of EU-wide standards set out to objectively evaluate the commissioning and outcome of the new infrastructure in Crete. These standards were commonly followed in all projects run by the Information Society (Information Society, 2004).

However, in an interview with the IT Director of the Regional Health Authorities in July 2006, it became clear that users were demanding that they be left alone to make decisions concerning which network to join, which software suites should stay and which should be replaced, as well as which databases of electronic patient records should be retained.

The resistance of the users was primarily an outcome of their exclusion from collective-choice rights which was further aggravated by the various technical and legal constraints imposed by the Information Society on the new information infrastructure (aimed at clarifying legal terms of use and avoiding the confusion that preceded technological innovation in the region). Due to the history of this technological innovation, users in this region exhibited high levels of IT literacy and thus had more expectations from the technology.

The consequence of the policy constraints to property right claims imposed by the Information Society on the Regional Health Authorities, and by extension the users, questioned the legitimacy of the new information infrastructure and generated network externalities for reviving parts of the HEALTHnet project as an alternative to the solution offered by CompeTech. "Generally, a lot of people have put pressure on us to take action towards ensuring that our systems stay in Crete," a senior engineer from CreteTech told us in July 2006. This reflects the comment by the director of IT services at the Regional Health Authorities, who said that the region might be better served with what already exists, whether that means HEALTHnet or any of the solutions previously installed by other IT vendors.

It is very difficult to determine what the possible outcomes and consequences of these

contested claims to ownership will be for the involved parties, but there is a strong indication that unless these claims are negotiated and enabling conditions agreed upon, the new information infrastructure will suffer a similar fate as that of HEALTHnet. At the time of the last fieldtrip (July 2006), evidence suggested that many healthcare professionals, including the Regional Health Authorities, felt that their best interests were not being considered. Furthermore, the "transparent mechanisms" employed by the Information Society were seen as not accounting for the values and existing practices of the users, and as hindering the whole initiative.

In February 2011, the new Director of IT at the Regional Health Authorities provided some quantitative data on the outcomes of the development of the new information infrastructure in Crete in the eight hospitals in the region (no data could be provided on primary healthcare centers). The data showed that almost all of the eight hospitals had complete installations of administrative modules (accounting, payroll, inventory control, etc.) and all of those modules were being used regularly. However, the electronic healthcare records module, although installed, was not being used in any of the hospitals (this included medical tests and laboratory data, with some exceptions). These data justify the concerns raised by various stakeholders during earlier fieldtrips in the region and pose serious questions around the governance of the project in Crete. The next section provides a discussion on the consequences of the project outcomes for Greece, and more broadly, for European Information Society programmes.

CONCLUSION

During both the HEALTHnet pilot and the Information Society initiative, the development of a regional information infrastructure in Crete was contested by user organizations, who wanted to have a choice in deploying their own networks not at the regional level, but rather at the organizational level. A prime example was a handful of wealthy hospital directors in the region who, having completely lost faith in HEALTHnet and the Information Society, decided to act on their own best interests. Their key concern was in establishing hospital administrative systems for managing patient accounts that were not part of CreteTech's proposed solutions. The hospital directors were not interested in developments at the regional level, but rather at the hospital/organizational level. In the end, as recent quantitative data show, these powerful stakeholders got what they wanted: administrative modules dominated user adoption in the region whereas medical modules (intended to contribute to regional monitoring of patient care across user organizations) were not used at all. Thus, although the development of a regional information infrastructure in Crete was not a complete failure, it was not a complete success either, rather there were multiple outcomes based on the heterogeneity of community attributes, the overarching property right regimes, and the negotiations around proposed infrastructure solutions.

Similar outcomes were observed in other regions in Greece that have undergone Information Society competitions for various information infrastructure projects (Greek Observatory for Information Society, 2010). In particular, only 61 percent of projects reported to have achieved the majority of targets originally set, with the main cause of failure being the "adjustment to difficulty by end-users," which totalled 77 percent (Greek Observatory for Information Society, 2010, p. 7). Other important causes of failure were "lack of specialized staff and technical support," and "inefficiency of the winning consortium" of IT providers (Greek Observatory for Information Society, 2010, p. 8). As a result, projects were found to be 69 percent "fully operational," 21 percent "partly operational," and 10 percent "non operational yet" (Greek Observatory for Information Society, 2010, p. 9).

Most importantly, the key problem with most projects was that very few of them were successful in implementing electronic patient records, a key aim not only of the Information Society initiative in Greece, but also of the European Commission's i2010 initiative on eHealth (2008/594/EC)[3]. Like in Greece, implementations of electronic patient records in other EU Members suffered similar outcomes (EHTEL, 2008). Specifically, as a follow-up to the publication of the European Commission Recommendation on cross-border interoperability of electronic health record systems, a short questionnaire survey[4] was sent to EU Member States. The questionnaire responses revealed extreme variance in the experiences of the Member States in relation to eHealth, with challenges faced at the local, regional, and national levels (EHTEL, 2008). The responses of the Member States with regard to future directions for eHealth at a European level "show, implicitly or explicitly, a degree of synergy with current discussions on governance in relation to eHealth" (EHTEL, 2008, p. 5). Organisationally, a number of propositions have been put forward to address issues of governance, cooperation, and join action, including propositions for European-level coordination project office, competence networks or centres, and consultative/advisory bodies (EHTEL, 2008, p. 5).

Despite good intentions, these propositions struggle to strike a balance between institutional rules imposed from national and supranational (e.g. European) institutions and the freedom of choice of involved communities. Efforts to strike a balance between institutional rules and freedom of choice was a key concern of the Mandelkern Group on Better Regulation, a panel of consultants appointed to review the conclusions of the European Council Lisbon Summit in 2000 (Mandelkern Report, 2001). In considering "co-regulation" as an alternative regulatory format, the Mandelkern Report highlighted the responsibilities undertaken by different actors, whose role could both be "top down" as original rule-makers, or "bottom up," implementing state rules in what has been called the "cooperative approach." The *European Governance* white paper (European Commission, 2001) supported this recommendation by arguing that the effectiveness of EU policies depends on ensuring wide participation throughout the policy chain. This led to the *Inter-Institutional Agreement on Better Law-Making* (European Commission, 2001), which requires multi-stakeholder representation and transparency in the procedures followed within a co-regulatory scheme (Marsden, 2008).

These policy developments are certainly a welcome shift from centralized regulation and the often strict constraints imposed on the development of information infrastructures across Europe. However, when implemented in practice, such co-regulatory schemes actually fail to achieve intended outcomes. For example, in the Crete case study, by instituting a number of 'transparent evaluation mechanisms,' the Information Society essentially operated on a co-regulatory scheme, seeking multi-stakeholder representation and transparency in the procedures followed in the regional competition. Although, at first, such a co-regulatory scheme might be seen to strengthen the position of user organizations in decisions made around the choice of IT providers, there were serious concerns whether this scheme took user needs specifically into account. In fact, the regulatory rules seemed to place their primary attention on *ex post* enforcement (e.g. monitoring the performance of the winning IT consortium). However, there was limited (if any) *ex ante* regulatory rules for safeguarding user interests by directly drawing on the input of local user communities. Instead, CompeTech was chosen through a tripartite committee of user representatives (covering legal, technical, and financial dimensions of bids), who were centrally appointed by the Information Society. In the end, although multi-stakeholder representation and transparency was sought, the Information Society not only revised and redistributed property rights regimes in the region, but also set regulatory constraints in the evaluation, choice, and future maintenance of infrastructural solutions in the region.

While property rights-based co-regulatory schemes can partially solve the problem of how information infrastructures will be developed in Europe and elsewhere, these schemes simply cannot work flawlessly (see Benkler, 2006). Instead, there is now a widespread discussion across Europe that community-based, 'open' technological development can, in fact, lead to more creative solutions based on the local needs of user-producers (e.g. Bannon & Griffin, 2001; Gripenberg et al., 2004; Ferlander & Timms, 2001). In this discussion, it is argued that, rather than depending on centrally imposed regulatory schemes (even if those are supposed to be cooperative in nature), the development of new information and communication technologies should be based on sharing resources and outputs "among widely distributed, loosely connected individuals who cooperate with each other without relying on either market signals or managerial commands" (Benkler, 2006, pp.60).

This alternative mode of information infrastructure development will be explored in more detail in Chapters 6 and 7 while drawing on the findings from both the Crete case study and the English case study discussed next in Chapter 5.

REFERENCES

Abel-Smith, B., Calltorp, J., Dixon, M., Dunning, A., Evans, R., Holland, W., & Mossialos, E. (1994). *Report on the Greek health services*. Athens, Greece: Farmetrika.

Ballas, A., & Tsoukas, H. (2004). Measuring nothing: The case of the Greek national health system. *Human Relations, 57*(6), 661–690. doi:10.1177/0018726704044951

Bangemann, M., da Fonseca, E. C., Davis, P., de Benedetti, C., Gyllenhamman, P., & Hunsel, L. (1994). *Europe and the global information society: Recommendations for the European Council.* Brussels, Belgium: European Council.

Bannon, L. J., & Griffin, J. (2001). New technology, communities, and networking: Problems and prospects for orchestrating change. *Telematics and Informatics, 18*(1), 35–49. doi:10.1016/S0736-5853(00)00021-6

Benkler, Y. (2006). *The wealth of networks.* New Haven, CT: Yale University Press.

Close, D. H. (2002). *Greece since 1945.* London, UK: Longman.

Constantelou, N. (2001). *In search of a vision: Information society policies in peripheral and middle-income countries.* Athens, Greece: National Technical University of Athens.

Constantinides, P., & Barrett, M. (2006). Negotiating ICT development and use: The case of a regional telemedicine system in Crete. *Information and Organization, 16*(1), 27–55. doi:10.1016/j.infoandorg.2005.07.001

Council of the European Union. (2000). *Conclusions of the Lisbon European Council.* Lisbon, Portugal.

Davaki, K., & Mossialos, E. (2005). *Plus ça change*: Health sector reforms in Greece. *Journal of Health Politics, Policy and Law, 30*(1–2), 143–167. doi:10.1215/03616878-30-1-2-143

Dutta, S., & Jain, A. (2006). An assessment of the relative level of development of an information society in the enlarged European Union. In Dutta, S., De Meyer, A., Jain, A., & Richter, G. (Eds.), *The information society in an enlarged Europe* (pp. 7–44). Munich, Germany: Springer, Roland Berger Strategy Consultants. doi:10.1007/3-540-33156-5_2

Ερευνητικό Ακαδημαϊκό Ινστιτούτο Τεχνολογίας Υπολογιστών (ΕΑΙΤΥ). (2001). *Επιχειρησιακό σχέδιο για την ανάπτυξη της πληροφορικής στην υγεία & πρόνοια για το επιχειρησιακό πρόγραμμα κοινωνία της πληροφορίας του Γ' ΚΠΣ: δράση 7 – τυποποίηση δεδομένων.* Υπουργείο Υγείας και Πρόνοιας, (In Greek).

Ερευνητικό Ακαδημαϊκό Ινστιτούτο Τεχνολογίας Υπολογιστών (ΕΑΙΤΥ). (2008). *Η χρήση των ΤΠΕ στον ευρύτερο δημόσιο και ιδιωτικό τομέα.* Παρατηρητήριο για την ΚτΠ, (In Greek).

European Commission. (1994). *Europe's way to the information society: An action plan.* Brussels, Belgium: European Commission.

European Commission. (1999). *An information society for all: eEurope action plan.* Brussels, Belgium: Council and the European Commission for the Feira European Council, European Commission.

European Commission. (2001, July 25). *European governance.* COM (2001) 428 final.

European Commission. (2003). European parliament council commission: Inter-institutional agreement on better law-making. *Official Journal of the European Union, 46*(C 321/01).

European Commission. (2008). *Commission recommendation of 2 July 2008 on cross-border interoperability of electronic health record systems.* Retrieved from http://eur-lex.europa.eu/LexUriServ/LexUriServ.do?uri=CELEX:32008H0594:EN:NOT

European Health Telematics (EHTEL). (2008). *eHealth interoperability: State of play and future perspectives.* Retrieved from http://ec.europa.eu/information_society/activities/health/docs/cip/calliope_assessment_eu_countries_questionnaire-recomm.pdf

Eurostat. (2003). *Statistics on the information society in Europe*. Luxembourg, Luxembourg: Office for Official Publications of the European Communities.

Ferlander, S., & Timm, D. (2001). Local nets and social capital. *Telematics and Informatics, 18*(1), 51–65. doi:10.1016/S0736-5853(00)00018-6

Graham, S., & Marvin, S. (2001). *Splintering urbanism: Networked infrastructures, technological mobilities and the urban condition*. New York, NY: Routledge. doi:10.4324/9780203452202

Greek Ministry of National Economy. (2000). *Operational program for the information society*. Athens, Greece.

Greek Observatory for Information Society. (2010). *Έρευνα για την αποτύπωση, λειτουργία και αξιολόγηση των πληροφοριακών συστημάτων και των διαδικτυακών πυλών που χρηματοδοτήθηκαν κατά το Γ' ΚΠΣ από το Ε.Π. Κοινωνία της Πληροφορίας*. Παρατηρητήριο για την ΚτΠ, (In Greek).

Gripenberg, P., Skogseid, I., Botto, F., Silli, A., & Thunainen, V. K. (2004). Entering the European information society: Four rural development projects. *The Information Society, 20*(1), 3–14. doi:10.1080/01972240490269807

Hellenic Republic. (1995). *Greek strategy for the information society: A tool for employment, development and quality of life*. Athens, Greece: Author.

Hellenic Republic. (1999). *Greece in the information society: Strategy and actions*. Athens, Greece: Author.

Information Society. (2004). *Διακήρυξη έργου - «Πληροφοριακό Σύστημα Υγείας του Πε.Σ.Υ.Π. Κρήτης», Μέρος Α'*. Κοινωνία της Πληροφορίας Α.Ε., Αθήνα 24/11/2004 (In Greek).

Isacsson, A., Koutis, A. D., Cedervall, M., Lindholm, L. H., Lionis, C. D., Svenninger, K., & Fioretos, M. (1992). Patient-number-based computerised medical records in Crete: A tool for planning and assessment of primary health care. *Computer Methods and Programs in Biomedicine, 37*, 41–49. doi:10.1016/0169-2607(92)90027-5

Kyriopoulos, J., & Tsalikis, G. (1993). Public and private imperatives of Greek health policies. *Health Policy (Amsterdam), 26*(2), 105–117. doi:10.1016/0168-8510(93)90113-4

Mandelkern Report. (2001, November 13). *Mandelkern group on better regulation*. Retrieved February 22, 2011, from http://ec.europa.eu/governance/better_regulation/documents/mandelkern_report.pdf

Mansell, R. E., & Steinmueller, E. (2000). *Mobilizing the information society: Strategies for growth and opportunity*. New York, N.Y: Oxford University Press.

Marsden, C. (2008). Beyond Europe: The Internet, regulation, and multi-stakeholder governance: Representing the consumer interest? *Journal of Consumer Policy, 31*, 115–132. doi:10.1007/s10603-007-9056-z

OECD. (2001). *Regulatory reform in Greece*. Paris, France: Author.

Perrons, D. (2004). *Globalisation and social change: People and places in a divided world*. New York, NY: Routledge.

Rodrigues, M. J. (2002). Introduction for a European strategy at the turn of the century. In Rodrigues, M. J. (Ed.), *The new knowledge economy in Europe* (pp. 1–27). Cheltenham, UK: Edward Elgar.

Sancho, D. (2002). European national platforms for the development of the information society. In Jordana, J. (Ed.), *Governing telecommunications and the information society in Europe* (pp. 202–227). Cheltenham, UK: Edward Elgar.

Sissouras, A., & Souliotis, K. (Eds.). (2002). *Health, health care and welfare in Greece*. Greek Ministry of Health and Welfare and the Athens Office of the European Observatory on Health Care Systems.

Skalkidis, P. (1998). Implementation of a hospital information system in a Greek university hospital. In Iakovidis, I. (Eds.), *User acceptance of health telematics applications* (pp. 62–68). Amsterdam, Netherlands: IOS Press.

Sotiriou, A. (1998). Towards user acceptance of telemedicine services. In Iakovidis, I. (Eds.), *User acceptance of health telematics applications* (pp. 177–181). Amsterdam, Netherlands: IOS Press.

Theodorou, M., Sarris, M., & Soulis, S. (1995). *Health systems and the Greek reality*. Athens, Greece: Papazizis. (in Greek)

Tountas, Y., Karnaki, P., & Pavi, E. (2002). Reforming the reform: The Greek national health system in transition. *Health Policy (Amsterdam)*, *62*(1), 15–29. doi:10.1016/S0168-8510(01)00217-2

ADDITIONAL READING

Baldwin, R., Hood, C., & Scott, C. (1998). *Socio-legal reader on regulation*. Oxford, UK: Oxford University Press.

Baumard, P., & Starbuck, W. H. (2005). Learning from failures: Why it may not happen. *Long Range Planning*, *38*(3), 281–298. doi:10.1016/j.lrp.2005.03.004

Blount, S., & Janicik, G. A. (2001). When plans change: Examining how people evaluate timing changes in work organizations. *Academy of Management Review*, *26*(4), 566–585.

Brown, N., Rappert, B., & Webster, A. (Eds.). (2000). *Contested futures: A sociology of prospective techno-science*. Aldershot, UK: Ashgate.

Cave, J., Marsden, C., Klautzer, L., Levitt, R., van Oranje-Nassau, C., Rabinovich, L., & Robinson, N. (2007). *Responsibility in the global information society: Towards multi-stakeholder governance*. Santa Monica: RAND, TR-472. Retrieved February 23, 2011, from http://www.rand.org/pubs/technical_reports/TR472/

Dutta, S., De Meyer, A., Jain, A., & Richter, G. (Eds.). (2006). *The information society in an enlarged Europe*. Munich, Germany: Springer, Roland Berger Strategy Consultants. doi:10.1007/3-540-33156-5

Fincham, R. (2002). Narratives of success and failure in systems development. *British Journal of Management*, *13*(1), 1–14. doi:10.1111/1467-8551.00219

Goldsmith, J., & Wu, T. (2006). *Who controls the internet? Illusions of a borderless world*. Oxford, UK: Oxford University Press.

Healey, P., Magalhaes, C. De., & Madanipour, A. (1999). Institutional capacity building, urban planning and urban regeneration projects. *Futura*, *3*, 117-137.

Kooiman, J. (2003). *Governing as governance*. London, UK: Sage.

Kummer, M. (2004). The results of the WSIS negotiations on internet governance. In D. MacLean (Ed.), *Internet governance: A grand collaboration*, (pp. 53-57). New York, NY: United Nations ICT Task Force Series 5.

Marsden, C. (Ed.). (2000). *Regulating the global information society*. London, UK: Routledge.

Reidenberg, J. R. (1998). Lex informatica: The formulation of information policy rules through technology. *Texas Law Review*, *76*(3), 553–584.

Sabol, T. (2003, April 8). eGovernment in selected EU accession states. *Prisma Strategic Guideline*.

Senden, L. (2005). Soft law, self-regulation and co-regulation in European law: Where do they meet? *Electronic Journal of Comparative Law, 9*(1). Retrieved February 23, 2011, from http://www.ejcl.org/91/art91-3.PDF

Servaes, J., & Burgelman, J.-C. (2000). In search of a European model for the information society. *Telematics and Informatics, 17*(1-2), 1–7. doi:10.1016/S0736-5853(00)00001-0

Sterman, J. (2000). *Business dynamics: Systems thinking and modelling for a complex world.* New York, NY: McGraw-Hill/Irwin.

Tucker, A. L., & Edmondson, A. C. (2003, Winter). Why hospitals don't learn from failures: Organizational and psychological dynamics that inhibit system change. *California Management Review, 45*(2), 55–72.

Wilson, M., & Howcroft, D. (2002). Re-conceptualising failure: Social shaping meets IS research. *European Journal of Information Systems, 11*(4), 236–250. doi:10.1057/palgrave.ejis.3000437

ENDNOTES

[1]   Based on an interview with the director of the PHC in 2003

[2]   Based on an interview with the general practitioner responsible for the development of the system in 2003

[3]   See article 18 of the European Commission's Recommendation on cross-border interoperability of electronic health record systems (2008/594/EC).

[4]   Questions asked by the European Commission to Member States included: -To what extent has your national administration achieved the objectives outlined in the Recommendation on cross-border interoperability of electronic health record systems (2008/594/EC)*?; -To what extent does the Recommendation contribute to establishment of interoperability of electronic health records and eHealth in your own country?;-How far are activities in your country contributing to achieving the objectives on the implementation of cross-border interoperability outlined in the recommendation?; -What suggestions would your country make to the European Commission for improving, enhancing, or expanding the current set of recommendations?; -On what services relating to the implementation of cross-border interoperability of electronic health records would your country suggest the European Commission should concentrate?

[*]   It should be stressed here that this Recommendation placed great emphasis on the development of "electronic infrastructures," which are defined very much in accordance with the Bangemann report (Bangemann et al., 1994). Article 18 of the European Commission's Recommendation noted (paragraph 4): Achieving and maintaining cross-border interoperability of electronic health record systems implies managing a continuous process of change and the adaptation of a multitude of elements and issues within and across *electronic infrastructures* in Member States. These electronic infrastructures are necessary to exchange information, interact cooperate in order to ensure the highest possible levels of quality and safety in healthcare provision to patients. Implementing interoperability of electronic health record systems will require a complex set of framework conditions, organisational structures and implementation procedures involving all relevant stakeholders.

Chapter 5
The Development of the English National Health Information Infrastructure

ABSTRACT

This chapter draws on a secondary analysis of publicly available data on the development of the English National Program for IT (NPfIT). Using the theoretical framework discussed in Chapter 3, this analysis focuses on the multilevel context, action arena, and outcomes in the NPfIT case, placing great emphasis on the property rights put forward and negotiated between key stakeholder groups. The chapter concludes with an analysis of the consequences of these negotiations for the English NPfIT and other such national information infrastructure projects.

INTRODUCTION

Unlike the case in Greece and other European nations, England has kept its distance from European policies – despite an inevitable process of Europeanization (see Schneider & Aspinwall, 2001). This is particularly true in the English public healthcare sector where information and communication initiatives have always been

DOI: 10.4018/978-1-4666-1622-6.ch005

driven at the national level within the context of the English National Health System (NHS).

Alongside a government agenda of public sector reform, information and communication initiatives within the English NHS have increasingly been perceived as critical in making the NHS more efficient and cost-effective. This is evident through the annual expenditure on IT and services by the English government that has doubled since 1999, reaching a figure of around £14 billion, which is the highest in Europe (NAO, 2004). The growing use of large external IT service providers and smaller more specialized firms see much potential in developing skills and capabilities in the healthcare sector. The split between public (in-house) and private (external) markets for IT services now stands at around 55 percent and 45 percent respectively.

In 2002, the government pledged to spend around £6.2 billion on a National Programme for Information Technology (NPfIT) with the purpose of delivering four critical elements: (1) NHS Care Records Service, (2) Electronic Appointment Booking, (3) Electronic Transmission of Prescriptions, and (4) Electronic Transfer of Digital Images (e.g. X-rays and scans). The NPfIT is now the world's largest civil IT programme (Connecting for Health, 2004, pp. 33).

Despite intentions, the history of introducing IT into the NHS has produced varied outcomes (NAO, 2004, 2006). This variation can be explained by examining the tensions created by the infrastructural ideal of a government-controlled, standardized form of provision of infrastructure services, on the one hand, and the splintering of that ideal through market mechanisms and private involvement on the other. In particular, during its earlier phase, the NHS can be seen to be dominated by a concern with delivering free, standardized, integrated healthcare services to all at the point of use (Klein, 2000). After the reforms introduced by the two Blair governments in the 1990s, and the discourse of the "Third Way," the NHS can be seen to be dominated by an obsession with innovation and change through an encouragement of competitiveness among healthcare service providers (Greener, 2005). The NPfIT was conceptualized in the context of this second era, but – paradoxically – driven primarily by the logic of the first era, i.e. a centrally controlled information infrastructure to satisfy an increasing but *varied* demand for healthcare services according to the medical specializations and needs of each healthcare organization.

This chapter explores the various problems created as a consequence of this paradoxical development. The next section provides an analysis of the historical evolution of policies used to bring the NPfIT into existence by examining broader political discourses in the English NHS toward improving the provision of public sector healthcare services. Subsequently, the following section provides an analysis of publicly available data presented before the Committee of Public Accounts (CPA) assigned to examine the progress made by the English Department of Health in implementing the NPfIT (HC, 2007a, 2007b, 2007c, 2009). Using the commons framework discussed in Chapter 3, this analysis will focus on the multilevel context, action arena, and outcomes in the NPfIT case, placing great emphasis on the property rights put forward and negotiated between key stakeholder groups. The chapter will conclude with an analysis of the consequences of these negotiations for the English NPfIT and other such national information infrastructure projects.

THE ENGLISH NATIONAL HEALTH SYSTEM

The Early NHS (1948-1997)

After the Beveridge report (Beveridge, 1942), the concept of a centralized, integrated, government-funded hospital service was established and in 1948 the newly-elected government created a National Health Service (NHS). The fundamental principles underlying the NHS were, and still largely are, that services would be funded predominantly from general taxation and that they would, in general, be free at the point of use, and comprehensive and available to all, regardless of means to pay.

To support this initiative, a tripartite governance structure was put in place, namely, government owned hospitals, a national network of general practitioners (GP), and community or personal health services. The three strands were financed centrally but managed separately.

Firstly, hospitals were divided into 'natural' districts which were overseen by Hospital Management Committees, which in turn reported to Regional Hospital Boards that were meant to be responsible for the application of government policy, the development of strategy and budgetary control, as well as the development of medical specialties (Greener, 2009). The prevailing management style for hospitals was that of 'facilitating,' with central instructions being passed down a chain of authority from central government to local hospital boards (Klein, 2000). Hospital management essentially rested on various combinations of medical superintendents, nursing (matrons), and lay administrators. Lay administration was primarily about enabling hospitals to function in clean, well-supplied, and well-maintained buildings, without questioning medical or nursing practice unless something went wrong (Harrison & Pollitt, 1994; Traynor, 1996). In fact, medical professionals had a special relationship with the state in that, the latter depended on the former to run the NHS in terms of rationing healthcare services within it (Greener, 2009). At the same time, the doctors depended on the state for employment as it became the monopoly employer with the founding of the NHS (Greener, 2009).

Community services were also centrally controlled by the state but with the difference that these services were under the management of the elected local government. In contrast, GPs were independent contractors and could not be 'managed' in this sense, but were influenced through a centrally agreed national contract for services. Thus, GPs functioned as gatekeepers to different healthcare services as they not only offered primary services to patients, but also referred the latter for tertiary services (Klein, 2000).

Through this gatekeeping, patients were essentially excluded from any participation in service choices in the NHS. Specifically, it was rather difficult for patients to change their GP once they had made their initial choice. In fact, in the early years of the NHS, GPs lobbied to prevent patients from changing their registered doctor on the grounds that such change would 'abuse' the system. This lobbying eventually resulted in a rule change in 1950 that required the written consent of the existing doctor before a change could occur (Ministry of Health, 1950, cited in Greener, 2009, pp.184). GPs, in their gatekeeper role, effectively controlled whether or not prescriptions would be written, and whether patients were referred to hospitals for specialist care (Greener, 2009).

The 'New' NHS (1997-2007)

Between the 1970s and 1990s there were a series of healthcare reforms introduced by the various governments of the time that sought to tackle some of the problems emerging from the early years of the NHS (see Klein, 2000). However, the most important change – and the focus of this chapter – came in 1997 with the succession of the Labour government after the Conservative rule since 1979.

The election of the first Blair Government in May 1997 brought a new approach to the NHS with a pledge to abolish earlier reforms. A white paper issued by the Department of Health (DoH), "The New NHS – Modern and Dependable" put forward a "Third Way" of running the service "based on partnership and driven by performance" (DoH, 1997, paragraph 1) as opposed to the focus on the hierarchical structures of past governments. Further reforms by the Blair Government were announced in July 2000 under the title "The NHS Plan" (DoH, 2000), which provided a radical action plan for the next 10 years setting out measures to put patients and people at the heart of the health service (e.g. letters about an individual patient's care were to be copied to the patient to increase transparency and empower patient choice). The NHS Plan was conceptualized in an effort to address such problems as the lack of national standards, old-fashioned demarcations between doctors and administrators and barriers between services, a lack of clear incentives and levers to improve performance, and over-centralization and disempowered patients.

Through these reforms, the tripartite structure introduced during the earlier years was revised to encourage partnerships between different service providers, whilst implementing a series of performance standards by which such partnerships would be evaluated. Specifically, GPs would still operate on independent contracts, but were now under increasing pressure to become more responsive to patient needs (i.e. become more flexible in their referrals and give patients alternative choices for tertiary care). In addition, hospitals were encouraged to become more autonomous by forming Foundation Trusts (i.e. partnerships). NHS Foundation Trusts[1] were established by the National Health Service Act 2006 in an effort to increase local ownership rather than centralized control from the DoH. All NHS Trusts could apply for Foundation status; however, the process was a very rigorous one monitored by an independent regulator and based on strict performance standards (e.g. on patient waiting times, mortality, and morbidity rates, etc.) and requiring the support of the Secretary of State. Finally, community or personal health services received more resources to help provide collaborative environments for diverse public lifestyles.

What is striking about these reforms is the increasing interest in defining the inputs and processes of participation mechanisms for service providers and patients. Despite these interests, patient participation, as well as the involvement of local health authorities in broader health care processes is still found to be "at the mercy of the increasing tendency for governments to define the outputs through performance targets, national service frameworks, and central regulatory functions as any other aspect of the NHS" (Peckham et al., 2005, pp. 227). The government's centralized efforts towards performance management have also had an impact on the everyday management

and operation of hospital care. The administrators of the early NHS have now been replaced by managers and chief executives, who are supposed to implement the performance measures enforced by the DoH as well as other national audit centers such as the National Institute for Clinical Excellence (NICE). This change in management came out of an effort to implement national standards, but also to break up the historical demarcation in the division of labor by placing lay administrators in control of specialized doctors and hospital care. However, "things may appear to be continuing much as before between the two groups," since, even though "the present wave of reforms have given the former group a greater ability to make decisions in the NHS... they still do not have the autonomy or power that the state apparently believes" (Greener, 2005, pp.107). In the end, despite the good intentions behind the more recent reforms in the NHS, these have only exacerbated existing problems by feeding the struggle between the managers and the doctors to win over each other, as opposed to helping them improve patient care. In this struggle the managers are clearly in a worse position, as – because of the historical division of labor – more considerable sanctions are possible for them for either failing in their performance by not securing an adequate 'star' rating for their respective hospital, or by straying too far from an acceptable practice in reporting their performance (Blackler, 2006; Greener, 2005).

Thus, there is a paradox: even though the reforms introduced by the two Blair governments aimed at decentralizing the NHS, breaking up historical demarcations of work, and empowering the patients, the NHS now seems to be under more scrutiny and control from the DoH (i.e. performance management), relationships with local doctors have not changed dramatically, and most patients would find it difficult to identify any changes.

THE NATIONAL PROGRAM FOR IT IN THE ENGLISH NHS (1998 - 2010)

The concept of a national IT system for the NHS was born in the midst of this paradox (Constantinides & Blackler, 2008). Specifically, as part of the reforms implemented by the Blair government in the NHS in 1998, the NHS Executive set a target for all NHS trusts to have electronic patient records in place by 2005. The central vision of the NPfIT was to standardize the previously fragmented IT delivery in all NHS organizations by introducing an integrated system (Currie & Guah, 2007). Thus, in contrast to previous NHS IT strategies, the procurement for new systems and services was carried out at the national level rather than by individual NHS organizations.

The NPfIT consisted of two main elements. The first was the local detailed clinical record, for use within local healthcare communities where the overwhelming majority of patient care is delivered. This was intended to integrate and coordinate the information which needs to be available to community care centers, GP practices, and hospitals (such as pathology test results, drugs prescribed, or hospital discharge notification), while enabling both managers and medical professionals to deliver better quality services. The second element was the national summary clinical record which aimed, for example, to support emergency care for people injured or taken ill while away from home. The NPfIT was also intended to provide additional services, such as electronic transmission of prescriptions, an email and directory service for all NHS staff (NHSmail), computer accessible X-rays and other medical files (Picture Archiving Communications Systems), a facility for patients to book first outpatient appointments electronically (Choose & Book) and a broadband network.

The majority of new systems would be installed in local NHS organizations, but IT contractors would be answerable to Connecting for Health, a national body that took over the responsibility for the NPfIT from the DoH in 2005. The strategy adopted was to break the program into five clusters, as evident in Figure 1.

Contracts were then put out to tender for systems-integrator-led consortia to act as Local Service Providers (LSP) for each cluster. The five LSP contracts were originally awarded to four different companies, with Accenture holding two of the five contracts. However, Accenture withdrew from the program in 2007 and its two LSP contracts were transferred to Computer Sciences Corporation (CSC) Alliance, one of the existing LSP. Thus, CSC Alliance now holds three of the five LSP contracts, including the North West and West Midlands cluster, and the North East and Eastern cluster. The remaining two regions were London and the South. Fujitsu held the South region until 2008 when its contract was terminated due to disagreements on the price and commercial terms of use of its proposed solutions (HC, 2009). The South region contract was transferred to BT, which also holds the London region contract. Additionally BT holds the two major contracts for supplying services at the national level, those for the New National Network (N3) network and the National Data Spine (hereafter the Spine), the backbone of national databases and functions such as security and authentication, as illustrated in Figure 2.

LSP have subcontracted some areas of their work to smaller, more specialized companies. In particular, in the three clusters now under CSC, the Lorenzo PAS system is being provided by iSoft. In the London and Southern cluster, a common solution project was initially formed between BT and Fujitsu to procure PAS systems from the U.S. software supplier IDX. However, the partnership was subsequently dissolved and BT switched from IDX to another U.S. firm, Cerner, as their main PAS system supplier. Cerner will supply the Millennium PAS system.

The next section presents an analysis of the development of the NPfIT by examining publicly available data from meetings between NPfIT project leaders and policymakers (HC, 2007a; 2007b;

Figure 1. The five clusters of the English National Program for IT. Source: adapted from HC (2007a)

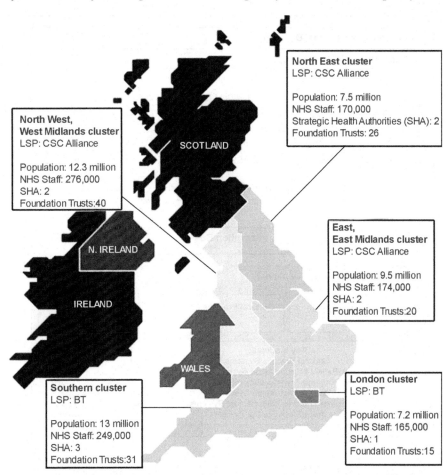

2007c; 2009). Table 1 provides a summary of the key themes derived from the analysis of the data.

The Multilevel Context

Material Characteristics of the Infrastructure

The NPfIT's initial aims involved major upgrades to existing network infrastructures, including the creation of N3, a private broadband network to link all NHS organizations, as well as the development of the Spine – both supplied by BT (in partnership with various network and service providers including Oracle) – to store information centrally, linking local and national IT systems and hosting national systems such as the patient care record[2]. The Spine first went live in June 2004 (HC, 2007a).

Responsibility for building local IT systems fell largely on the LSPs operating within each of the five regional clusters. LSPs were responsible both for the upgrading of large numbers of local IT systems, and for ensuring the interoperability between systems required to support the detailed patient care record by following a number of Spine compliance guidelines approved by Connecting for Health (NHS, 2004). The main projects undertaken by LSPs were as follows: (1) the replacement of hospital Patient Administration System (PAS) software (with the Millennium system supplied in the London and Southern clusters by the U.S. company Cerner; and the Lorenzo

Figure 2. The Conceptual Architecture of the NPfIT in 2002-2004

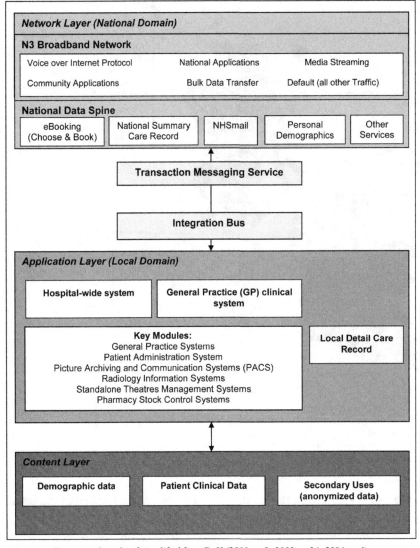

Sources: adapted and simplified from DoH (2002,pp.2; 2003,pp.34; 2004,pp.6)

system supplied in the other three clusters by the UK company iSoft); (2) the introduction of new PAS systems for community and mental health providers; (3) the replacement or upgrade of some GP practice IT systems; (4) the installation of Picture Archiving and Communications Systems (PACS) in all hospitals; and (5) the provision of more sophisticated clinical systems, particularly in hospitals (e.g. systems for cardiology).

In an effort to increase the standardisation of clinical information, Connecting for Health also secured the agreement of all IT providers to introduce the Systemized Nomenclature of Medicine, also known as SNOMED CT, across the NHS. SNOMED CT is a single comprehensive database of codes covering diseases, operations, treatments, drugs, and a number of other areas (HC, 2007a). In addition, the Spine was built on HL7v3 standards for data management and messaging.

Table 1. Key themes from the findings

Analytical focus	The Development of the NPfIT (1998-2010)
Multilevel Context	Material characteristics of the infrastructure • *Network facilities*: N3 & Spine architecture supplied by BT in partnership with Oracle and built on open standards • *Applications*: one main application – PAS (Millenium system supplied in the London and Southern clusters by the U.S. company Cerner; Lorenzo system supplied in the other three clusters by the UK company iSoft) – with a focus on both national and local patient records • *Content:* administrative, patient, & other medical data Institutional rules (property rights) Formal rights regimes specified by Connecting for Health: • *Operational rights* granted to users • *Collective choice rights* granted to directors of NHS Trusts • *Constitutional right* reserved by Connecting for Health on behalf of the NHS; NHS Foundation Trusts given right to overrule the constitutional right of Connecting for Health under certain conditions Communal attributes (right holders) • *Users* (healthcare professionals & administrative/management staff) • *Providers* (BT, CSC Alliance, and their partners) • *Policymakers* (English government – Department of Health & Connecting for Health)

Action Arena (also see Figure 3)	1. Questions over how users will access, store, and exchange information resources locally and nationally
	2. lack of participation in provider selection and resistance to the co-production model prescribed by Connecting for Health and the main IT providers (i.e. BT and CSC alliance) by authorized users (i.e. healthcare professionals, administrators)
	3.
	    o concerns over cost and timeline of the NPfIT project (return on investment issues)
	    o concerns over competence of providers to meet project demands and NHS needs especially after the withdrawal of Accenture and the termination of Fujitsu's contract
	4. concerns over whether the centralized solution will increase security gaps over the handling of private, confidential patient data
	5. disruption of temporal and spatial patterns of use
	6. unintended consequences (e.g. NHS Foundation Trusts opting for alternative "interim" applications, fragmentation)
	7. possible alienation of the information resources and the NPfIT
	8. alienation of relationships between users and main ICT providers

Outcomes	• some increase/improvement in knowledge exchange among some users in some Trusts of the English NHS • concerns about non participation in the centralized procurement strategy of the NPfIT and related future implementation plans • confused/unclear efficiency of NPfIT due to the various competing technologies deployed in the region primarily because of various "local ownership" initiatives • questions around the sustainability of NPfIT and its possible fragmentation due to a change of strategy at Connecting for Health for locally-led procurement of IT solutions

Both SNOMED CT and HL7v3 are approved by European (CEN TC251) and International (ISO 215) Standards' Bodies in health informatics.

Institutional Rules (Property Rights)

Connecting for Health instituted a number of rules to ensure both a strong competition for the contracts and the necessary mechanisms with which to ensure the security of those contracts. For the main contracts (N3, the Spine, and the 5 LSP), there were 160 responses to the notice published in the Official Journal of the European Union which signified the start of the competitive process (NAO, 2006). The number of IT providers was reduced as each procurement stage progressed. All of the contracts were procured in under a year between February 2003 and February 2004 – and most were concluded within ten months.

Connecting for Health required the final bidders to undertake "Proof of Solution" tests in a simulated environment with users, to show whether their systems could meet a number of predetermined scenarios (NAO, 2006). Connecting for Health also undertook due diligence on the winning bidders to establish their ability and capacity to deliver the contracts they were to be awarded with. According to the NAO report (2006, pp. 35-40), the longer IT providers took to deliver, the longer it took before they got paid. IT providers who missed key milestone dates were required to pay agreed amounts, "delay deductions," into an escrow account on which interest was earned. For example, BT did not meet a number of milestones within Phase 1 Release 1 of the Spine and agreed to make a payment, without any admission of liability, into an escrow account. Subsequently BT won these deductions back because they met specified service commencement dates. If delays were the fault of Connecting for Health, caused by acts or omissions of other IT providers or outside of the effective control of the relevant provider, they could claim "delay events," which, if agreed or determined, would allow later delivery of services and, in some cases, payment of compensation to the affected provider (NAO 2006, pp. 35-40). Providers who failed to meet agreed levels of service accrued "performance deductions," and had to pay into an escrow account amounts depending on the severity of the performance failure and its repetition (NAO 2006, pp. 35-40). If a provider rectified its failure for the following three months, the performance deductions were refunded with interest. If that was not the case then Connecting for Health was entitled to keep the money.

All the aforementioned mechanisms were put in place to transfer financial and delivery risk to the prime contractors. With these mechanisms, Connecting for Health reserved the constitutional right to step in and manage the supply chain, if and when required, and to control and audit the performance of providers. Moreover, the Department of Health was the formal owner of all software, hardware, and content (NAO, 2006). The prime contractors (BT and CSC Alliance) were responsible for delivering the hardware and the software (with associated penalties if they missed

key milestones or failed to perform as specified in the requirements) but they did not own anything; they were just contractors on a pre-agreed fee. Collective choice rights of removal, management, and exclusion were granted to the directors of NHS Trusts. Finally, the users (i.e. healthcare professionals and administrative/management staff) were granted operational rights of access, contribution, and extraction of content from various applications offered by the NPfIT.

Community Attributes (Property Right Holders)

The English NHS serves the needs of 50 million people across five clusters and 10 Strategic Health Authorities (SHA) as evident from Figure 1. In each cluster, one of the Chief Executives of the SHA (only the London cluster has one SHA) was appointed as the Senior Responsible Owner (SRO) for the implementation of the NPfIT (NAO, 2006). Cluster, SHA, and local health community programmes were established and the DoH allocated resources to SHAs to pump-prime local implementation activities through the network of local programmes. Through this network, many NHS staff members were engaged in the delivery of the NPfIT locally. For example, in each cluster, Clinical Advisory Groups were set up to obtain clinical input on specific systems as they were being developed, which included medical, nursing, and other clinical professions as well as IT managers and administrative staff.

In addition, in November 2004, the then Director of IT Service Implementation appointed seven National Clinical Leads to champion four healthcare professional groups in the NHS: GPs, hospital doctors, nurses, and allied health professionals. The National Clinical Leads have engaged directly with national organisations through the National Advisory Group and demonstrated their influential role. For example, the GP Clinical Leads highlighted the demand from GPs for a wider choice of systems and facilitated the resolution of the issues around offering a wider choice of GP IT systems.

Despite these efforts to engage the various communities of the NHS, however, there were mixed reactions as to the objectives and value of the NPfIT among both the users and the policymakers. Even though the user communities varied in size, level of wealth, and presented great heterogeneity in their needs and practices (healthcare professionals vs. administrative staff), some of them were powerful enough to resist the implementation of the NPfIT. In particular, Foundation Trusts (including hospitals, mental health centers, and GP practices) – because of their relative autonomy in the NHS – did not only raise their concerns about the NPfIT but also proceeded to the procurement and implementation of alternative solutions. The key concerns raised by Foundation Trusts, as well as smaller groups of healthcare professionals and administrative staff, were around (1) the centralized procurement and delivery of national IT services by a single provider (i.e. BT); (2) the competency of the LSP to deliver on time and within the budget, especially after the withdrawal of Accenture and

the termination of the Fujitsu contract; (3) the engagement of the healthcare professionals, who were already voicing their concerns about the lack of information and participation in the decisions around the local NPfIT solutions; and finally (4) the security and confidentiality of patient data. These concerns were initially highlighted in the NAO report on the NPfIT (NAO, 2006) and later scrutinized by the Committee of Public Accounts in a number of consecutive meetings (HC, 2007a, 2007b, 2007c, 2009).

The next section provides an in-depth analysis of the negotiations that took place around these concerns, while highlighting the bargaining power of some communities over others and the dynamic distribution of property rights among them.

The Action Arena

The negotiation problems that occurred during this phase are illustrated in Figure 3 and discussed in more detail below.

Figure 3. Problems during the development of the NPfIT (2006-2010)

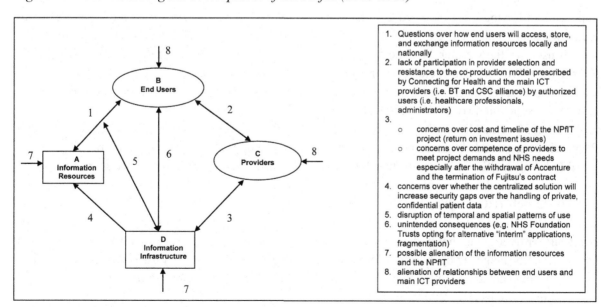

1. Questions over how end users will access, store, and exchange information resources locally and nationally
2. lack of participation in provider selection and resistance to the co-production model prescribed by Connecting for Health and the main ICT providers (i.e. BT and CSC alliance) by authorized users (i.e. healthcare professionals, administrators)
3.
   - concerns over cost and timeline of the NPfIT project (return on investment issues)
   - concerns over competence of providers to meet project demands and NHS needs especially after the withdrawal of Accenture and the termination of Fujitsu's contract
4. concerns over whether the centralized solution will increase security gaps over the handling of private, confidential patient data
5. disruption of temporal and spatial patterns of use
6. unintended consequences (e.g. NHS Foundation Trusts opting for alternative "interim" applications, fragmentation)
7. possible alienation of the information resources and the NPfIT
8. alienation of relationships between end users and main ICT providers

Centralized Procurement and Delivery of National IT Services

Firstly, in relation to the centralized procurement of national IT services, the decision to award both the N3 and the Spine to BT arose from an effort to centralize control and mitigate security risks whilst also minimizing costs to future upgrades, as the Chief Operating Officer for the NPfIT, said (HC, 2009, Ev12³):

... one of the values of using a common system that is of good quality is that it is going to be resilient and have disaster recovery built in... but also, every time you come to upgrade it, the fewer systems there are to upgrade, the cheaper it is, and the less risky it is.

Both the Department of Health and the Managing Director of BT Health also offered strong assurances about technical security levels, arguing that unlawful access to the Spine would be nearly impossible (HC, 2007c, Ev121, & Ev89 respectively).

However, doubts were raised by executive managers of Trusts and individual healthcare professionals about the decision to create a national Spine for storing and transferring information, as opposed to allowing individual Trusts to handle their own data locally. For example, a group of 13,500 users in the Greater Manchester region (North West, West Midlands cluster) argued that they were getting real benefits by sharing a divided system across hospital Trusts (HC, 2007c, Ev121, Ev89, & Ev55). In addition, the UK Computing Research Council added that a single system accessible by all NHS employees from all Trusts maximizes rather than minimizes the risk of a security breach (HC, 2007c, Ev121, Ev89, & Ev125). The British Computer Society took this point further by arguing that higher levels of security would be achieved by storing information in a "distributed database" rather than on centralized storage systems (HC, 2007c, Ev121, Ev89,

& Ev38). However, the Director General of IT in 2007 was dismissive of this idea, admitting that (HC, 2007c, Ev121, Ev89, & Ev10):

None of the leading suppliers of solutions in this space who are willing to bid and take financial and completion risk around the delivery came up with that [distributed] architecture.

Evidently, a distributed architecture would seriously compromise BT's (and its subcontractors) intellectual property rights over the technical and financial control of proposed solutions. At the same time, though, this claim raised the question as to how much scope there was for the NHS and for individual Trusts to renegotiate contracts for national services. The following is a discussion from the second CPA meeting pointing at this very issue (HC, 2009, Ev11):

CPA member: If I earmark a hospital, I do not really have an option other than to go to BT for the core services, do I? ... On the national data Spine, again you are using the Oracle database server platform for that, and presumably at some point in time that might become very expensive to use. Is it a realistic option to find another supplier?

Chief Operating Officer for the NPfIT: Bearing in mind that we have an enterprise-wide agreement with Oracle to supply unlimited—within the parlance it is all you can eat— so as much of the Oracle products as you can buy at a fixed price.

CPA member: That may be a very good deal, but if you do not like the deal you are offering is it realistic or sensible or highly disruptive to go elsewhere?

Chief Operating Officer for the NPfIT: It would be disruptive. That particular decision as to which database platform they use is the supplier's, since they are getting it for nothing effectively.

CPA member: So in one case you are stuck with BT, in the other you are stuck with Oracle.

In fact, in both cases, BT was the major supplier and, thus, essentially, the NPfIT was 'stuck' with BT for national IT services. Through the maxim of 'centralized and secured' networks and 'all you can eat' database systems, NPfIT project leaders presented BT as the best option among alternative IT options.

However, irrespective of whether the NPfIT was 'stuck' with BT for national IT services, all NPfIT contracts contained obligations on suppliers to comply with comprehensive security requirements, to report any breach of the security requirements, and to make recommendations for the remedy of any such breaches. As mentioned earlier, Connecting for Health had the freedom to call in a third party to monitor its IT providers and had the right to terminate a contract immediately if the provider failed to meet any of the specified requirements at any given time, without any compensation (HC, 2007c, Ev152).

Competency of the LSP

Secondly, in relation to the competency of the LSP to deliver on time and on budget, there was more avid resistance by user organizations, and possibly non-interoperable systems.

In the first CPA meeting (HC, 2007a), the Chairman began the discussion by asking the then Acting Chief Executive of the NHS to explain the reasons why the program was running late and whether it was, in fact, too ambitious. The Acting Chief Executive of the NHS attempted to shift the responsibility around the delays to the NPfIT by directing the blame to the LSP's incompetency of meeting project demands (HC, 2007a, Ev2). Although the CPA members were sceptical about the Acting Chief Executive's arguments, by the time of the second CPA meeting (HC, 2009) one LSP had left the programme (i.e. Accenture) and the contract of another LSP was terminated (i.e.

Fujitsu). There were, thus, questions to be raised against the competency of the LSP to meet project demands on time and cost, as evident from the following exchange (HC, 2009, Ev1):

Chairman of the CPA: Why have you withdrawn? What has gone wrong?

Group Director UK Public Services, Fujitsu: As I think the Committee knows, there has been a very long period of renegotiation called the contract re-set discussion, at the end of which the two parties ... were unable to agree on the price and the commercial terms.

Later in the meeting, it became clear that the disagreement on price and commercial terms came down to payment for deployment and repeated requests for system customizations not agreed in the initial contracts (HC, 2009, Ev15-16). The two parties have since been discussing the arrangements to take place to help both Fujitsu and the NPfIT transition out, a process which had been repeated a year earlier with Accenture. The failure to meet the demands of the IT providers meant that the NPfIT has now been left with two providers with significant "implications for the Programme's capacity and capability, and for the Department's [of Health] leverage" (HC, 2009, pp.3).

Beyond issues of contractual agreements on commercial terms of use, the major issue was that of standardization vs. customization, as argued above by the Group Director UK Public Services, Fujitsu. Because of the various LSP and their sub-contractors, and, most importantly, the repeated requests of individual NHS Trusts for systems customized to their local needs, standardization seemed like an impossible feat.

Specifically, there were significant delays to the two main hospital applications, Millennium and Lorenzo, supplied by BT and CSC Alliance respectively. The former Director General of IT commented that one cause of the delays had been difficulties in "anglicizing" Millennium, which is primarily used in the U.S., so that it could operate in the NHS (HC, 2007c, Ev15). Regarding the Lorenzo system, the former Director General of IT stated that the sheer complexity of building a new software system from scratch had delayed the project (HC, 2007c, Ev15). The former Director General of IT also pointed out that the process of actually deploying new hospital PAS software, irrespective of who the provider was, had proved more difficult than expected, particularly because of the need to move data from old systems onto new ones without causing excessive disruption to the delivery of care (HC, 2007c, Ev11).

All these problems led some Trusts to choose different 'interim' solutions in an effort to minimize disruptions to work practices until all the problems with the LSP solutions were resolved. Some of these interim solutions were gaining increasing support by Trusts, which raised questions of liability for the NPfIT (HC, 2009, Ev3-4).

The root of the problem was a number of local ownership initiatives that compromised the control that the DoH had over different healthcare service providers. For example, the DoH had no power over Foundation Trusts, which could choose to completely withdraw from any participation in the NPfIT (HC, 2009). The bargaining power of Foundation Trusts was further strengthened by the NPfIT Local Ownership Programme (NLOP), which was implemented following a review of the management of NPfIT in October 2006. NLOP devolves responsibility for implementing local systems, and for some elements of the management of LSP contracts, from Connecting for Health to the 10 Regional Strategic Health Authorities of the NHS and their respective Foundation Trusts (HC, 2007c, Ev107).

In addition, GP Systems of Choice (GPSoC), another initiative towards local ownership launched in March 2006, allowed individual GPs to choose their own software provider. Providers would be subject to approval by Connecting for Health according to interoperability standards, but individual practices could choose from a number of accredited software systems (HC, 2007c, Ev11-12).

Despite their apparent immunity, however, even Foundation Trusts and GPs were subject to the constitutional right of the DoH (HC, 2009, Ev3):

Chief Executive of the NHS: ... As far as foundation trusts are concerned, the first thing ... is that as part of their license, whatever system they agree to take at the end of the day has to be connected to the main system. That is the first thing. Secondly, they are, like all of us, subject to Treasury rules, which are very clear about taking account of the impact on the wider public sector finances.

In other words, even though Foundation Trusts could choose to buy an alternative system, there were legal-technical control mechanisms, which were enforced to ensure that no actions worsened conditions in the NPfIT and more broadly the NHS – i.e. by adding to interoperability problems and by increasing the financial burden of the public sector. For example, among speculations that four Trusts in the southern cluster might choose not to have the Millennium system installed, it was recently reported that the NHS would be liable to pay £44m to BT – 60 percent of the £73m contract originally agreed with BT (Hoeksma, 2009). The money would come out of the total allocation for NHS IT in the South, meaning there would be £44m less to buy other systems for those Trusts. Thus, even though individual Trusts have a choice, their choice is very tightly governed by extant control mechanisms (HC, 2009, Ev9).

Engagement of Healthcare Professionals

Thirdly, in addition to problems with the national and local delivery of IT services, the NPfIT project leaders were criticized for failing to effectively engage the medical professionals in the development of various applications. An appraisal commissioned by the National Audit Office of the development of the IT specification requirements found that it was developed after engagement with a broad spectrum of NHS stakeholders but that there was no recorded link between the detailed items in the specification and the person or group making that contribution (NAO, 2006). The problem was that there was no good audit trail for clinical input into the production of the specification (HC, 2007a, Ev5):

Director General of IT: ... I fully accept the criticism that is made in the NAO Report that we failed to map input from every single clinician who had input—there were thousands of them—into a requirements document.

The project leaders responded that "there is very much more to do" in terms of engaging the medical professionals, but a lot of it depended on the latter understanding the new clinical functionality that the implemented applications introduced in their practices (HC, 2007a, Ev22). They then provided evidence of how a number of medical professionals were already embracing the NPfIT and there were no expressed concerns that applications were developed outside their own needs and work practices (HC, 2007a, Ev42):

Radiology manager Hillingdon Hospitals NHS Trust: ... Doctors I've never met before are coming up to me and saying how great the system is, and how good it is to have quick access to images.

Consultant psychiatrist Oxleas NHS Foundation Trust: We've implemented the new systems in one directorate and look forward to rolling it out over the next few months across the remainder of a large mental health trust.

Despite these positive outcomes, however, many medical professional groups still complained that NPfIT project leaders did not do much to engage them in both the specification and the implementation phase. For example, in 2006 the Royal College of Nurses' (RCN) survey of 4,500 members found 65 percent had not received adequate information or any information at all about NPfIT; while 74 percent said there had been inadequate consultation or no consultation (HC, 2007a, Ev97). Similarly in another survey conducted by Ipsos MORI for Connecting for Health in February 2006, 64 percent of GPs answered that they were "unaware" of when they would be expected to start uploading their patients' clinical details to the national database as part of the Care Records Service, 12 percent of them were "unsure," and 8 percent said there was "insufficient information to comment" – with only 16 percent giving more positive answers (HC, 2007a, Ev158).

This evidence indicates that a lot needs to be done to regain the support of the medical professionals for the NPfIT. The proper engagement of the various medical professional groups will be a huge (about 700,000 people would have to be involved) and costly task, made particularly difficult due to its commencement so long after the project was announced. Nonetheless, unless this is done, it is hard to see how medical professionals can be persuaded that the NPfIT can provide extensive clinical functionality (HC, 2009, Ev7, Ev10) and that serious and effective action is being taken to protect the confidentiality of patient records, which is discussed next.

Security & Confidentiality of Patient Data

Finally, from the outset of the NPfIT, there were increasing concerns about the security and confidentiality of patient data. The CPA – drawing on the increasing concerns of healthcare service providers – argued that the prospect of nationally shared patient care records tended to raise more concerns about possible security breaches than that of locally shared patient care records. Extant security mechanisms for secondary uses of clinical data were questioned as being inefficient (HC, 2007c, Ev47):

Chairman of the CPA: ... Is there a risk that the use of data by secondary users will end up in the European courts?

Professor of International Law, London Metropolitan University: I will say yes... The issue hinges on identifiability. ... Only totally anonymized data or very seriously pseudonymised data can ever be passed on without with the consent of the individual. In many studies the level of security against re-identification is not sufficient.

In response to these concerns, the Royal College of GPs argued for "organizational boundaries around information" so that data could not be shared between organizations without the patient's explicit consent (HC, 2007c, Ev93). This suggestion was also put forward by the British Medical Association and the British Computer Society (HC, 2007c, Ev43 & Ev38 respectively).

The DoH pointed out that an increasing amount of information, particularly from hospitals, would be stored electronically on LSP servers, something which would make it impossible to prevent patient-identifiable information from being placed on LSP records systems (HC, 2007c, Ev6). The Department also commented that local "sealed envelopes" – securely 'locked' information, opened only after the patient's explicit consent – would be available to safeguard particularly sensitive information held in electronic patient records systems (HC, 2007c, Ev7). However, CSC Alliance stated that exact policy specifications for "sealed envelopes" had not yet been given to LSP by Connecting for Health and that any solution would have to wait for implementations at the Spine (HC, 2007c, Ev58-59). There were, thus, very strong interdependencies between solutions implemented at the national and local service levels with explicit links to national policy on data access, distribution, and manipulation.

One proposal to address the problem of data security and confidentiality was to implement role-based access through smart cards, which would add an e-GIF security level 3, the highest level of security in government terminology, as Chief Operating Officer for the NPfIT explained (HC, 2009, Ev 8). The question, however, was whether, in the end, people would follow proper procedures irrespective of any installed technologies. The response of the Chief Executive of the NHS was that the NHS has issued "a huge amount of guidance... [and] have put it high up on the responsibilities of all chief executives in the NHS" to ensure that people would take corrective action when something goes wrong (HC, 2009, Ev 13). This response was also supported by the Clinical Director of Patient Care Records at the Department of Health, and the Chief Clinical Officer of the NHS Connecting for Health (HC, 2009, Ev 13-14). Both referred to standards and an "information governance toolkit," but those were still meant to be implemented locally, something which again raised questions of managing security breaches at the national level (HC, 2009, Ev 14).

One clinician described the complexity of the architecture envisaged by listing the steps (11 in total) required to access various local and national data depositories and, in turn, offered an analysis of emerging issues (HC, 2007c, Ev 136-141). Instead, he suggested, clinicians should retain their servers and the governance of the data locally and Connecting for Health should run an offsite encrypted backup service (HC, 2007c, Ev 138). "This would also alleviate the problem of narrow broadband connections which cannot support off-site serving of clinical systems on a large scale" and would resonate to BT's suggestion "that no clinical system should be dependent on N3/internet connections to function," in contrast to the demands of Connecting for Health (HC, 2007c, Ev 138). Thus, once again, there was a dilemma of centralized vs. decentralized procurement and standardized vs. customized services.

Outcomes

As evident from the above discussion, despite efforts from the NPfIT project leaders and NHS executives, the NPfIT still faces significant problems and scrutiny by NHS healthcare professionals and administrative staff, as well as policymakers.

As reported in the more recent National Audit Office report (NAO, 2011), there has been variable success in delivering local systems in the NPfIT, with some systems partly delivered (e.g. 53 percent of Acute Trusts in London), and yet others removed from the scope of the program altogether (e.g. Ambulance and GP systems in London and the South) (NAO, 2011, pp.12). The progress with delivering national systems favoured a better outcome, with the N3 broadband network and the Data Spine having been fully delivered, but with the National Summary Care Record only delivered in 10 percent of Trusts (NAO, 2011, pp.17).

In addition, the scrutiny of policymakers (and the CPA especially) seems to have been driven by short-term performance targets to satisfy re-election campaigns with little patience for goals that required long time horizons (Greener, 2009). The implications of the negotiating strategy of the policymakers were that, very often, they were ready to criticize NPfIT leadership if outcomes were not readily measurable, and to introduce new reforms to address limitations (Brennan, 2007).

The NPfIT project leaders and NHS executives were the first to face the scrutiny of the policymakers, with the former feeling pressured by an effort to exceed NPfIT project limitations and pursue unrealistic goals due to both their insecurity of potentially losing their job and their ambition to become heroes (see Blackler, 2006; Greener, 2005). The implications were that NPfIT project leaders and NHS executives were often found to fall in the trap of committing to unrealistic and unachievable timetables and objectives with detrimental consequences such as losing their jobs – as in the example of the Director General of IT in 2007 (Curry & Guah, 2007; also see HC,

2007 on NPfIT leadership issues). At the same time, however, their 'irrational' behavior was also found to push the learning curve of participant organizations, including the NHS as a whole, to new levels.

Specifically, the DoH has recently announced that, having learned from mistakes made in the past, it is now changing the whole strategy behind the NPfIT to one that is more local and needs-led than centrally controlled (DoH, 2010; also see Cruickshank, 2010). Evidently, while such a change seeks to address concerns about non participation in the centralized procurement strategy of the NPfIT, it confirms concerns about the efficiency of NPfIT and nurtures the distributed and fragmented deployment locally-led IT solutions.

In particular, the ability to implement alternative, local solutions fed into the efforts of Foundation Trusts toward complete independence from the DoH in terms of executive decisions on IT investments (see HC, 2009). For example, Newcastle Foundation Trust has signed a contract with Pittsburgh Medical Centre in the United States for a Patient Administration System, including clinical functionality and order communications (HC, 2009, Ev24). The contract is for five years with an option to extend for two years and, although there is a possibility of later migrating to NPfIT solutions, there are strong indications that 'interim' solutions implemented in this and other Trusts across the NHS will be hard to replace as time goes by. The negative implication of this outcome was that (NAO, 2011, pp.8):

With fewer systems being provided through the Programme and more use being made of a variety of existing systems, there is an increased risk of not achieving adequate compatibility across the NHS to effectively support joined up healthcare. The Department estimates that achieving interoperability will cost at least £220 million.

This was exactly what the NPfIT project leaders feared the most and fought against: that too much choice would lead to interoperability problems and more costs. However, based on figures provided by the National Audit Office, even with a series of agreed reductions in the number of systems being delivered by the remaining suppliers, "under the terms of the current contracts it is unlikely that the remaining work can be completed by the end of the contracts in 2015-16" (NAO, 2011, pp.10). In fact, there has been a strong opposition to the NPfIT by the coalition government formed by the Conservatives and the Liberal Democrats, when elected into power in 2008. The new government essentially argued that investments made in relation to the NPfIT do not represent value for money and the program should therefore be scrapped altogether (Hoeksma, 2011).

In addition, the NPfIT was met with strong resistance by the majority of healthcare professionals within the NHS. Healthcare professionals in the NHS have always been driven by status and the ability to exercise control over decisions taken in their professionally dominated arena and are always ready to dispute any efforts to change that could compromise their position in the division of labor (Blackler, 2006; Greener, 2005, 2009). Using the excuse that they did not understand the scale and objectives of the service innovations proposed by the NPfIT, primarily due to a lack of engagement by the NPfIT leaders – even though, both the former Acting Chief Executive of the NHS and the Director General of IT deny such allegations (see HC, 2007a) – they posed strong resistance to the NPfIT often criticising it in public forums (e.g. Penney, 2005; Ford, 2005).

The LSPs found themselves in the midst of the aforementioned conflicting agendas, which did not align with their interests and needs that are very much tied into market dynamics – i.e. they have to develop and deliver products and services to a wide population of potential customers with diverse needs, not just the NHS. So, their big dilemma was whether to jeopardize their competitive positioning by consuming valuable time and resources for a national project that is conditioned by constant political pressures. This dilemma was what eventually forced both Accenture and Fujitsu to withdraw from the NPfIT, while raising concerns about the remaining LSP.

In summary, against a backdrop of continuous change in the NHS, the NPfIT is currently halfway through its planned implementation. It is too early to predict whether the NPfIT will achieve its overall aims and objectives, but publicly available data show that the NPfIT is consistently missing the original performance targets (Hendy et al., 2005; NAO, 2006; NAO, 2011) and is also seemingly becoming increasingly fragmented. The current delays and shortcomings around the delivery of various applications are not merely confined to technical issues, but extend to poor engagement and communication between those who seek to enforce this system and the various user groups it is intended to serve. An increase in 'user engagement' is currently being advocated and implemented by Connecting for Health (NAO, 2006; HC, 2009). However, the analysis of the data illustrate a more fundamental and intransigent problem between an infrastructural ideal of centralized, integrated, and standardized services, on the one hand, and an effort to strike a more flexible procurement of services through local partnerships between NHS Trusts and private companies. Against the aforementioned competing procurement models, defining the aims and objectives of the NPfIT has become increasingly difficult, as conflicting and contradictory agendas gain and lose momentum within the English NHS.

CONCLUSION

Previous research has pointed to the ways in which complex technologies like the NPfIT compel organizations like the NHS to develop complex structures and complex management processes (Perrow, 1999). However, these complex structures and processes involve gaps in coordination and communication with the consequence that organizations have more difficulty managing those technologies effectively. Farjoun and Starbuck (2007) discuss the example of NASA's space shuttle, which, because of its multiple and diverse technologies, has inhibited NASA from replacing unreliable and legacy components. Instead, this technological complexity has pushed NASA to add "hierarchical layers and occupational specialties that have narrowly defined functions," which have, in turn, resulted in poor and inappropriate responses to even small, incremental changes (Farjoun & Starbuck, 2007, pp.551).

The need to add more organizational structures to address the emerging technological complexity is also observed in the NPfIT. For example, in 2003, before the English NHS was divided into five clusters and 10 Strategic Health Authorities (SHA), there were 28 SHAs and there was an expectation that 28 IT service providers would be appointed – one for each SHA – for the procurement of the NPfIT (Brennan, 2007). If this change had been implemented, each local provider would be dealing with less than half a dozen Trusts; work would have started much sooner; the relationships between Trusts and providers would have been easier to manage, and the latter could have been in a better position to deal with time and budget limitations as well as software customization requests. Instead, the governance of the NPfIT was structured on a rather complex and potentially unmanageable model – from the DoH, to Connecting for Health, to clusters, SHA, local programs, senior responsible owners, LSP, and Trusts, all being assigned a piece of the governance of the project.

Some commentators have argued that the problem started with a change in the strategy for electronic patient records (Brennan, 2005). Beginning with the national EPR Program (1994-1997) and the follow-up ERDIP Program, electronic patient records were to be built at the level of local clinical communities. Such a program would have consisted of integrated clinical and administrative systems. These would have produced a passive

record held locally. A national summary record would have been fed from these local systems as part of future functionality upgrades, but not as a pre-requisite. Despite this early formulated strategy, however, NPfIT project leaders and NHS executives decided that the main objective of their program was a single national electronic record. Most of the problems with the Programme can be traced to that fundamental re-interpretation of what the NHS needed (Brennan, 2005). It might have been workable if this was allowed to evolve over time, so long as the program's primary objective was left untouched – to put in place effective, workable local systems that support the way that healthcare professionals work in local organisations.

Granted there is a need for national electronic patient records. However, during the early days, patients would have tended to choose what they knew and it might have been more sensible to deliver local solutions and a local record first before worrying about the national electronic record that appears to be driven by political need rather than a clinical or public need (cf. Graham & Marvin, 2001 on national infrastructure procurement and the political agendas behind such projects). In fact, there is a strong clinical case now for the implementation of local systems to support the clinicians in what they do and in helping them produce a local electronic record (Cruickshank, 2010). It may have been more pragmatic to implement these local clinical systems first and in time pull their outputs together in a large, single national database.

So, the NPfIT has been and is still torn between two possible solutions: a nationally- vs. a locally-led solution. In the first option, the NPfIT will supposedly be more secure, it will save time and money, and it will achieve integration of services. In the second option, the NPfIT will supposedly offer more flexibility to local Trusts and NHS authorities to choose systems according to their individual needs and by doing so it could potentially speed up the deployment of IT in the English NHS.

Ironically, England has found itself in a similar situation in the past. In the 19th century, England followed the broad consensus of the time that infrastructures through which services were distributed were most effectively managed through "natural monopolies" by a single supplier. By the 1920s, after a series of reforms, England found itself unable to integrate its many, incompatible local electricity suppliers (Hughes, 1983). Instead of integration, England, like other major cities across the world, deregulated the market and allowed the splintering of electricity infrastructures through public-private partnerships (see Graham & Marvin, 2001, pp.237-239). The NPfIT seems to be going through a similar splintering process at the moment.

In the USA, there have been similar efforts to develop a national health information infrastructure with a technological trajectory that exhibits a striking resemblance to the trajectory of the NPfIT. Like the 1998 NHS Executive white paper, *Information for Health* (NHS Executive, 1998), in 1998, the National Committee on Vital and Health Statistics (NCVHS), a U.S. federal advisory committee composed of private sector experts, reported that the USA's information infrastructure could be an essential tool for promoting the nation's health in its seminal white paper, *Assuring a Health Dimension for the National Information Infrastructure* (NCVHS, 1998). Then, and again in striking similarity to the English Department of Health's strategy document, *Delivering 21st Century IT Support for the NHS – National Strategic Programme* (DoH, 2002), the USA's NCVHS delivered its own white paper, *A Strategy for Building the National Health Information Infrastructure* (NCVHS, 2001).

The aims and objectives of the USA white papers follow the same logic as the English white papers for developing a national health information infrastructure, with a focus on standardized, patient-centric information, toward improving the quality of national healthcare services offered to their respective populations. Like in the case of the English NPfIT, several organizational structures were established to govern the emerging technological complexity of the USA's national health information infrastructure (CMS, 2010; Thompson & Brailer, 2004; U.S. DHHS, 2005; also see USA Congress, 2010). The key difference between the two countries is that, the USA has a stronger private healthcare provider model (Burns, 2002) and, thus, structures established accounted for the public-private relationships between healthcare producers, purchasers, and providers.

However, the challenges faced in the English NPfIT are also faced by the USA's national health information infrastructure, including interoperability issues between disparate systems, engagement of the healthcare professionals (especially in relation to the functionality of proposed systems), and privacy of patient data (e.g. see Fernandopulle & Patel, 2010; Karsh et al., 2010; Nutting et al., 2009). Further, actual use of electronic patient records systems are also at very low levels. Specifically, in 2008 and 2009, the USA's National Center for Health Statistics (NCHS) conducted two national surveys on the use of electronic medical record/electronic health records (Hsiao, et al., 2009). Despite an effort to present the findings from a more positive angle, in 2009, only 6.3 percent of physicians reported having systems of a fully functional system, and 20.5 percent of them reported having systems that met the criteria of a basic system (comparable figures for 2008 were 4.4 percent and 16.7 percent respectively) (Hsiao, et al., 2009). In fact, actual use (partial or otherwise) of these systems remained at below 50 percent (Hsiao, et al., 2009).

The key reason behind these poor statistics is that–as in the English NPfIT–the rising costs of health care services and healthcare technologies, coupled with the complexities of centrally allocating budgets and establishing institutional rules for governing the infrastructure, make it almost impossible to satisfy all stakeholders (Kaushal et al., 2005)[4]. In the end, evidence shows that current developments in the USA have focused on local efforts through entities such as regional health information organizations (RHIOs)–the corresponding organizations to the Strategic Health Authorities of the English NHS. RHIO-driven strategies are thought to have a greater likelihood of success than a centralized strategy, because RHIOs can act as independent third parties, bringing stakeholders together and supporting health information exchange between them (Adler-Milstein et al., 2008). Even such strategies, however, will only be successful if they are "built around sustainable business models, [something] which requires both profitability and value creation for participants" (Adler-Milstein et al., 2008, pp. 61).

As historical analyses of early infrastructure development have shown, there is no *best* solution. There are advantages and disadvantages with every solution, but these have to be evaluated against the consequences each solution generates for different communities. It is because of this need to evaluate the consequences of an infrastructural solution against the local needs of various communities that there is now a widespread discussion that community-based, 'open' technological development can, in fact, lead to more creative solutions based on the local needs of user-developers (e.g. Lessig, 2001; Litman, 2001; Benkler, 2006).

This alternative mode of information infrastructure development will be explored in more detail next, in Chapters 6 and 7, while drawing on the findings from both the Crete and the English case studies, and other such regional and national efforts.

REFERENCES

Adler-Milstein, J., McAfee, A. P., Bates, D. W., & Jha, A. K. (2008). The state of regional health information organizations: Current activities and financing. *Health Affairs*, 27(1), 60–69. doi:10.1377/hlthaff.27.1.w60

Benkler, Y. (2006). *The wealth of networks*. New Haven, CT: Yale University Press.

Beveridge, W. (1942). *Social insurance and allied services. Cm 6404*. London, UK: HMSO.

Blackler, F. (2006). Chief executives and the modernization of the English National Health Service. *Leadership*, 2(1), 5–30. doi:10.1177/1742715006060651

Brennan, S. (2005). *The NHS IT project: The biggest computer programme in the world… ever!* Oxford, UK: Radcliffe Publishing.

Brennan, S. (2007). The biggest computer programme in the world ever! How's it going? *Journal of Information Technology*, 22(3), 202–211. doi:10.1057/palgrave.jit.2000104

Burns, L. R. (2002). *The health care value chain: Producers, purchasers and providers*. San Francisco, CA: Jossey Bass.

Centers for Medicare & Medicaid Services. (CMS). (2010). Medicare and Medicaid programs; electronic health record incentive program. Final rule. *Federal Register*, 75(144), 44313–44362.

Connecting for Health. (2004). *Business plan*. Retrieved February 20, 2011, from http://www.connectingforhealth.nhs.uk

Constantinides, P., & Blackler, F. (2008). Co-orienting the object: An activity theoretical analysis of a public report on the UK's National Program for IT. In Barrett, M., Davidson, E., Middleton, C., & DeGross, J. (Eds.), *Information technology in the service economy: Challenges and possibilities for the 21st century* (pp. 259–270). Boston, MA: Springer. doi:10.1007/978-0-387-09768-8_18

Cruickshank, J. (2010). *Fixing NHS IT: A plan of action for a new government*. Retrieved February 20, 2011, from http://www.2020health.org/export/sites/2020/pdf/2020itdocA4MASTERlow27-04.pdf

Currie, W. L., & Guah, M. (2007). Conflicting institutional logics: A national program for IT in the organisational field of healthcare. *Journal of Information Technology, 22*(3), 235–247. doi:10.1057/palgrave.jit.2000102

Department of Health (DoH). (1997). *The new NHS: Modern, dependable. Cm 3807*. London, UK: Author.

Department of Health (DoH). (2000). *The NHS plan: A plan for investment, a plan for reform. Cm 4818-I*. London, UK: Author.

Department of Health (DoH). (2002). *Delivering 21st century IT support for the NHS–national strategic programme*. Retrieved February 20, 2011, from http://www.connectingforhealth.nhs.uk/resources/policyandguidance/delivery_21_century_it.pdf

Department of Health (DoH). (2003). *Integrated care records service: Introduction to the output based specification*. Retrieved February 20, 2011, from http://www.dh.gov.uk/prod_consum_dh/groups/dh_digitalassets/@dh/@en/documents/digitalasset/dh_4055049.pdf

Department of Health (DoH). (2004). *National programme for IT: Initial guidance for existing system suppliers*. Retrieved February 20, 2011, from http://www.ehiprimarycare.com/img/document_library0282/NPfITsuppliersguide.pdf

Department of Health (DoH). (2010). *The future of the national programme for IT*. London, UK: Author.

Executive, N. H. S. (1998). *Information for health: An information strategy for the modern NHS 1998–2005: A national strategy for local implementation*. London, UK: Department of Health.

Farjoun, M., & Starbuck, W. H. (2007). Organizing at and beyond the limits. *Organization Studies, 28*(4), 541–566. doi:10.1177/0170840607076584

Fernandopulle, R., & Patel, N. (2010). How the electronic health record did not measure up to the demands of our medical home practice. *Health Affairs, 29*(4), 622–628. doi:10.1377/hlthaff.2010.0065

Ford, S. (2005). Letter: Challenges to implementing NPfIT: Nothing counts except what is in front of the clinician to use. *British Medical Journal, 331*, 516. doi:10.1136/bmj.331.7515.516

Graham, S., & Marvin, S. (2001). *Splintering urbanism: Networked infrastructures, technological mobilities and the urban condition*. New York, NY: Routledge. doi:10.4324/9780203452202

Greener, I. (2005). Health management as strategic behaviour: Managing medics and performance in the NHS. *Public Management Review, 7*(1), 95–110. doi:10.1080/1471903042000339437

Greener, I. (2009). *Healthcare in the UK: Understanding continuity and change*. Bristol, UK: Policy Press.

Harrison, S., & Pollitt, C. (1994). *Controlling health professionals: The future of work and organization in the national health service*. Milton Keynes, UK: Open University Press.

Hoeksma, J. (2009, October 1). South liable for greenfield penalties. *E-Health Insider*.

Hoeksma, J. (2011, May 18). NAO says NPfIT is not value for money. *E-Health Insider*.

House of Commons (HC). (2007a). Department of health: The national programme for IT in the NHS. *Twentieth Report of Session 2006-07*, HC 390. House of Commons, Committee of Public Accounts. Retrieved February 20, 2011, from http://www.publications.parliament.uk/pa/cm200607/cmselect/cmpubacc/390/390.pdf

House of Commons (HC). (2007b). The electronic patient record. *Sixth Report of Session 2006-07, Vol II–Written Evidence*, HC 422-II. House of Commons, Health Committee. Retrieved February 20, 2011, from http://www.publications.parliament.uk/pa/cm200607/cmselect/cmhealth/422/42202.htm

House of Commons (HC). (2007c). The electronic patient record. *Sixth Report of Session 2006-07, Vol III–Oral & Written Evidence*, HC 422-III. House of Commons, Health Committee. Retrieved February 20, 2011, from http://www.publications.parliament.uk/pa/cm200607/cmselect/cmhealth/422/42202.htm

House of Commons (HC). (2009). The national programme for IT in the NHS: progress since 2006. *Second Report of Session 2008-09*, HC 153. House of Commons, Committee of Public Accounts. Retrieved February 20, 2011, from http://www.publications.parliament.uk/pa/cm200809/cmselect/cmpubacc/153/15302.htm

Hsiao, C.-J., Beatty, P. C., Hing, E. S., Woodwell, D. A., Rechtsteiner, E. A., & Sisk, J. E. (2009). *Electronic medical record/electronic health record use: United States, 2008 and preliminary 2009*. Atlanta, GA: National Center for Health Statistics, Center for Disease Control and Prevention.

Hughes, T. P. (1983). *Networks of power: Electrification in Western society, 1880-1930*. Baltimore, MD: Johns Hopkins.

Karsh, B. T., Weinger, M. B., Abbott, P. A., & Wears, R. L. (2010). Health information technology: Fallacies and sober realities. *Journal of the American Medical Informatics Association, 17*(6), 617–623. doi:10.1136/jamia.2010.005637

Kaushal, R., Blumenthal, D., Poon, E. G., Jha, A. K., Franz, C., & Middleton, B. (2005). The costs of a national health information network. *Annals of Internal Medicine, 143*(3), 165–173.

Klein, R. (2000). *The new politics of the NHS*. Harlow, UK: Longman.

Lessig, L. (2001). *The future of ideas: The fate of the commons in a connected world*. New York, NY: Random House.

Litman, J. (2001). *Digital copyright*. Amherst, NY: Prometheus Books.

NAO. (2006). *Department of health: The national programme for IT in the NHS. Report by the Comptroller and Auditor General: Session HC 1173*. London, UK: NAO.

NAO. (2011). *The national programme for IT in the NHS: An update on the delivery of detailed care records systems. Report by the Comptroller and Auditor General: Sesion HC 888*. London, UK: NAO.

National Audit Office (NAO). (2004, November 5). Improving IT procurement. *Report by the Comptroller and Auditor General, Session 2003–4*, HC 877. London, UK: The Stationery Office Limited.

National Health Service (NHS). (2004, October 4). *National program for IT: Initial guidance for existing system suppliers*.

National Health Service (NHS). (n.d.). *Foundation trust directory*. Retrieved on January 13, 2011, from http://www.monitor-nhsft.gov.uk/home/about-nhs-foundation-trusts/nhs-foundation-trust-

NCVHS. (2001). *Information for health: A strategy for building the national health information infrastructure*. Washington, DC: US Dept of Health and Human Services.

Nutting, P. A., Miller, W. L., Crabtree, B. F., Jaen, C. R., Stewart, E. E., & Stange, K. C. (2009). Initial lessons from the first national demonstration project on practice transformation to a patient-centered medical home. *Annals of Family Medicine, 7*(3), 254–260. doi:10.1370/afm.1002

Peckham, S., Exworthy, M., Greener, I., & Powell, M. (2005). Decentralizing health services: More local accountability or just more central control? *Public Money and Management, 25*(4), 221–228. doi:10.1111/j.1467-9302.2005.00477.x

Penney, T. M. (2005). Letter: Challenges to implementing NPfIT: Clinicians are becoming increasingly more influential. *British Medical Journal, 331*, 516. doi:10.1136/bmj.331.7515.516-a

Perrow, C. (1999). *Normal accidents: Living with high risk technologies.* Princeton, NJ: Princeton University Press.

Schneider, G., & Aspinwall, M. (Eds.). (2001). *The rules of integration: The institutionalist approach to the study of Europe.* Manchester, UK: European Policy Research Unit Series, Manchester University Press.

Thompson, T. G., & Brailer, D. J. (2004). *The decade of health information technology: Delivering consumer-centric and information-rich health care: Framework for strategic action.* Washington, DC: U.S. Department of Health and Human Services.

Traynor, M. (1996). A literary approach to managerial discourse after the NHS Reforms. *Sociology of Health & Illness, 18*(3), 315–340. doi:10.1111/1467-9566.ep10934667

U.S. Congress. (2010). Patient protection and affordable care act. *111ᵗʰ Congress United States, Federal Statute,* HR 3590. Retrieved November 20, 2012, from http://burgess.house.gov/UploadedFiles/hr3590_health_care_law_2010.pdf

U.S. Department of Health and Human Services (US DHHS). (2005). *Summary of nationwide health information network (NHIN) request for information (RFI) responses.* Washington, DC: U.S. Department of Health and Human Services Office of the National Coordinator for Health Information Technology.

ADDITIONAL READING

Aldrich, H. E. (1999). *Organizations evolving.* London, UK: Sage Publications.

Baumard, P., & Starbuck, W. H. (2005). Learning from failures: Why it may not happen. *Long Range Planning, 38*(3), 281–298. doi:10.1016/j.lrp.2005.03.004

Blount, S., & Janicik, G. A. (2001). When plans change: Examining how people evaluate timing changes in work organizations. *Academy of Management Review, 26*(4), 566–585.

Brown, N., Rappert, B., & Webster, A. (Eds.). (2000). *Contested futures: A sociology of prospective techno-science.* Aldershot, UK: Ashgate.

Chisholm, D. (1989). *Coordination without hierarchy: Informal structures in multi-organizational systems.* Berkeley, CA: University of California Press.

Conlon, D. E., & Garland, H. (1993). The role of project completion information in resource allocation decisions. *Academy of Management Journal, 36*(2), 402–413. doi:10.2307/256529

Fincham, R. (2002). Narratives of success and failure in systems development. *British Journal of Management, 13*(1), 1–14. doi:10.1111/1467-8551.00219

Gerstner, L. V. Jr. (2002). *Who says elephants can't dance? Inside IBM's historic turnaround.* New York, NY: Harper Business.

Grabowski, M., & Roberts, K. H. (1996). Human and organizational error in large scale systems. *IEEE Transactions on Systems, Man, and Cybernetics. Part A, Systems and Humans, 26*(1), 2–16. doi:10.1109/3468.477856

Heath, C., & Staudenmayer, N. (2000). Coordination neglect: How lay theories of organizing complicate coordination in organizations. In Staw, B. M., & Sutton, R. I. (Eds.), *Research in organizational Behavior* (pp. 153–191). New York, NY: Elsevier Science. doi:10.1016/S0191-3085(00)22005-4

Heimann, C. F. L. (1997). *Acceptable risks: Politics, policy, and risky technologies.* Ann Arbor, MI: University of Michigan Press.

Jervis, R. (1997). *System effects: Complexity in political and social life.* Princeton, NJ: Princeton University Press.

Miller, D. (1990). *The Icarus paradox: How exceptional companies bring about their own downfall.* New York, NY: HarperCollins.

Miller, D. (1993). The architecture of simplicity. *Academy of Management Review, 18*(1), 116–138.

Starbuck, W. H., & Farjoun, M. (2005). *Organization at the limit: Lessons from the Columbia disaster.* Oxford, UK: Blackwell Publishing.

Sterman, J. (2000). *Business dynamics: Systems thinking and modelling for a complex world.* New York, NY: McGraw-Hill/Irwin.

Tucker, A. L., & Edmondson, A. C. (2003, Winter). Why hospitals don't learn from failures: Organizational and psychological dynamics that inhibit system change. *California Management Review, 45*(2), 55–72.

Weick, K. E., & Sutcliffe, K. M. (2001). *Managing the unexpected: Assuring high performance in an age of complexity.* San Francisco, CA: Jossey-Bass.

Wilson, M., & Howcroft, D. (2002). Re-conceptualising failure: Social shaping meets IS research. *European Journal of Information Systems, 11*(4), 236–250. doi:10.1057/palgrave.ejis.3000437

ENDNOTES

[1] There are currently 132 NHS Foundation Trusts, of which 40 are Mental Health Trusts.

[2] For more detailed information on the architecture of the NPfIT see the iinitial gguidance provided by the NHS to ICT providers (NHS, 2004), the National Audit Office report (2006), and evidence presented before the Committee of Public Accounts by BT Health (HC, 2007c, Ev127-128).

[3] 'Ev' refers to both oral and written evidence submitted to the CPA. Quotations without the 'Ev' refer to page numbers.

[4] In comparing the USA's investment plans for a national health information infrastructure to those of England and Canada (estimated at £8million and $1.5million respectively, in 2005), Kaushal et al., (2005, pp.170-1) found that: We identified the critical providers, functional domains, and interoperability requirements for a model NHIN. In sum, $156 billion in capital investment and $48 billion in annual operating costs would be required to achieve a model NHIN in 5 years… If we continue on our current trajectory of IT adoption, the health care system will spend about one quarter of the costs of the functionalities of a model NHIN and will probably not even begin to address issues of interoperability. These findings suggest that

policy initiatives are needed if we are to close this gap.... A major barrier to widespread IT adoption is that costs are generally incurred by a few entities, while benefits accrue too many. For example, hospitals make an initial multimillion-dollar investment in CPOE [computerized physician order entry] systems, although financial benefits accrue too many. Institutions tend to invest in areas with direct financial benefits to themselves, such as new equipment or facilities. It seems unlikely that the private sector will move forward rapidly to adopt IT without public sector investment or incentives, both in terms of money and leadership, although this incurs the risk that public dollars will substitute for private dollars targeted to acquire IT functionalities over the next 5 years.

Chapter 6
Challenges to the Development of Information Infrastructures:
A Synthesis of the Findings

ABSTRACT

In Chapters 4 and 5, two case studies involving the development of new information infrastructures were described and analyzed using the commons perspective and associated theoretical framework. Although the two case studies exhibited great differences in scope (regional versus national), context (Greek versus English health system), and time frame, each involved a set of contextual characteristics, an action arena, and a set of outcomes. The purpose of this chapter is to synthesize the findings from the analysis of the two case studies, while also drawing links with findings from other settings. This synthesis leads to some theoretical implications while establishing stronger associations between the literature on information infrastructures and traditional commons arrangements.

INTRODUCTION

The presentation of the two case studies in the order they appear was deliberate in order to illustrate the challenges of developing an information infrastructure from a pilot across a region (Crete case study), to a fully-scaled national information

DOI: 10.4018/978-1-4666-1622-6.ch006

infrastructure (English case study). Both case studies contribute to extant research by demonstrating how a commons perspective can enrich our understanding of negotiations and relevant outcomes in information infrastructure development across different scales.

Extant research has certainly offered useful conceptualizations of information infrastructure development by focusing, on the one hand, on the ways that organizations can achieve strategic business-IT integration (e.g. Weill & Broadbent, 1998; Weill & Ross, 2004), and on the other, the ways by which integration efforts often lead to (un)intended consequences and drift (e.g. Bowker & Star, 1999; Ciborra & associates, 2001; Hanseth et al., 2006; Sahay et al., 2009).

As Sahay et al., (2009) critically note, however, we have little empirical knowledge about *why* and *how* negotiations occur in order to better understand these (un)intended consequences. In their own analysis of a health information systems project (HISP) in India, Sahay et al., (2009) propose a focus on different sets of actors (large and powerful vs. small and relatively powerless), the systems these actors seek to introduce within the same context, and the political capacity and credibility each of these actors bring into the negotiations. They present a compelling narrative of how a small actor–a local NGO–struggles against a large powerful actor–state health authorities–to develop a local/regional health information infrastructure, and discuss how consequences unfold.

The commons framework adopted in this book builds upon and extends studies focusing on negotiations that take place between key actors in the development of information infrastructures. In particular, the commons framework offers greater insight into the role of different actors, as well as the power asymmetries between them, by focusing on different actors' property rights and the consequences those rights generate in the ordering of relationships between key actors, as well as the successful or failed development of information infrastructures.

In the Crete case study, the HEALTHnet pilot was initiated by a small actor, CreteTech, who, by giving hardware and software for free, and engaging a small community of key healthcare professionals in the region of Crete, sought to establish political-technical credibility in the region. Like the early pilots in the HISP project in India (Sahay et al., 2009), and other developing countries (see Braa et al., 2004), the HEALTHnet

pilot encountered user resistance partly due to the lack of support from the government agencies, something which brought the legitimacy of the project into question among users.

However, the fiercest form of resistance arose from contestations around the property rights of different communities on the implemented technologies. These varied from an IP rights dispute between CreteTech and a once collaborating general practitioner, to a questioning of the collective choice rights of individual hospitals to remove HEALTHnet applications and manage their own self-funded projects, and a constitutional right dispute between CreteTech and other IT providers in the region with the Regional Health Authorities of Crete over who had control over which technologies implemented in the region. The negotiations between these various actors and the property rights they claimed over the various technologies led to processes of so called "reflexive standardization"–i.e. alternative outcomes than the intended objective of 'standardized' or 'integrated' systems (Hanseth et al., 2006).

Similarly, but at a different scale of development, in the English case study, the NPfIT was initiated with the full support of the English Department of Health and a clear plan of development and implementation. Still, the NPfIT was met with resistance from various communities at different levels, from Strategic Health Authorities (SHA), Foundation Trusts, GP Practices, individual healthcare professionals, and administrative staff. This resistance came from concerns over the centralized procurement of the NPfIT, the competency of the Local Service Providers (LSP), the poor engagement of the healthcare professionals, and the security and confidentiality of patient data. The root of all these concerns was the distribution of property rights across interested and affected communities. Some key questions asked were: why should procurement be centralized and not decentralized, allowing each local Trust to rightfully choose its customized solution? Why should LSP be contracted nationally by clusters and not rightfully so by each SHA? Why should healthcare professionals be told which application would best suit their needs, instead of allowing them to rightfully decide what worked best for them? Why should patient records be built on a national model–with all the security issues associated with such a model–and not on a local (distributed) model?

The findings from the two case studies point to some well reported issues in the literature, such as the contrast between the global or national and local development of an information infrastructure (Rolland & Monteiro, 2002), the tensions between top-down control and bottom-up alignment (Ciborra & Hanseth, 2001), and the often negative impact of political reforms and the complexity of negotiations around the development of information infrastructures across different time periods (e.g. Bowker & Star, 1999; Sahay et al., 2009). The commons perspective, though, goes a step further in analyzing the changing dynamics of these historical negotiations.

In particular, past studies have argued that a new information infrastructure is never developed from scratch but rather evolves on the existing installed base. This argument holds that early design and adoption decisions, as well as the early relationships different actors form with adopted technologies, create a future path for an information infrastructure (Hanseth, 2001). This argument may be valid in some cases, but multiple and diverse trajectories are more likely to be created because of the complexity of the public-private properties of an information infrastructure and the changes in the property rights of different actors.

In the Crete case study, the Information Society initiative challenged the extant installed base in the region of Crete, by instituting new rules (e.g. 'transparent evaluation mechanisms,' licenses, property rights) and by awarding the contract for a new information infrastructure to CompeTech–an IT provider with no previous history in the region. Through this new set of institutional rules, the Information Society not only revised and redis-

tributed each actor's property rights in the region, but also set regulatory constraints when evaluating and keeping parts of the installed base. In this instance, the commons perspective illustrates vividly the power asymmetries between different actors and the consequences that manifest for the installed base across time.

Similarly, in the English case study, after the systematic scrutiny of the National Audit Office and the Committee of Public Accounts on the NPfIT–including a public outcry from individual NHS healthcare professionals and executives–the NPfIT seems to be drifting into multiple trajectories away from the original plan of a centralized, national information infrastructure. Although N3 and the Spine will most probably remain (but perhaps adjusted)[1], the whole strategy behind the NPfIT has already been altered to one that is more local and needs-led than centrally controlled (Cruickshank, 2010; DoH, 2010; NAO, 2011). There are strong indications that 'interim' solutions being implemented at various Trusts across the NHS will be hard to replace as time goes by.

Reflecting on these findings, it becomes clear that the development and evolution of information infrastructures, like traditional commons, is embedded in deep-seated clashes of interest which are usually mediated by property right regimes, power asymmetries, and (in turn) the tribalism of participant communities.

To resolve these clashes of interest, key actors often attempt to negotiate solutions either by privatizing parts of the infrastructure (as in the case of CreteTech during the HEALTHnet pilot) or by centrally controlling the infrastructure (as in the latter phase in the Crete case study and in the English case study). However, both types of solutions involve significant issues that are difficult to resolve, such as: excessive administrative and policing costs in the case of centralized control (e.g. the various mechanisms and audit checks imposed by both the Greek and the English government in the management of contracts around the procurement of IT solutions), and negotiating costs over the transfer of benefits emanating from intellectual property (IP) rights in the case of private ownership (e.g. the dispute between the Regional Health Authorities of Crete and CreteTech over IP rights emanating from the I-EHR module in the Crete case study). Clearly, the challenges to the development of information infrastructures are multifaceted. The ways in which different communities adapt to these challenges are as unique as the circumstances in which they occur.

The following sections of this chapter will provide a detailed discussion of the challenges and various adaptation strategies that participant communities employ in the development of information infrastructures. This discussion is organized around two main themes observed in the two case studies: namely, the multiple levels through which an information infrastructure becomes developed, from national to local and across networks of communities of practice; and the ownership of information infrastructure resources and the need for contractual agreements.

MULTIPLE LEVELS OF INFORMATION INFRASTRUCTURE DEVELOPMENT

The first theme refers to challenges in devising appropriate institutions to account for the development of an information infrastructure at different levels. A key challenge will involve resolving potential conflicts that occur among stakeholders at different levels with respect to their perceptions of the infrastructure and the most appropriate use of offered services. The diversity of perceptions among stakeholders at different levels will often lead to a shift from (or a hybrid of) national-local control of the infrastructure, in an effort to develop new institutions for local management and enforcement.

For example, consider the difficulty and associated contestations between individual Trusts

and Connecting for Health in deciding whether to integrate national care records with local electronic patient records across the NHS. As discussed in the analysis of the English case study, conflicts occur when users at different levels do not have the same understanding of the characteristics of resources being accessed and exchanged and the associated risks of such exchange (e.g. breach of security, privacy of data).

As reported in traditional commons studies (Acheson & Brewer, 2003), initial conflicts over resource boundaries at a local level (such as patient data) and the inability of local users to defend these boundaries results in a shift of authority over a resource from a local to a higher level, usually national, but possibly global level. The conflicts are usually over areas along the boundaries of adjacent users of the resource. For example, consider the problems of one Trust sharing patient data with another Trust in the same cluster, including losing patients to one another, but also giving the opportunity to each Trust to scrutinize healthcare services offered by another. In this case, the challenge is to defend the boundaries and to reduce incentives for adjacent users to infringe upon the territory held by a particular community of users. In the NPfIT, this was to be achieved through smart cards, role-based access, and a number of information governance guidelines, all of which would secure the usage boundaries of each local Trust and each local user, while at the same time enforcing mechanisms of non-intrusion by other Trusts and users.

This example illustrates the evolving symbiotic relationship between state and local actors, neither of which could have managed resources effectively without the other. Connecting for Health would have had little political legitimacy to impose state-mandated regulations on local Trusts without their explicit agreement to give up some of their authority–hence the NPfIT Local Ownership Program (NLOP). In turn, local Trusts would have had little ability to control access to national databases in the face of changing technology without the enforcement and organizational ability of the state. Whether this hybrid system of national and local control will eventually take advantage of complementarities at different levels, however, remains to be seen. In fact, the current NPfIT structure seems to provide more incentives for local actors to place the priorities of their users over those of the rest of the NHS. For example, some Foundation Trusts' capacity to opt out of the NPfIT while meeting the necessary Treasury requirements and technical standards can cause significant problems to the interests of the NPfIT in the rest of the NHS.

On the other hand, in the Crete case study, the constant change of government and the introduction of repeated political reforms, illustrates how top-down conventional regulation and control provides classic incentive problems that can lead to conflicts. Such conflicts have been well reported in the commons literature, where the visibility and strength of specific interests have been found to shape the structure and participation in stakeholder forums, the content of the debate, and eventual outcomes in the governance of a commons (Anderson et al., 2002; Birner & Wittmer, 2003; Dolšak & Ostrom, 2003). Despite the fact that, in these cases, the legitimate tool for establishing political strength and gaining the support of diverse user communities is the state, the latter has also been found to exercise great control over local needs. This was also true in the Crete case study. For example, during the HEALTHnet pilot years, CreteTech struggled to gain legitimacy in the region of Crete by seeking the support of the government, as this was what the majority of users expected. With the Information Society initiative, however, the Greek government showed that it had no interest in dialogue, as new contracts for regional information infrastructures were to be developed top-down with limited participation from local authorities and users.

The two case studies show, each in their own light, the historical political legacies that have continued to be salient in information infrastruc-

ture development. These are legacies related to the nature of the policy-making processes, and public administration, as well as cultural characteristics which also have historical underpinnings. On the one hand, the English NHS has historically been torn by a complex relationship between the state and healthcare organizations (including doctors) whereby the latter were originally given more autonomy over services offered and management decisions, but were later stripped of that autonomy toward more centralized control and performance management (Greener, 2009). On the other hand, the Greek NHS, from its initiation, has been torn by corruption, lack of planning and structure, poor financing mechanisms, and industrial unrest among healthcare professionals (Ballas & Tsoukas, 2004). These national variations between the two case studies illustrate how the development of information infrastructures is a contested process that comes up against historical political legacies. These legacies can act as impediments and barriers to development, but there is no reason to doubt that they can also contribute to the eventual evolution of an information infrastructure at different levels (as historical studies in more conventional infrastructure development have also shown–see Chapter 1).

More importantly, the two case studies illustrate how an information infrastructure is developed not just at the national or local levels but also in hybrids of the two, as well as in networks of communities of practice that draw on expert as well as local, experience-based knowledge (cf. Ostrom, 1999). These different levels of information infrastructure development seem to signal the collapse of coordinated public-sector planning and administration. They reflect an abandonment of the (problematic) ideal of an integrated, standardized information infrastructure that can be characterized as having some kind of organic unity (cf. Graham & Marvin, 2001). Instead, these different levels of information infrastructure development have fuelled efforts toward a definition of ownership of information infrastructure resources to accommodate diverse (and often conflicting) needs.

OWNERSHIP OF INFORMATION INFRASTRUCTURE RESOURCES

The key resources of an information infrastructure are the information resources created, stored, and shared across different users. Defining the ownership of these information resources will usually involve challenges in devising regulative mechanisms, while managing the heterogeneity of interests involved.

Devising regulative mechanisms for information resources (i.e. assuring that rights are not exceeded and that the institutional rules governing rights are not violated) is challenged by the difficulties involved in ascribing the source of any particular information resource. That is, information resources are difficult to localize because of their ubiquity and mobility. By contrast, the impacts of more traditional (natural) resources such as fish or trees, though extensive, tend to be more localized. In turn, the extraction (including the source of extraction) of natural resources is more readily observable, something which makes monitoring easier (e.g. see Ostrom, 1990; Wade, 1994). With information resources, a disjoint between the source and the impact complicate the ability to penalize or enforce sanctions on the correct actor. Furthermore, regulation of an externality that is not confined within the borders of particular (usually local) authorities weakens the potential for enforcement. Even if one could make an accurate link between the source of information extraction and the impact, the rules set by one local authority cannot be imposed on authorities located elsewhere.

The English case study illustrates this challenge in the attempts of Connecting for Health to enforce security standards on the access and use of national care records. After an inquiry by the Committee of Public Accounts (CPA) in 2007 over

who would have access to locally and nationally held information and under what circumstances, it became evident that operational security over the use of national care records would be impossible primarily because of the "nature of the environment" in the NHS, as BT management noted (HC, 2007a, pp.39). BT management referred to the way NHS organizations are freely accessible to the public and IT security is unlikely to be closely monitored in busy hospital departments. As a consequence, a number of regulative mechanisms were to be introduced to address operational security concerns including a registration process for the production of smartcards based on role-based access, as well as the establishment of the legitimacy of the relationship between a patient and a user. However, soon after these mechanisms were announced there was a lot of criticism that in different localities where there is a lot of changing roles, it would be extremely difficult to deal with all the individual decisions that are being made as to who should have what role and what privilege (HC, 2007a, pp.40). Some healthcare professionals also noted that these regulative mechanisms interfered with their (more important) medical work and that, as a consequence, many would find ways of working around those mechanisms (HC, 2007a, pp.41).

The key to the challenge is that information resources hold the ability to cross boundaries and affect many types of institutions and stakeholders. In fact, even definitions of stakeholders become contested, for it is difficult to place clear boundaries on who is affected by the use of the resource. This is why regulative mechanisms such as those proposed in the NPfIT appear as the only way forward toward the acceptability of the overarching property rights regime as well as the equity of outcomes. However, this generally means that rights are allocated only to current users, usually based on existing levels of use, which favors some while generating problems for others (cf. Bowker & Star, 1999). In turn, if historic uses form the basis for allocating rights on a particular resource, those individuals or institutions that have used the resource in the past, gain control over that resource. Opposition may be generated in allowing some individuals or institutions to benefit in this way.

These findings illustrate how the characteristics of information resources (i.e. their ubiquity and mobility) have prompted greater attention to property rights over those resources. In fact, the apparent need for more regulative mechanisms to address possible security issues has increasingly raised concerns of ownership around information resources (e.g. patient data). One GP providing evidence to the CPA on the NPfIT noted (HC, 2007b, Ev182):

As advances in electronic hardware have permitted greater volumes of information and scanned images to be held for rapid retrieval, we have moved to the point where many practices in the UK have become either paper-light or even paper free. Throughout this period of transition we have become increasingly aware of the **issues of ownership** *of patient data. Many patients view their data as being their own, despite the protestations of successive Secretaries of State, either in print at the foot of our old Lloyd-George record cards, or through a tacit assumption that provision of electronic hardware confers* **intellectual property rights** *to the data held therein. This paradox is at the heart of the present anxiety about the right to withhold personal data from the State, which is not viewed in all quarters as entirely benign in its intentions, at all times. (emphasis added)*

This view was also held by many information and IT managers in the NHS who were found to be unconvinced that the balance between what was held centrally and what was held locally was appropriate (HC, 2007b, Ev84-85).

Contestations over issues to ownership were also observed in the Crete case study. Although these contestations varied from an IP rights over the development of the I-EHR module, to overall ownership over the various technologies imple-

mented in the region during the HEALTHnet pilot, the core of the conflicts was around who owned information resources (i.e. patient data) in the region through a conferred control of the information infrastructure.

Issues of ownership over patient data have recently been discussed by a panel of experts convened by the American Medical Informatics Association (AMIA) in relation to U.S. efforts to develop national electronic patient records. The panel discussed a full range of issues related to data transparency, consumer awareness and understanding, technical issues and challenges of identity management and user authentication, commercialization and sale of patient data, and oversight (Safran et al., 2007). The panel stressed the importance of "consensus-building meetings encompassing a broad constituency" that would focus on data access and control but *not* ownership (Safran et al., 2007, pp.6). The panel experts acknowledged that despite privacy regulations set by public policies such as the Health Insurance Portability and Accountability Act of 1996 (HIPAA), attention on property right solutions gives way to uses of health data that hinders patient privacy and erodes public trust. The panel identified the need "to explicitly address issues of health data access and control throughout data life cycles" and asserted that the "development and execution of patient choice options involving explicit authorization for use of their own data (opting in/opting out)" is perhaps the only way to mitigate patient privacy issues (Safran et al., 2007, pp.6). Further, the panel stressed the importance of leadership at state and national levels to mediate public-private interests towards "legal/regulatory remedies" on the use, abuse, and misuse of health data (Safran et al., 2007, pp.6).

Although not arguing directly for a contractual solution to the problem of health data creation and exchange, the panel's recommendations implicitly lead towards such a solution. In fact, it would be easier to authorize use of health data and to require informed consent through contractual agreements that are negotiated at the point of use at each health organization. In other words, the creation and exchange of health data would be agreed upon through contractual agreements at different levels of use. Such a solution would be most appropriate both to the Crete and the English case studies since it would offer strong incentives to accommodate the different stakeholders' best interests.

At the same time, however, individual contracts would have to be negotiated and agreed upon between the IT providers, the content providers (e.g. healthcare organizations), and the end users (e.g. doctors, patients). Such negotiations, as both case studies have illustrated, however, would depend on a number of factors shaping the capacity for collective action among these distinct interest groups.

For example, in the Crete case study, during the HEALTHnet pilot, the Regional Health Authorities of Crete and the majority of users expected and trusted the government to act as a neutral arbiter and regulator of contracts with IT providers, including CreteTech. However, after the completion of the Information Society program, there were concerns against the decision to award the contract to CompeTech because of the reluctance of the government to allow the local government and the local users to participate in the chosen technological solution. The government's increased role in the negotiation and regulation of the contract eroded the trust that less-powerful stakeholders such as CreteTech and the users once had in the government. Therefore, the success of negotiating contracts for regulating common resources will depend on whether the various parties can establish sufficient trust among themselves to enable cooperation and political consensus.

Yet heterogeneity of interests among actors may be so extensive that it is impossible to achieve cooperation or collective action even where it was once successful. For example, during its early phase, the HEALTHnet pilot was a great success with CreteTech receiving a European e-health award. However, the success of the pilot was never scaled up because of the reasons already discussed, including healthcare reforms at the national level affecting regional policy, IP rights disputes, and lack of trust. Such collective-action failures that compromise the information infrastructure may call for intervention at the central level in setting and enforcing desired outcomes, though methodologies for achieving those outcomes may be conducive to more localized decision making–a process which Ciborra and Hanseth (2001) have called drifting: more top-down control leading to more resistance and bottom-up alignment, which in turn leads to a perception of a need for more control and so on.

Another approach may rest with efforts to (re) build trust and to reduce interest heterogeneity and thereby pave the way for successful collective action. The NPfIT case suggests that great caution should be used in resorting to flexible mechanisms in regulating the development of an information infrastructure because of those mechanisms' potential to undermine cooperation and sharpen heterogeneity of interests, as in the examples of the contracts with Accenture and Fujitsu. In the end, though, property rights can get concentrated in the hands of a few powerful rights holders (as in the case of BT and CSC Alliance), causing equity concerns, as powerful property right holders have greater capacity to assume the transaction costs of tradable rights.

As the above discussion suggests, it is impossible to write down every possible contingency in a contract (Grossman & Hart, 1986; Hart & Moore, 1990). Rather, contracts are always incomplete in that there are contingencies left out (Han et al., 2004). Because of this, some stakeholders may attempt to behave opportunistically by withholding relevant information if they believe they can gain advantages by doing so. In turn, different stakeholders negotiating contract agreements will usually try to enforce complex contracts to protect themselves against contingencies and the opportunistic behaviour of the others–as both the

Crete and English case studies so vividly illustrate. Certainly full owners will have more bargaining power relative to authorized users (Bakos & Nault, 1997). However, the latter will always find ways to resist and work around extant property rights regimes, as in the examples of various Foundation Trusts in the English NHS opting for alternative systems than those proposed by either BT or CSC Alliance. Similar workarounds were observed in Crete during the HEALTHnet pilot, with wealthy hospitals in the region opting for alternative systems.

In summary, despite efforts to regulate and govern the development of information infrastructures, the complexity of the multilevel context of an information infrastructure and the heterogeneity of interests involved, often lead to outcomes that are contested with significant consequences for the infrastructure itself and the communities that depend on it. Complex contractual agreements in joint with government regulation are enforced in an effort to anticipate and address many of the contingencies that emerge in the process. However, the development of information infrastructures often leads to unintended consequences and drift (e.g. Bowker & Star, 1999; Ciborra & associates, 2001; Hanseth et al., 2006; Sahay et al., 2009).

CONCLUSION & IMPLICATIONS

Information infrastructures, due to their combined private and public good properties and associated network externalities, have traditionally justified or encouraged centralized control, usually from the state (Sahay et al., 2009), but also from corporations–in the case of corporate information infrastructures (Ciborra & associates, 2001).

One motivation for centralized control is the tendency to monopolize the development of information infrastructures. This tendency arises because many information infrastructures have the characteristics of a so-called natural monopoly, which are a combination of durable and immobile

investments and strong economies of scale. The economies of scale denote that the cheapest way to serve a community is with a single company (as in the example of BT for national IT services in the NPfIT). Moreover, the durability and immobility of the investments increase the risk for new entrants who seek to challenge the incumbent. Concern over monopoly often leads the state to either provide infrastructure services itself or to regulate the prices and quality of service of private infrastructure companies through complex contracts.

A second motivation for centralized control is that some types of information infrastructure generate benefits beyond those that accrue to its immediate users. For example, in national health information infrastructure projects such as those in England, Australia, Canada, and the USA, the key objective was to standardize the previously fragmented IT systems in healthcare organizations by introducing a national IT infrastructure while improving clinical governance and performance toward higher quality services (ACHI, 2001; DoH, 2002; NCVHS, 2001; NHIMAC, 2001). Thus, the benefits of the proposed information infrastructures were thought to cut through their immediate users and spill over to the whole population. In this context, information infrastructures are viewed as important ingredients to local economic development while ensuring universal access to a basic level of infrastructure services (e.g. healthcare) and the protection of equal opportunities for individual citizens. These developmental and equity considerations have led the state and other powerful actors (e.g. the World Health Organization) to promote the centralized procurement of information infrastructure development, so as to ensure better control over fees and costs, while cross-subsidizing lower tariffs for poorer user organizations. For example, more recently the World Health Organization has announced its commitment to the creation of national enterprise architectures intended to facilitate better access to universal, integrated infrastructural services across national health systems (Stansfield et al, 2008, pp.1, cited in Sahay et al., 2009, pp.401):

The enterprise architecture is the next level of elaboration of the [framework] where general lessons, standards, and processes can be aggregated and documented for knowledge sharing. A well-thought-out and collaboratively supported architecture enables systems to be built and implemented using consistent standards for data collection, management, reporting, and use. The components of the enterprise architecture will be adapted from or collaboratively generated with the global disease programs whose buy-in and endorsement is crucial to its success. Investments in health information systems can be aligned and leveraged around such architectures to build stronger core health information systems supporting better local health services management, health policy, and ultimately stronger health systems.

In addition to the above, a third motivation for centralized control in information infrastructure development is to reduce security concerns around the access and exchange of information resources. As evident from both case studies, access and exchange of patient data is a highly sensitive and contested issue due to the confidentiality of private information. Because security risks over the access of such sensitive information usually rests on non-users (i.e. patients), the government often feels justified in imposing a number of regulatory rules on their behalf (e.g. see the cases in Australia, Canada, and the USA–ACHI, 2001; NCVHS, 2001; NHIMAC, 2001). And even if security risks fall on users (e.g. doctor-patient confidentiality), the state intervention may be warranted if users are not sufficiently informed to judge the risks that they are being exposed to (see Kosseim & Brady, 2008, for the Canadian experience; & Safran et al., 2007, for the USA example).

Centralized control often leads to relationship-specific investments due to the inevitable conse-

quences of the socio-technical arrangements involved in information infrastructure development (Monteiro, 2001). These relationship-specific investments refer to various contractual agreements, which usually involve a mediating agency (e.g. the state) but they are negotiated between IT providers and individual user organizations. The mediating role of a previously centrally-controlling agency (e.g. the state) will come in the form of regulation, enforced when it is too costly or difficult for the IT providers and user organizations to reach individual agreements. Typically, the regulator will monitor the negotiations between the IT providers and the users because of the possibility that one may take advantage of its position.

However, the involvement of the regulator may complicate even more the drafting of these contractual agreements. In effect, the regulator becomes a third party to an already complicated contractual relationship and may be influenced by special interests towards specific directions (Gómez-Ibáñez, 2003). Concerns about the regulator being influenced by special interests were raised in both the Crete case study (by CreteTech on failing to win a contract during the Information Society competition) and the English case study (by Fujitsu on delivering services and products beyond the original contract agreements). In both cases, the special interests involved had a more direct impact on the users than either the state or the IT providers, primarily by causing disruptions on, and uncertainty on the future of, the users' work practices. That is, on the one hand, there were legal ways for the state to influence IT providers, but, on the other, IT providers also typically had stronger incentives and more resources to press their cases than the users did[2]. In effect, this becomes a problem of collective action whereby it is difficult to organize a large heterogeneous group to pursue policies of collective benefit (Olson, 1965), while also balancing the shift of power between the state and private companies.

The complex institutional arrangements aimed at better governance of an information infrastructure and the efforts of diverse user communities toward collective action have increased the capacity for decentralized coordination (as opposed to centralized control). The outcome (as in the NPfIT case) has been a pronounced splintering of information infrastructures–i.e. their *vertical*, *horizontal*, and *virtual* fragmentation (Graham & Marvin, 2001). This has also meant service tiering, with wealthy user communities contracting their own systems and receiving premium, highly reliable services (e.g. Foundation Trusts), while poor user communities must rely on slow deployment of services or complete exclusion from decisions around infrastructural development (e.g. most hospital trusts in the NHS). Evidence of such splintering can also be found in the USA (Adler-Milstein et al., 2008), but also in India (Sahay et al., 2009), and other developing countries (Braa et al., 2004).

The consequence of this splintering of information infrastructures is the emergence of multiple layers of infrastructure spaces, constructed for economically affluent users, which are increasingly separated and partitioned from surrounding spaces–spaces where basic functionality and connections may become increasingly problematic. In effect, while information infrastructures are intended to integrate and standardize previously fragmented and isolated organizational and computer-based information systems, their splintering achieves the exact opposite result. In turn, less economically affluent users will lag behind important infrastructure investments and will eventually be excluded from access to infrastructure services altogether, as in the case of less economically affluent and institutionally powerless hospitals in the NHS (cf. Castells, 2010).

Access to infrastructure services will never be institutionally and politically unified, even among more economically affluent users. Powerful coalitions of users, IT providers, and policymakers often meet internal as well as external resistance. For example, in the Crete case study, during the Information Society initiative, the CompeTech solution was resisted by both the Regional Health Authorities, different groups of users (especially GPs in primary healthcare centres), and CreteTech. Their resistance might not have been forceful, but as recent data show, their silent resistance (in the form of non-participation) may have serious implications for the sustainability of the CompeTech solution.

Certainly, because of the increased interdependencies between different nodes across an information infrastructure, including the network externalities that accrue from such interdependencies, connectivity will continue to be maintained whether through standardized services or through "patchwork interfaces" (Ellingsen & Monteiro, 2003). In this context, an information infrastructure becomes saturated by different, sometimes non-interoperable information systems that later need to be 'patched up,' interfaced, and made to interconnect. As a consequence, strategies and policies to control the boundaries of infrastructure services become impossible, as the sociotechnical fluidity created by the resistance against dominant forms of information infrastructure development begins to break down the separate structures which powerful coalitions strive to enforce. Instead, the diversity of organizational practices offers channels through which both the logic of centralized control and the logic of splintering information infrastructures can be resisted and transgressed (Ciborra, 2007; Hanseth et al., 2006; Osei-Joehene & Ciborra, 2007; Rolland & Monteiro, 2002, 2007). Such practices tend to resist any normalizing attempt by powerful actors and may shape the construction of spaces in between the two dominant logics; such practices can serve to balance the extreme tendencies of the two dominant logics with more synergistic development and governance strategies.

Beyond Engagement and Participation: Co-Production and Synergy in Information Infrastructure Development

The above synthesis of the findings from the two case studies and the analogies drawn with other regional and national information infrastructures point to the realization that the latter cannot rely on a single great architect (e.g. the state, a single IT provider) nor on totally distributed, locally-driven processes. Rather, information infrastructures should be developed through co-production and synergy across all stakeholders.

Engagement and participation in IT development has long been pioneered through participatory design approaches (Beyer & Holtzblatt, 1998; Ehn & Kyng, 1991; Greenbaum & Kyng, 1991; Merkel et al., 2004; Muller, 2002; Schuler & Namioka, 1993). Despite their merits, such approaches are often undertaken without considering the political and cultural context within which participation is sought to take place (but see Enid Mumford's ETHICS approach, Mumford, 1983, 1995)[3]. "Participatory processes have been increasingly approached as technical, management solutions to what are basically political issues" (Gujit & Shah, 1998, pp.3). In particular, there are clear cases where the culture and politics of an organization prevent participative processes from producing truly participative outcomes by constraining who can say what and how within any kind of group activity (Biggs & Smith, 1998). In fact, many organizations often feel forced to create an impetus for participation even if they perceive it to be contextually non-viable, in order to please certain powerful interests (e.g. those who are funding a project) (Heeks, 1999).

In addition, participatory design projects have varied with respect to *how* and *why* workers will and should participate (Kensing & Blomberg, 1998). At one end of the spectrum, worker participation is limited to providing designers with access to workers' skills and experiences. At the other end of the spectrum workers participate, not only because their skills and experience are considered valuable, but also because their interests in the design outcome are acknowledged and supported. These two extremes point to the fact that workers usually have little or no control over the design process or its outcome. Rather projects are usually initiated at the behest of managers or design professionals. Workers are asked to participate in those aspects of the project where their input is viewed as valuable (e.g. description of current work practices and testing/evaluation of technology) but left out of most of the decisions that are technology-related. In many participatory design projects it is not even possible for all those affected by the design effort to fully participate. This limited level of participation is viewed by many participatory design researchers as insufficient to meet the goals of a participatory design project. What is missing is a commitment to the possibility of real worker influence over the direction and outcome of the IT development effort, as well as its future sustainability (Bødker, 1996).

Research in traditional commons has proposed an alternative approach to development that aims at addressing some of the aforementioned issues. Unsatisfied with the dominant theories of urban governance underlying policy recommendations of massive centralization, commons scholars argued that, the production of a commons is difficult without the active participation of those supposedly benefiting from the commons. Thus, they developed the term "co-production" to describe the potential relationship that could exist between the 'producer' (e.g. the state) and 'clients' (e.g. users of the commons) (Ostrom, 1996). Co-production is a way through which synergy can occur between what a government does and what citizens do. Ostrom (1996, pp.1073) explains:

The "regular" producer of education, health, or infrastructure services is most frequently a government agency. Whether the regular producer is the only producer of these goods and services depends both on the nature of the good or service itself and on the incentives that encourage the active participation of others. All public goods and services are potentially produced by the regular producer and by those who are frequently referred to as the client. The term "client" is a passive term. Clients are acted upon. Co-production implies that citizens can play an active role in producing public goods and services of consequence to them.

Through this definition, it becomes evident that, co-production moves beyond engagement and participation toward co-governance of a development project (Bode, 2007; Brandsen & Pestoff, 2006). To understand this difference, Ostrom (1996) suggests we break down the production of a good or service into its constituent parts, i.e. its production functions and associated incentive structures.

Ostrom (1996, pp.1079-1080) uses the example of waste disposal, and offers two production functions toward achieving the former: sending a public truck on a regular route to collect garbage or recyclable materials versus requiring that citizens take garbage or recyclables to a designated location. She argues that the choice over the two functions depends on the wage rate paid to public officials as compared to the opportunity costs facing citizens for spending their time in transport. If the wage rate of public officials is lower than the opportunity cost of citizens then the most efficient form of production is located entirely in the public sector. Maximum output could be achieved entirely by the public officials, assuming they are fully motivated to work up to their capacity. Alternatively, if the opportunity costs of citizens were comparably lower than the wage rate of public officials, maximum output could be entirely produced by citizens alone, again assuming full motivation to perform to capacity. In a third scenario, when the inputs from public officials and citizens are complementary, output is best produced by some combination of input from both sources (i.e. varying degrees of oppor-

tunity costs for citizens and wage rates for public officials). Co-production, it is argued, offers very clear possibilities with potentially better (higher) benefits for both 'regular' producers and 'clients.'

Arguably, though, co-production will not be possible for all development projects. Even in situations where it is possible, there are challenges in inducing successful co-production (Mayo & Moore, 2002; Taylor, 2003).

The first key challenge is that co-production may dilute accountability, blurring the boundaries between the public and private agencies acting as 'regular' producers and the 'clients.' Yet there is a paradox here–the very act of participation in governance can better clarify the lines of accountability and responsibility (Mayo & Moore, 2002). Moreover, as co-production almost always means a redistribution of power among stakeholders, the very process of moving to greater co-production is necessarily highly political and calls into question participatory processes (Baiocchi, 2003).

The second key challenge is who participates in co-production and why. There is much evidence that command over community resources and social capital are disproportionately in the hands of better-off members of the community (Taylor, 2003), and some communities do not always want to run their own services (Goetz & Gaventa, 2001). This evidence highlights the need to explore the balance of costs and benefits experienced by co-producing users and communities. This balance may mean that, for many users and citizens, co-production will not be appealing.

Finally, co-production will usually be met by professional resistance. Many professional groups are found to assume that gains in status among co-producing clients might come at their expense (Crawford, Rutter, & Thelwall, 2004). Professional groups are often reluctant to hand over discretion to service users and their support networks, not trusting them to behave responsibly (Barnes et al., 1999), and often they lack the skills to work closely with users and communities (Schachter & Aliaga, 2003).

Exactly because of the aforementioned challenges and the need to support multiple (instead of bilateral) relationships among different stakeholders, it has been argued that, inducing co-production is more likely to be successful if polycentric governance structures (rather than monocentric or highly centralized) are instituted. A polycentric governance structure offers opportunities to organize not one, but many, governing units, with each of those units being able to exercise independent authority to make and enforce rules within a specified area for particular policy areas (see McGinnis, 1999; Ostrom, Schroeder, & Wynne, 1993). The key advantage of a polycentric governance structure is that, rules can be written in a general form that can then be tailored to local circumstances. In other words, many more actions tailored to local arenas can be authorized in a polycentric governance structure than in a monocentric structure that tries to establish uniform rules for all settings (Ostrom, 1996).

The development of information infrastructures can learn from the experiences gained from more traditional commons studies, specifically in relation to efforts to induce co-production. The next chapter explores in more detail the ways by which co-production can be successfully instituted, by examining a set of principles toward a polycentric governance structure for information infrastructure development.

REFERENCES

Acheson, J., & Brewer, J. (2003). Changes in the territorial system of the Maine lobster industry: Implications for management. In Dolšak, N., & Ostrom, E. (Eds.), *The commons in the new millennium: Challenges and adaptations* (pp. 37–60). Cambridge, MA: MIT Press.

Adler-Milstein, J., McAfee, A. P., Bates, D. W., & Jha, A. K. (2008). The state of regional health information organizations: Current activities and financing. *Health Affairs, 27*(1), 60–69. doi:10.1377/hlthaff.27.1.w60

Advisory Committee on Health Infostructure (ACHI). (2001). *Tactical plan for a pan-Canadian health infostructure, 2001 update*. Ottawa, Canada: Office of Health and the Information Highway, Health Canada.

Anderson, C. L., Nugent, R. E., & Locker, L. B. (2002). Microcredit, social capital, and common-pool resources. *World Development, 30*(1), 95–105. doi:10.1016/S0305-750X(01)00096-1

Baiocchi, G. (2003). Participation, activism, and politics: The Pôrto Alegre experiment. In Fung, A., & Wright, E. O. (Eds.), *Deepening democracy: Institutional innovations in empowered participatory governance* (pp. 45–76). London, UK: Verso.

Bakos, J. Y., & Nault, B. R. (1997). Ownership and investment in electronic networks. *Information Systems Research, 8*(4), 321–341. doi:10.1287/isre.8.4.321

Ballas, A., & Tsoukas, H. (2004). Measuring nothing: The case of the Greek national health system. *Human Relations, 57*(6), 661–690. doi:10.1177/0018726704044951

Barnes, M., Harrison, S., Mort, M., Shardlow, P., & Wistow, G. (1999). The new management of community care: Users groups, citizenship and co-production. In Stoker, G. (Ed.), *The new management of British local governance* (pp. 112–127). Houndmills, UK: Macmillan.

Benkler, Y. (2006). *The wealth of networks*. New Haven, CT: Yale University Press.

Beyer, H., & Holtzblatt, K. (1998). *Contextual design*. San Francisco: Morgan Kaufmann.

Birner, R., & Wittmer, H. (2003). Using social capital to create political capital: How do local communities gain political influence? A theoretical approach and empirical evidence from Thailand. In Dolšak, N., & Ostrom, E. (Eds.), *The commons in the new millennium: Challenges and adaptations* (pp. 291–334). Cambridge, MA: MIT Press.

Bode, I. (2007). Co-governance within networks and the nonprofit-forprofit divide. In Pestoff, V., & Brandsen, T. (Eds.), *Co-production: The third sector and the delivery of public services* (pp. 81–98). London, UK: Routledge.

Bødker, S. (1996). Creating conditions for participation: Conflicts and resources in systems development. *Human-Computer Interaction, 11*(3), 215–236. doi:10.1207/s15327051hci1103_2

Bowker, G., & Star, S. L. (1999). *Sorting things out–Classification and its consequences*. Cambridge, MA: MIT Press.

Brandsen, T., & Pestoff, V. (2006). Co-production, the third sector and the delivery of public services. *Public Management Review, 8*(4), 593–601. doi:10.1080/14719030601022874

Brennan, S. (2007). The biggest computer programme in the world ever! How's it going? *Journal of Information Technology, 22*(3), 202–211. doi:10.1057/palgrave.jit.2000104

Ciborra, C. U. (Ed.), & associates (2001). *From control to drift: The dynamics of corporate information infrastructures*. Oxford, UK: Oxford University Press.

Ciborra, C. U. (2007). When is an Intranet? The topsy-turvy unfolding of a web-based information system. In Hanseth, O., & Ciborra, C. (Eds.), *Risk, complexity and ICT* (pp. 183–210). London, UK: Edward Elgar.

Ciborra, C. U., & Hanseth, O. (2001). Introduction. In Ciborra, C. U. (Ed.), *From control to drift: The dynamics of corporate information infrastructures* (pp. 1–14). Oxford, UK: Oxford University Press.

Crawford, M., Rutter, D., & Thelwall, S. (2004). *User involvement in change management: A review of the literature*. London, UK: Imperial College.

Cruickshank, J. (2010). *Fixing NHS IT: A plan of action for a new government*. Retrieved March 1, 2011, from http://www.2020health.org/2020health/research/nhsit.html

Department of Health (DoH). (2002). *Delivering 21st century IT support for the NHS–National strategic programme*. London, UK: Author.

Department of Health (DoH). (2010). *The future of the national programme for IT*. London, UK: Author.

Dolšak, N., & Ostrom, E. (2003). The challenges of the commons. In Dolšak, N., & Ostrom, E. (Eds.), *The commons in the new millennium: Challenges and adaptations* (pp. 3–34). Cambridge, MA: MIT Press.

Ehn, P., & Kyng, M. (1991). Cardboard computers: Mocking-it-up of hands-on the future. In Greenbaum, J., & Kyng, M. (Eds.), *Design at work* (pp. 169–196). Hillsdale, NJ: Erlbaum.

Ehn, P., & Löwgren, J. (1997). Design for quality-in-use: Human–computer interaction meets information systems development. In Helander, M., Landauer, T. K., & Prabhu, P. (Eds.), *Handbook of human–Computer interaction* (pp. 299–313). Amsterdam, Netherlands: Elsevier.

Ellingsen, G., & Monteiro, E. (2003). A patchwork planet. Integration and cooperation in hospitals. *Computer Supported Cooperative Work, 12*(1), 71–95. doi:10.1023/A:1022469522932

Goetz, A. M., & Gaventa, J. (2001). *Bringing citizen voice and client focus into service delivery*. Institute of Development Studies, Working Paper No. 138. Retrieved November 24, 2011, from http://www.ids.ac.uk/go/idspublication/bringing-citizen-voice-and-client-focus-into-service-delivery

Gómez-Ibáñez, J. A. (2003). *Regulating infrastructure: Monopoly, contracts, and discretion*. Cambridge, MA: Harvard University Press.

Graham, S., & Marvin, S. (2001). *Splintering urbanism: Networked infrastructures, technological mobilities and the urban condition*. New York, NY: Routledge. doi:10.4324/9780203452202

Greenbaum, J., & Kyng, M. (Eds.). (1991). *Design at work: Cooperative design of computer systems*. Hillsdale, NJ: Erlbaum.

Greener, I. (2009). *Healthcare in the UK: Understanding continuity and change*. Bristol, UK: Policy Press.

Grossman, S. J., & Hart, O. D. (1986). The costs and benefits of ownership: A theory of vertical and lateral integration. *The Journal of Political Economy, 39*, 691–719. doi:10.1086/261404

Han, K., Kauffman, R. J., & Nault, B. R. (2004). Information exploitation and interorganizational systems ownership. *Journal of Management Information Systems, 21*(2), 109–135.

Hanseth, O. (2001). The economics of standards. In Ciborra, C. U. (Ed.), *From control to drift: The dynamics of corporate information infrastructures* (pp. 56–70). Oxford, UK: Oxford University Press.

Hanseth, O., Jacucci, E., Grisot, M., & Aanestad, M. (2006). Reflexive standardization: Side effects and complexity in standard making. *Management Information Systems Quarterly, 30*, 563–581.

Hart, O., & Moore, J. (1990). Property rights and the nature of the firm. *The Journal of Political Economy, 98*(6), 1119–1158. doi:10.1086/261729

Heeks, R. (1999). The tyranny of participation in information systems: Learning from development projects. *Developing informatics: Working paper series*. Manchester, UK: Institute for Development Policy and Management, University of Manchester.

House of Commons (HC). (2007a). The electronic patient record. *Sixth Report of Session 2006-07, Vol I - Written Evidence*, HC 422-I. House of Commons, Health Committee. Retrieved February 24, 2011, from http://www.publications.parliament.uk/pa/cm200607/cmselect/cmhealth/422/42202.htm

House of Commons (HC). (2007b). The electronic patient record. *Sixth Report of Session 2006-07, Vol II - Written Evidence*, HC 422-II. House of Commons, Health Committee. Retrieved February 24, 2011, from http://www.publications.parliament.uk/pa/cm200607/cmselect/cmhealth/422/42202.htm

Kensing, F., & Blomberg, J. (1998). Participatory design: Issues and concerns. *Computer Supported Cooperative Work, 7*(3-4), 167–185. doi:10.1023/A:1008689307411

Kosseim, P., & Brady, M. (2008). Policy by procrastination: Secondary use of electronic health records for health research purposes. *McGill Journal of Law and Health, 2*, 5–45.

Mayo, E., & Moore, H. (Eds.). (2002). *Building the mutual state: Findings from the virtual thinktank*. London, UK: New Economics Foundation/Mutuo.

McGinnis (Ed.). (1999). *Polycentric governance and development: Readings from the workshop in political theory and policy analysis*. Ann Arbor, MI: Univ. of Michigan Press.

Merkel, C., Xiao, L., Farooq, U., Ganoe, U. H., Lee, R., Carroll, J. M., & Rosson, M. B. (2004). Participatory design in community computing contexts: Tales from the field. In *Proceedings of the Eighth Conference on Participatory Design: Artful Integration: Interweaving Media, Materials and Practices-Volume 1*, (pp. 1-10).

Muller, M. J. (2002). Participatory design: The third space in HCI. In Jacko, J. A., & Sears, A. (Eds.), *The human computer interaction handbook: Fundamentals, evolving technologies and emerging applications* (pp. 1051–1068). Mahwah, NJ: Lawrence Erlbaum.

Mumford, E. (1983). *Designing Human Systems–The ETHICS Method*. Manchester, UK: Manchester Business School.

Mumford, E. (1995). *Effective systems design and requirements analysis: The ETHICS approach*. Basingstoke, UK: Macmillan.

Mumford, E. (2006). The story of socio-technical design: Reflections on its successes, failures and potential. *Information Systems Journal, 16*, 317–342. doi:10.1111/j.1365-2575.2006.00221.x

National Committee on Vital and Health Statistics (NCVHS). (2001). *Information for health: A strategy for building the national health information infrastructure*. Washington, DC: U.S. Department of Health and Human Services.

National Health Information Management Advisory Council (NHIMAC). (2001). *Health online: A health information action plan for Australia* (2nd ed.). Australian Institute of Health and Welfare.

Osei-Joehene, D., & Ciborra, C. U. (2007). The duality of risk and the evolution of danger in global ICT integration. In Hanseth, O., & Ciborra, C. (Eds.), *Risk, complexity and ICT* (pp. 154–182). London, UK: Edward Elgar.

Ostrom, E. (1990). *Governing the commons: The evolution of institutions for collective action*. New York, NY: Cambridge University Press.

Ostrom, E. (1996). Crossing the great divide: Co-production, synergy and development. *World Development, 24*(6), 1073–1087. doi:10.1016/0305-750X(96)00023-X

Ostrom, E. (1999). Coping with tragedies of the commons. *Annual Review of Political Science, 2*, 493–535. doi:10.1146/annurev.polisci.2.1.493

Ostrom, E., Schroeder, L., & Wynne, S. (1993). *Institutional incentives and sustainable development: Infrastructure policies in perspective*. Boulder, CO: Westview Press.

Pain, D., Owen, J., Franklin, I., & Green, E. (1993). Human-centred systems design: A review of trends within the broader systems development context. In Green, E., Owen, J., & Pain, D. (Eds.), *Gendered by design? Information technology and office systems*. London, UK: Taylor & Francis.

Ritter, T. (2010, February 10). Fujitsu settlement of NPfIT dispute unlikely in next year, says Cerner. *Computer Weekly.com*. Retrieved February 18, 2011, from http://www.computerweekly.com/blogs/public-sector/2010/02/fujitsu-settlement-of-npfit-di.html

Rolland, K. H., & Monteiro, E. (2002). Balancing the local and the global in infrastructural information systems. *The Information Society, 18*(2), 87–100. doi:10.1080/01972240290075020

Rolland, K. H., & Monteiro, E. (2007). When 'perfect' integration leads to increasing risks: The case of an integrated information system in a global company. In Hanseth, O., & Ciborra, C. (Eds.), *Risk, complexity and ICT* (pp. 97–117). London, UK: Edward Elgar.

Safran, C., Bloomrosen, M., Hammond, M., Labkoff, S., Markel-Fox, S., Tang, P., & Detmer, D. (2007). Toward a national framework for the secondary use of health data: An American Medical Informatics Association white paper. *Journal of the American Medical Informatics Association, 14*(1), 1–9. doi:10.1197/jamia.M2273

Sahay, S., Monteiro, E., & Aanestad, M. (2009). Configurable politics and asymmetric integration: Health e-infrastructures in India. *Journal of the Association for Information Systems, 10*(5), 399–414.

Schachter, H. L., & Aliaga, M. (2003). Educating administrators to interact with citizens: A research note. *Public Organization Review, 3*(2), 191–200. doi:10.1023/A:1024292931120

Schuler, D., & Namioka, A. (Eds.). (1993). *Participatory design: Principles and practices.* Hillsdale, NJ: Erlbaum.

Spohrer, J., & Riecken, D. (2006). Services science. *Communications of the ACM, 49*(7), 31–32.

Stansfield, S., Orobaton, N., Lubinski, D., Uggowitzer, S., & Mwanyika, H. (2008). The case for a national health information system architecture: A missing link to guiding national development and implementation. Paper presented at the *Making the ehealth connection*, Bellagio, Italy, July 13–August 8, 2008.

Taylor, M. (2003). *Public policy in the community.* Houndmills, UK: Palgrave Macmillan.

Vargo, S. L., & Lusch, R. E. (2004). Evolving to a new dominant logic for marketing. *Journal of Marketing, 68*(1), 1–17. doi:10.1509/jmkg.68.1.1.24036

Wade, R. (1994). *Village republics: Economic conditions for collective action in South India.* Oakland, CA: ICS Press.

Weill, P., & Broadbent, M. (1998). *Leveraging the new infrastructure: How market leaders capitalize on information.* Boston, MA: Harvard Business School Press.

Weill, P., & Ross, J. (2004). *IT governance: How top performers manage IT decision rights for superior results.* Boston, MA: Harvard Business School Press.

ADDITIONAL READING

Abbate, J. (1999). *Inventing the Internet.* Cambridge, MA: MIT Press.

Aldrich, H. E. (1999). *Organizations evolving.* London, UK: Sage Publications.

Arias, E. G., Eden, H., Fischer, G., Gorman, A., & Scharff, E. (2000). Transcending the individual human mind–creating shared understanding through collaborative design. *ACM Transactions on Computer-Human Interaction, 7*(1), 84–113. doi:10.1145/344949.345015

Baldwin, R., Hood, C., & Scott, C. (1998). *Socio-legal reader on regulation.* Oxford, UK: Oxford University Press.

BCS/RAE. (2004). *The challenges of complex IT projects.* British Computer Society and Royal Academy on Engineering Report. Retrieved March 1, 2011, from http://www.bcs.org/content/conWebDoc/1167

Beniger, J. (1986). *The control revolution: Technological and economic origins of the information society.* Cambridge, MA: Harvard University Press.

Bijker, W., Hughes, T., & Pinch, T. (1987). *The social construction of technological systems.* Cambridge, MA: MIT Press.

Carmel, E., Whitaker, R., & George, J. (1993). PD and joint application design: A transatlantic comparison. *Communications of the ACM, 36*(4), 40–48. doi:10.1145/153571.163265

Cave, J., Marsden, C., Klautzer, L., Levitt, R., van Oranje-Nassau, C., Rabinovich, L., & Robinson, N. (2007). *Responsibility in the global information society: Towards multi-stakeholder governance*. TR-472. Retrieved February 23, 2011, from http://www.rand.org/pubs/technical_reports/TR472/

Chisholm, D. (1989). *Coordination without hierarchy: Informal structures in multi-organizational systems*. Berkeley, CA: University of California Press.

Clement, A., & Van den Besselaar, P. (1993). A retrospective look at PD projects. *Communications of the ACM, 36*(4), 29–37. doi:10.1145/153571.163264

Dietz, T., Ostrom, E., & Stern, P. (2003). The struggle to govern the commons. *Science, 302*, 1907–1912. doi:10.1126/science.1091015

Dourish, P. (2001). *Where the action is: The foundations of embodied interaction*. Cambridge, MA: MIT Press.

Dutton, W. H. (Ed.). (1996). *Information and communication technologies: Visions and realities*. Oxford, UK: Oxford University Press.

Edwards, P. N., Jackson, S. J., Bowker, G. C., & Knobel, C. P. (2007). Understanding infrastructure: Dynamics, tensions, and design. Report of a Workshop on *History & theory of infrastructure: Lessons for new scientific cyberinfrastructures*. NSF, Office of Cyberinfrastructure.

Fitzgerald, B. (2000). System development methodologies: The problem of tenses. *Information Technology & People, 13*(3), 17–185. doi:10.1108/09593840010377617

Gerstner, L. V. Jr. (2002). *Who says elephants can't dance? Inside IBM's historic turnaround*. New York, NY: Harper Business.

Grabowski, M., & Roberts, K. H. (1996). Human and organizational error in large scale systems. *IEEE Transactions on Systems, Man, and Cybernetics. Part A, Systems and Humans, 26*(1), 2–16. doi:10.1109/3468.477856

Janis, I. (1983). *Groupthink*. Boston, MA: Houghton Mifflin.

Janssen, M. (2003). Sunk-cost effects and vulnerability to collapse in ancient societies. *Current Anthropology, 44*(5), 722–728. doi:10.1086/379261

Jervis, R. (1997). *System effects: Complexity in political and social life*. Princeton, NJ: Princeton University Press.

Keen, P. W. (1991). *Shaping the future: Business redesign through information technology*. Boston, MA: Harvard Business School Press.

Kooiman, J. (2003). *Governing as governance*. London, UK: Sage.

Lyytinen, K., & Robey, D. (1999). Learning failure in information systems development. *Information Systems Journal, 9*(2), 85–101. doi:10.1046/j.1365-2575.1999.00051.x

Mackay, C. (1993). *Extraordinary popular delusions and the madness of crowds*. New York, NY: Barnes and Noble.

Miller, D. (1993). The architecture of simplicity. *Academy of Management Review, 18*(1), 116–138.

Olson, G. M., Malone, T. W., & Smith, J. B. (Eds.). (2001). *Coordination theory and collaboration technology*. Mahwah, NJ: Lawrence Erlbaum Associates.

Ostrom, E., Gardner, R., & Walker, J. (1994). *Rules, games, and common-pool resources*. Ann Arbor, MI: University of Michigan Press.

Raghvendra, R. C., & Sahay, S. (2006). Computer-based health information systems-projects for computerization or health management? Empirical experiences from India. In Gascó-Hernandez, M., Equiza-López, F., & Acevedo-Ruiz, M. (Eds.), *Information communication technologies and human development: Opportunities and challenges* (pp. 2209–2231). Hershey, PA: Idea Group Publishing.

Starbuck, W. H., & Farjoun, M. (2005). *Organization at the limit: Lessons from the Columbia disaster*. London, UK: Blackwell Publishing.

Sterman, J. (2000). *Business dynamics: Systems thinking and modelling for a complex world*. New York, NY: McGraw-Hill/Irwin.

Tainter, J. (1988). *The collapses of complex societies*. Cambridge, MA: Cambridge University Press.

Turner, W., Bowker, G., Gasser, L., & Zackland, M. (2006). Information infrastructures for distributed collective practices. *Computer Supported Cooperative Work*, 1–18.

ENDNOTES

[1] The Spine itself has been criticised as "an ill-conceived venture in that it does not support adequately the legal framework of the national health service in the UK, nor does it have parallels overseas" (HC, 2007a, pp.101).

[2] The NHS is still in a court dispute with Fujitsu with the latter claiming up to £700 million fees in compensation.

[3] Even Mumford's ETHICS approach has been criticized for not being truly participative or democratic, but rather too managerial (Ehn & Löwgren, 1997; Pain et al., 1993). This criticism was acknowledged by Mumford herself in a paper written towards the end of her life (Mumford, 2006), where she

recognized that the humanistic values and democratic ethos of the sociotechnical approach to IT development was ill-suited to the more punishing business context of the 1980s and 1990s, when companies chose methods such as lean production and business process reengineering to gain competitive advantage and maximize profit and growth opportunities. Human values and democratic processes seemed more of an obstacle to this business context and were thus abandoned.

While acknowledging the criticisms to the sociotechnical approach, however, Mumford (2006) points out that, since the early 2000s, there has been a dramatic change from hierarchical organizations to networked organizations and decentralized structures as a result of new technological developments. For example, the open software movement has provided a powerful paradigm for opening up access to proprietary software systems and applications, thus allowing people to add, mix, edit, and adapt code for all kinds of purposes not intended by the original developers. In addition, the advent of Web 2.0 technologies and services allow for the emergence of new forms of social media and "open innovation." These changes have led to great resistance to structured–non-human oriented–business objectives, poor economic gains, and conflicting organizational directions (see Chapter 8 in this book).

Mumford (2006) describes two alternative scenarios of how this complexity can be effectively managed in the future, as proposed by the British Department of Trade and Industry (DTI). In the first scenario, "networks of self-employed individuals come together via the internet to work on *common* projects based on temporary contracts" (Mumford, 2006, pp.335, emphasis added). In this scenario, because many individuals will be self-employed, they will have to become skilled at promoting themselves, running their own lives, and protecting their knowledge. People will not be seeking jobs, but will be seeking customers to whom they will sell their skills and knowledge. In the second scenario–which is strongly linked to the first–"stable, relatively large organizations…prosper through the collection of knowledge. This means they place a high value on the development of knowledge, and they are anxious to keep the employees who possess this" (Mumford, 2006, pp. 336). In both scenarios, Mumford (2006) is essentially referring to the now booming service economy in which intangibility, exchange processes, and relationships are central (Vargo & Lusch, 2004). In the service economy, services are defined as "the application of specialized competences (knowledge and skills) through deeds, processes, and performances for the benefit of another entity or the entity itself" whether that means an individual or an organization (Vargo & Lusch, 2004, pp.2). Further, it is argued that new information and communication technologies have helped create products with a higher service component than in previous decades, as in recent examples of software-as-a-service offerings by companies such as IBM (Spohrer & Riecken, 2006).

The success of these service-oriented or knowledge-based arrangements depends on the creation of secure communications structures and also on the development of human relationships based on trust. In turn, systems of social support and protection such as community groups, professional associations, or new kinds of trade unions will need to be created and established (Mumford, 2006). It is argued that these systems of social support will pave new avenues of sociotechnical development.

Mumford's arguments resonate with a commons-approach to IT development while supporting human values and democratic processes, although she does not directly reference any studies from the commons literature. The key difference between Mumford's arguments (and associated ETHICS principles–see Mumford 1983, 1995) is that, a commons-approach does not require participants to have skilled knowledge (including being a member of a skilled professional or unionist group), but rather it focuses on more fundamental issues of collective action toward co-production (discussed in this Chapter of the book) and polycentric governance structures (discussed in Chapter 7).

Chapter 7
The Governance of Information Infrastructures

ABSTRACT

This chapter continues on from the discussion in Chapter 6 by exploring the notions of co-production and polycentric governance structures in the development of information infrastructures. Drawing on Ostrom's (1990) original principles toward commons governance, as well as more recent developments from commons studies (Anderies et al., 2004; Hess & Ostrom, 2007), this chapter builds on and extends extant research on the governance of information infrastructures and concludes with implications for further research into IT governance through a commons perspective.

INTRODUCTION

Information technology (IT) governance has traditionally been tied to decision making processes toward the effective procurement of IT resources (Dean & Sharfman, 1996; Devaraj & Kohli, 2003; Sambamurthy & Zmud, 1999; Weill & Ross, 2004). Decisions are made across different domains including business strategy, IT architecture and infrastructure, business application needs, and IT investment prioritization options

DOI: 10.4018/978-1-4666-1622-6.ch007

(Weill & Ross, 2004). In each of these domains, stakeholder constituencies take different lead roles and responsibilities for IT decision making, and each generates different benefits and challenges (Weill & Ross, 2004).

Traditionally, three configurations have been distinguished for IT governance (Sambamurthy & Zmud, 1999). In each configuration, stakeholder constituencies take different lead roles and responsibilities for IT decision making. In the *centralized* configuration, corporate IT management has IT decision-making authority concerning infrastructure, applications, and development. In the *decen-*

tralized configuration, division IT management and business-unit management have authority for infrastructure, applications, and development. In the *federal* configuration (a hybrid configuration of centralization and decentralization), corporate IT has authority over infrastructure, and division IT and business-units have authority over applications and development. In general, it is argued that centralization provides greater efficiency and standardization, while decentralization improves business ownership and responsiveness (Brown, 1997). The literature suggests that the federal configuration provides the benefits of both centralization and decentralization (Hodgkinson, 1996; Von Simson, 1990), and research indicates that organizations adopt a federal configuration when pursuing multiple competing objectives (Brown & Magill, 1998; Sambamurthy & Zmud, 1999).

Despite the merits of approaching IT governance as the selection and use of decision making procedures for the effective procurement of IT resources, research in information infrastructure development suggests that IT governance cannot be solely concerned with the formal allocation of IT decision-making authority (see in particular Ciborra et al., 2001). Irrespective of the locus of control, mechanisms for lateral coordination need to be included for IT governance. For example, the findings from both the Crete and English case studies indicate that, in more dynamic environments, effective IT governance is more likely to resemble a network of relationships rather than classical hierarchical structures. In such complex, interdependent decision-making environments, there is considerable uncertainty and ambiguity arising from within distributed communities of users, providers, and policymakers, among others (cf. DeSanctis et al., 1999; Jarvenpaa & Ives, 1994).

Given the increasingly large scale nature of information infrastructure projects, it is essential that individuals (and the communities they represent) at multiple levels are engaged in the decision making process, to ensure that IT resources meet the needs of all constituencies. A key objective of

IT governance is to ensure such synergies occur and associated benefits are reaped, not solely at the procurement level, but more importantly at the level of implementation.

The theoretical framework discussed in Chapter 3 of this book holds possibilities for addressing this objective. The key differentiating factor of this theoretical framework and other frameworks found in the IT governance literature is exactly its focus on the multilevel context of IT resources and the dynamic negotiations around the diverse property rights of various right holders.

The purpose of this chapter will be to explore a set of commons-based governance principles for developing information infrastructures by drawing on Ostrom's (1990) original work. The following sections in this chapter will extend Ostrom's (1990) original set of governance principles by applying them in the context of the two case studies presented in Chapters 4 and 5 and analyzed in Chapter 6. These principles will also be contrasted to extant research on IT governance and more recent developments from commons studies (Anderies et al., 2004; Hess & Ostrom, 2007). This chapter concludes with implications for further research into information infrastructure governance through a commons perspective.

GOVERNANCE PRINCIPLES FOR INFORMATION INFRASTRUCTURE DEVELOPMENT

The analysis of the two case studies in Chapter 6 points to a well reported challenge in the commons literature, namely, how a collection of individuals can "organize and govern themselves to obtain collective benefits in situations where the temptations to free-ride and to break commitments are substantial" (Ostrom, 1990, pp.27).

To address this challenge, Ostrom and her colleagues (e.g. Anderies et al., 2004; Constanza et al., 2001; Hess & Ostrom, 2007; Ostrom, 1990; Ostrom et al., 1994) studied a wide range

Table 1. Governance principles for information infrastructure development

1. *Defining Boundaries*	The boundaries of the information infrastructure and those of individuals or groups with rights to infrastructure resources should be clearly defined.
2. *Balancing the Benefits and Costs of Resource Usage*	Operational rights specifying the types of infrastructure resources that a user can access should be directly linked to local needs and conditions concerning work practices, available technologies, information, and/or money inputs.
3. *Monitoring & Sanctioning Resource Usage*	A system for monitoring resource usage should be implemented by the users themselves. Users who violate rules of use should receive graduated sanctions (depending on the seriousness & context of the offense) from other users and/or officials accountable to these users (i.e. by constitutional right holders).
4. *Devising & Modifying Resource Usage*	Users should have rights to devise and modify the rules determining the use of infrastructure resources. These rights should not be imposed by external authorities (e.g. the state)
5. *Conflict-Resolution Mechanisms*	Users and their officials should have rapid access to low-cost, local arenas to resolve conflict among users, between users and officials, and between users, their officials, and infrastructure providers.

Source: adapted from Ostrom (1990) and Anderies et al (2004)

of communities, some of which had a long history of successfully producing and maintaining collective goods, while others had failed partially or completely in meeting this challenge. In comparing the successes and the failures, Ostrom and colleagues found that groups which are able to organize and govern themselves are marked by a set of governance principles.

These principles are used as an organizing device for the discussion that follows. The discussion extends Ostrom and colleagues' original points and applies them to the context of information infrastructure development. The five governance principles are directly linked to the theoretical framework discussed in Chapter 3 and are grouped under three categories. The first category is *group size and boundaries*, in which the first principle is discussed, focusing on issues around the group size of stakeholders participating in information infrastructure development, along with the importance of defining the boundaries of the infrastructure itself. The second category is that of *rights and rules of resource usage*, in which the second, third, and fourth principles are discussed, focusing on operational, collective-choice and constitutional rights. Finally, the third category is that of *conflict resolution,* in which the fifth principle is discussed, focusing on the importance of establishing arenas for resolving

conflicts amongst stakeholders participating in information infrastructure development.

The adapted principles are summarized in Table 1 and discussed below in more detail.

Group Size & Boundaries

One of the most commonly accepted tenets in the literature on collective action is that "the larger the group, the less it will further its common interests" (Olson, 1965, pp. 36). Researchers have identified a number of reasons why collective action may be more difficult as group size increases. First, as the group becomes larger, the costs of an individual's decision to free-ride are spread over a greater number of people (Dawes, 1980). If an individual's action does not appreciably affect others, the temptation to free-ride increases. More generally, the larger the group, the more difficult it may be to affect others' outcomes by one's own actions. Thus, an individual may be discouraged from participating in collective action if his or her actions do not affect others in a noticeable way. Second, it is often the case that as group size increases, anonymity becomes increasingly possible and an individual can free-ride without others noticing his or her actions (Dawes, 1980). Third, the costs of organizing are likely to increase (Olson, 1965), i.e., it becomes more difficult to communicate with others and coordinate the activities of members in order to provide collective goods and discourage free-riding.

In many ways this principle is difficult to apply in the context of information infrastructures because the costs and effectiveness of defection, social control, and coordination are very different than groups that interact without computer-mediated communication. A key difference is that one's behavior within the 'boundaries' of an information infrastructure is visible to every other user, whether there are 10 users or 1000. Thus, the costs of free-riding by, for example, exploiting existing information resources without contributing to the creation of new ones (e.g. new electronic health records), are not diffused as the number of users increases. Indeed, one could argue that the effects of free-riding increase as user membership increases, because there are a greater number of participants to be inconvenienced or infuriated by such actions. This characteristic of information infrastructure use creates new challenges but also new possibilities for those wishing to establish cooperative communities. The fact that every user's behavior is visible and identifiable discourages free-riding among those who only free-ride when they can do so anonymously. By recording and monitoring user behaviour, an information infrastructure can make individual actions more visible, while raising issues of responsibility and accountability; an information infrastructure acts as a proxy for the development of governance and control of users across functional units (cf. Power, 1999).

At the same time, an information infrastructure can reduce the costs of communication and coordination, by allowing users to produce and maintain collective goods that would otherwise be too expensive. In particular, communicating with a thousand people involves essentially the same personal costs as sending a message to a single individual. Also, a great number of members can participate in discussions involving numerous topics–although information overload can become a

problem–and a historical record of users' interactions is automatically produced. Thus, there may be the potential to sustain cooperation in much larger groups than is possible without computer-mediated communication.

For example, in the English case study, the NPfIT aimed at providing several thousand users scattered around different regions in England with access to national summary care records, thus, enabling a lifelong monitoring of patient pathways within the NHS. While this could have been achieved in face-to-face meetings at the Strategic Health Authority and/or NHS network level, via the NPfIT, users can interact more frequently, at a lower cost, and among a larger and more widespread group than could be sustained otherwise. However, as evident from the findings and analysis of this case study, these intended features of the NPfIT did not solely guarantee successful collective action. There are other governance principles that also seem to be necessary if an information infrastructure is to work effectively.

Ostrom (1990) found that one of the most important features of successful collective action around a commons is for the collective good to have clearly defined boundaries. Ostrom (1990, pp.91) explained:

Without defining the boundaries of the [collective good] and closing it to 'outsiders,' local appropriators face the risk that any benefits they produce by their efforts will be reaped by others who have not contributed to those efforts. At the least, those who invest in the [collective good] may not receive as high a return as they expected. At the worst, the actions of others could destroy the resource itself.

Boundaries are also important in that they encourage frequent, ongoing interaction among group members. This is critical because repeated interaction is perhaps the single most important factor in encouraging successful collective action (Axelrod, 1984). If individuals are not likely to interact in the future, there is a huge temptation to behave selfishly and to free-ride. On the other hand, knowing that one will be interacting with others on a continual basis can lead to the creation of reputations and serve as a powerful deterrent to short-run, selfish behavior.

In the context of information infrastructures, boundaries are often hard to define, without clear mechanisms for sufficiently warding off those who would exploit the resources produced by others, as in the example of Web 2.0 and interdependent, mixable web services. Some have argued, though, that by specifying exactly the globally shared resources of an information infrastructure and the local applications that sit on top of those, IT professionals can effectively define an information infrastructure's boundaries (e.g. see Weill & Broadbent, 1998; Weill & Ross, 2004). However, beyond the architectural boundaries of an information infrastructure, actual usage can be extremely fluid. In fact, while there are many technical resources to construct access boundaries around an information infrastructure, many of these boundaries exist only by voluntary compliance and are easily violated.

For example, in the NPfIT there were concerns around the sharing of patient data between NHS Trusts, including losing patients to one another, but also giving the opportunity to each Trust to scrutinize healthcare services offered by another. In this case, the challenge was to defend the boundaries and to reduce incentives for adjacent users to infringe upon the territory held by a particular community of users. This was to be achieved through smart cards, role-based access, and a number of information governance guidelines, all of which would secure the usage boundaries of each local Trust and each local user, while simultaneously enforcing mechanisms of non-intrusion by other Trusts and users. However, soon after these mechanisms were announced there was a lot of criticism that in different localities where there are many changing roles, it would be extremely difficult to deal with all the individual decisions that are being made as to who should have what role and what privilege. Some healthcare professionals also noted that these regulative mechanisms interfered with their (more important) medical work and that, as a consequence, many would find ways of working around those mechanisms–i.e. violating the boundaries.

As this example shows, defining (and in the process restricting) access to different resources and categorizing the user base according to different roles (e.g. user, power user, administrator, etc.) is not the sole determining factor for setting clear boundaries around an information infrastructure. What is important to note here is that organizational participants will make a number of choices around their information infrastructure arrangements in order to try to leverage their negotiating power in the larger social order. However, their choices will be constrained by available resources and organizational practices that are defined outside the formal boundaries of their organizations, as in the example of a number of hospital directors in Crete opting for alternative systems during the HEALTHnet pilot: even though they made a choice to opt out of the HEALTH pilot, their choice was already constrained and later questioned after CompeTech won the contract for the development of a completely new information infrastructure for the region.

Thus, to understand these choices, the larger situational boundaries must be identified. These boundaries involve not just the resource–i.e. the information infrastructure–but also the social-political context in which it is developed. These boundaries can only be defined in relation to the participants of this larger negotiating context and their rights to the information infrastructure. These rights are discussed next.

Rights & Rules of Resource Usage

As argued throughout the book, successful collective action will depend on a set of rights for governing how information infrastructure resources should be used and who should be responsible for producing and maintaining those. These rights are negotiated, established, resisted, and revised according to the set of institutional rules that define them (Ostrom, 1990). It is, thus, important that these rights are tailored to the specific needs and circumstances of participant communities.

This is another governance principle that is considered to be a feature of cooperative communities–i.e. that there is a good match between the goals and local conditions of a group and the rights that govern the actions of the group's members. Research in traditional commons indicates that there is often great variation from community to community in the details of the rights for governing collective goods, which highlights the need to carefully assess the relevance and appropriateness of applying specific rights of a successful group to another (Constanza et al., 2001).

Similarly, in the context of information infrastructure governance, it is argued that rights should be well-matched to local conditions, something which can encourage different stakeholders to trust each other's rights and to become committed in following them. More importantly, individuals affected by rights governing IT use should be allowed to participate in modifying the rules that determine those rights. It is argued that this feature results in better designed rules because the individuals with the knowledge of the day-to-day work practices of the group and the challenges the group faces could modify the rules over time to better fit local conditions. In contrast, rules that are centrally created and forced upon a community by outside authorities (e.g. the state) often fail miserably because the rules do not take into account knowledge of local conditions or because the same set of rules are applied in a procrustean fashion to many communities despite important differences between them.

This was exactly the point that the Director of IT services at the Regional Health Authorities of Crete raised, when he complained that the CompeTech solution–and associated rights–was imposed on

the region by the Information Society. Instead, he argued, local authorities and users should have been allowed to devise their own rules for determining the processes, by which the infrastructure solution was chosen, as well as the operational and collective-choice rights for governing the usage of associated IT resources. External authorities such as the Information Society should have not been allowed to intervene and challenge any of the locally-determined rules.

These findings are well reported in the information infrastructure literature where such centrally imposed rules are often found to constrain the development and sustainability of an information infrastructure (e.g. Bowker & Star, 1999; Rolland & Monteiro, 2002). Bowker & Star's (1999) seminal study of the development of the International Classification of Diseases (ICD), a global information infrastructure administered by the World Health Organization (WHO), illustrates vividly the historical struggles between different institutions (e.g. the WHO, the U.S. National Library of Medicine) and professional healthcare communities (e.g. nurses, general practitioners, etc) to define the rules of the ICD.

Indeed, in the original studies by Ostrom and colleagues, successful collective action was marked by user participation in devising and refining the rules (Ostrom et al., 1994). Most importantly, the rules were well-matched to local conditions, something which encouraged most members to trust the rules and to become committed in following them. However, this does not seem to be adequate in ensuring cooperative relations. Some type of system to monitor and sanction members' actions was a feature of every successful community (Ostrom, 1990).

Monitoring and sanctioning is important not simply as a way of punishing rule-breakers, but also as a way of assuring members that others are doing their part in using common resources effectively. More specifically, in commons studies, successful communities were found to implement systems for monitoring and sanctioning of people's behaviour, rather than assigning such tasks to external authorities (Ostrom et al., 1994). These successful communities employed a graduated system of sanctions, whereby the initial sanction for breaking a rule was often very low. This was so because community members realized that even a well-intentioned person might break the rules when facing an unusual situation or extreme hardship. Severely punishing such a person might alienate him or her from the community, causing greater problems. For example, a large monetary fine imposed on a person facing an unusual problem may produce resentment and unwillingness to conform to the rules in the future. Graduated punishments ranging from insignificant fines all the way to banishment, applied in settings in which the sanctioners know a great deal about the personal circumstances of the other appropriators and the potential harm that could be created by excessive sanctions, may be far more effective than a major fine imposed on a first offender (Ostrom, 1990, pp.98).

Other researchers (e.g. Levi, 1988) have argued that many individuals are willing to comply with a set of rules governing collective goods if they believe the rules are efficacious and that most others are complying with the rules. That is, many people are contingent cooperators, willing to cooperate as long as most others do.

This was observed in the Crete case study. Initially, the HEALTHnet pilot enjoyed small-scale success by attracting a good user base of general practitioners from primary care centres. However, after a series of disputes over ownership rights with the Regional Health Authorities, these general practitioners gradually abstained from any use of the HEALTHnet applications. An illustrative example of such a decline in use was that of a general practitioner, who was initially one of the most enthusiastic users of the integrated electronic health records module, but who later switched back to using paper-based records.

As this example illustrates, an information infrastructure makes monitoring much easier, but poses special problems for sanctioning. While monitoring can be accomplished at a very low cost (almost as a side effect of IT resource use and non-use–an IT administrative task), sanctioning a participant's behavior is far more challenging. Social order can be enforced by ensuring that all users have a clear common understanding of what should and should not occur in their interactions. Thus, there needs to be a clear and situated transition from this global understanding to actual implementation in local practices.

For example, in the NPfIT, an "information governance toolkit" was proposed in an effort to ascertain that the use of different applications was clearly defined at the level of each Trust, whilst also complying with related data protection legislation at the national NHS level. However, as the members of the Committee of Public Accounts (CPA) rightly pointed out, there was no guarantee that users in each Trust would follow the rules so the security and confidentiality of patients' records was ensured. The NPfIT project leaders, however, argued that security and related rules of resource usage were dealt with at the technical level and that, apparently the security of the NPfIT could be compared with that found in banks. One NHS patient acting as a witness in one of the CPA meetings responded to this comment (HC, 2007, pp. Ev32):

I feel at some points we are not looking at the way that technology is happening outside this little world of NHS IT and the way that can have an impact on people, but that is not a problem the banks have. So, if you are trying to make comparisons, I think another useful one might be to look at the kind of internal audit system you will tend to have in a bank and the rather specialised and skilled people that they would employ to do that; and I can find no evidence that within the NHS we have an equivalent kind of privacy skilled auditor internally who can do the sort of investigation and monitoring which forms a part of this social total structure of security which will make me start to believe some of these things in the Care Record Guarantee. What we do have is a steady drizzle of bureaucracy coming out of the Information Governance Toolkit.

...

I think you could learn a good deal of lessons from the banks because they have been doing it for longer and there are certain types of people I can identify working in the banking system who are in some ways a worthy adversary for many of the people who attack systems. They are able to think the way they do... so that they are thinking into the mindset. They are not relying on: "We comply with rule 206 in the information toolkit," they are thinking themselves into the problem.

This comment, by an NHS patient, strikes at the heart of devising, modifying, and enforcing rules of resource usage. It emphasizes the need to identify and involve end users, in each locality, who would not only participate in the definition of rules, but more importantly put those rules into practice. It is not enough to say that one complies with X rule in a governance toolkit; it is more important to assign–within local communities– individuals who would be responsible for making sure that their locality complies with rule X. And if there is a violation of that rule by a community member, again the community, in joint with an official agency, should decide on the graduated sanctions to be enforced on violators. Such an arrangement would be more easily perceived by users as legitimate, and the rules of resource usage would tend to be followed without high costs of monitoring and enforcement. Some long-lived traditional commons arrangements are examples of such successful arrangements (Coward, 1980; Siy, 1982).

As research in information infrastructure development has shown, however, such an arrangement would most probably lead to conflicts between richer and poorer user groups because

there may be a mismatch between the costs and benefits of receiving different parts of the information infrastructure (Weill & Broadbent, 1998). For example, Weill and Broadbent (1998) provide evidence to suggest that half of the firms they studied engage in a "deal making process," which focuses on the negotiations between richer and poorer business units and their immediate needs. As Weill & Broadbent (1998) argue, the pressure on costs and dominance in the deal making process may prevent negotiating parties from valuing the flexibility inherent in infrastructure resources. Consequently, it is important to have some method to resolve the conflicts that will inevitably arise.

Conflict Resolution

Beyond the case of small, homogeneous groups involved in a pattern of mutual reciprocity to produce an obvious collective benefit, negotiations become more difficult. The more the composition of the users and their choice of infrastructure providers differ, the more complex incentive structures become. In an extreme case, when there is great heterogeneity in the user base and the composition of infrastructure providers, there will be great diversity in the contract agreements, including the costs of developing an information infrastructure. As in the example of the NPfIT, such heterogeneity led to issues of standardization vs. customization and the default of two infrastructure providers, Accenture and Fujitsu. Such collective-action failures that compromise the information infrastructure may call for a centralized approach in setting and enforcing desired outcomes, though methodologies for achieving those outcomes may be conducive to more localized decision making. Between the two extremes of small and large homogeneous groups multiple variations exist.

In one variation, the infrastructure providers may be chosen through open call for tenders by the state or a state-governed agency, combined with input from representatives of the user population. As all parties involved will benefit from the development of infrastructure resources, there is an incentive to invest in an information infrastructure. However, problems with budgets and contractual agreements (often influenced by special interests of private companies towards specific directions–as discussed in Chapter 6) may cause problems in pursuing policies of collective benefit. In this case, infrastructure providers may behave as bandits, who have some incentive for investing in improvements because they will reap some return from those improvements, without, however, any regard for the welfare of the users and vice versa.

Accenture and Fujitsu's termination of their NPfIT contract was based exactly on fears that they were behaving as 'bandits,' even though both companies argued otherwise (HC, 2009). Also, in the Crete case study, when CreteTech senior managers were asked as to whether they would be interested and keen to find ways to collaborate with CompeTech so that some of their systems could stay in the region, the answer was negative. Beyond issues of interoperability between CreteTech's and CompeTech's architecture, the more serious issue for both vendors was that of possible benefits (or lack thereof) emanating from combining their technological solutions irrespective of user needs. In such cases, it becomes important how the link between users and providers is implemented (Link 2 in Figure 1 in Chapter 3), so that both users and infrastructure providers equally experience the consequences of each other's decisions and choices.

In a second variation, users and infrastructure providers may possess different information sets: users may have better knowledge concerning resource dynamics, but the infrastructure providers may have better knowledge of larger-scale processes (Nandhakumar & Avison, 1999). In turn, infrastructure providers may design different rules for resource usage in their provided IT applications without sufficient understanding of the resource dynamics, and thus may generate

unintended consequences. In one example, Hanseth et al (2002) describe how, although initially the central division management staff at Norsk Hydro initiated an SAP project while drawing on input from various user groups, there were diverse sets of resource dynamics that escaped their knowledge and span of control which eventually caused a number of unintended consequences. These resource dynamics included (Hanseth et al., 2002, pp. 45-46):

differences in national legislation concerning accounting, taxes, environmental issues, multiple transport systems in different nations/regions (railway, ships, trucks, river boats, etc.) ... [as well as] differences in business cultures and market structures in those nations and regions.

Consequently, the SAP infrastructure ended up being customized for each individual site; "the SAP solution had changed from one coherent common system to a complex, heterogeneous infrastructure" (Hanseth et al., 2002, pp.46). This is exactly what is happening to the NPfIT, with individual Trusts now negotiating local variations to the original NPfIT solution.

As these and other examples (e.g. Puri & Sahay, 2003) illustrate, infrastructure providers and the state or corporate agencies that sponsor them are often unable to directly observe the diverse dimensions of infrastructure resources in complex cases due to disparate information sets. They can, however, derive information about the functioning of the resource in different ways. For example, users who directly experience resource dynamics (Link 1 in Figure 1 in Chapter 3) may provide the information to the infrastructure providers (Link 2 in Figure 1). This is exactly what was proposed in the latest report to the NPfIT, where better engagement of healthcare professionals was argued for (HC, 2009). Alternatively, infrastructure providers may also employ analysts or others who examine information resources (Link 5 in Figure 1), and report back to them (Link 3 in Figure 1). At the same time, however, it is acknowledged that all these indirect methods of deriving information about resource dynamics may lead to errors in translation.

In turn, some have argued that better knowledge integration can be achieved through processes of communicative action based on the following conditions (Hirschheim & Klein, 1994):

- provide equal opportunities to all participants to raise issues, points, and counterpoints to other views, thus placing perceived disagreements on the open agenda for discussion;
- all participants to be placed on equal footing to give or refuse orders, insist on gaining deeper understanding through clarifications that must be provided, aimed at diffusing asymmetrical power distribution among participants;
- all participants to have the opportunity to question clarity, veracity, sincerity, and social responsibility of the actions proposed, aimed at testing legitimacy and correctness of "factual, instrumental, and normative claims" (Hirschheim & Klein, 1994, pp.90)–a condition which would also help address problems identified in the first variation above;
- all participants to have an equal opportunity to articulate feelings of doubts or concerns, aimed at exposing manipulative intents, ulterior motives etc., and also ensure that members who lack the felicity of expression are also heard.

While applying these conditions as a theoretical device to examine the integration of disparate knowledge systems around GIS-based applications in different regions of India, Puri and Sahay (2003) found that local users were able to interact with the more powerful communities involved in the project by expressing their views relatively freely. This communicative action approach influ-

enced the "design processes to be taken up in more participatory ways at two levels: (i) consultation between local GIS teams and the communities, and (ii) development of GIS based on local needs, while, simultaneously, utilizing the scientific knowledge and technical infrastructure of the scientific institutions for building the final GIS database" (Puri & Sahay, 2003, pp.195). As Puri and Sahay (2003) argue, the relative success of this rural development project came about through the effective building of institutional rules, which enabled decentralized decision-making, and integration with locally-understood work practices in which indigenous knowledge was given equal consideration with more specialized, scientific knowledge (Puri & Sahay, 2003, pp.196).

The need to provide access to low-cost conflict resolution mechanisms in the development of information infrastructures is clear: for the reasons already discussed, conflicts between users and infrastructure providers, including mediating agencies, such as the state, are fairly common. In fact, in some cases, some groups seem to be dedicated entirely to on-going conflicts. For example, in one longitudinal case study, Howcroft and Light (2006) focused on packaged software selection and procurement. Their analysis highlighted both overt and covert power issues involved in the procurement of software and illustrated the interplay of power between senior management, IT managers, IT providers, and users. Similar issues are reported by Howcroft and McDonald (2007) in the process of IS investment evaluation in a large international financial institution.

These examples, like the ones discussed earlier, illustrate the need for conflict resolution mechanisms without resorting to external authorities. Resolution has to come from the participants in the development process. Only then will participants find the resolution legitimate and trustworthy to commit to it (Ostrom, 1990).

CONCLUSION & IMPLICATIONS

The governance principles proposed by Ostrom and colleagues were originally conceptualized for more traditional commons arrangements such as irrigation systems and forests. Many scholars have since independently examined the relevance of these principles for explaining the difference between sustainably vs. unsustainably governed commons arrangements (Guillet, 1992; Abernethy & Sally, 2000; Kaijser, 2002). In this chapter, it has been argued that, with some adaptation, these governance principles also apply in the development of information infrastructures. These principles can be used as a method for analyzing the internal dynamics within the components of an information infrastructure, including the important links between them.

In summary, clearly defined boundaries (principle 1) help identify who should receive benefits and who should incur related costs in developing an information infrastructure. If boundaries are not clearly defined, users will be less willing to trust one another and the infrastructure providers. Defining a fair balance between the benefits a user obtains and his or her contributions to the information infrastructure (principle 2) leads to equity and trust among different participants (Isaac et al., 1991). Specifically, arrangements that are considered fair reduce the chance that the users will try to challenge, avoid, or disrupt the information policies of the infrastructure providers (i.e. how information resources are to be used). In addition, enabling users to establish institutional rules (principle 3) of resource usage also encourage better and fairer participation in regulating use. Furthermore, rules that are established by most of the users themselves are better known, understood, and perceived as being legitimate. These first three principles together help solve core problems associated with subtractability of resource usage. They do not by themselves necessarily improve the sustainability of an information infrastructure, because rules made to solve these

problems are not self-enforcing. Thus, incorporating monitoring, graduated sanctioning (principle 4), and conflict-resolution mechanisms (principle 5) as part of the overall governance for developing an information infrastructure provides continuous mechanisms for invoking and interpreting rules and finding ways of imposing sanctions that increase common knowledge and agreement.

These principles can collectively be thought of as a feedback control for resource usage. They transform information about the state of an information infrastructure into actions that influence its use. However, an information infrastructure can become fragile due to conflicts over the interpretation of rules, rule breaking, and the nature of the appropriate sanction. Without regular access to low-cost and rapid conflict-resolution mechanisms to mediate these interactions, the common understanding about what rules mean can be lost. Graduated sanctions preserve a sense of fairness by allowing flexible punishment when there is disagreement about rule infractions. Without these mechanisms, the incentives to free-ride (i.e. overuse without contributing to the creation and management of information resources) may again dominate individual practices against collective action. Recognizing the formal rights of users to accomplish the above prevents those who want to harm or abstain from any participation in collective action, from claiming a lack of legitimacy regarding the information infrastructure.

Despite these normative suggestions, however, it is acknowledged that implementing the proposed governance principles is no easy task. While drawing on the analysis of the findings from the Crete and the English case study and contrasting those to other research on information infrastructure development, a key lesson is that, unlike more traditional commons, a computer-based commons has a double edge: monitoring the behavior of others becomes easier while sanctioning undesirable behavior becomes more difficult; the costs of communication between members of a large group are decreased while the effects of defecting are often amplified; and the existence of several thousand users makes it easy for individuals to find others who share specific interests and goals, but also makes those who want to disrupt those groups able to find them. Moreover, community relations may include both symbiotic and destructive interactions: communities are never entirely homogeneous. Instead, there are often socio-economic and socio-political tensions within a community. Furthermore, not all communities have the capability to make their own rules or to regulate themselves. Communities in some organizations have a culture for autonomous decision-making and therefore have a better ability to self-organize. Communities in other organizations, however, have little cultural background for collective action. Thus, there is no simple conclusion to developing information infrastructures, and normative governance principles must always be approached critically.

To strengthen the possibilities of successful collective action in large scale systems and establish a solid ground upon which the aforementioned governance principles can be implemented, commons scholars suggest nesting a set of local institutions into a broader network of institutions (Ostrom, 1990; Anderies et al., 2004). This 'nesting of institutions' essentially refers to the notion of polycentric governance structures (rather than monocentric or highly centralized), which, as was mentioned at the end of Chapter 6, offer opportunities to organize not one, but many, governing units, with each of those units being able to exercise independent authority to make and enforce rules within a specified area for particular policy areas (see McGinnis, 1999; Ostrom, Schroeder, & Wynne, 1993). The next subsection examines the notion of polycentric governance structures in more detail, while developing implications for the governance of information infrastructures.

The 'Nesting of Institutions': Polycentric Information Infrastructure Governance

As discussed in the beginning of this chapter, research on IT governance has been a priority in the field as it has traditionally been tied to decision making processes toward the effective procurement of IT resources (Brown, 1997; Dean & Sharfman, 1996; Devaraj & Kohli, 2003; Hodgkinson, 1996; Sambamurthy & Zmud, 1999; Von Simson, 1990; Weill & Ross, 2004).

One of the most cited IT governance frameworks is Weill and Ross's (2004) "governance arrangement matrix," which provides suggestions as to *what* decisions must be made to ensure effective IT governance, and *who* should make those decisions (Weill & Ross, 2004, pp.11). According to this matrix, there are five key IT decisions, namely, regarding *IT principles* (i.e. identifying the business role of IT), *IT architecture* (i.e. defining integration and standardization requirements), *IT infrastructure* (i.e. determining shared and enabling services), *business application needs* (i.e. specifying the business need for IT applications), and *IT investment and prioritization* (i.e. choosing which IT initiatives to fund and how much to spend) (Weill & Ross, 2004, pp.54-55). These five decisions are made in succession in that IT principles drive the IT architecture that leads to a specific IT infrastructure and so on. However, as Weill and Ross (2004, pp.11-12) note:

One or more people are responsible for making each of these decisions. Typically, [however] many more people provide input to these decisions. IT governance involves defining who will be responsible for both input and decision making for each decision.

Thus, for the rows in their matrix, they define a set of "archetypes" for specifying decision rights. Each archetype identifies the group of people involved in making an IT decision, including *busi-*

ness monarchy (i.e. top managers), *IT monarchy* (i.e. IT specialists), *feudal* (i.e. each business unit making independent decisions), *federal* (i.e. combination of the corporate center and the business units with or without IT people involved), *IT duopoly* (i.e. IT group and one other group such as top management or business unit leaders), and *anarchy* (i.e. isolated individuals or small groups making decisions) (Weill & Ross, 2004, pp.59). The key challenge, it is argued, is "for every enterprise to determine where it wants to locate both input and decision-making responsibility for each type of governance decision" (Weill & Ross, 2004, pp.12). In addition, Weill and Ross (2004) argue that there is another challenge around how decisions will be made and monitored, reflecting the need for governance mechanisms such as *decision-making structures* (e.g. committees, teams, etc), *alignment processes* (e.g. evaluation processes, service-level agreements, etc.), and *communication approaches* (e.g. announcements, advocates, etc.) (Weill & Ross, 2004, pp.87). In the end, as the authors admit, "IT governance can be messy" (Weill & Ross, 2004, pp.85).

Arguably, Weill and Ross's (2004) framework, in joint with the empirical material they provide, offers a lot of insights into implementing effective IT governance. However, their framework has been developed with top executives or unit managers in mind, and, thus, seems to work in a top-down flow. More importantly–for the purpose of this section–their framework seems to suggest that the proposed governance mechanisms are linked to one another through networks of hierarchical interactions (e.g. from a business unit manager to a top executive), rather than inside one another (i.e. nested).

The nesting of governance principles into a broader network of institutions is thought to break governance into a series of layers, with each layer dealing with the same types of issues but at a progressively larger scale and lesser level of detail, thus, distributing decision-making across all stakeholders (McGinnis, 1999; Ostrom, Schro-

eder, & Wynne, 1993). Nesting is thus used as a mechanism for linking together small-scale local interactions to develop actions on the large scale. In other words, nesting helps smaller units become part of a more inclusive system without giving up their essential autonomy (Marshall, 2005).

The value of nesting lower-level, smaller units, rather than absorbing or sidelining them, follows from the vertical assurance problems that arise as governance becomes multi-levelled. Introducing a higher level assists lower-level stakeholders with their horizontal assurance problems only to the extent that they trust the higher level not to fail them (Marshall, 2005; Putnam, 1993). Retaining units that different stakeholders have self-organized, and minimizing restrictions on their autonomy, helps with vertical assurance problems since stakeholders can be expected to place greater trust in units they create for themselves and in which they maintain collective-choice property rights (Ostrom, 1999).

In the context of information infrastructure development, there is an added value of nesting, since optimal governance decisions cannot be identified precisely at the outset (Bowker & Star, 1999; Ciborra et al., 2001). The positive network externalities driving the evolution of information infrastructures can splinter them non-linearly from one configuration to another, with the timing and direction of splintering events rarely being predictable (Hanseth, 2001). There is value, therefore, in developing nesting (or polycentric) governance structures that contribute towards the sustainability and scalability of information infrastructures.

Implementing nested governance structures can be summarized into two key challenges. The first is to decide how to assign governance tasks across the different levels. The second is to manage the cross-level interactions, or 'vertical interplay,' arising from any assignment. Young (2002) proposed that the best strategy for addressing these challenges lies in assigning tasks to the appropriate level of organization and acting then to ensure that the resulting cross-level interactions yield actions that are complementary rather than conflicting.

The focus on the problem of assigning tasks across governance levels has revolved largely around the principle of "subsidiarity". The principle of subsidiarity was established in EU law by the Treaty of Maastricht, which entered into force on 1 November 1993. The present formulation is contained in Article 5(3) of the Treaty on European Union (consolidated version following the Treaty of Lisbon, which entered into force on 1 December 2009). Under the principle of subsidiarity, any particular task should be decentralized to the lowest level of governance with the capacity to conduct it satisfactorily. This conviction implied that a higher level of organization should refrain from undertaking tasks that could be performed just as well by a grouping closer to the individual. The principle is now also widely thought to have practical advantages for large-scale collective action problems.

At a more practical level of discussion, McKean (2002, pp.10) proposed a further refinement of the subsidiarity principle, by arguing that 'the lowest possible level of governance' can be defined according to the following rule: an individual subunit of the governance system is free to undertake all the tasks that do not affect anyone in another subunit, "but we move up a notch to a higher level if a subunit wants to engage in behaviour that will affect any other subunit." Hence, a task is centralized to higher levels until a level is reached where all individuals with a substantive interest in the task are represented adequately.

This proposal assumes that a subunit's capacity to perform a task depends only on whether the task can be fulfilled without generating spillovers upon other subunits. However, the capacity of any subunit to perform a task at the same standard as a higher-level subunit will normally depend also on additional factors (Marshall, 2005). A subunit may be able to perform a particular task without generating spillovers, yet may be at a disadvantage compared with a higher-level subunit in access-

ing all the physical, financial, human, and social capacities needed to conduct that task adequately (Marshall, 2005). As observed by commons scholars (see Dietz et al., 2003; McGinnis, 1999), it is a common mistake of governments and other policy makers (e.g. corporate) to underestimate the capacities of subunits at any level to self-organize governance arrangements for which they are currently 'too small.' It can sometimes be possible for subunits to deal with higher-level (i.e., spatially broader) problems by reconstituting themselves to represent all key interests at that higher level. Otherwise, they may be capable of closing mismatches of this kind by cooperating voluntarily with one or more other units operating at a similar level towards a federated solution. Denial of opportunities for such participation runs the risk of disenfranchising the lower-level subunits, leading them to cooperate less voluntarily with higher level decisions than would otherwise be the case (Marshall, 2005).

More importantly, building the capacity for a subunit at any level to implement the subsidiarity principle involves a "chicken and egg problem" (Ribot, 2002, pp.15). Typically, there is reluctance to decentralize tasks to lower-level subunits before their capacity has been proven, even though it is impossible to establish such proof until decentralization has occurred. One solution to this problem is to begin by decentralizing simpler tasks for which lower-level capacity is clearly evident and/or the costs of failure would not be severe. Most importantly, for people to perceive that participation in capacity-building activities (e.g. developing local electronic patient records databases) will further their goals, they must have secure rights to reap benefits from exercising the capacities developed.

In the context of information infrastructure development, such favourable conditions are unlikely to exist at the outset. This is so, because the resources being developed are often not valued highly by those whose participation is sought. For example, in both the Crete and the

English case studies–but also in the case of the U.S. National Health Information Infrastructure (e.g. see Fernandopulle & Patel, 2010; Karsh et al., 2010; Nutting et al., 2009)–the proposed aims and functionalities of electronic patient records modules were seriously questioned by healthcare professionals. As discussed in Chapters 4-6, even though there are real advantages in decentralizing property rights for mobilizing local units, building their capacities, and increasing the value of local IT solutions, these advantages are often undermined by the policymakers.

The more fundamental part of the problem, however, is usually opposition to effective decentralization from parties with vested interests in preserving the status quo. Governments and other stakeholders that ordinarily have benefited from centralized collective-choice property rights regimes are reluctant often to relinquish or share them, because doing so would mean losing their power and access to political influence. This is exactly why, many infrastructure development projects have been traditionally centrally controlled (see Graham & Marvin, 1999; Sassen, 2001). Also see the examples of information infrastructure development in SKF, Roche, and IBM (Ciborra et al., 2001).

From the above discussion, it becomes evident that achieving wide legitimacy is the most pervasive scale-related obstacle to success with polycentric governance (Armitage, 2008; Berkes, 2006; Carlsson & Sandstorm, 2008). Such legitimacy can only be achieved through lengthy social processes to build horizontal and vertical linkages across different stakeholders (Berkes, 2006; Young, 2002), as well as to foster learning (Folke et al., 2005). On the one hand, it has been argued, "greater attention to vertical and horizontal linkages," should help different stakeholders "respond to change, adapt and cope with uncertainty by improving communication, coordination, and collaboration" (Armitage, 2008, pp.14). Building such vertical and horizontal linkages will benefit from a variety of institutional forms such as, epistemic communities, boundary organizations, policy networks, and institutional interplay (Berkes, 2006). On the other hand, processes of learning can also help achieve wide legitimacy. Inducing learning across a population will benefit from institutional arrangements toward collaborative decision-making structures, flexible policy conditions, and social organization in which the role of social capital, and relationships and trust-building are emphasized (Armitage, 2005; Folke et al., 2005).

More recently, Wang and Ramiller (2009) have proposed a framework for community-based learning towards successful IT innovation that takes on board the points raised above. Wang and Ramiller (2009) start by analyzing the nature of learning *in* a collective (i.e. in an epistemic community) and learning *by* a collective (i.e. by storing, processing, and instituting 'best practices' across the collective), as well as *learning by doing* (i.e. materially engaging with a technology) and *learning about* (i.e. making sense of information that is available about the technology). By applying this multilevel framework in the context of the diffusion of innovation of enterprise resource planning (ERP) systems, Wang and Ramiller (2009) provide evidence to suggest that "organizational learning associated with IT innovation will eventually be better understood when it can be placed in the context of learning processes on the community scale"; that such learning "is needed for staging and understanding actions subsequently undertaken" in innovation processes; and that such understanding helps in "charting the evolution and dynamics of innovation-related learning at the community level" (Wang & Ramiller, 2009, pp. 727).

Wang and Ramiller's (2009) learning framework could be applied in the context of information infrastructure development for instituting appropriate learning processes across different stakeholders at multiple levels. Indeed, Wang and Ramiller (2009, pp.728-729) offer a number of conjectures based on their analysis of ERP innovation that point to the possibilities of their learning framework in also helping to build horizontal and vertical linkages across different stakeholders–the second factor deemed important in achieving wide legitimacy in polycentric governance. In particular, it is argued that, in learning about the technology, community members will "provide the first public articulation of the corresponding innovation's *know-why* and *know-what*," which will push them to "seek advice and counsel on the issue of *know-how*," with technology vendors and consultants gradually becoming active contributors to the discourse, until the technology is implemented and the cycle of learning by doing starts (Wang & Ramiller, 2009, pp.728). These communicative interactions can help build the appropriate horizontal and vertical linkages across different stakeholders, while further feeding the learning process.

In conclusion, as was previously stated, "IT governance can be messy" (Weill & Ross, 2004, pp.85), and no monolithic approach can provide absolute answers. In this chapter, a set of general governance principles were proposed in an effort to distribute decision-making, monitoring and sanctioning, and conflict resolution across all stakeholders. In this effort, it was also argued that, the deployment of these governance principles will benefit greatly if institutions of governance are nested, thus, helping smaller units become part of a more inclusive system without giving up their essential autonomy. Such nesting, however, is no easy task and will depend on the continuous building of horizontal and vertical linkages across all stakeholders, while inducing multilevel learning processes. At its core, governance is an attempt to "shape human conduct by calculated means," by educating desires, configuring habits, aspirations, and beliefs (Li, 2006, pp.3; citing Foucault). Governance, thus, involves an understanding of human behaviour and can only be administered on a case by case basis, according to contextual attributes, situational practices, and associated politics.

REFERENCES

Abernethy, C. L., & Sally, H. (2000). Experiences of some government-sponsored organisations of irrigators in Niger and Burkina Faso, West Africa. *Journal of Applied Irrigation Science*, *35*(2), 177–205.

Anderies, J. M., Janssen, M. A., & Ostrom, E. (2004). A framework to analyze the robustness of social-ecological systems from an institutional perspective. *Ecology & Society*, *9*(1), 18–34.

Armitage, D. (2005). Adaptive capacity and community-based natural resource management. *Environmental Management*, *35*(6), 703–715. doi:10.1007/s00267-004-0076-z

Armitage, D. (2008). Governance and the commons in a multi-level world. *International Journal of the Commons*, *2*(1), 7–32.

Axelrod, R. (1984). *The evolution of cooperation*. New York, NY: Basic Books.

Berkes, F. (2006). From community-based resource management to complex systems: The scale issue and marine commons. *Ecology and Society*, *11*(11), 45–59.

Bowker, G., & Star, S. L. (1999). *Sorting things out–Classification and its consequences*. Cambridge, MA: MIT Press.

Brown, C. V. (1997). Examining the emergence of hybrid IS governance solutions: Evidence from a single case site. *Information Systems Research*, *8*(1), 69–94. doi:10.1287/isre.8.1.69

Brown, C. V., & Magill, S. L. (1998). Reconceptualizing the context-design issue for the information systems function. *Organization Science*, *9*(2), 177–195. doi:10.1287/orsc.9.2.176

Carlsson, L., & Sandstrom, A. (2008). Network governance of the commons. *International Journal of the Commons*, *2*(1), 33–54.

Ciborra, C. U., & Hanseth, O. (2001). Introduction. In Ciborra, C. U. (Ed.), *From control to drift: The dynamics of corporate information infrastructures* (pp. 1–14). Oxford, UK: Oxford University Press.

Costanza, R., Low, B. S., Ostrom, E., & Wilson, J. (Eds.). (2001). *Institutions, ecosystems, and sustainability*. New York, NY: Lewis Publishers.

Coward, E. W. Jr., (Ed.). (1980). *Irrigation and agricultural development in Asia: Perspectives from the social sciences*. Ithaca, NY: Cornell University Press.

Dawes, R. (1980). Social dilemmas. *Annual Review of Psychology*, *31*, 169–193. doi:10.1146/annurev.ps.31.020180.001125

Dean, J., & Sharfman, M. (1996). Does decision process matter? A study of strategic decision-making effectiveness. *Academy of Management Journal*, *39*(2), 368–396. doi:10.2307/256784

DeSanctis, G., Staudenmayer, N., & Wong, S. (1999). Interdependence in virtual organizations. In Cooper, C., & Rousseau, D. M. (Eds.), *Trends in organizational behavior* (pp. 81–104). New York, NY: John Wiley & Sons.

Devaraj, S., & Kohli, R. (2003). Performance impacts of information technology: Is actual usage the missing link? *Management Science*, *49*(3), 273–289. doi:10.1287/mnsc.49.3.273.12736

Dietz, T., Ostrom, E., & Stern, P. C. (2003). The struggle to govern the commons. *Science*, *302*(5652), 1907–1912. doi:10.1126/science.1091015

Fernandopulle, R., & Patel, N. (2010). How the electronic health record did not measure up to the demands of our medical home practice. *Health Affairs*, *29*(4), 622–628. doi:10.1377/hlthaff.2010.0065

Folke, C., Hahn, T., Olsson, P., & Norberg, J. (2005). Adaptive governance of social-ecological systems. *Annual Review of Environment and Resources*, *30*, 441–473. doi:10.1146/annurev.energy.30.050504.144511

Graham, S., & Marvin, S. (2001). *Splintering urbanism: Networked infrastructures, technological mobilities and the urban condition*. New York, NY: Routledge. doi:10.4324/9780203452202

Guillet, D. W. (1992). Comparative irrigation studies: The Orbigo Valley of Spain and the Colca Valley of Peru. *Poligonos*, *2*, 141–150.

Hanseth, O., Ciborra, C., & Braa, K. (2002). The control devolution: ERP and the side-effects of globalization. *The Data Base for Advances in Information Systems*, *32*(4), 34–46. doi:10.1145/506139.506144

Hess, C., & Ostrom, E. (2007). *Understanding knowledge as a commons: From theory to practice*. Cambridge, MA: MIT Press.

Hirschheim, R., & Klein, H. K. (1994). Realizing emancipatory principles in information systems development: The case for ETHICS. *Management Information Systems Quarterly*, *18*(1), 83–109. doi:10.2307/249611

Hodgkinson, S. T. (1996). The role of the corporate IT function in the federal IT organization. In Earl, M. J. (Ed.), *Information management: The organizational dimension* (pp. 247–260). Oxford, UK: Oxford University Press.

House of Commons (HC). (2007). The electronic patient record. *Sixth Report of Session 2006-07, Vol III–Oral & Written Evidence*, HC 422-III. House of Commons, Health Committee. Retrieved February 20, 2011, from http://www.publications.parliament.uk/pa/cm200607/cmselect/cmhealth/422/42202.htm

House of Commons (HC). (2009). The national programme for IT in the NHS: Progress since 2006. *Second Report of Session 2008-09*, HC 153. House of Commons, Committee of Public Accounts. Retrieved February 20, 2011, from http://www.publications.parliament.uk/pa/cm200809/cmselect/cmpubacc/153/15302.htm

Howcroft, D., & Light, B. (2006). Reflections on issues of power in packaged software selection. *Information Systems Journal, 16*(3), 215–235. doi:10.1111/j.1365-2575.2006.00216.x

Howcroft, D., & McDonald, R. (2007). An ethnographic study of IS investment appraisal. *International Journal of Technology and Human Interaction, 3*(3), 69–86. doi:10.4018/jthi.2007070106

Isaac, R. M., Mathieu, D., & Zajac, E. E. (1991). Institutional framing and perceptions of fairness. *Constitutional Political Economy, 2*(3), 329–370. doi:10.1007/BF02393135

Jarvenpaa, S. L., & Ives, B. (1994). The global network organization of the future: Information management opportunities and challenges. *Journal of Management Information Systems, 10*(4), 25–57.

Kaijser, A. (2002). System building from below: Institutional change in Dutch water control systems. *Technology and Culture, 43*(3), 521–548. doi:10.1353/tech.2002.0120

Karsh, B. T., Weinger, M. B., Abbott, P. A., & Wears, R. L. (2010). Health information technology: Fallacies and sober realities. *Journal of the American Medical Informatics Association, 17*(6), 617–623. doi:10.1136/jamia.2010.005637

Levi, M. (1988). *Of rule and revenue*. Berkeley, CA: University of California Press.

Li, T. M. (2006). Neo-liberal strategies of government through community: The social development program of the World Bank in Indonesia. *IILJ Working Paper*. Global Administrative Law Series. New York, NY: Institute for International Law and Justice, New York University School of Law.

Marshall, G. R. (2005). *Economics for collaborative environmental management: Renegotiating the commons*. London, UK: Earthscan Publications.

McGinnis (Ed.). (1999). *Polycentric governance and development: Readings from the workshop in political theory and policy analysis*. Ann Arbor, MI: Univ. of Michigan Press.

McKean, M. A. (2002). Nesting institutions for complex common-pool resource systems. In J. Graham, I. Reeve, & D. Brunckhorst (Eds.), In *Proceedings of the 2nd International Symposium on Landscape Futures*. Armidale, Australia: Institute for Rural Futures, University of New England.

Nutting, P. A., Miller, W. L., Crabtree, B. F., Jaen, C. R., Stewart, E. E., & Stange, K. C. (2009). Initial lessons from the first national demonstration project on practice transformation to a patient-centered medical home. *Annals of Family Medicine, 7*(3), 254–260. doi:10.1370/afm.1002

Olson, M. (1965). *The logic of collective action: Public goods and the theory of groups*. Cambridge, MA: Harvard University Press.

Osei-Joehene, D., & Ciborra, C. U. (2007). The duality of risk and the evolution of danger in global ICT integration. In Hanseth, O., & Ciborra, C. (Eds.), *Risk, complexity and ICT* (pp. 154–182). London, UK: Edward Elgar.

Ostrom, E. (1990). *Governing the commons: The evolution of institutions for collective action*. Cambridge, UK: Cambridge University Press.

Ostrom, E. (1999). Coping with tragedies of the commons. *Annual Review of Political Science, 2*, 493–535. doi:10.1146/annurev.polisci.2.1.493

Ostrom, E., Gardner, R., & Walker, J. (1994). *Rules, games, and common-pool resources*. Ann Arbor, MI: University of Michigan Press.

Ostrom, E., Schroeder, L., & Wynne, S. (1993). *Institutional incentives and sustainable development: Infrastructure policies in perspective*. Boulder, CO: Westview Press.

Power, M. (1999). *The audit society: Rituals of verification*. Oxford, UK: Oxford University Press.

Puri, S. K., & Sahay, S. (2003). Participation through communicative action: A case study of GIS for addressing land/water development in India. *Information Technology for Development, 10*, 179–199. doi:10.1002/itdj.1590100305

Putnam, R. D. (1993). *Making democracy work*. Princeton, NJ: Princeton University Press.

Ribot, J. C. (2002). *Democratic decentralization of natural resources: Institutionalizing popular Participation*. Washington, DC: World Resources Institute.

Rolland, K. H., & Monteiro, E. (2002). Balancing the local and the global in infrastructural information systems. *The Information Society, 18*(2), 87–100. doi:10.1080/01972240290075020

Sambamurthy, V., & Zmud, R. (1999). Arrangements for information technology governance: A theory of multiple contingencies. *Management Information Systems Quarterly, 23*(2), 261–290. doi:10.2307/249754

Sassen, S. (2001). *The global city* (2nd ed.). Princeton, NJ: Princeton University Press.

Siy, R. Y. Jr. (1982). *Community resource management*. Quezon City, Philippines: University of the Philippines Press.

Star, S. L., & Ruhleder, K. (1996). Steps toward an ecology of infrastructure: Design and access for large information spaces. *Information Systems Research, 7*(1), 111–134. doi:10.1287/isre.7.1.111

Von Simson, E. M. (1990, July-August). The centrally decentralized IS organization. *Harvard Business Review*, 158–162.

Wang, P., & Ramiller, N. C. (2009). Community learning in IT innovation. *Management Information Systems Quarterly, 33*(4), 709–734.

Weill, P., & Ross, J. (2004). *IT governance: How top performers manage IT decision rights for superior results*. Boston, MA: Harvard Business School Press.

Young, O. R. (2002). Institutional interplay: The environmental consequences of cross-scale interactions . In Ostrom, E., Dietz, T., Dolšak, N., Stern, P. C., Stonich, S., & Weber, E. U. (Eds.), *The drama of the commons* (pp. 263–291). Washington, DC: National Academy Press.

ADDITIONAL READING

Ciborra, C. (2002). *The labyrinths of information*. Oxford, UK: Oxford University Press.

Dourish, P. (2001). *Where the action is: The foundations of embodied interaction*. Cambridge, MA: MIT Press.

Hickson, D. J., Butler, R. J., Cray, D., Mallory, G. R., & Wilson, D. C. (1986). *Top decisions: Strategic decision making in organizations*. San Francisco, CA: Jossey Bass.

Mackay, C. (1993). *Extraordinary popular delusions and the madness of crowds*. New York, NY: Barnes and Noble.

Mintzberg, H. (1973). Strategy making in three modes. *California Management Review, 16*(2), 44–53.

Mintzberg, H., Raisinghani, D., & Theoreet, A. (1976). The structure of 'unstructured' decision processes. *Administrative Science Quarterly, 21*(2), 246–275. doi:10.2307/2392045

Pettigrew, A. M. (1973). *The politics of organizational decision making*. London, UK: Tavistock Institute.

Pfeffer, J., & Salancik, G. R. (1978). *The external control of organizations: A resource dependence perspective*. New York, NY: Harper Row.

Sillince, J. A. A., & Mouakket, S. (1997). Varieties of political process during systems development. *Information Systems Research, 8*(4), 368–397. doi:10.1287/isre.8.4.368

Tainter, J. (1988). *The collapses of complex societies*. Cambridge, UK: Cambridge University Press.

Van Grembergen, W. (Ed.). (2003). *Strategies for information technology governance*. Hershey, PA: Idea Group Publishing. doi:10.4018/978-1-59140-140-7

Weill, P. (2004). Don't just lead, govern: How top-performing firms govern IT. *MIS Quarterly Executive, 3*(1), 1–17.

Weill, P., & Ross, J. (2005). A matrixed approach to designing IT governance. *Sloan Management Review, 46*(2), 26–34.

Section 3
Further Research

Chapter 8
New Information Infrastructure Commons

ABSTRACT

This chapter explores the characteristics of new and emerging information infrastructures. In particular, the chapter focuses on Free and Open Source Software (FOSS) projects, exploring what makes individuals and communities contribute code and ideas towards a FOSS product, but also how they negotiate and eventually agree on a set of institutional rules for structuring their collective action. The chapter also examines the emerging attributes of mashup projects and the ways that, once again, individuals and communities design and structure their contribution. The chapter concludes with some implications for further research on and around these new information infrastructures.

INTRODUCTION

Since the 1960s when ARPANET was created, researchers have looked for ways to continue to formulate new approaches for global collaboration. As a result, over the last two decades or so, the Internet has moved from a domain utilized primarily by high-skilled computer scientists, engineers, and others in high-tech industries to a network of users with diverse expertise and

educational background. This environment, where digital files can be copied and transferred globally in an instant and at very little cost, makes it much easier to treat information as a global public good. However, while general information can be considered a public good, specific information leading to the development of a product, e.g. software code, is a form of intellectual property. There are, however, new, alternative models of global Internet-based collaboration that represent a form of commons (Dietz, Ostrom, & Stern, 2003).

DOI: 10.4018/978-1-4666-1622-6.ch008

Free and Open Source Software (FOSS) is an exemplar of such models, where communities of skilled users operate collectively to produce a good (i.e. the software) through a common property regime (Benkler, 2002; Boyle, 2003; Schweik, 2007). This means that the development of FOSS is based on property rights (McGowan, 2001), whereby some individuals involved have rights to how the code is written (i.e. operational rights), have control over what goes into future versions of the code (i.e. collective-choice rights), and can exclude others from submitting new code to a new release (i.e. constitutional rights) (Schweik, 2005). One gains rights to a FOSS project by either: (1) being the person or group who started the project from scratch; (2) being someone who has received authority from the original owner to take the lead in future maintenance and development efforts; (3) being a person who takes over a project that is widely recognized as abandoned and makes a legitimate effort to locate the original author(s) and gets permission to take over ownership; and (4) a "hostile takeover"–where the project can be hijacked or "forked" (i.e. two competing versions of the same project) because of the "new derivative works" permissions provided by the license (Raymond, 2001; McGowan, 2001).

These rights are configured by determining three groups of attributes: the design and structure of institutional rules; the community of FOSS participants; and the material characteristics of the information infrastructure that supports their interaction. As in the two empirical case studies discussed earlier in the book, these attributes will be negotiated in ongoing interactions between new and old participants and their interests. Similarly, it is argued that (Weber, 2004, pp.189):

the open source process is an ongoing experiment. It is testing an imperfect mix of leadership, informal coordination mechanisms, implicit and explicit norms, along with some formal governance structures that are evolving and doing so at a rate that has been sufficient to hold surprisingly complex systems together.

Another example of a new information infrastructure commons is the technological capability provided by web applications and tools to weave data from different sources into a new data source or service–i.e. mashups. The term 'mashups' implies easy and fast combination, aggregation, and visualization of diverse sources of raw data–most often using open application processing interfaces (API) and data sources (Bolin et al., 2005; Faaborg & Lieberman, 2006; Fujima et al., 2004). Mashups are a direct evolution of Web 1.0 Internet models, through which providers used to store user data on portals and then updated them regularly. Providers controlled all user data, and users had to utilize their products and services to retrieve the information. With the advent of Web 2.0 a new proposition has been created, using Web standards that are commonly and widely adopted across infrastructures, while allowing users to mix and match existing services to create new ones. These include business mashups (e.g. enterprise mashups that expose actionable information from diverse internal and external information sources) (Schroth & Christ, 2007), consumer mashups (e.g. Wikipedia), and data mashups (i.e. combination of diverse resources to create a new and distinct Web service that was not originally provided by either source) (Benslimane et al., 2008; Sheth et al, 2007).

Mashups are becoming increasingly widespread, especially in the context of combining geographic data and displaying such integrated data on maps. For example, HealthMap was developed by the Children's Hospital Informatics Program in Boston to integrate disparate data sources within Google Maps toward a unified and comprehensive view of the current global state of infectious diseases and their effect on human and animal health. This freely available web service integrates outbreak data of varying reliability, ranging from media sources (e.g. Google News) to personal accounts (e.g. ProMED), and more valid alerts (e.g. World Health Organization) (see Boulos et al., 2008).

Although the mashup model is still relatively new in comparison to FOSS, it too, is dependent on the configuration and structure of institutional rules, community attributes, and the material characteristics of the underlying information infrastructure. In a recent book, Lessig (2008) takes on the challenge to map out these attributes for the mashup model by offering examples from everyday life. Lessig (2008) explores the different types of hybrid property regimes that will most probably survive in the future by examining the rights of the original creator of digital content (e.g. an artist), the remixer (e.g. a user), and the infrastructure provider (e.g. movie studio).

This chapter will explore the particular attributes of these new information infrastructures and compare and contrast them with more conventional ones. The next section will examine in more detail the attributes of FOSS projects, including what makes individuals and communities contribute code and ideas towards a FOSS product, but also how they negotiate and eventually agree on a set of institutional rules for structuring their collective action. The section that follows this discussion will examine the emerging attributes of mashups projects and the ways that, once again, individuals and communities design and structure their contribution. The chapter will conclude with some implications for further research on and around these new information infrastructures.

FREE AND OPEN SOURCE SOFTWARE

The terms "free" and "open source" software refer to software products distributed under terms that allow users to use, modify, and redistribute the software in any manner they see fit, without requiring that they pay the author(s) of the software a royalty or fee for engaging in the aforementioned

activities[1]. In general, such terms of distribution also protect the moral right of the software's author(s) to be identified as such (Lessig, 2004). Products such as the GNU/Linux operating system, the Apache Web server, the Mozilla Web browser, the PHP programming language, and the OpenOffice productivity suite are all well-known examples of this kind of software.

What makes the FOSS "movement"–as it is sometimes called (Lerner & Tirole 2001; Stallman 1999)–interesting to study is the simple fact that large numbers of highly skilled software developers (and users) dedicate tremendous amounts of time and effort to the creation, expansion, and ongoing maintenance of free and open products and services.

In one of the most widely cited papers in the FOSS research literature, Lerner and Tirole (2002) employ an economic rationale of cost and benefit in explaining why developers choose to participate in FOSS projects. As long as benefits exceed costs, it makes sense for a developer to participate in a project. Costs to the developers are defined mainly as opportunity costs in time and effort spent participating in creating a product where they do not retrieve a direct monetary reward for their participation. Additional costs are also borne by organizations where these developers work if they are contributing to FOSS projects during work hours. Lerner and Tirole propose that the net benefit of participation consists of immediate and delayed payoffs. Immediate payoffs for FOSS participation can include meeting user needs for particular software (where working on the project actually improves performance) and the enjoyment obtained by working on a "cool" project. Delayed benefits to participation include career advancement and ego gratification. Participants are able to indicate to potential employers their superior programming skills and talents by contributing code to projects where their performance can be monitored by any interested observer. Developers may also care about their reputation within the software community, and thus contribute code to earn respect. In either case, delayed payoffs are a type of signalling incentive for potential and actual contributors to FOSS projects.

In a survey of more than 2,700 FOSS developers conducted as part of a European Commission research project, Ghosh and Glott (2002) report that more than 53 percent of the respondents indicated "social" motivations to join and continue in the community. The single most important motivation was "to learn and develop new skills." About 31 percent of the respondents noted career and monetary concerns, 13 percent indicated political motivations, and 3 percent indicated product requirements. Contrary to many altruism-based explanations of participation, Ghosh and Glott (2002) report that 55 percent of respondents note "selfish" reasons to participate; that is, they state that they take in more than they contribute. Interestingly, this study finds no difference in participation levels in projects between those that are motivated by social concerns and those that are motivated by career/monetary concerns. This study also showed that a majority of the developers are male, and that more than 60 percent are under the age of 26.

In a more recent survey of 684 developers in 287 FOSS projects on sourceforge.net, Lakhani and Wolf (2005) report that the largest and most significant determinant of effort (hours/week) expended on a project was an individual sense of creativity felt by the developer. They surveyed and found that more than 60 percent rated their participation in the projects as the most (or equivalent to the most) creative experience in their lives. Respondents expressed a diverse range of motivations to participate, with 58 percent of them noting user need for software (work and non-work-related) as being important. Intellectual stimulation while coding (having fun), improving programming skills, and an ideological belief that software should be free/open were also important reasons for participating in a FOSS project.

The findings from both surveys described above indicate an inherent source of strength within the global FOSS community. By allowing individuals with multiple motivation types to coexist and collaborate, the global FOSS community can and does attract a wide range of participants. Individuals can join for their own idiosyncratic reasons, and the global FOSS community does not have to be overly concerned about matching motivations to incentives.

There are, however, questions to be asked regarding the skills of FOSS community members, the security and reliability of the software, and the sustainability of FOSS economic and business models, amongst other issues (Anderson, 2005; Agerfalk & Fitzgerald, 2008; Fitzgerald & Kenny, 2003; Neumann, 2005; Rusovan, Lawford, & Parnas, 2005). FOSS has been noted to depart wildly from established software business models, and indeed FOSS companies–including hybrid proprietary-FOSS companies–have had to create new value offers predicated on software as a service, value of software use rather than value of software purchase, and so on. Weinstock and Hissam (2005) examine these challenges by presenting data from five case studies on how FOSS is developed, and how it fits into the general practice of software engineering. Weinstock and Hissam (2005) conclude that FOSS is a viable source of components from which to build systems, but such components should not be chosen over other sources simply because the software is free/open source. They caution adopters not to embrace FOSS blindly, but to carefully measure the real costs and benefits involved.

OSS 2.0: Property Rights & Governance Issues

Fitzgerald (2006) argues that the opportunities offered by FOSS need to be understood in terms of the evolution of free/open software development practices. He argues that since the early FOSS projects, FOSS companies have now moved into a more commercially viable model, which he calls OSS 2.0. So, it is argued, where (Fitzgerald, 2006, pp.591):

[early] FOSS products were targeted primarily at horizontal infrastructure where requirements and design issues were largely part of the established wisdom, thus facilitating a global developer base... in OSS 2.0... the analysis and design phases have become more deliberate... [where] paid developers will be assigned to work on open source products in vertical domains.

In fact, although early FOSS projects attracted large groups of participants, more recent projects have only managed to attract a handful of participants (Dempsey et al., 2002) who were paid to participate (Ghosh & Glott, 2002).

This commoditization of open source and free software has created new opportunities for many projects, but has also created new dilemmas such as, how to treat different contributions of code and how to enforce terms for software modification and distribution within a user and developer population that keeps growing larger but also more diverse in its attitudes toward commercial software. This is because contributors may not share a common employer and have few rights to the code.

During its early phase, FOSS was based on the principle of "copyleft," which differs from traditional software licensing in how it allocates the entitlements in copyright law. Copyleft provides users of the software the right to (a) access and read the program source code, (b) copy and redistribute the software, and (c) make modifications to the source code (Stallman, 1999). Stallman, one of the pioneers of FOSS, implemented these copyleft rules by creating the GNU General Public License (GPL) and the Free Software Foundation to promote the GPL (see http://www.gnu.org).

However, over time as FOSS evolved into OSS 2.0 with more commercial objectives in mind, the concept of open source licensing emerged with the intention to minimize the freedom of the users and increase the potential exploitation of benefits

from for-profit organizations. McGowan (2005, pp.361-362) explains:

When developers write code and fix it in a tangible medium, copyright law gives them the exclusive right to reproduce the code, distribute it, and make works derived from their original work. Subject to some important exceptions such as fair use, persons who would like to do these things with code need the author's permission. Authors grant such permission through licenses. The terms "free" software or "open source" software refer to software distributed under licenses with particular sorts of terms. A common reference guide to such licenses is the "Open Source Definition (OSD)," which ... is now maintained by the Open Source Initiative (OSI).

There are now over seventy OSI-approved licenses, all of which satisfy the general conditions of the OSD, but have variations in the rights provided to software users[2]. These variations demonstrate that FOSS authors have a more complex decision to make when considering how to license their software. Under this copyleft licensing model, FOSS projects are not treated as public goods (as was the original intention of Stallman), but rather authors have the choice to keep some of their intellectual property rights and relinquish others through the licensing. In this sense, FOSS is developed as a commons (Schweik, 2007).

In this new licensing model, FOSS projects can easily become "quilts of code" from many different authors, each of whom owns rights as to which the others are licensees (McGowan, 2005). In addition to ownership, this arrangement means that authors have the right to terminate a project at will, and/or assign rights to third parties willing to police license violations, for example (e.g. the Free Software Foundation serves this role for some projects) (McGowan, 2005). At the same time, however, the authors' right to alienate a FOSS project or to allow a third party to do so, goes against the FOSS values of independence and individual autonomy, something which may, in the end, push the FOSS community to withdraw from participating in the project altogether (O' Mahony, 2005).

Consider the following example (McGowan, 2005, pp.371): If B wrote a derivative[3] work that used A's code, and if A may terminate the GPL rights he grants to licensees including B, then A may prevent B from distributing A's original code in B's derivative work. Termination would also be effective against persons receiving B's work under the GPL. However, B could continue to distribute his/her own code, as to which he/she holds the rights. Whether A's termination was a large blow to the project as a whole would depend on how important his/her original code was. Whether B's code would be worth anything without A's would depend on the same thing. Thus, whether A–the original author–would be likely to terminate would depend at least in part on whether he/she needed to use B's code, because a termination by A could invite reciprocal termination by B.

This example shows how, although the termination of FOSS projects is a possibility, projects that incorporate code from many authors seem unlikely candidates for unilateral termination. And for projects to which the community has chosen not to contribute its efforts, privatization might do little to disrupt community norms (O' Mahony, 2005).

Despite the presence of such community norms, however, there is no reason to expect future FOSS development to free itself from copyrights (Benkler, 2002). There will always be opportunistic persons or firms who might try to appropriate a base of FOSS code for use in a proprietary program. FOSS development will always have to rely on the right to exclude being vested in a person or entity willing to wield that right to enforce community norms and prevent appropriation of the community's work. Otherwise developers might find themselves underwriting someone else's profit margins. Developers might conduct quite a lot of work simply for the joy of

it, but their views might change if someone else were free-riding to profit from their labor.

The Free Software Foundation defends the proposition that authors should not have to share the product of their labor with people who will not share with them. The key concept here is the consent of the author (who is free to negotiate a deal under different terms if he/she chooses), so one could generalize this proposition to say that authors should not be forced to allow others to use their code in cases where authors do not consent to the use. This proposition, in turn, could be justified by Locke's theory of property, which holds that individuals have property rights in themselves, thus in their labor, and thus in the products of their labor–at least, so long as their production does not diminish the quality or quantity of inputs in the commons and is available to others (Gordon, 1993; Waldron, 1993). However, copyright is more often described as a utilitarian reward system than the embodiment of Lockean theory, and there are utilitarian objections to this approach (Benkler, 2001).

These debates over FOSS development practices and licenses point to the fact that, unlike cases of more traditional commons where governance is central for the success and sustainability of a commons (Dietz, Ostrom & Stern, 2003), in the FOSS context, governance is poorly understood (Schweik & Semenov, 2003) and conflict-ridden (Shaikh & Cornford, 2003).

Although the debate over how to best govern FOSS projects is still open, current FOSS development practices and licenses confirm the wide versatility of the FOSS model that creates general property rights and allows individuals to deploy them in the ways that best suit their needs. This is partly because FOSS development practices and licenses are supported by an 'open' information infrastructure that helps FOSS participants coordinate the collaborative effort. For example, the FOSS project-management website, sourceforge. net, provides group communication functions and software version-control systems, which help archive versions of software, enable new submissions and the retrieval of modules, protect against overwrite and elimination of code, and provide analysis functions, among other support practices (Schweik, 2007).

Because of this 'open' attribute of the information infrastructure (cf. Hanseth, 2001) that supports FOSS development, some have argued that, only by examining next-generation applications "we can begin to understand the true long-term significance of the open source paradigm shift" (O'Reilly, 2005a, pp.463). The next section specifically focuses on such next-generation applications.

MASHUPS AND PROCESSES OF ONLINE SOCIAL PRODUCTION

With the advent of fourth generation programming languages such as PHP and JSP, and client-side, web technologies such as Asynchronous JavaScript and XML (Ajax), web services and applications have evolved from the static hyperlinks of the Web 1.0 era to the rich, interactive, user-generated content of the Web 2.0 era (O'Reilly, 2005b). Web 2.0 is a service-oriented architecture that utilizes existing and new protocols (e.g. HTTP and Dynamic HTTP) and open standards (e.g. SOAP and REST) to enable users to leverage and integrate the content, presentation, or application functionality of disparate Web sources. The aim is to combine–i.e. mashup–these sources towards providing a set of much richer applications or services.

The term mashup was borrowed from the pop music scene, where a mashup is a new song that is mixed from vocal and instrumental tracks from two different source songs (usually belonging to different genres). Like these mixed songs, a mashup is an innovative composition of content, presentation (i.e. interface), and application functionality.

In addition to the more well-known types of map mashups (e.g. Google's Maps API, Microsoft's Virtual Earth, Yahoo Maps, AOL's MapQuest, etc), there are video and photo mashups, search and shopping mashups, and news mashups, among others. For example, the emergence of photo hosting and social networking sites like Flickr with APIs for photo sharing has led to a variety of interesting mashups, including the ability to include metadata on the digital content being hosted such as, who took the picture, what it is a picture of, where and when it was taken, and more. Also comparative shopping tools such as BizRate, PriceGrabber, MySimon, and Google's Froogle use combinations of business-to-business APIs to aggregate comparative price data. Finally, news sources such as the New York Times, the BBC, and Reuters use syndication technologies like RSS and Atom to disseminate news feeds related to various topics. Syndication feed mashups can aggregate a user's feeds and present them over the Web creating a personalized newspaper that caters to the reader's particular interests.

The logic behind the development of these mashup infrastructures is the following. Due to rapidly changing market dynamics, a significant amount of business collaborations tend to last for a few months. With the average application integration effort taking from three to six months, there's little room left for a return on investment (see Culnan et al., 2010; Nambisan & Baron, 2009). The industry needs solutions that can be built rapidly and cost effectively to solve immediate and specific business problems, yet be considered disposable when the market moves on (Nambisan & Baron, 2009). To this end, the next generation of new information infrastructures have put mashup infrastructures in the hands of the users (non-developers) so they can build solutions in a manner that can overcome return on investment issues. To achieve this, the development of new information infrastructures has become significantly more affordable and expedient, while empowering end users to quickly integrate disparate services and applications together–i.e. to become developers or co-producers of business value (Nambisan & Baron, 2009). Considering the fact that end users are already familiar with the capabilities of many Web services and content, mashup infrastructures allow for extremely rapid application development.

The Architecture of a Mashup Infrastructure

A mashup infrastructure is architecturally comprised of three different elements that are logically and physically disjoint (i.e. they are separated by both network and organizational boundaries): API/content providers (e.g. Flickr), the mashup site, and the client's Web browser (Merrill, 2009).

First, API/content providers could vary from for-profit technology companies such as Flickr to non-for-profit organizations such as a research organization providing content for public health purposes (see Boulos, 2008). To facilitate data retrieval, providers often expose their content through web-protocols such as REST, SOAP, and RSS/Atom. In addition, mashups that extract content from sites like Wikipedia and virtually all government and public domain web sites do so by a technique known as *screen scraping*. Screen scraping denotes the process by which a tool attempts to extract information from the content provider by attempting to parse the provider's Web pages, which were originally intended for human consumption (Merrill, 2009).

Second, the mashup site is where the mashup is actually hosted. Interestingly, just because this is where the mashup logic resides, it is not necessarily where it is executed. On the one hand, mashups can be implemented similarly to traditional Web applications using server-side dynamic content generation technologies like Java servlets, CGI, PHP, or ASP. Alternatively, mashed content can be generated directly within the client's browser through client-side scripting (i.e. JavaScript) or applets. This client-side logic is

often the combination of code directly embedded in the mashup's Web pages as well as scripting API libraries or applets referenced by these Web pages. The benefits of client-side mashing include less overhead on behalf of the mashup server (i.e. data can be retrieved directly from the content provider) and a more seamless user-experience (i.e. pages can request updates for portions of their content without having to refresh the entire page). Often mashups use a combination of both server and client-side logic to achieve their data aggregation (Yu et al., 2008).

Finally, the client's Web browser is where the application is rendered graphically and where user interaction occurs. As described above, mashups often use client-side logic to assemble and compose the mashed content. Today's browsers incorporate several technologies focused around the asynchronous loading and presentation of content including XHTML and CSS for style presentation, the Document Object Model (DOM) API for dynamic display and interaction, XML for asynchronous data exchange, and JavaScript for browser-side scripting. When used together, the goal of these technologies is to create a smooth, cohesive Web experience for the user by exchanging small amounts of data with the content servers rather than reload and re-render the entire page after some user action (Yu et al., 2008).

From Proprietary & Hierarchical to Heterogeneous & Multilayered Infrastructure Development

Through this flexible architectural design, mashups take the development of information infrastructures from proprietary and hierarchical to heterogeneous and multilayered structures (Benkler, 2006; Lessig, 2008). In a proprietary and hierarchical structure, an information infrastructure is developed as a private good, which is owned by a single entity (e.g. Microsoft) and then licensed for a fee to lay users as a packaged product (e.g. Microsoft Windows products) with very clear usage rights, and with the owner always in control. In a heterogeneous and multilayered structure, an information infrastructure is developed as a commons, where common-pool resources can be creatively used by individuals with a variety of motivations without any single person or entity asserting rights to exclude either from the contributed components or from the resulting whole (Benkler, 2006).

In order to avoid having commons projects (e.g. a photo album on Flickr) appropriated by any single party, participants usually retain copyrights in their contribution, but license them to anyone under a Creative Commons license (see creative-commons.org) that combines a universal license to use the materials with licensing constraints that make it difficult, if not impossible, for any single contributor or third party to appropriate the commons projects. This model of licensing is the most important institutional innovation of the new and emerging information infrastructures and requires anyone who modifies commons projects and distributes the modified version to license it under the same free terms as the original software (Lessig, 2008).

For example, Flickr's API is a very powerful tool that allows user-developers to build services and tools that access Flickr and use the images there in new ways, while ensuring intellectual property rights. Users can use the API to tag, categorize, and keyword each photo. In fact, many photographers often post photos with the very intention of grabbing the top image search of specific Google keywords or phrases and then linking their professional website in their Flickr comment section. For a wedding photographer in a small market, being able to have one of his/her images come up first when someone searches for photographer in that market can be a great way his/her work is found by potential clients. It may even make up the bulk of their marketing efforts and source of clients. For these and many other reasons, Flickr's powerful API is one of the critical factors that both developers and users enjoy

the infrastructure, and Flickr's ability to interact with other services has been critical to its success.

To manage copyrighted content, Flickr has incorporated Creative Commons (CC) licensing options into its user interface, giving photographers and other users around the world the easy ability to share photos on terms of their choosing. Currently there are well over 200 million CC-licensed content on the site, establishing Flickr as the Web's single largest source of such content (see www.creativecommons.org).

The sharing of CC-licensed content is monitored and policed through community norms, i.e. by the users themselves. Inappropriate content gets flagged by community moderators and any content violating community rules is reported.

Certainly, it can be argued that the companies behind the new information infrastructures (e.g. Flickr) are still the owners of the technology upon which lay-users and expert developers are able to develop new commons projects. However, it needs to be stressed that, without the content creators (i.e. the user-developers), these companies would not have a viable business model. That is, the value that companies like Flikr create for themselves comes from the value individual users create through their interactions with other users over different time periods (Keen, 2007). Thus, the success of these new information infrastructures is not controlled by the companies themselves, but from an architectural design that produces value as a by-product of people getting what they want (Bricklin, 2006).

In addition, the success of these new information infrastructures also comes from the possibilities they offer toward "LEGO-ized innovation," i.e. the ways by which the functionality of these mashups gets turned into a block that others can add to their own Web services and content (Lessig, 2008). Tapscott and Williams (2008, pp.183) discuss the example of Google Maps:

Google Map mashups, for example, have emerged to do everything from pinpointing the locations of particular crime sites, to outing celebrity home-steads, to enabling fitness buffs to measure their daily running distance. Or, for the price conscious, there's CheapGas, a service that mashes Google Maps and GasBuddy together to identify gas stations with the lowest pump prices.

The integration is often transparent (cf. Star & Ruhleder, 1996) while enabling the sharing of powerful functionality across many different sites. Web services enable the invention and the building to be shared among many different entities.

There is, however, a key challenge faced by these new information infrastructures and that is the trade-off between the protection of intellectual property and personal or corporate interests versus fair-use and the free flow of information. Anil Dash, a vice president with Six Apart, articulated this trade-off in the following question: "Should Flickr compensate the creators of the most popular pictures on its site?" (Tapscott & Williams, 2008, pp.205). Caterina Fake, cofounder of Flickr, gave the following answer (Tapscott & Williams, 2008, pp.206):

[T]here are systems of value other than, or in addition to, money, that are very important to people: connecting with other people, creating an online identity, expressing oneself—and, not least, garnering other people's attention. She continued on, saying that the Web—indeed the world—would be a much poorer place without the collective generosity of its contributors. The culture of generosity is the very backbone of the Internet.

Despite this response, however, it is hard for many to see how a "culture of generosity" can coexist with an ethic of profit. If the work of individual users-developers was plainly a contribution to the development of a private good (e.g. the development of the new Windows infrastructure), then the answer would be easy: they should be paid otherwise they would stop contributing. However,

the work of these users-developers is a contribution to the development of a commons project, and so there is no clear answer to the trade-off (Lessig, 2008). There is not a single social contract for all digital contributions, whether that is software code or cultural works, including photos, videos, or text (Benkler, 2006).

Thus, as in the case of OSS 2.0, there is a need for a more in-depth understanding of the challenges of governing mashups around the institutional rules of participation (see Constantinides, 2012).

CONCLUSION & IMPLICATIONS FOR FURTHER RESEARCH

As evident from the above discussion, the development of new information infrastructures has placed social production and exchange centre stage, sidetracking the more dominant property- and market-based production. In turn, these new information infrastructures are developed less like a product and more like a collective endeavour where no single group or individual has full control over property rights. *Everyone* is potentially a user-developer, and information infrastructures, including the services and content they provide, are derived from previous technologies and ideas–mashups. At the same time, increased participation is faced with the trade-off between the protection of intellectual property and personal or corporate interests versus fair-use and the free flow of information. Benkler (2006, pp.92) notes:

It is the feasibility of producing information, knowledge, and culture through social, rather than market and proprietary relations—through cooperative peer production and coordinated individual action—that creates the opportunities for greater autonomous action, a more critical culture, a more discursively engaged and better informed republic, and perhaps a more equitable global community.

This new era of information infrastructure development will require researchers to inquire deeper into governance issues by examining (a) the reasons that motivate people to participate in these online enterprises of social production, (b) the norms and policies (e.g. licences) that keep them together, including how those norms and policies are negotiated and implemented in practice, and (c) whether or not such development is efficient.

There is certainly a wide range of theoretical approaches that could help researchers understand the reasons that motivate people to participate in new information infrastructure development; however, what is most important is to understand the dynamic between a "commercial" and a "sharing" economy (Lessig, 2008). In a "commercial" economy, money is the central means of motivation and exchange (Benkler, 2004). For example, anyone wanting a copy of proprietary software has to pay a price to acquire it. In contrast, a "sharing" economy is different. Of all the possible terms of exchange within a sharing economy, the single term that is not appropriate is money. One can demand that a friend spend more time with them, and the relationship is still a friendship. However, if one demands payment for the time he/she spends with another, the relationship is no longer a friendship. Lessig (2008, pp.119) argues:

Viewed like this, we all live in many different commercial and sharing economies, all at the same time. These economies complement one another, and our lives are richer because of this diversity.

New information infrastructures are developed in the midst of the complementarities generated by a commercial and a sharing economy. Thus, there needs to be recognized that there is some form of social and psychological motivation that is neither interchangeable with financial incentives nor simply cumulative with those. Transacting within a commercial economy through monetary rewards may either increase or decrease the social-psychological rewards of a sharing economy (be

they intrinsic or extrinsic, functional or symbolic) and vice versa. In other words, money-oriented motivations are different from socially oriented motivations: sometimes they align; sometimes they collide. Which of the two will be the case is contingent to the historical-cultural context of information infrastructure development. Consider the example of the early initiation of the FOSS movement, which was primarily based on a sharing economy, and the evolution to OSS 2.0, where many individual contributions are based on monetary rewards. Moreover, it is important to recognize that individuals are not monolithic agents. Some people are more focused on making money, whereas others are more driven by social standing and esteem, yet others by a psychological sense of well-being. While it is possible to distinguish different personality types based on what motivates them, the reality is that most people are a composite of different personality types. What needs to be understood is under what conditions the many and diverse desired rewards of different individuals can turn into an important modality of social production.

In addition to theories of motivation and participation, researchers will have to explore the role of new information and communication technologies and next-generation applications in mobilizing and directing processes of social production or not. The modular architecture of new information infrastructures provides individual users more autonomy and flexibility with which to define the nature, extent, and timing of their participation in the development of those infrastructures. However, researchers need to be critical in their exploration of the impact of these new technologies and applications. Researchers need to examine both how these new technologies and applications increase and decrease processes of social production by enabling some users while inhibiting others, since, as Star (1999, pp. 380) has noted, "one person's infrastructure is another's difficulty." The distinction may not be as clear cut as a simple recognition of what enables and what constrains. Instead, there needs to be a more in-depth exploration and analysis of how different parts of these new technologies and applications may help to mobilize and scale-up processes of social production while at the same time those very parts may create confusion and conflict.

This is exactly what is happening now across various social networking sites such as Flickr and YouTube, whereby participation is faced with the trade-off between the protection of intellectual property and personal or corporate interests versus fair-use and the free flow of information.

This is why researchers need to inquire deeper into the norms and policies (e.g. licences) that keep people participating, including how those norms and policies are negotiated and implemented in practice. Such research may have to take a broader, more global perspective into current laws and regulations concerning the ownership and licensing of creative works. There has been extensive research in this area, primarily at the policy level (e.g. Benkler, 2001, 2002, 2004, 2006; Lessig, 2004, 2006; McGowan, 2001, 2005; Schweik, 2005, 2007; Tapscott & Williams, 2008), with researchers usually acknowledging the complexity involved and abstaining from making any recommendations, suggesting instead great sensitivity to context. Thus, there is, a need for more ethnographically-informed research to understand how international laws and regulations concerning the ownership and licensing of creative works applies in particular contexts and under specific circumstances.

This need is made evident from the long legal disputes over peer-to-peer file sharing, which has neither stopped illegal sharing nor found a way to make sure artists are compensated for unauthorized sharing (Lessig, 2004). This example shows how the law is just one part of the problem. A bigger part is the new and emerging norms and expectations of individual users around the control of creative works, norms that are radically different from the norms found at the time when the law was originally established. Movements like the Creative Commons were specifically initiated to help people see the difference between legal and social norms of commons development. Creative Commons gives authors free legal (copyright licenses) and technical tools (metadata and simple marking technology) to mark their creativity with the freedoms they intend their creative works to carry. Lessig (2008, pp.278) argues:

In the five years since this project launched, millions of digital works have been marked to signal this freedom rather than control. Some have used them to help spread their work. Others have used them simply to say, "This is the picture of creativity I believe in." And as the tools have been used, they have begun to define an alternative, privately built copyright system: Almost two- thirds of the licenses restrict commercial use but permit non-commercial use. The vast majority permit free derivatives, though half of those require that the derivatives be released freely as well. This is a picture of a much more balanced regime, built by volunteers, one license at a time.

The Creative Commons is an exemplar of how communities can self-regulate their actions and, consequently, self-govern their commons without the interference of either the state and/or powerful private actors (Lessig, 2004, 2008; Benkler, 2006). However, the Creative Commons is only a step toward copyright reform; it is not itself an ultimate solution.

Alongside the Creative Commons there is another 'solution': a widespread, global culture of ignoring altogether exclusive property rights. This culture has developed a discourse of justification that focuses on the overreaching of the copyright industries and on the ways in which the artists themselves are being exploited by rights holders. While in parts of the world such as the United States this is considered illegal, there are places where courts have sporadically treated participation in file sharing practices as copying for private use, which is exempted in some countries, including a number of European countries. In any event, the sheer size of this movement and its apparent refusal to disappear in the face of lawsuits and public debate present a genuine alternative to both the legal copyright model and the Creative Commons.

Researchers need to inquire deeper into the efficiency, and consequently the sustainability of these norms and policies. The first thing to recognize is that markets, firms, and social relations are three distinct transactional frameworks (Benkler, 2006). For example, in (a) a market transactional framework, one buys software resources online; in (b) a firm transactional framework one utilizes the software resources available within a firm he or she is employed; and in (c) a social transactional framework one 'borrows' software resources from a 'friend.' Comparing and improving the efficiency of (a) and (b), respectively, has been a central project in transaction-costs organization theory, where, for example, the costs of processing an individual order are compared to the costs of planning for the average, common needs of a group of people. Because of this, some stakeholders may attempt to behave opportunistically by withholding relevant information if they believe they can gain advantages by doing so. In turn, different stakeholders negotiating contract agreements will usually try to enforce complex contracts to protect themselves against contingencies and the opportunistic behaviour of the others (Grossman & Hart, 1986; Hart & Moore, 1990; Han et al., 2004). Certainly full owners will have more bargaining power relative to authorized users (Bakos & Nault, 1997). However, (c) is also an alternative transactional framework, where one develops a set of social relations, rather than market- or firm-based relations to address a set of needs. Benkler (2006, pp.108) argues:

The point is that most of economics internally has been ignoring the social transactional framework as an alternative whose relative efficiency can be accounted for and considered in much the same way as the relative cost advantages of simple markets when compared to the hierarchical organizations that typify much of our economic activity—firms.

Because of these new and emerging information infrastructures, researchers will need to explore the social relations that motivate and organize individual and community contributions beyond the standard categories of evaluating efficiency considered to be appropriate for market- and firm-based relations. Rather, researchers will need to explore the notion of efficiency in the context of the ways in which individual human creativity and social relationships impact the development of new information infrastructures.

REFERENCES

Agerfalk, P., & Fitzgerald, B. (2008). Outsourcing to an unknown workforce: Exploring open sourcing as a global sourcing strategy. *Management Information Systems Quarterly, 32*(2), 385–410.

Anderson, R. (2005). Open and closed systems are equivalent (that is, in an ideal world). In Feller, J., Fitzgerald, B., Hissam, S., & Lakhani, K. (Eds.), *Perspectives on free and open source software* (pp. 127–142). Cambridge, MA: MIT Press.

Benkler, Y. (2001). Siren songs and Amish children: Information, autonomy and law. *N.Y.U. Law Review, 76*(23), 59–77.

Benkler, Y. (2002). Coase's penguin, or Linux and the nature of the firm. *The Yale Law Journal, 112*(3), 1–42. doi:10.2307/1562247

Benkler, Y. (2004). Sharing nicely: On shareable goods and the emergence of sharing as modality of economic production. *The Yale Law Journal, 114*, 273–358. doi:10.2307/4135731

Benkler, Y. (2006). *The wealth of networks: How social production transforms markets and freedom.* New Haven, CT: Yale University Press.

Benslimane, D., Dustdar, S., & Sheth, A. (2008). Services mashups: The new generation of Web applications. *Internet Computing, IEEE, 12*(5), 13–15. doi:10.1109/MIC.2008.110

Bolin, M., Webber, M., Rha, P., Wilson, T., & Miller, R. C. (2005). Automation and customization of rendered Web pages. In *Proceedings of UIST '05 the 18th annual ACM symposium on user interface software and technology*, 163-172.

Boulos, M. N. K., Scotch, M., Cheung, K. H., & Burden, D. (2008). Web GIS in practice VI: A demo playlist of geo-mashups for public health neogeographers. *International Journal of Health Geographics, 7*(38), 1–16.

Boyle, J. (2003). The second enclosure movement and the construction of the public domain. *Law and Contemporary Problems, 66*(1-2), 33–75.

Bricklin, D. (2006). The cornucopia of the commons: How to get volunteer labor. Retrieved April 5, 2011, from http://www.bricklin.com/cornucopia.htm

Constantinides, P. (2012). (forthcoming). The development and consequences of new information infrastructures: The case of mashup platforms. *Media Culture & Society.*

Culnan, M. J., McHugh, P., & Zubillaga, J. (2010). How large U.S. companies can use Twitter and other social media to gain business value. *MIS Quarterly Executive, 9*(4), 243–259.

Dempsey, B., Weiss, D., Jones, P., & Greenberg, J. (2002, February). Who is an open source developer? *Communications of the ACM, 45*(2), 67–72. doi:10.1145/503124.503125

Dietz, T., Ostrom, E., & Stern, P. (2003). The struggle to govern the commons. *Science, 302*(5652), 1907–1912. doi:10.1126/science.1091015

Faaborg, A., & Lieberman, H. (2006). A goal-oriented Web browser. In *Proceedings of CHI '06 the SIGCHI conference on Human Factors in computing systems*, 751-760.

Fitzgerald, B. (2006). The transformation of open source software. *Management Information Systems Quarterly, 30*(3), 587–598.

Fitzgerald, B., & Kenny, T. (2003). Open source software in the trenches: Lessons from a large-scale implementation. In *Proceedings of the 24th International Conference on Information Systems (ICIS)*, 316-326.

Fujima, J., Lunzer, A., Hornbaek, K., & Tanaka, Y. (2004). Clip, connect, clone: Combining application elements to build custom interfaces for information access. In *Proceedings of UIST '04 the 17th annual ACM symposium on User interface software and technology*, 175-184.

Ghosh, R. A., & Glott, R. (2002). *Free/libre and open source software: Survey and study.* Retrieved March 30, 2011, from http://www.flossproject.org/index.htm

Gordon, W. J. (1993). A property right in self-expression: Equality and individualism in the natural law of intellectual property. *The Yale Law Journal, 102*, 1533–1543. doi:10.2307/796826

Keen, A. (2007). *The cult of the amateur: How today's internet is killing our culture.* New York, NY: Doubleday/Currency.

Lakhani, K. R., & Wolf, R. (2005). Why hackers do what they do: Understanding motivation and effort in free/open source software projects. In Feller, J., Fitzgerald, B., Hissam, S., & Lakhani, K. (Eds.), *Perspectives on free and open source software* (pp. 3–22). Cambridge, MA: MIT Press. doi:10.2139/ssrn.443040

Lerner, J., & Tirole, J. (2001). The open source movement: Key research questions. *European Economic Review, 45*(4-6), 819–826. doi:10.1016/S0014-2921(01)00124-6

Lerner, J., & Tirole, J. (2002). Some simple economics of open source. *The Journal of Industrial Economics, 50*(2), 197–234. doi:10.1111/1467-6451.00174

Lessig, L. (2004). *Free culture: How big media uses technology and the law to lock down culture and control creativity*. New York, NY: The Penguin Press.

Lessig, L. (2008). *Remix: Making art and commerce in the hybrid economy*. New York, NY: The Penguin Press. doi:10.5040/9781849662505

McGowan, D. (2001). Legal implications of open source software. *University of Illinois Review, 241*(1), 241–304.

McGowan, D. (2005). Legal aspects of free and open source software. In Feller, J., Fitzgerald, B., Hissam, S., & Lakhani, K. (Eds.), *Perspectives on free and open source software* (pp. 361–392). Cambridge, MA: MIT Press.

Merrill, D. (2009). *Mashups: The new breed of Web app*. Retrieved April 6, 2011, from http://www.ibm.com/developerworks/xml/library/x-mashups/index.html

Nambisan, S., & Baron, R. (2009). Virtual customer environments: Testing a model of voluntary participation in value co-creation activities. *Journal of Product Innovation Management, 26*(4), 388–406. doi:10.1111/j.1540-5885.2009.00667.x

Neumann, P. G. (2005). Attaining robust open source software. In Feller, J., Fitzgerald, B., Hissam, S., & Lakhani, K. (Eds.), *Perspectives on free and open source software* (pp. 123–136). Cambridge, MA: MIT Press.

O'Mahony, S. (2005). Non-profit foundations and their role in community-firm software collaboration. In Feller, J., Fitzgerald, B., Hissam, S., & Lakhani, K. (Eds.), *Perspectives on free and open source software* (pp. 393–414). Cambridge, MA: MIT Press.

O'Reilly, T. (2005a). The open source paradigm shift. In Feller, J., Fitzgerald, B., Hissam, S., & Lakhani, K. (Eds.), *Perspectives on free and open source software* (pp. 461–482). Cambridge, MA: MIT Press.

O'Reilly, T. (2005b). *What is Web 2.0: Design patterns and business models for the next generation of software*. Retrieved May 8, 2011, from http://www.oreillynet.com/pub/a/oreilly/tim/news/2005/09/30/what-is-web-20.html

Open Source Initiative. (n.d.). *Open source licenses*. Retrieved from http://www.opensource.org/licenses

Raymond, E. S. (2001). *The cathedral and the bazaar: Musings on Linux and open source by an accidental revolutionary*. Sebastopol, CA: O'Reilly.

Rusovan, S., Lawford, M., & Parnas, D. L. (2005). Open source software development: Future or fad? In Feller, J., Fitzgerald, B., Hissam, S., & Lakhani, K. (Eds.), *Perspectives on free and open source software* (pp. 107–122). Cambridge, MA: MIT Press.

Schroth, C., & Christ, O. (2007). Brave new Web: Emerging design principles and technologies as enablers of a global SOA. In *Proceedings of the IEEE International Conference on Services Computing, (SCC 2007)*, 597-604.

Schweik, C. M. (2005, June). An institutional analysis approach to studying libre software commons. *Ugrade: The European Journal for the Informatics Professional*, 17-27.

Schweik, C. M. (2007). Free/open-source software as a framework for establishing commons in science. In Hess, C., & Ostrom, E. (Eds.), *Understanding knowledge as a commons: From theory to practice* (pp. 277–310). Cambridge, MA: MIT Press.

Schweik, C. M., & Semenov, A. (2003). The institutional design of open source programming. *First Monday, 8*(1). Retrieved September 11, 2011, from www.firstmonday.org.

Shaikh, M., & Cornford, T. (2003). Version management tools: CVS to BK in the Linux kernel. In J. Feller, B. Fitzgerald, S. Hissam, & Lakhani, K. (Eds.), In *Proceedings of ICSE'03 International Conference on Software Engineering.*

Sheth, A. P., Gomadam, K., & Lathem, J. (2007). SA-REST: Semantically interoperable and easier-to-use services and mashups. *IEEE Internet Computing, 11*(6), 91–94. doi:10.1109/MIC.2007.133

Stallman, R. (1999). The GNU operating system and the free software movement. In DiBona, C., Ockman, S., & Stone, M. (Eds.), *Open sources: Voices from the open source revolution.* Sebastopol, CA: O'Reilly. doi:10.1109/ICSM.2006.68

Star, S. L. (1999). The ethnography of infrastructure. *The American Behavioral Scientist, 43*(3), 377–391. doi:10.1177/00027649921955326

Star, S. L., & Ruhleder, K. (1996). Steps toward an ecology of infrastructure: Design and access for large information spaces. *Information Systems Research, 7*(1), 111–134. doi:10.1287/isre.7.1.111

Tapscott, D., & Williams, A. (2008). *Wikinomics: How mass collaboration changes everything.* London, UK: Atlantic Books.

Waldron, J. (1993). From authors to copiers: Individual rights and social values in intellectual property. *Chicago-Kent Law Review, 68*, 841–850.

Weber, S. (2004). *The success of open source.* Cambridge, MA: Harvard University Press.

Weinstock, C. B., & Hissam, S. A. (2005). Making lightning strike twice. In Feller, J., Fitzgerald, B., Hissam, S., & Lakhani, K. (Eds.), *Perspectives on free and open source software* (pp. 143–160). Cambridge, MA: MIT Press.

Yu, J., Benatallah, B., Casati, F., & Daniel, F. (2008, September-October). Understanding mashup development. *IEEE Internet Computing, 13*(5), 44–52. doi:10.1109/MIC.2008.114

ADDITIONAL READING

Brooks, F. (1975). *The mythical man month.* Reading, MA: Addison-Wesley.

Dalle, J.-M., & Jullien, N. (2003). "Libre" software: Turning fads into institutions? *Research Policy, 32*(1), 1–11. doi:10.1016/S0048-7333(02)00003-3

David, P. A. (1998). Common agency contracting and the emergence of "open science" institutions. *The American Economic Review, 88*(2), 15–21.

Fielding, R. T. (1999). Shared leadership in the apache project. *Communications of the ACM, 42*(4), 42–43. doi:10.1145/299157.299167

Frey, B. (1997). *Not just for the money: An economic theory of personal motivation.* Brookfield, VT: Edward Elgar.

Hars, A., & Ou, S. (2002). Working for free? Motivations for participating in open source projects. *International Journal of Electronic Commerce, 6*(3), 25–39.

Hissam, S., Plakosh, D., & Weinstock, C. (2002). Trust and vulnerability in open source software. *IEEE Proceedings-Software, 149*(1), 47–51. doi:10.1049/ip-sen:20020208

Kogut, B., & Metiu, A. (2001). Open-source software development and distributed innovation. *Oxford Review of Economic Policy, 17*(2), 248–264. doi:10.1093/oxrep/17.2.248

Lakhani, K. R., & von Hippel, E. (2003). How open source software works: "Free" user-to-user assistance. *Research Policy, 32*(6), 923–943. doi:10.1016/S0048-7333(02)00095-1

Ljungberg, J. (2000). Open source movements as a model for organising. *European Journal of Information Systems, 9*(4), 208–216. doi:10.1057/palgrave/ejis/3000373

Melucci, A. (1996). *Challenging codes: Collective action in the information age*. Cambridge, UK: Cambridge University Press. doi:10.1017/CBO9780511520891

Moody, G. (2001). *Rebel code: Inside Linux and the open source revolution*. New York, NY: Perseus Press.

Nakakoji, K., & Yamamoto, Y. (2001). Taxonomy of open-source software development. Making sense of the bazaar: Proceedings of the 1st workshop on open source software engineering. *IEEE Computer Society*, 41–42.

O'Mahony, S. (2003). Guarding the commons: How community-managed software projects protect their work. *Research Policy, 1615*, 1–20.

Ostrom, E. (1990). *Governing the commons: The evolution of institutions for collective action*. Cambridge, UK: Cambridge University Press.

Ostrom, E., Gardner, R., & Walker, J. (1994). *Rules, games, and common-pool resources*. Ann Arbor, MI: University of Michigan Press.

Raymond, E. (1996). *The new hacker's dictionary* (3rd ed.). Cambridge, MA: MIT Press.

Sandler, T. (1992). *Collective action: Theory and applications*. Ann Arbor, MI: University of Michigan Press.

Scacchi, W. (2002). Understanding the requirements for developing open source software systems. *IEEE Software, 149*(1), 24–39. doi:10.1049/ip-sen:20020202

Shepsle, K. A. (1979). Institutional arrangements and equilibrium in multidimensional voting models. *American Journal of Political Science, 23*, 27–59. doi:10.2307/2110770

Shepsle, K. A. (1989). Studying institutions: Some lessons from the rational choice approach. *Journal of Theoretical Politics, 1*, 131–149. doi:10.1177/0951692889001002002

Thompson, K. (1999). Unix and beyond: An interview with Ken Thompson. *IEEE Computer, 32*(5), 58–64. doi:10.1109/MC.1999.762801

Torvalds, L., & Diamond, D. (2001). *Just for fun: The story of an accidental revolutionary*. New York, NY: Harper Collins.

Touraine, A. (1981). *The voice and the eye: An analysis of social movements*. Cambridge, UK: Cambridge University Press.

von Hippel, E. (2005). *Democratizing innovation*. Cambridge, MA: MIT Press.

von Hippel, E., & von Krogh, G. (2003). Open source software and the private collective innovation model: Issues for organization science. *Organization Science, 14*(2), 209–223. doi:10.1287/orsc.14.2.209.14992

von Krogh, G., Spaeth, S., & Lakhani, K. R. (2003). Community, joining, and specialization in open source software innovation: A case study. *Research Policy, 32*, 1217–1241. doi:10.1016/S0048-7333(03)00050-7

Wall, L. (1999). The origin of the camel lot in the breakdown of the bilingual Unix. *Communications of the ACM, 42*(4), 40–41. doi:10.1145/299157.299166

Wiegers, K. (2002). *Peer reviews in software: A practical guide*. Boston, MA: Addison-Wesley.

Williams, S. (2002). *Free as in freedom: Richard Stallman's crusade for free software*. Sebastopol, CA: O'Reilly.

ENDNOTES

[1] More detailed, formal definitions for the terms *free* and *open source* are offered by the Free Software Foundation (FSF) and Open Source Initiative (OSI). The decision to use one of these terms rather than the other is generally ideological, rather than functional; the FSF prefers the use of a term that explicitly refers to freedom, while the OSI believes that the dual meaning of the English word 'free' (*gratis* or *libertas*) is confusing, and instead prefers the emphasis on the 'open' availability and modifiability of source code. In Europe the French-English construct *libre software* has been widely adopted to unambiguously capture the connotation intended by the FSF.

[2] See (Open Source Initiative)

[3] Derivative work is any work containing the original code or a portion of it either verbatim or with modifications and/or translated into another language (McGowan, 2005).

Chapter 9
The Consequences of New Information Infrastructures

ABSTRACT

This chapter builds on the discussion in Chapter 8 by exploring the dynamics of social participation in the development of new information infrastructures. Specifically, this chapter focuses on the consequences of social participation and 'free choice' – if indeed individuals are free, i.e. without any external influence – into different types of interaction offered by new information infrastructures. The WikiLeaks information infrastructure is used as an example to set the ground for examining how new information infrastructures generate a number of consequences for the 'freedom' of individual users, and for those seeking to monitor and control infrastructure use. This discussion raises a number of ethical issues which are explored by drawing on Foucault's notion of governmentality. The chapter concludes with some implications for further research on the ethical governance of information infrastructure development.

INTRODUCTION

Recent developments in Web-based technologies, the increasing bandwidth, and the shift toward more compact and efficient (online) media production and delivery channels have given way to new information infrastructures that transcend various business contexts into the social domain as central hubs of communication and entertainment. These new developments have been referred to as Web 2.0, which enable the participative and modular building of virtual applications, whilst mashing-up data and functionality from a number of different sources (Grossman, 2006; O'Reily, 2005).

These developments have brought information and communication power that was previously the preserve of corporations within the reach of every motivated individual. In 2006, *Time* magazine's

DOI: 10.4018/978-1-4666-1622-6.ch009

Person of the Year was 'You,' 'Me,' 'Everyone' (Grossman, 2006):

And we are so ready for it. We're ready to balance our diet of predigested news with raw feeds from Baghdad and Boston and Beijing. You can learn more about how Americans live just by looking at the backgrounds of YouTube videos—those rumpled bedrooms and toy-strewn basement rec rooms—than you could from 1,000 hours of network television. And we didn't just watch, we also worked. Like crazy. We made Facebook profiles and Second Life avatars and reviewed books at Amazon and recorded podcasts. We blogged about our candidates losing and wrote songs about getting dumped. We camcordered bombing runs and built open-source software.

Web 2.0 is, thus, more of a cultural phenomenon that emerged from developments surrounding Web-based technologies and which pushed for collective mobilizations of people and resources. This push was exacerbated by advances in computer networking combined with powerful home computers and modern operating systems and increased streaming bandwidths. In turn, we have now moved to a new era of virtual communication whereby one can create new content which can be communicated to others in real-time.

This new generation of Web-based technologies is coupled by a new model of amassing the computing powers of distributed computers. Grid computing functions by connecting geographically remote computers into a single network to create a virtual supercomputer and in the process combining the computational power of all computers on the grid (as well as the software applications embedded therein) (Foster & Kesselman, 1999; Foster, 2002, 2003). In this way, grid computing takes advantage of idle resources as most computers use their central processing units on average only 25 percent of the time.

An exemplar of this new form of virtual creation and communication is manifested in Sec-

ond Life. Second Life (SL) is built on a unique combination of grid computing and streaming technologies that allow it to constantly expand (SL website, 2008):

Second Life exists on a scalable server grid running Linux, capable of supporting thousands of simultaneous Second Life Residents. Each server represents a unique geographic region—so the world can grow infinitely in any direction, just by adding off-the-shelf Linux boxes... Second Life keeps evolving, even when you're gone—while you're sleeping, your neighbor can build a new house, a castle, or something you never would have imagined.

The uniqueness of SL comes from the combination of grid computing with real-time, three dimensional streaming technology allowing all content (e.g. objects, textures, audio, video, and motion) to be streamed to personal computers around the globe in real-time at broadband bandwidths. Further, as the above quote from the SL website suggests, by building on a scalable grid server and by giving the opportunity to SL residents to create their own content, SL is constantly at a moment of *singularity* whereby the (virtual) world expands ex nihilo; there are no predetermined boundaries- rather space is filled as it is being created (Ondrejka, 2007). In this context, SL wants everyone to become their own creator (SL website, 2008):

Create anything you can imagine with powerful, highly flexible building tools, using geometric primitives and a simple, intuitive interface. Build right in Second Life—no separate tools to learn or applications to load. Build in-world in real time with other Residents... A simple yet powerful in-world scripting language lets you add behaviors and special effects to your objects. It's easy for non-programmers to pick up, since you can easily modify and edit existing scripts. Or make your own scripts—lock your house with a private password, make a music box, or invent a pet that follows you around.

Like the mash-up examples discussed in Chapter 8, the ready availability of computational and design resources offered by SL exemplifies the concept of virtualization – an information infrastructure with ready functions hidden behind an interface that conceals the details of how those functions were put together and implemented, but which the end user is able to use with relatively no difficulty (Foster, 2003).

To this end, some view these new information infrastructures as *technologies of freedom* since they enhance the freedom of choice for individuals and intensify horizontal (bottom-up) relations in networks of organizations and individuals (Poole, 1983; Morrisett, 2003; Hay & Packer, 2004). The focus here is on the manifestation of "freedoms conceived in terms of a complicated conjunction of social and physical [technological] bodies in space" (Hay & Packer, 2004, pp.212-213). For example, SL is a virtual environment that offers opportunities to freely create, socialize, and trade as one wishes, even including the possibility to play digital games within SL itself. As in the example of FOSS and mashup applications, residents of SL create digital resources and carry out different types of transactions of their creations with other residents.

Yet, others claim that since the development of these new information infrastructures is determined by leaders in governments, public administrations, businesses, and other organizations, they are primarily *technologies of surveillance and control* (Beniger, 1996; Garfinkel, 2000; Lyon, 2001). For example, massive multiplayer online role-playing games (MMORPG) (see Turkle, 1995, 2005), like SL, are the brainchild of large, property-owning corporations who monitor and sanction potentially unlawful or harmful behavior.

In reality, these new information infrastructures function simultaneously as technologies of freedom *and* as technologies of surveillance and control[1] (Van Dijk, 2006). As discussed in Chapter 8 of this book, unlike more traditional common arrangements, new information infrastructures are not used by commoners under clear governance rules. In consequence, although separate commoners act collectively, their actions are not collective in the sense of the early commons studies; rather their actions are instigated under complex motivational structures approaching mathematical chaos (see Wilson et al,. 1994), whereby no single user or group of users have absolute information of all likely combinations of future events (Ostrom, 2009). Thus, although there are now technological advances for better monitoring and controlling the actions of the commoners, the latter also have more freedom to roam about and create havoc in those commons, as in the recent examples of hackers attacking large corporations such as MasterCard (Addley & Halliday, 2010) and Sony (Gaudin, 2011).

The key of the 'problem' (if indeed it is a problem) is that, although there are privately owned, corporate information infrastructures (like those of MasterCard and Sony), these are accessible through a global electronic commons: the World Wide Web and the Internet. In fact, once security structures collapse (as they often do), all privately owned and public information infrastructures become interconnected (and vulnerable) under the global electronic commons. This creates a huge governance challenge, not just for large corporations and government agencies, but – more importantly for the purposes of this book – also for those groups of people that manage a common-pool resource (e.g. a FOSS project, WikiLeaks).

This chapter will explore the challenge of governing the consequences of new information infrastructures. To set the ground for the discussion, the next section will use the WikiLeaks example to examine how new information infrastructures generate a number of consequences for the 'freedom' of individual users, and for those seeking to monitor and control infrastructure use. In the following section, these consequences will be explored through the notion of governmentality (Foucault, 1984, 1991) – i.e. of how people seek to govern their own choices and those of other individuals, and to what ends[2]. The chapter will conclude with some implications for further research on the ethical governance of information infrastructure development.

KEY CONSEQUENCES OF NEW INFORMATION INFRASTRUCTURES: THE CASE OF WIKILEAKS

WikiLeaks: Structure, Objectives, and Associated Challenges

WikiLeaks is an international non-profit organization that relies on contributions from independent, anonymous, news sources, news leaks, and whistleblowers, to publish private, secret, and classified media content (WikiLeaks website, 2011, 'About' page). The original wikileaks.org website was launched in 2006 and claimed a database of more than 1.2 million documents within a year of its launch (Calabresi, 2010). The creators of WikiLeaks have not been formally identified, although Julian Assange has been reported to be the founder and spokesperson for the organization (Burns & Somaiya, 2010).

Initially, WikiLeaks allowed any willing individual to post a document on the site, anonymously and untraceably. Users could publicly discuss documents and analyze their credibility and veracity, while formulating collective publications a la Wikipedia. However, unlike Wikipedia, WikiLeaks established an editorial policy that accepted only documents that were "of political, diplomatic, historical, or ethical interest" (and excluded "material that is already publicly available" (WikiLeaks website, 2008). As of 2010, it is no longer possible for anybody to post on the WikiLeaks website or edit a document. Instead, submissions are regulated by an internal review process and some are published, while documents not fitting the editorial criteria are rejected by anonymous WikiLeaks reviewers (WikiLeaks website, 2008).

Technically, WikiLeaks is based on several software packages, including MediaWiki, Freenet, Tor, and PGP (McLachlan & Hopper, 2009). The WikiLeaks website has been available on multiple servers around the world and different domain names following a number of denial-of-service attacks and its severance from different Domain Name System (DNS) providers (Randall & Cooper, 2010). Until August 2010, WikiLeaks was hosted by PRQ, a Sweden-based company, which is said to have "almost no information about its clientele and maintains few if any of its own logs" (Goodwin, 2008). "WikiLeaks maintains its own servers at undisclosed locations, keeps no logs, and uses military-grade encryption to protect sources and other confidential information" (Goodwin, 2008).

After the site became the target of a denial-of-service attack from a hacker on its old servers, Julian Assange told Swiss public television TSR that he was seriously considering to seek political asylum in neutral Switzerland and setting up a WikiLeaks foundation in the country to move the operation there (Nebehey, 2010). The search for 'neutrality' and of political asylum came after a series of releases by WikiLeaks which caused an outcry from the international community as it revealed secret information and data on military tactics, political relationships, and high-profile socio-economic developments around the world.

In brief, the key releases of WikiLeaks were a video from the Baghdad airstrike in 12 July 2007, in which Iraqi civilians and journalists were killed by an Apache helicopter (known as the *Collateral Murder* video); the Afghan War Diary, a compilation of more than 76,900 documents about the war in Afghanistan not previously available for public review; the Iraq War Logs, a package of almost 400,000 documents, which helped to map every death in Iraq, and across the border in Iran; the U.S. State department diplomatic cables, which caused the biggest outcry from the international community; and finally, the Guantanamo Bay files, a package of 779 secret files relating to prisoners detained in the Guantanamo Bay detention camp (WikiLeaks website, 2011, 'Main' page).

In an interview, Assange explained that these releases came about in an effort to regulate government and protect freedom of speech (Khatchadourian, 2010). At the same time, Assange acknowledged that the practice of posting largely unfiltered classified information online could one day lead the Web site to have "blood on our hands" (Khatchadourian, 2010). He expressed the view that the potential to save lives, however, outweighs the danger to innocents (Khatchadourian, 2010).

Right about the time of this comment, the U.S. Justice Department opened a criminal probe on WikiLeaks and founder Julian Assange, primarily because of the leak of the U.S. State diplomatic cables (Savage, 2010). In December 2010, Assange was captured in Britain after the Swedish authorities had issued a European Arrest Warrant (EAW) to extradite him to Sweden for questioning for an alleged sex assault. Although Assange denied allegations, his capture was followed by a series of threats by various governments toward Assange and the integrity of WikiLeaks. These threats led to some legal experts to question whether Assange had become the target of a global smear campaign to demonise him as a criminal or as a terrorist, without any legal basis (Lauder, 2010; Savage, 2010), while the Center for Constitutional Rights issued a statement highlighting its alarm at the "multiple examples of legal overreach and irregularities" in his arrest (CCR, 2010).

Consequences of WikiLeaks

A few months prior to Assange being captured–specifically, on 29 July 2010–WikiLeaks added a 1.4GB "Insurance File" to the Afghan War Diary page. The file was AES encrypted and has been speculated to serve as insurance in case the WikiLeaks website or its spokesman Julian Assange are incapacitated, upon which the passphrase could be published (Ward, 2010). Following the first few days' release of the U.S. State diplomatic cables starting 28 November 2010, the U.S. television broadcaster *CBS* predicted that "If anything happens to Assange or the website, a key will go out to unlock the files. There would then be no way to stop the information from spreading like wildfire because so many people already have copies" (Palmer, 2010). *CBS* correspondent Declan McCullagh stated, "What most folks are speculating is that the insurance file contains unreleased information that would be especially embarrassing to the U.S. government if it were released" (Palmer, 2010).

In addition to the Afgan War "Insurance File," on 19 July 2010, during a televised interview, Assange showed a document WikiLeaks had on an Albanian oil well blowout, and said they also had material from inside BP on the recent oil well blowout in the Gulf of Mexico (Anderson, 2010). During another *CNN* broadcast he said that WikiLeaks was "getting enormous quantity of whistle-blower disclosures of a very high calibre," but added that they have not been able to verify and release the material because they do not have enough volunteer journalists (Galant, 2010). Further, in December 2010, Assange told *Forbes* that WikiLeaks was planning another "megaleak" early in 2011 from inside the private sector, involving "a big U.S. bank" and revealing an "ecosystem of corruption" (Greenberg, 2010). Bank of America's stock price fell by 3 percent as a result of this announcement, and Assange commented on the possible impact of the release that "it could take down a bank or two" (De la Merced, 2010).

Although these announcements could have been part of a media strategy to counter the threats on Assange's own life, but also the political pressure on WikiLeaks, they generated a number of responses from state governments, but also big corporations.

For example, since December 2010, all U.S. federal government employees and contractors have been forbidden from accessing classified documents publicly available on WikiLeaks and other websites (MacAskill, 2010a). Although Hillary Clinton refused to comment on specific reports, she claimed that the leaks "put people's lives in danger" and "threatens national security" (Calabresi, 2010).

Also, in Iceland in August 2009, Kaupthing Bank succeeded in obtaining a court order preventing Iceland's national broadcaster, RÚV, from broadcasting a risk analysis report showing the bank's substantial exposure to debt default risk (Sigurgrimsdottir, 2009). This information had been leaked by a whistleblower to WikiLeaks and remained available on the WikiLeaks site (Sigurgrimsdottir, 2009). Consequently, WikiLeaks has been credited with inspiring the Icelandic Modern Media Initiative, a bill meant to reclaim Iceland's 2007 *Reporters Without Borders* ranking as first in the world for free speech (BBC, 2010). It should be noted that the chief sponsor of the initiative is former volunteer for WikiLeaks and member of the Icelandic parliament (BBC, 2010).

At the same time, several companies severed ties with WikiLeaks. For example, PayPal permanently cut off the account of the Wau Holland Foundation, the main fund-raising organization for WikiLeaks. PayPal alleged that the account violated its "Acceptable Use Policy," stating specifically that the account was used for "activities that encourage, promote, facilitate, or instruct others to engage in illegal activity" (Satter & Svensson, 2010). In addition, Moneybookers, which collected donations for WikiLeaks, terminated its relationship with the site. Moneybookers affirmed that its decision had been made "to comply with money laundering or other investigations conducted by government authorities, agencies, or commissions" (Leigh & Evans, 2010). During the same period, MasterCard and Visa announced that they would no longer accept payments to and from WikiLeaks pending "further investigations"

(Satter & Svensson, 2010). Finally, Amazon severed its ties with WikiLeaks, to which it was providing infrastructure services, after an intervention by an aide of U.S. Senator Joe Lieberman (MacAskill, 2010b).

In the days following these developments, numerous mirrors of the WikiLeaks site appeared, and the Anonymous group of Internet activists called on supporters to attack the websites of companies which opposed WikiLeaks under the banner of Operation Payback, which was previously aimed at anti-piracy organisations (Somaiya, 2010).

In another move of support for WikiLeaks, XIPWIRE established a way to donate to WikiLeaks, and waived their fees (Webster, 2010). Datacell, the Swiss-based IT company that enabled WikiLeaks to accept credit card donations, announced that they would take legal action against Visa Europe and MasterCard, in order to resume allowing payments to the website (Webster, 2010). In addition, the UN High Commissioner for Human Rights stated that Visa, MasterCard, and Amazon may be "violating Wikileaks' right to freedom of expression" by withdrawing their services (Pillay, 2010).

In 2010, in the midst of these developments, Julian Assange received the Sam Adams Award and was named the Readers' Choice for *TIME's Person of the Year* in 2010 (Friedman, 2010). The UK Information Commissioner also stated that "WikiLeaks is part of the phenomenon of the online, empowered citizen" (Curtis, 2010). Finally, supporters of WikiLeaks in the media and academia have commended it for exposing state and corporate secrets, increasing transparency, supporting freedom of the press, and enhancing democratic discourse while challenging powerful institutions (Medb, 2010).

More importantly, the releases of U.S. diplomatic cables inspired the splintering of a number of other information infrastructures based on the WikiLeaks model. These include, OpenLeaks created by the former deputy to Assange, Daniel Domscheit-Berg, who said the intention was to be more transparent than WikiLeaks (Nordstrom, 2010); BrusselsLeaks, which is focused on the European Union as a collaborative effort of media professionals and activists that seek to "pull the shady inner workings of the EU system out into the public domain. This is about getting important information out there, not about BrusselsLeaks [or any other 'leaks' for that matter]" (Piven, 2010); TradeLeaks, which was created to "do to trade and commerce what WikiLeaks has done to politics," by ensuring that "individuals and businesses should attain values from others through mutually beneficial and fully consensual trade, rather than force, fraud, or deception" (Piven, 2010); Indoleaks, an Indonesian site that seeks to publish classified documents primarily from the Indonesian government (Piven, 2010); and many more.

THE GOVERNMENTALITY OF NEW INFORMATION INFRASTRUCTURES

At first, WikiLeaks may seem as an extreme example of a niche type of information infrastructure. However, after a closer look, WikiLeaks is not very far off the open source movement (Feller et al., 2005) discussed in Chapter 8. Like the early FOSS projects and more recent mash-ups, the WikiLeaks information infrastructure is developed based on a commons model: there is no central body governing the rights to access, use, and redistribute whatever resources are stored, produced, and consumed in the commons, rather the communities of users make up the rules of their interaction in practice, according to the resources and the mode of distribution. The only major difference is that WikiLeaks deals with resources that are not necessarily bound to intellectual property regimes (although they could), but rather with resources that are sensitive, confidential, secret, and critical to the integrity and *governance of a state*, as well as the *governance of individuals*, whether those are politicians, bankers, 'criminals,' or citizens.

A useful concept for analyzing how governance manifests in these new information infrastructures is that of *governmentality* (Foucault, 1991). With this term, Foucault opens up the problems of governance beyond those of the disciplinary society, to the conditions of emergence of the "mentality of government" or the "conduct of conduct" (Gordon, 1991). The verb *to conduct* is critical in understanding the true meaning of governmentality as it points to both the act of leading and of behaving, of conducting others and of conducting oneself (Foucault, 1982, pp.220-221). Thus, Foucault juxtaposes an analysis of the 'practices of government' to the 'practices of the self,' two relatively independent, yet interdependent domains that bring together the micro and macro-levels of power.

The practices of government begin with an underlying, historical political rationality, which does not simply arise from the 'rulers' and their interests, but from historically developed and modified forms of rationality (Dean, 1997). That is, government rationality has–over several centuries[3]–become imbricated in the "things" that humans occupy themselves with–wealth, resources, territory, customs, habits, and so on (Foucault, 1991, pp.93). These "things" can be categorized into sets of *techniques* (e.g. systems of accounting, forms of surveillance, etc.) and *technologies* (e.g. bodies of expertise, bodies of ownership), which help to implement governance across a population (Dean, 1997). This set of techniques and technologies seek to 'align' the happiness of the population with the strength of the state[4] through the implementation of new rationalities for the practices of the self (Foucault, 1988, pp.82-83). There is, thus, "circularity" between practices of government and practices of the self, where the individual's demands for the enhancement of civil, political, and social rights are responded to by the creation of more governmental practices to secure, defend, protect, and foster those rights. Foucault (1993, pp.203-4) notes:

Governing people is not a way to force people to do what the governor wants; it is always a versatile equilibrium, with complementarity and conflicts between techniques which assure coercion and processes through which the self is constructed or modified by himself.

Especially in today's Web 2.0 era, individuals are constructed, not as citizens who obey rules and address problems they share with others, but as rational and calculating *entrepreneurs*[5] who are not only capable of, but also responsible for caring for themselves. That is, practices of government operate through a tacit or explicit conception of freedom of choice on the practices of the self. However, it is exactly on the premises of such freedom of choice that the population can be 'manipulated' through various government practices. "*Free* subjects" are "those that exercise some type of choice," but they are also "free *subjects*, whose subjection operates through the exercise of choice" (Dean, 1997, pp.193). In this sense, (Foucault, 1991, pp.95):

government is defined as a right manner of disposing things so as to lead not to the form of the common good, as the jurists' texts would have said, but to an end which is 'convenient' for each of the things that are to be governed.

New information infrastructures have increased the centralization of institutions, procedures, calculations, and tactics towards a convenient end of government, by enabling a further concentration of power and increased surveillance of free subjects. At the same time, however, new information infrastructures are, by definition, the opposite of centralization, and as a result, a conflict between the practices of government and the practices of the self is inevitable.

For example, increasingly more and more organizations encourage their employees to use online social networking sites such as Facebook, Flickr, Twitter, etc., in an effort to create opportunities for increased business value (Culnan et al., 2010). At the same time, however, these same organizations have developed strict social media policies "both for their protection and to provide guidelines to employees on the safe and savvy use of internal and external social platforms" (Donston-Miller, 2011). For example, the National Library of Australia cautions its employees to adhere to the following guidelines when using social networking sites such as YouTube and Flickr (NLA, 2011):

...users must not access inappropriate material on the Internet via a Web browser or other software tool.... It is possible that Library employees may have a work related need to access material that may be deemed inappropriate. In these cases the employee must notify their supervisor of this variance prior to, or immediately after, accessing this information... should be aware of laws covering libel, defamation, privacy, and the protection of intellectual property... must be apolitical, impartial and professional, and avoid any statements that might be interpreted as advocating government policies or criticising the policies of political parties or groups... employees should take note of any copyright/Creative Commons notices attached to content they wish to use/repurpose. Additionally employees should cite or otherwise acknowledge content sources when they are known.

....

*Employees who participate in online communication deemed not to be in the best interest of the Library will be **subject to disciplinary action** under the Library's Managing Misconduct Policy. The Library will remove, or request the employee to remove, any material where there is a breach of the Values and Code of Conduct or a breach of the controls detailed in the Library's Social Media Policy and Guidelines... (emphasis added)*

This form of disciplinary action against behavior that may be deemed unlawful or violating the interests of different stakeholder groups is exactly what happened in the WikiLeaks example discussed earlier, when companies like PayPal, Moneybookers, and Amazon, in joint with government agencies, blocked all WikiLeaks resources as violating their information policies and threatening national security.

As these examples illustrate, modern forms of control are not exclusively carried out by recourse to institutionalized violence or threats of violence like imprisonment, financial penalties, and so on. The prime function of modern form of control is not to repress, but to make most of the population conform voluntarily to norms, policies, or rules, by making these publicly available for everyone to access. In this way, user-developer communities are encouraged to self-discipline themselves and their members by continuously monitoring and reporting instances when community norms, policies, or rules are violated (Constantinides, 2012). This is why, for Foucault (1979, pp.195):

[We] must cease once and for all to describe the effects of power in negative terms, it "excludes," it "represses," it "censors," it "abstracts," it "masks," it "conceals." In fact power produces: it produces reality; it produces domains of objects and rituals of truth.

In this new Web 2.0 era, each individual becomes the end at which power has effects; each individual becomes "productive" in the exercise of power. The actual objective is the self-implementation of disciplining techniques and technologies by the entire population with the aim "to reform conduct... and deconstruct settled ways of mental and physical behavior, and to produce and then govern new forms of habitual conduct in belief and action" (Tully, 1993, pp. 179). This new governmentality indicates that an individual's mode of being is constructed by a process of normalization whose purpose is to create "a state of conscious and permanent vis-

ibility that assures the automatic functioning of power" (Foucault, 1979, pp. 201).

The most efficient disciplining technology is the one the disciplined apply to themselves. This is achieved by giving individuals and groups an identity through the very techniques they employ in everyday life such as user and developer blogs and forums, where individuals constantly construct their identity by building up their status as 'expert' contributors.

The normalization of human subjectivities prompts them to act in congruence with–but also in resistance against–the objectives of a normalizing process. In this sense, one can claim that "modern society has no control center" and that power can be conceptualized instead as a "field of power" in which power relations are exercised in a determinist yet open-ended fashion (Beck, 1992). This was exactly what happened in the WikiLeaks case where, the power exercised by various national governments and corporations against Assange and WikiLeaks was later met by the resistance of the Anonymous group of hackers, independent legal experts, patches of the global journalist community, and a splintering of the WikiLeaks model into multiple other similar sites. Techniques such as hacking and denial of service (both for and against WikiLeaks) were already available and made ready-to-hand through new web technologies.

Certainly, after the capture of Assange, many journalists and online wiki users came under tremendous pressure to conform to the normalizing influences inherent in this deployment of electronic power (Ungerleider, 2011). Although considerable resistance is evident, the fear of reprisals from "legitimate" authority and self-appointed Internet "police" shape the behavior of many. Policing becomes a case of "state security" when resources exchanged on the Internet are thought to contain confidential and even secret information, as in the case of WikiLeaks. This is when the instruments of government go beyond legislation, manifesting into new techniques and technologies of control.

A primary example of such a manifestation of state power is the USA Patriot Act, legislation passed by Congress six weeks after the September 11th attacks, which broadened the U.S. government's surveillance powers in several areas including records searches and intelligence searches. "Project Carnivore," is a networked surveillance technology developed for the Federal Bureau of Investigation for the purposes of implementing the Patriot Act. Although some members of the legal community have argued in favor of the use of Carnivore (Dunham, 2002; Strauss, 2002), most legal scholars agree that Carnivore has the potential to intrude on the civil liberties of individuals (Haas, 2001; Holmes, 2001; Merl, 2001; Tountas, 2003). Ventura et al (2005, pp.63-64) argue that:

At the most general level, as a system of deeply penetrating surveillance, Carnivore represents a means of correct training which Foucault (1977, pp.170-194) describes as an 'examination,' i.e., a method of disciplinary power that is able to see and record every move and thought of each and all, but that itself cannot be seen... the very fact that the FBI has the potential to monitor communications on a website may lead Internet users to believe that they are constantly being watched... The FBI's position on the Carnivore software, the published official statements regarding the project, and the very name of the Project all suggest a culture in the ranks of social control agents that advocates a 'by-any-means-necessary' mindset that fits well with the totalizing aspirations of disciplinary power.

The 'by-any-means-necessary' mindset– i.e. governmentality–of electronic disciplinary power is also evident in the WikiLeaks case, from a total denial of access of resources from WikiLeaks and other websites to U.S. federal employees (MacAskill, 2010a), to the permanent cut-off of WikiLeaks' financial accounts (Satter &

Svensson, 2010; Leigh & Evans, 2010), and the criminal probe on Julian Assange (Lauder, 2010; Savage, 2010), all instituted under questionable circumstances.

Individuals are encouraged to self-censure their practices in new information infrastructures like WikiLeaks, not just to avoid being censured and penalized by state and corporate governance technologies, but also because of the other users' potential gaze and recourse to electronic disciplining techniques. Besides the more common forms of privacy intrusion such as spamming, denial of service, and computer virus attacks, as well as the stealing of credit card information, there are other virtual forms of illegal activity. In one example, in 2003, Chinese courts were presented with a complaint filed by a user of the Red Moon virtual world who had gathered an array of virtual weapons sufficient to render him effectively invincible in the virtual world (Fairfield, 2005). According to the user, a hacker broke into his account and stole his weapons. The Red Moon administrator refused to provide him with the identity of the thief and the user turned to the courts. In one of the first decisions of its kind, the court in *Li Hongchen v. Beijing Arctic Ice Technology Development Co.* ruled that the user was entitled to compensation from the administrator in the form of the return of the stolen (virtual) weapon (Fairfield, 2005).). In a similar incident, in 2006, a Second Life user called her local police in Kansas because her avatar had been stolen by an online scam artist (Quarmby, 2009). Even though the user did not lose her real world money, she lost her in-game Linden Dollars. Not knowing where to turn to, she called the local police who did not know what to do or how to handle the matter (Quarmby, 2009).

To this end, new information infrastructures, including mobile computing and telephony[6], have generated a new intimacy with technology and, in consequence, a new state of the self, itself. As Sherry Turkle (2008, pp.122, emphasis added) has noted:

*We are tethered to our "always-on/always-on-you" communications devices and the people and things we reach through them: people, Web pages, voice mail, games, artificial intelligences (non-player game characters, interactive online "bots"). These very different objects achieve a certain sameness because of the way we reach them. Animate and inanimate, they live for us through our tethering devices, always **ready-to-mind and hand**.*

And added that (Turkle, 2008, pp.130, emphasis added):

*Always-on/always-on-you technology takes the job of **self-monitoring** to a new level. We try to keep up with our lives as they are presented to us by a new **disciplining technology**.*

In this new era of 'always-on/always-on-you' information infrastructures, Foucault's panopticon becomes the distributed sources of observation of the behavior of individuals and–more importantly–how they respond to various rules and technical commands. In other words, the panopticon needs not be a centralized data collection system, since the surveillance of individual and collective conduct occurs within the mini-panopticons that individuals use on a daily basis: smart phones, PCs, and touch-pad computers, but also the very APIs *ready-to-hand* from the Web sites they visit.

These mini-panopticons entrench surveillance into the ownership of an information infrastructure, and thus have self-normalizing effects on many users. That is, while the various discourses of ownership–including copyright, intellectual property rights, and the like–have promoted ideals of choice, freedom, autonomy, and individualism, the reality is that individuals are more and more subject to the unforgiving demands of a government rationality based on a new intimacy with technology (Turkle, 2006). In fact, it has been argued that the recent increase in intellectual property disputes of digital content illustrate not the failure of what sometimes has been called the "ownership society" (see Singer, 2006), but rather its success in instituting a moralizing principle of punishing those who have not amassed sufficient ownership (Hamann, 2009).

CONCLUSION & IMPLICATIONS FOR FURTHER RESEARCH

In this chapter, it has been argued that new information infrastructures–from social networking sites, to FOSS projects, mash-ups, and wiki-based journalism–function simultaneously as technologies of freedom *and* as technologies of surveillance and control (Van Dijk, 2006). That is, although there are now technological advances for better monitoring and control of the actions of different infrastructure users, the latter also have more freedom to roam about and create havoc across interconnected information infrastructures, whether those are privately owned or public. This creates a huge governance challenge, not just for large corporations and government agencies but–more importantly for the purposes of this book–also for those groups of people that manage a common-pool resource (e.g. a FOSS project, WikiLeaks).

While drawing on the notion of governmentality (Foucault 1984, 1991), this chapter has argued that the Web 2.0 era has brought about a new form of government rationality, whereby every individual is pushed to become an entrepreneur. (Hammann 2009, pp.38) defines such an entrepreneur as:

a free and autonomous atom of self-interest who is fully responsible for navigating the [online] social realm using rational choice and cost-benefit calculation to the express exclusion of all other values and interests.

Foucault's notion of governmentality makes visible the practices of government on populations and the practices of the self that individuals perform upon themselves in order to become certain kinds of subjects.

New information infrastructures provide individual users with numerous technological choices for entrepreneurial activity, but at the same time, those choices generate consequences not just for individual users but for the networked population at large. Whether the population chooses to conform to or resist the governing structures of these new information infrastructures becomes irrelevant since either choice will render them subjects of the underlying rationality. To repeat an earlier quote "*free* subjects" are "those that exercise some type of choice", but they are also "free *subjects*, those whose subjection operates through the exercise of choice" (Dean, 1997, pp.193, emphasis in original). The reasons for conforming and resisting, thus, refer to the historical constitution of position takings including the conditions that made them possible–a historical process that strikes at the heart of efforts to govern oneself and others (Foucault, 1995).

This conclusion points to some implications for further research in relation to the ethical governance of new information infrastructures.

Governance issues were discussed extensively in Chapters 6 and 7 of this book by focusing on the enabling conditions in the relationship between the material characteristics of an information infrastructure, institutional rules, and community attributes, as well as the impact of the external environment (e.g. state policy, technological developments) on those relationships. However, the focus was on more contained communities, as found in specific organizations (e.g. a hospital, a primary healthcare centre). In the context of new information infrastructures such as the ones described in Chapter 8 and this Chapter (e.g. a FOSS project, WikiLeaks, etc.), different individuals are usually found to be members of multiple communities simultaneously, and even the boundaries of the communities themselves are hard to define.

There is, thus, a need for further research that moves beyond a focal community, a focal unit of analysis, towards an analysis of the benefits of the social sacrifices to be widely shared by most individuals, who take entrepreneurial risks inside new information infrastructures. In such an endeavor, the focus should be the ethical and political dilemmas that generate contestations around shared infrastructure resources, which are produced, stored, distributed, and mashed-up across a wide population of user-developers.

Both in this Chapter and in Chapter 8, the new possibilities for social interaction made possible by new information infrastructures were discussed (e.g. participating in FOSS projects) and the positive and negative consequences were explored (e.g. creative mash-ups of digital content, whistle-blowing, violations of freedom of speech). These consequences lead one to ask whether these new information infrastructures threaten some of the important values underlying community life.

Some have already argued that the Internet enables a reconfiguration of communities based on individual choices provided to users (Graham, 1999). Therefore, one advantage of online communities is that they empower the individual to choose a community in which to interact instead of simply having to accept the default community or society in which individuals are already situated. That is, new information infrastructures act as technologies of freedom providing individuals with greater choice and freedom with respect to joining different communities. Values involving freedom, choice, openness, and so forth, certainly would seem to favor democratic ideals. However, others see the relationship between the Internet and democracy quite differently. For instance, some argue that the Internet has both democracy-enhancing and democracy-threatening aspects (Sunstein, 2002). On the one hand, the Internet enhances democracy in the sense that it provides greater access to information by lowering the costs involved in finding and getting information; on the other hand, though, because that information can be filtered so easily, the Internet can be seen to also threaten democracy–who decides which information gets filtered, how, and why. As a study by Introna and Nissenbaum (2000) reveals, the criteria by which search engines filter information are not transparent, and particular sites systematically are excluded. In turn, new information infrastructures can be seen to facilitate political and social fragmentation by isolating individuals and insulating groups–as in the case of WikiLeaks. These factors tend to increase polarization and breakup communities into small groups and even individual users.

Thus, a key question for further research is whether community should continue to be the focal unit of analysis, or whether we now need to shift the focus onto the individual, while placing great attention on socio-cultural factors of the development of the self. More specifically, we need to focus on the social-historical self while acknowledging that individuals are not independent, autonomous agents (Foucault, 1979, 1982, 1988). That is, the self is not an entity that can be fully grasped as a single instant; the self is diachronically structured in that its elements exist in and over time and always in relation to other selves (Foucault, 1979, 1982, 1988; also see Turkle, 1995, 2005). Moreover, as argued earlier through the notion of governmentality, selves should be seen as to a large extent formed by factors not under the control of individual agents themselves. Most of the central elements of our existence are things that were not (and in many cases could not be) chosen by us–even though, through our choices, we generate consequences for our very existence.

In order to understand the ethical governance of new information infrastructures we, thus, need to carry out historical studies of the construction of individual and collective selves by first rejecting the assumption that individuals (e.g. Chief Technology Officers) hold superhuman

abilities to fashion themselves and their worlds through simple choices in the present (e.g. see Weill & Broadbent, 1998; Weill & Ross, 2004; for 'best' IT governance and leadership practices). Instead, we should focus more cautiously on the social-historical elements, which have made those choices available in the first place. In other words, we cannot escape our past because it is already embodied in our present choices and future directions.

At the same time, while acknowledging that individuals are not independent, autonomous agents, further research should explore how *self-governance* could be defended as a fundamental normative notion–a central tenet in commons studies (see Ostrom, Walker, & Gardner, 1992). Foucault (1979, 1982, 1988) has already argued that to understand what it means to be self-governing, it is necessary to inquire into the diachronic processes that gave rise to our current condition. That is, we need to inquire into those processes that enable individuals to *self-reflect* on their choices, so that the broad range of characteristics that make up the self will come into focus. When we begin to view autonomous individuals as able to reflectively appraise their value commitments (and the conditions within which those commitments were made), then we can also begin to understand how those commitments count as important factors in governing their interactions with one another inside new information infrastructures.

Such a view would also require researchers to inquire deeper into processes of social acceptance, since the value commitments of individual agents will only become valid if they become acceptable by those governed by them. For example, as discussed in Chapter 8, FOSS projects are usually based on the principle of "copyleft" (Stallman, 1999). Unlike copyright, copyleft is more of a value commitment than a property right, in that, any FOSS released under copyleft can be accessed, copied, and modified by others only if they accept the value commitments of the original author. In the event that the author makes the choice to alienate a FOSS project or to allow a third party to do so, users can withdraw from participating in the project altogether, since such a value commitment would go against the FOSS values of individual autonomy (O' Mahony, 2005). This is true for any project instituted under a Creative Commons license (Lessig, 2008).

A focus on the socio-historical construction of individual and collective selves, their efforts toward self-governance, and their acceptance or rejection of different value commitments would also bring to the surface the power relations that shape those dynamics. Research into the power relations that shape the construction of the self and any value commitments to self-governance would need to explore how acceptance is achieved through political and moral legitimacy. For example, despite WikiLeaks' good intentions and its value commitment to free speech, one could question whether WikiLeaks has the right to act on behalf of the cause it claims to act for. On the other hand, one could also question whether other individuals and organizations have the right to mute WikiLeak's actions through any means necessary on grounds of justice. In other words, anyone may claim to represent good morals or to stand for justice, but how do they gain moral and political legitimacy and what implications does such legitimacy have on the choices of different individuals–not just for WikiLeaks, but potentially for other information infrastructures? Once again, the focus should not be on ideal principles or 'best practice guidelines,' but rather on processes through which choices are made, reflected upon, accepted or rejected, and closure is temporarily reached, only to be questioned again.

The next and final chapter of this book continues this ethical discussion by placing emphasis on the role of the researcher in researching new information infrastructures.

REFERENCES

Addley, E., & Halliday, J. (2010, December 8). Operation payback cripples MasterCard site in revenge for WikiLeaks ban. *The Guardian*. Retrieved April, 27 2011, from http://www.guardian.co.uk/media/2010/dec/08/operation-payback-mastercard-website-wikileaks

Anderson, C. (2010, July). Julian Assange: Why the world needs WikiLeaks. *TED*. Retrieved May 8, 2011, from http://www.ted.com/talks/julian_assange_why_the_world_needs_wikileaks.html

BBC. (2010, February 12). Iceland's journalism freedom dream prompted by Wikileaks. *BBC Online*. Retrieved May 8, 2011, from http://news.bbc.co.uk/2/hi/technology/8510927.stm

Beck, U. (1992). *Risk society: Toward a new modernity*. London, UK: Sage.

Beniger, J. R. (1996). Who shall control cyberspace? In Strate, L., Jacobson, R., & Gibson, S. (Eds.), *Communication and cyberspace* (pp. 49–58). Cresskill, NJ: Hampton.

Benkler, Y. (2006). *The wealth of networks*. New Haven, CT: Yale University Press.

Burns, J. F., & Somaiya, R. (2010, October 23). WikiLeaks founder on the run: Trailed by notoriety. *The New York Times*. Retrieved May 8, 2011, from http://www.nytimes.com/2010/10/24/world/24assange.html

Calabresi, M. (2010, December 2). WikiLeaks' war on secrecy: Truth's consequences. *TIME Magazine*. Retrieved May 8, 2011, from http://www.time.com/time/world/article/0,8599,2034276-3,00.html

CCR. (2010, December 7). CCR statement on arrest of WikiLeaks founder Julian Assange. *Center for Constitutional Rights*. Retrieved May 8, 2011, from http://ccrjustice.org/newsroom/press-releases/ccr-statement-arrest-of-wikileaks-founder-julian-assange

Constantinides, P. (2012). (forthcoming). The development and consequences of new information infrastructures: The case of mashup platforms. *Media Culture & Society.*

Culnan, M. J., McHugh, P., & Zubillaga, J. (2010). How large U.S. companies can use Twitter and other social media to gain business value. *MIS Quarterly Executive, 9*(4), 243–259.

Curtis, P. (2010, December 30). Ministers must 'wise up not clam up' after WikiLeaks disclosures. *The Guardian.* Retrieved May 8, 2011, from: http://www.guardian.co.uk/politics/2010/dec/30/wikileaks-freedom-information-ministers-government

De La Merced, M. (2010, November 30). WikiLeaks' next target: Bank of America? *The New York Times.* Retrieved May 8, 2011, from http://dealbook.nytimes.com/2010/11/30/wikileaks-next-target-bank-of-america/

Dean, M. (1997). *Critical and effective histories: Foucault's methods and historical sociology.* London, UK: Routledge.

Dreyfus, H. L., & Rabinow, P. (1982). *Michel Foucault: Beyond structuralism and hermeneutics.* Chicago, IL: The University of Chicago Press.

Dunham, G. S. (2002). Carnivore, the FBI's e-mail surveillance system: Devouring criminals, not privacy. *Federal Communications Law Journal, 54,* 543–566.

Fairfield, J. A. (2005). Virtual property. *Boston University Law Review. Boston University. School of Law, 85*(4), 1047–1102.

Feller, J., Fitzgerald, B., Hissam, S., & Lakhani, K. (Eds.). (2005). *Perspectives on free and open source software.* Cambridge, MA: MIT Press.

Foster, I. (2002). The grid: A new infrastructure for 21st century science. *Physics Today, 55*(2), 42–47. doi:10.1063/1.1461327

Foster, I. (2003). The grid: Computing without bounds. *Scientific American, 288*(4), 78–85. doi:10.1038/scientificamerican0403-78

Foster, I., & Kesselman, C. (1999). *The grid: Blueprint for a new computing infrastructure.* San Francisco, CA: Morgan Kaufmann.

Foucault, M. (1979). The history of sexuality: *Vol. 1. An introduction* (Hurley, R., Trans.). London, UK: Allen Lane.

Foucault, M. (1982). Afterword: The subject and power. In Dreyfus, H., & Rabinow, P. (Eds.), *Michel Foucault: Beyond structuralism and hermeneutics* (pp. 208–226). Brighton, UK: Harvester.

Foucault, M. (1988). Politics and reason. In Kritzman, L. D. (Ed.), *Politics, philosophy, culture: Interviews and other writings 1977-1984.* New York, NY: Routledge.

Foucault, M. (1991). Governmentality. In Burchell, G., Gordon, C., & Miller, P. (Eds.), *The Foucault effect* (pp. 87–104). Chicago, IL: University of Chicago Press.

Foucault, M. (1993). About the beginning of the hermeneutics of the self: Two lectures at Dartmouth. *Political Theory, 21*(2), 198–227. doi:10.1177/0090591793021002004

Foucault, M. (1995). *Discipline & punish: The birth of the prison* (2nd ed.). (Sheridan, A., Trans.). New York, NY: Vintage Books.

Friedman, M. (2010, December 15). Julian Assange: Readers' choice for TIME's Person of the Year 2010. *TIME Magazine.* Retrieved May 8, 2011, from http://newsfeed.time.com/2010/12/13/julian-assange-readers-choice-for-times-person-of-the-year-2010/

Galant, R. (2010, July 16). WikiLeaks founder: Site getting tons of 'high caliber' disclosures. *CNN Online.* Retrieved May 8, 2011, from http://edition.cnn.com/2010/TECH/web/07/16/wikileaks.disclosures/

Garfinkel, S. (2000). *Database nation: The death of privacy in the 21ˢᵗ century*. Sebastopol, CA: O'Reilly.

Gaudin, S. (2011, April 26). Sony warns users of data loss from PlayStation network hack. *ComputerWorld Online*. Retrieved April 27, 2011, from http://www.computerworld.com/s/article/9216191/Sony_warns_users_of_data_loss_from_PlayStation_network_hack?source=toc

Goodwin, D. (2008, February 21). Wikileaks judge gets Pirate Bay treatment. *The Register*. Retrieved April 28, 2011, from http://www.theregister.co.uk/2008/02/21/wikileaks_bulletproof_hosting/

Gordon, C. (1991). Governmental rationality: An introduction. In Burchell, G., Gordon, C., & Miller, P. (Eds.), *The Foucault effect* (pp. 1–51). Chicago, IL: University of Chicago Press.

Graham, G. (1999). *The Internet: A philosophical inquiry*. New York, NY: Rutledge.

Greenberg, A. (2010, November 29). An interview with WikiLeaks' Julian Assange. *Forbes*. Retrieved April 28, 2011, from http://blogs.forbes.com/andygreenberg/2010/11/29/an-interview-with-wikileaks-julian-assange/2/

Grossman, L. (2006, December 16). Time's Person of the Year: You. *Time Magazine*. Retrieved April 20, 2011, from http://www.time.com/time/magazine/article/0,9171,1569514,00.html

Haas, T. C. (2001). Carnivore and the Fourth Amendment. *Connecticut Law Review, 34*, 261–291.

Haliday, J. (2011, August 8). London riots: BlackBerry to help police probe Messenger looting 'role'. *The Guardian*. Retrieved November 1, 2011, from http://www.guardian.co.uk/uk/2011/aug/08/london-riots-blackberry-messenger-looting

Hay, J., & Packer, J. (2004). Crossing the media(-n): Auto-mobility, the transported self, and technologies of freedom. In Couldry, N., & McCarthy, A. (Eds.), *MediaSpace: Scale and culture in a media age* (pp. 209–232). New York, NY: Routledge.

Holmes, P. K. (2001). FBI's Carnivore: Is the government eating away our right of privacy? *Roger Williams University Law Review, 7*, 247–272.

Introna, L., & Nissenbaum, H. (2000). Shaping the Web: Why the politics of search engines matter. *The Information Society, 16*(3), 169–185. doi:10.1080/01972240050133634

Khatchadourian, R. (2010, June 7). No secrets. *The New Yorker*. Retrieved May 8, 2011, from http://www.newyorker.com/reporting/2010/06/07/100607fa_fact_khatchadourian?currentPage=9

Lauder, S. (2010, December 7). Law experts say WikiLeaks in the clear. *The World Today: ABC Radio*. Retrieved May 8, 2011, from http://www.abc.net.au/worldtoday/content/2010/s3086781.htm

Leigh, D., & Evans, R. (2010, October 14). WikiLeaks says funding has been blocked after government blacklisting. *The Guardian*. Retrieved May 8, 2011, from http://www.guardian.co.uk/media/2010/oct/14/wikileaks-says-funding-is-blocked

Lessig, L. (2008). *Remix: Making art and commerce in the hybrid economy*. London, UK: The Penguin Press. doi:10.5040/9781849662505

Lyon, D. (2001). *Surveillance society: Monitoring everyday life*. Buckingham, UK: Open University Press.

MacAskill, E. (2010a, December 3). "U.S. blocks access to WikiLeaks for federal workers. *The Guardian*. Retrieved May 8, 2011, from http://www.guardian.co.uk/world/2010/dec/03/wikileaks-cables-blocks-access-federal

MacAskill, E. (2010b, December 2). WikiLeaks website pulled by Amazon after U.S. political pressure. *The Guardian*. Retrieved May 8, 2011, from http://www.guardian.co.uk/media/2010/dec/01/wikileaks-website-cables-servers-amazon

McLuhan, M. (1962). *The Gutenberg galaxy: The making of typographic man*. Toronto, Canada: University of Toronto Press.

McLuhan, M. (1994). *Understanding media: The extensions of man*. Cambridge, MA: MIT Press. (Original work published 1964)

Medb, R. (2010, December 11). Where's the democracy in hunting Wikileaks off the Net? *The Irish Independent*. Retrieved May 1, 2011, from http://www.independent.ie/opinion/columnists/medb-ruane/medb-ruane-wheres-the-democracy-in-hunting-wikileaks-off-the-net-2456960.html

Merl, S. R. (2001). Internet communication standards for the 21st century: International terrorism must force the U.S. to adopt 'Carnivore' and new electronic surveillance standards. *Brooklyn Journal of International Law*, *27*, 245–284.

Morrisett, L. (2003). Technologies of freedom? In Jenkins, H., & Thorburn, D. (Eds.), *Democracy and new media* (pp. 21–31). Cambridge, MA: MIT Press.

National Library of Australia (NLA). (n.d.). *Social Media Policy*. Retrieved November 01, 2011, from http://www.nla.gov.au/policy-and-planning/social-media

Nebehey, S. (2010, November 4). WikiLeaks founder says may seek Swiss asylum. *Reuters*. Retrieved May 1, 2011, from http://www.reuters.com/article/2010/11/04/us-usa-wikileaks-idUSTRE6A369920101104

Nordstrom, L. (2010, December 10). Former WikiLeaks worker: Rival site under way. *The Washington Times*. Retrieved May 1, 2011, from http://www.washingtontimes.com/news/2010/dec/10/former-wikileaks-worker-rival-site-under-way/

O'Mahony, S. (2005). Non-profit foundations and their role in community-firm software collaboration. In Feller, J., Fitzgerald, B., Hissam, S., & Lakhani, K. (Eds.), *Perspectives on free and open source software* (pp. 393–414). Cambridge, MA: MIT Press.

O'Reilly, T. (2005, September 30). What is Web 2.0: Design patterns and business models for the next generation of software, *O'Reilly Network Online*. Retrieved May 8, 2011, from http://www.oreillynet.com/pub/a/oreilly/tim/news/2005/09/30/what-is-web-20.html

Ondrejka, C. (2007). Second Life: Collapsing geography. *Innovations: Technology, Governance, Globalization*, *2*(3), 27–55. doi:10.1162/itgg.2007.2.3.27

Ostrom, E. (1990). *Governing the commons: The evolution of institutions for collective action*. New York, NY: Cambridge University Press.

Ostrom, E. (2009, December 8). Beyond markets and states: Polycentric governance of complex economic systems. *The Sveriges Riksbank Prize in Economic Sciences in Memory of Alfred Nobel 2009*. Lecture conducted from Stockholm University, Aula Magna.

Ostrom, E., Walker, J., & Gardner, R. (1992). Covenants with and without a sword: Self-governance is possible. *The American Political Science Review*, *86*(2), 404–417. doi:10.2307/1964229

Palmer, E. (2010, December 2). WikiLeaks backup plan could drop diplomatic bomb. *CBS Online*. Retrieved May 8, 2011, from http://www.cbsnews.com/stories/2010/12/02/eveningnews/main7111845.shtml

Pillay, N. (2010, December 9). UN High Commissioner for human rights Navi Pillay voices concern at reports of pressure being exerted on private companies to halt financial or internet services for WikiLeaks. *UN TV*. Retrieved May 8, 2011, from http://www.unmultimedia.org/tv/unifeed/d/16541.html

Piven, B. (2010, December 17). Copycat WikiLeaks sites make waves. *Al Jazeera English*. Retrieved May 8, 2011, from http://english.aljazeera.net/indepth/features/2010/12/20101216194828514847.html

Pool, I. (1983). *Technologies of freedom*. Cambridge, MA: Harvard University Press.

Quarmby, B. (2009). Pirates among the Second Life islands–Why you should monitor the misuse of your intellectual property in online virtual worlds. *Cardozo Arts & Entertainment Law Journal, 26*, 667–694.

Randall, D., & Cooper, C. (2010, December 5). WikiLeaks hit by new online onslaught. *The Independent*. Retrieved May 8, 2011, from http://www.independent.co.uk/news/world/politics/wikileaks-hit-by-new-online-onslaught-2151570.html

Satter, R. G., & Svensson, P. (2010, December 3). WikiLeaks fights to stay online amid attacks. *Associated Press*. Retrieved May 8, 2011, from http://www.businessweek.com/ap/financialnews/D9JSHKUG0.htm

Savage, C. (2010, December 1). U.S. weighs prosecution of WikiLeaks founder, but legal scholars warn of steep hurdles. *The New York Times*. Retrieved April 28, 2011, from http://www.nytimes.com/2010/12/02/world/02legal.html

Sigurgrimsdottir, H. (2009, August 4). Iceland court lifts gag order after public outrage. *The Seattle Times*. Retrieved May 1, 2011, from http://seattletimes.nwsource.com/html/nationworld/2009597317_apeuicelandbankoutrage.html

Singer, J. W. (2006). The ownership society and takings of property: Castles, investments, and just obligations. *The Harvard Environmental Law Review, 30*, 309–338.

Somaiya, R. (2010, December 5). Hundreds of WikiLeaks mirror sites appear. *The New York Times*. Retrieved May 1, 2011, from http://www.nytimes.com/2010/12/06/world/europe/06wiki.html

Stallman, R. (1999). The GNU operating system and the free software movement. In DiBona, C., Ockman, S., & Stone, M. (Eds.), *Open sources: Voices from the open source revolution*. Sebastopol, CA: O'Reilly. doi:10.1109/ICSM.2006.68

Strauss, A. Y. (2002). A constitutional crisis in the digital age: Why the FBI's 'Carnivore' does not defy the Fourth Amendment. *Cardozo Arts and Entertainment Law Journal, 20*, 231–258.

Sunstein, C. R. (2002). *Republic.com*. Princeton, NJ: Princeton University Press.

Tountas, S. W. (2003). Carnivore: Is the regulation of wireless technology a legally viable option to curtail the growth of cybercrime? *Washington University Journal of Law and Policy, 11*, 351–377.

Tully, J. (1993). Governing conduct: Locke on the reform of thought and behavior. In Tully, J. (Ed.), *An approach to political philosophy* (pp. 179–241). Cambridge, UK: Cambridge University Press. doi:10.1017/CBO9780511607882.007

Turkle, S. (1995). *Life on the screen: Identity in the age of the Internet*. New York, NY: Simon and Schuster.

Turkle, S. (2005). *The second self: Computers and the human spirit*. Cambridge, MA: MIT Press.

Turkle, S. (2006). Always-on/always-on-you: The tethered self. In Katz, J. E. (Ed.), *Handbook of mobile communication studies* (pp. 121–138). Cambridge, MA: MIT Press.

Ungerleider, N. (2011, February 16). Leaked emails: Anti-WikiLeaks security firm targeted journalists. *Fast Company*. Retrieved May 9, 2011, from http://www.fastcompany.com/1728259/leaked-emails-anti-wikileaks-security-firm-targeted-journalists

Ventura, H., Mitchell, M., & Deflem, M. (2005). Governmentality and the war on terror: FBI project Carnivore and the diffusion of disciplinary power. *Critical Criminology*, *13*(1), 55–70. doi:10.1007/s10612-004-6167-6

Ward, V. (2010, December 3). WikiLeaks website disconnected as U.S. company withdraws support. *The Daily Telegraph*. Retrieved May 8, 2011, from http://www.telegraph.co.uk/news/worldnews/wikileaks/8178457/WikiLeaks-website-disconnected-as-US-company-withdraws-support.html

Webster, S. C. (2010, December 7). MasterCard, Visa shut down electronic donations to WikiLeaks. *The Raw Story*. Retrieved May 8, 2011, from http://www.rawstory.com/rs/2010/12/07/mastercard-shuts-donations-wikileaks-calling-site-illegal/

Weill, P., & Broadbent, M. (1998). *Leveraging the new infrastructure: How market leaders capitalize on information*. Boston, MA: Harvard Business School Press.

Weill, P., & Ross, J. (2004). *IT governance: How top performers manage IT decision rights for superior results*. Boston, MA: Harvard Business School Press.

WikiLeaks website (2008, April 19). *WikiLeaks' submissions page*. (archived from the original). Retrieved May 8, 2011, from http://classic-web.archive.org/web/20080419013425/http:/www.wikileaks.org/wiki/Wikileaks:Submissions

WikiLeaks website (2011). *WikiLeaks' main page*. Retrieved May 8, 2011, from http://www.wikileaks.ch/

Wilson, J. A., Acheson, J., Metcalfe, M., & Kleban, P. (1994). Chaos, complexity, and community management of fisheries. *Marine Policy*, *18*, 291–305. doi:10.1016/0308-597X(94)90044-2

ADDITIONAL READING

Abrahamson, J. B., Arterton, F., & Orren, G. (1988). *The electronic commonwealth: The impact of new technologies upon democratic politics*. New York, NY: Basic Books.

Adoni, H., & Nossek, H. (2001). The new media consumers: Media convergence and the displacement effect. *European Journal of Communication Research*, *26*(1), 59–83.

Arterton, C. F. (1987). *Teledemocracy: Can technology protect democracy?* Newbury Park, CA: Sage.

Barber, B. J. (1984). *Strong democracy: Participatory politics for a new age*. Berkeley, CA: University of California Press.

Barber, B. J. (1996). *Jihad versus McWorld: How the planet is both falling apart and coming together*. New York, NY: Ballantine.

Becker, T. L. (1981). Teledemocracy: Bringing power back to the people. *The Futurist*, *15*(6), 6–9.

Becker, T. L., & Slaton, C. (2000). *The future of teledemocracy*. Westport, CT: Praeger.

Beniger, J. R. (1986). *The control revolution: Technological and economic origins of the information society*. Cambridge, MA: Harvester.

Brown, D. (1997). *Cybertrends: Chaos, power and accountability in the information age*. London: Viking.

Castells, M. (2010). *The power of identity* (2nd ed.). London, UK: Blackwell.

Frissen, P. H. A. (1999). *Politics, government, technology: A postmodern narrative on the virtual state*. London, UK: Edward Elgar.

Joinson, A. (2001). Self-disclosure in computer-mediated communication: The role of self-awareness and visual anonymity. *European Journal of Social Psychology, 31*(2), 177–192. doi:10.1002/ejsp.36

Katz, J. E., & Rice, R. E. (2002). *Social consequences of Internet use, access, involvement, and interaction*. Cambridge, MA: The MIT Press.

Negroponte, N. (1995). *Being digital*. New York, NY: Knopf.

Spears, R. (1994). Panacea or panopticon? The hidden power of computer-mediated communication. *Communication Research, 21*(4), 427–459. doi:10.1177/009365094021004001

Tsagarousianou, R. (1999). Electronic democracy: Rhetoric and reality. *Communications: The European Journal of Communication Research, 24*(2), 189–208.

Tsagarousianou, R., Tambini, D., & Bryan, C. (1998). *Cyberdemocracy, technology, cities and civic networks*. New York, NY: Routledge. doi:10.4324/9780203448847

Webster, F. (2001). The information society revisited. In L. Lievrouw (Ed.), *Handbook of the new media*, (pp. 22–33). London, UK: Thousand Oaks.

ENDNOTES

[1]   This view is reminiscent of the work of Marshall McLuhan (1962, 1964). Though the World Wide Web was invented after his death, McLuhan prophesied the Web back in the 1960s, prompting a critical problematization of both the positive and negative attributes of this new medium. McLuhan said of the future positive aspects of this new medium (McLuhan, 1964, pp.61):

The next medium, whatever it is-it may be the extension of consciousness-will include television as its content, not as its environment, and will transform television into an art form. A computer as a research and communication instrument could enhance retrieval, obsolesce mass library organization, retrieve the individual's encyclopedic function and flip into a private line to speedily tailored data of a saleable kind.

But he also warned that (1962, pp.32):

Instead of tending towards a vast Alexandrian library, the world has become a computer, an electronic brain, exactly as an infantile piece of science fiction. And as our senses have gone outside us, Big Brother goes inside. So, unless aware of this dynamic, we shall at once move into a phase of panic terrors, exactly befitting a small world of tribal drums, total interdependence, and superimposed co-existence. [...] Terror is the normal state of any oral society, for in it everything affects everything all the time. [...]

[2]   This is a direct reference to Foucault's cautionary suggestion that "People know what they do; they frequently know why they do what they do; but what they don't know is what they do does" (Dreyfus & Rabinow, 1982, pp.187).

[3]   Foucault traces "the problem of government" from the sixteenth century to today offering a critical analysis of the genealogy–i.e. the historical development–of "how to govern oneself, how to be governed, how to become the best possible governor" (Foucault, 1991, pp.87). In his series of lectures on the subject, he gives examples of the government of the state by a prince (citing Machiavelli's *The Prince*), the government of children, the government of pedagogy, the government

of the family, and many more (see Gordon, 1991).

4   By 'state,' Foucault referred to the nation state. This definition, though, could also be extended to the government state of 'new' organizations and 'new' information infrastructures

5   A select number of Second Life users have already made judicious use of their time in Second Life to become highly successful in-world entrepreneurs (see Quarmby, 2009).

6   In August 2011, the instant messenger service offered through BlackBerry mobile phones–in joint with messages posted on Facebook and Twitter–played a key role in organising riots in London. Once again, these technologies played a dual role–both as technologies of freedom, but also as technologies of surveillance and control–since Scotland Yard later contacted the BlackBerry developers, who immediately complied with the request to provide access to private messages, despite user complaints (Halliday, 2011).

Chapter 10
The Role of the Researcher in New Information Infrastructure Research

ABSTRACT

In this chapter, the role of the researcher in new information infrastructure research is explored. The key ideas informing this chapter are drawn from a critical reflection on trends in information systems (IS) research and the need for a more pragmatic approach (Constantinides et al., 2012). The focus is on developing a better understanding of the consequences of research choices by drawing on the notion of phronesis – the reflective development of prudent knowledge that is continuously shaped by and imbued with situated values and interests (Flyvberg, 2001). Specifically, it is argued that, IS researchers must recognize that research involves not just choices about how to conduct a study (i.e. theoretical and methodological choices), but also about why we study what we study and who is affected by our work (i.e. the desirable outcomes and long-term impact of research).

INTRODUCTION

As researchers, we all strive to produce relevant knowledge, and, thus, we are all preoccupied with the question of 'which body of practice is my research concerned with?'

DOI: 10.4018/978-1-4666-1622-6.ch010

In many ways, relevant knowledge may refer to those practices which are specific to a particular organizational, social, economic, political, and business context (Pettigrew, 1985; Walsham, 1993). Contextualist research provides the necessary links between theory and practice, thus contributing to relevant knowledge. At the same time, however, it can also be argued that contextualist research eschews generalizability in favour of a descriptive and analytical understanding of the concerns, beliefs, and practices of particular contexts (Lee & Baskerville, 2003). Yet contextualists argue that generalized knowledge is far too removed from any specific context to be immediately relevant, and to shape it towards very different interpretive, political, and ethical worlds would be difficult. Giddens (1984, pp.42) supports this claim by stating, "[t]he problem in the study of human activity is that every attempt at a context-free definition of an action, that is, a definition based on abstract rules or laws, will not necessarily accord with the pragmatic way an action is defined by the actors in a concrete social situation." In other words, generalized knowledge fails to directly inform and direct practitioners who find the remoteness of theoretical language and generalized rules-of-thumb to lack immediate relevance to their everyday practices (Lee, 1999). Instead, practitioners draw upon other sources of knowledge, particularly popular business magazines, which ironically provide short and to-the-point advice about present and future trends.

Despite these debates, the problem of relevant knowledge is not about whether to choose generalizability over contextuality and vice versa. The problem of relevant knowledge rests with the fact that researchers and practitioners live predominantly in different worlds (Flyvbjerg, 2001) and enact different language games[1] (Astley & Zammuto, 1992).

Social science and organizational researchers often strive for *episteme* – or knowledge of universals through abstract generalizations of social practices. The concern with episteme is meant to generate theoretical constructs and language that are meaningful to the research community that will (hopefully) read them in relevant publications. However, these "theoretical constructs are not mirrors reflecting the 'true' nature of reality" (Astley & Zammuto, 1992, pp. 445), but reflections of the concerns, hopes, and fears of a research community and its particular views of the world. As such, these theoretical constructs are not immediately relevant to the practice fields from which they were drawn. In particular, Bennis and O'Toole (2005) suggest that scientific rigor (i.e. episteme) has dominated relevance. They ask "why have business schools embraced the scientific model of physicists and economists rather than the professional model of doctors and lawyers?"[2] (Bennis & O'Toole, 2005, pp. 96). They argue that, business schools should focus more on technical knowledge and professional skills (i.e. *techne*), and, likewise, social science and organizational research should focus on how such knowledge and skills are acquired and nurtured in practice.

Techne is the form of knowledge that practitioners are most interested in and refers to the production of skills together with the tools and artifacts that are required for their expression (Flyvbjerg, 2001). Some areas of IS research have focused on a generalized form of techne through, for example, design science and systems analysis and design methods. Still, though, only a few studies have examined the techne of systems analysis and design in practice (cf. Fitzgerald, 1997), suggesting that this knowledge of systems analysis and design may itself be an attempted episteme of techne. Practitioners are also indirectly concerned with another form of knowledge – *phronesis* – which points to an ethical "activity by which instrumental rationality is balanced by value-rationality" (Flyvbjerg, 2006, pp. 370). Phronesis is intimately concerned with nuanced action that is timely, specific, ethical, and contextually relevant. Put simply, phronesis is practical common sense "concerned with deliberation about values and interests" (Flyvbjerg, 2006, pp. 371). In other words, whereas episteme is concerned with theoretical know-why and techne denotes technical know-how, phronesis emphasizes practical knowledge and ethics.

According to Flyvbjerg (2001, 2004, 2006), the problem with relevant social science research is that the development and concern for phronesis has been lost in contemporary approaches in research and practice. Similarly, it has been argued that to date, the IS field "has focused almost the entirety of its resources on theoretical and technical knowledge, ignoring ethical and applicative knowledge" (Hirschheim & Klein, 2003, pp. 268). Similar arguments have also been made elsewhere acknowledging that "the core IS field… is under representative of ethics and IS" (Mingers & Walsham, 2010, pp.2).

The result has been a dominant focus on episteme or techne, or a combination of the two, in most academic research. In other words, in addressing the problem of contextualization through a search for general knowledge, it appears that social science researchers have lost the importance of ethics. With the exception of some critical studies in IS which focus on values and interests, the majority of IS research seems to ignore the crucial relevance of phronesis (see Hirschheim & Klein, 2003). In response, Flyvbjerg suggests a need to turn towards studies of phronesis through a form of situational ethics[3] which would consider value-rational questions in specific organizational and practical settings.

Recently, Constantinides, Chiasson, and Introna (2012) have drawn on Flyvbjerg's (2001, 2004, 2006) contemporary conceptualization of phronesis, in addition to Peirce's (1931-58) approach to *phronetic research* (i.e. ethical-applicative, value-informed), to develop a pragmatic framework for IS research. This framework is used to identify key questions IS researchers should ask in engaging the different ends of research inquiry. These include the anticipated and desired outcomes of the research, the collective and long-term impact of the research for the communities IS researchers serve and inform, and the ways in which research choices are fostered, shaped, and restricted by power relations.

This chapter uses this pragmatic framework to raise a number of important questions in new information infrastructure research. The key argument is that, research should be approached as a series of conflicting choices and value judgments,

individually and collectively made. These options shape the research projects researchers choose to pursue and have significant consequences for those affected by this work – that is, practitioners and other researchers. The chapter ends with a set of practical recommendations with which researchers can carry out phronetic research on new information infrastructures.

A PRAGMATIC FRAMEWORK FOR PHRONETIC IS RESEARCH

In line with Flyvberg's (2001) critique of social science research – and Hirschheim and Klein's (2003) similar critique of IS research – as being primarily concerned with episteme and techne at the expense of phronesis, Constantinides, Chiasson, and Introna (2012) develop a pragmatic framework for phronetic IS research.

They start with Peirce's conceptualization of three interdependent normative sciences, with *logic* (i.e. approaches to reasoning) presupposing conclusions about *ethics* (i.e. methods of conduct), which, in turn, presuppose conclusions about *aesthetics* (i.e. the anticipated and desirable outcomes of a research study). They offer a quote from Peirce (CP 5.611)[4] to explain this interdependency:

What does right reasoning consist in? It consists in such reasoning as shall be conducive to our ultimate aim. What, then, is our ultimate aim? [...] It would seem to be the business of the moralist to find this out, and that the logician has to accept the teaching of ethics in this regard. But the moralist, as far as I can make it out, merely tells us that we have a power of self-control, that no narrow or selfish aim can ever prove satisfactory, that the only satisfactory aim is the broadest, highest, and most general possible aim; and for any more definite information, as I conceive the matter, he (sic) has to refer us to the aesthetician, whose business it is to say what is the state of things which is most admirable in itself.

In the context of IS research, it is stressed that "beyond the question of whether practitioners will read and use research results arising from certain theoretical assumptions and methodologies, the entire effort rests on choices concerned with the ethical conduct of researchers, and a deliberation about the anticipated and desirable outcomes worth pursuing in IS research" (Constantinides et al., 2012, pp.3). In other words, choices of logic presuppose questions and answers about ethics and aesthetics.

These interdependent choices are thought to emerge in a continuous inquiry within a community of inquirers (CP 1.574), which comes to realize the highest good of their collective efforts (CP 1.191). This highest good refers to how people within the community come to collectively think, act and feel (CP 8.315). The highest good, thus, is directly related to the generation of relevant knowledge by directing and shaping attention towards those collections of thoughts (logic), actions (ethical conduct), and feelings (aesthetics) worth pursuing by the majority within a community of inquirers (Apel, 1995).

The process of realizing the highest good and transforming communal practices and values was referred to by Peirce as "critical common-sensism," a productive reflective-learning process whereby ideas and practices are understood in terms of their anticipated and actual consequences (Liszka, 1978). "That is, meaning is not ascribed in a priori terms; rather, it is identified by anticipating 'what if' consequences to potential actions and conduct" (Elkjær & Simpson, 2006,3) towards an evaluation of possible solutions "which would hold in the long run" (CP 5.209-211).

Critical common-sensism has strong affiliations to the notion of phronesis as both are concerned with deliberation about the values and interests of a broader community of inquiry (Flyvberg, 2001, 2004, 2006). However, as Con-

stantinides et al (2012) note, Peirce is largely silent about power and its influence on the determination of the ends of research inquiry. Flyvbjerg (2006) offers a way forward by arguing for a broader, more inclusive community of stakeholders. Beyond an effort towards more plurality in research inquiry, Flyvberg raises the critical question of "[w]ho gains and who loses, and by which mechanisms of power?" (Flyvberg, 2006, pp.374). Drawing on Nietzsche and Foucault, Flyvberg (2001, chapters 7 & 8) understands power to be exercised through various government rationalities that shape and determine communal values and choices around research inquiry. Ascribing to this view, Constantinides et al (2012) suggest that power governs the development and reconfiguration of research practices including the very strategies by which different researchers interact with one another, as well as where they choose to do their research, around which topics, and published in which outlets.

Based on these ideas, Constantinides et al (2012) propose a pragmatic framework (as illustrated in Figure 1) which calls on researchers to individually and collectively question the various ends of IS research.

The framework focuses on the choices and value judgements IS researchers make around logical ends (i.e. approaches to reasoning), ethical ends (i.e. methods of conduct), aesthetic ends (i.e. the anticipated and desirable outcomes), and the highest good (i.e. the long-term impact of the collective body of research beyond a single site and the concerns of a local community). The highest good occupies the middle of the figure because it is the emergent and collective realization of what is produced and meaningful to a community of inquiry, through its diverse and collective practices (CP 5.433). At the same time, because these ends are shaped by and within power relations, as manifested in various rationalities of action, including publication policies, funding schemes, etc. (Flyvberg, 2001), such power relations are thought to surround the other

Figure 1. A Pragmatic Framework for Questioning the Ends of IS Research

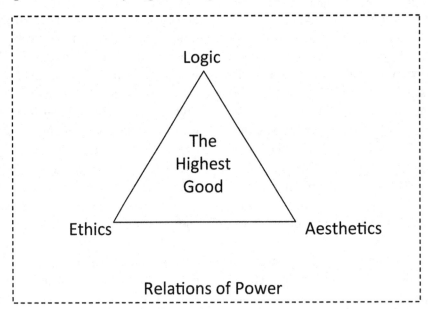

four ends. By placing the four ends in a triangle, Constantinides et al (2012, pp.6) "emphasize the strong interdependencies between them, and the complementary and competing relationships among them."

Beyond a call for more reflective research practices, the pragmatic framework heightens research sensitivity by probing into the history and consequences of various research choices leading towards a more informed understanding and potential transformation of the situated ends of IS research.

QUESTIONING THE ENDS OF NEW INFORMATION INFRASTRUCTURE RESEARCH

This section uses the pragmatic framework to question the ends of new information infrastructure research. The key objective is to reveal the set of value judgments researchers make about their choice of topics, the ways of designing and executing their research studies, and the ways of representing their results in publication outlets.

By revealing these sets of value judgments and choices, the intention is to spur researchers to critically engage the consequences of their research. Table 1 provides a summary of this critical engagement, which is explored in more depth below.

Choosing an Information Infrastructure Topic

Information infrastructure research has historically been informed by disciplinary traditions, such as sociotechnical (interpretivist) studies (e.g. Hanseth & Monteiro, 1997; Star & Ruhleder, 1996) and functionalist studies (e.g. Weill & Broadbent, 1998). In turn, these disciplinary traditions are found to determine the topics of information infrastructure research by defining the logic, ethics, aesthetics, and the highest good of research studies. For example, sociotechnical studies tend to focus on the development of information infrastructures through ethnographic methods and science and technology studies (STS) concepts and theories, toward an understanding of the trajectory of the technology and the various communities of practice involved (see Chapter

Table 1. Questioning the ends of new information infrastructure research

Key Sets of Research Choices	Logic: *the theories and methodologies we use to structure knowledge*	Ethics: *the ethical methods of conduct we employ to carry out research*	Aesthetics: *the desirable outcomes of our research*	Highest Good: *the long-term impact of the research beyond a single site and topic area*
Choosing an information infrastructure topic	How do disciplinary assumptions affect the topics researchers can study, and how do they restrict a more 'open' view of those topics?	Does the researcher's disciplinary tradition force topics too quickly into pre-existing methods of conduct, and how does it exclude participant influence over topics?	How can disciplinary knowledge produce a more general form of knowledge about new information infrastructures?	How can a single discipline lead to an understanding of the long-term impact of new information infrastructures?
>Power Relations	*What are the power relations that are shaping answers to these questions (e.g. funding, publication, disciplinary control)?*			
Designing & Executing the research	How can researchers break free from extant disciplinary assumptions to study new information infrastructure phenomena (e.g. social production)?	How are research participants served by, and involved in, the research?	How do researchers help to institute the transformations desired by the communities they wish to serve?	How can researchers contribute to an understanding of the long-term impact of new information infrastructures given the change in contexts, practices, and technologies?
>Power Relations	*How are the participants' behaviour shaped by the power asymmetries in the research (e.g. use of students in research)?*			
Representing knowledge from the research	How should researchers represent the complex realities they wish to portray and inform?	How do extant (technical) ways of representing methods of conduct affect the ability to report deeper ethical issues (e.g. power asymmetries among participants)?	How can knowledge from a single research study become generalized across research settings?	How can the long-term impact of the research be represented in ways that will be comprehendible and exploitable in future research?
>Power Relations	*Was the representation of the research results shaped by asymmetrical relations of power (e.g. funding, publication, supervisory relations, disciplinary control)?*			

Adapted from Constantinides, Chiasson, and Introna (2012, pp.7)

2 in this book). These studies contribute to the highest good of a more nuanced understanding of the sociotechnical relations involved in information infrastructure research, while revealing the possible (un)intended consequences of those relations. Functionalist studies tend to focus on the development of information infrastructures through more quantitative methods and theories, toward an analysis and evaluation of various financial and operational decisions regarding different technological choices. These studies contribute to the highest good of 'better' leadership and more 'effective' management of information infrastructure investments (see Chapter 2).

Whilst insightful, each in its own way, these groups of information infrastructure studies are already implicated in the rationalities of their respective disciplines. That is, they contribute to their disciplinary tradition by pursuing topics that are considered relevant within that tradition, and according to well-established logic, ethics, and aesthetics, and their targeted highest good. Certainly, researchers may continue to carry out their research within these rationalities, whether intentionally or unintentionally, as they may view such research as satisfying their objectives and intentions. In other words, research along disciplinary traditions should still be defended along certain parameters of relevance.

However, if researchers are interested in carrying out phronetic research into new information infrastructures they need to question (a) whether disciplinary assumptions affect the topics they can study by restricting a more 'open' view of those topics (i.e. logic); (b) whether their disciplinary tradition force topics too quickly into pre-existing methods of conduct, while (potentially) excluding participant influence over topics (i.e. ethics); (c) whether knowledge within the discipline alone can productively transform a more general form of knowledge about new information infrastructures (i.e. aesthetics); (d) whether a single discipline can lead to an understanding of the long-term impact of new information infrastructures (i.e. highest good); and (e) which power relations shape answers to these questions?

A general response to these questions by phronetic researchers would be to embrace post-paradigmatic, "problem-driven" rather than "methodology-driven" research in the name of a more relevant, civic-minded scholarship that can challenge power and change social relations for the better (Flyvberg, 2001; Shapiro, 2005). Such a response would be particularly useful in new information infrastructure research, where advances in new information and communication technologies in joint with new forms of online, social interactions call for pluralism in the methodologies and theoretical assumptions adopted, as those grow out of the practices in specific contexts. For example, research in FOSS projects and mashups (see Chapter 8 in this book) would be restricted to specific topics if viewed from a single disciplinary perspective (e.g. contractual agreements around FOSS projects approached through transaction cost theory or the theory of incomplete contracts). In contrast, if pluralism is adopted, the research would open up possibilities for probing into multiple topics and phenomena within the same field of studies. For instance, topics in and around FOSS projects include motivation and participation in such projects, project management, community formation and alternative

means of production outside monetary rewards, contractual agreements and the management of intellectual property rights, service innovation, knowledge production and knowledge management, hacker culture, and the list goes on.

At the same time, by adopting pluralism, researchers will generate more channels of communication with research participants, thereby enabling a dialogue around the ethical methods of conducting the research. In the case of mashups, such pluralism would be particularly relevant and useful as it would help to set the boundaries of participation and conduct prior to instigating the research and, thus, taking a proactive stance against potential disputes around intellectual property rights, privacy of information, and corporate interests, among others.

Breaking free from disciplinary traditions would help researchers to approach topics and phenomena from multiple points of view, thus, enabling the production of a more general form of knowledge about new information infrastructures. Researchers carrying out studies on new information infrastructures should be open to multiple forms of generalized knowledge emerging from their research, including new *concepts* (e.g. social production), new *theory* (e.g. information infrastructures as commons), *specific implications* (e.g. on governance of new information infrastructures), or *rich insights* (e.g. moving from the governance of technology to the governance of the self) (see Walsham, 1995 for an explanation of these forms of generalized knowledge).

Choosing to acknowledge and reflect on these multiple forms of generalized knowledge will have implications for the highest good that a research study strives to achieve. Constantinides et al. (2012, pp.8) explain that:

The highest good of the research is distinct from aesthetic ends in that it refers to implications beyond a single research paper and topic area and a short period of time, opening up a space for debating broader concerns across the IS field.

Broader concerns in the IS field include producing research results that are relevant and useful to other disciplines such as public policy, sociology, and computer science, all of which have a strong interest on the impact of new information infrastructures on state governance and public affairs, social values and norms, and new technological advances. While it may be hard to anticipate the long-term impact of a research study, considering what could be the highest good of the research early on, would force researchers to inquire deeper into how topics are chosen, maintained, or dropped.

Such questioning would lead to a consideration of the power relations that condition research choices across logic, ethics, and aesthetics, as well as the highest good. For example, as discussed in Chapter 8 of this book, although FOSS projects were initially driven by ideological beliefs around free and open software, more recently, FOSS projects have moved into more commercially viable models with large corporations like Microsoft providing both monetary and professional incentives for participation (see Fitzgerald, 2006). This evolution of FOSS projects means that many research choices are conditioned by power relations including funding for research projects, as well as how research should be carried out and which outcomes should be reported or not. WikiLeaks is another example of a new information infrastructure that has been conditioned by power relations (see Chapter 9 in this book) and research choices around topics such as knowledge management, privacy, social production, etc., would need to be questioned against the possible consequences for the communities affected by the research.

Designing and Executing the Research

As discussed above, extant information infrastructure research tends to follow specific disciplinary traditions when choosing a topic. These traditions are also found to inform the design and execution of research studies, whether that is a case study

approach (Ciborra & associates, 2001), a historical analysis (Abbate, 1999; Bowker & Star, 1999), or a statistical analysis of questionnaires and surveys across different industries (Byrd & Turner, 2000; Duncan, 1995). Each of these approaches provides rich insights for the specific logic, ethics, aesthetics, and highest good deemed relevant within each tradition.

However, if researchers are interested in conducting phronetic research in new information infrastructures they need to question (a) how researchers can break free from extant disciplinary assumptions to study new information infrastructure phenomena (i.e. logic), (b) how research participants are served by, and involved in, the research (i.e. ethics), (c) how researchers help to institute the transformations desired by the communities they wish to serve (i.e. aesthetics), (d) how researchers contribute to an understanding of the long-term impact of new information infrastructures given the change in contexts, practices, and technologies (i.e. highest good), and (e) how the participants' behaviors are shaped by the power asymmetries in the research.

A general response to the above questions can be provided through a pluralist approach to IS research, as Mingers (2001, pp.240-241) argues in the following quote:

IS is much more than simply the development of computer-based business systems–electronic and information technology is now so fundamental within society that IS as a discipline must concern itself with the general evolution of human communication… Thus, it has to draw upon a very wide range of disciplines–technology, psychology, economics, sociology, mathematics, linguistics, semiotics–that encompass very different research traditions. This puts IS in a position similar to other management areas such as organizational studies, which are also characterized by a plurality of research paradigms, each with particular research methods. Consideration then turns to the possible relations between these paradigms…

different research methods (especially from different paradigms) focus on different aspects of reality and therefore a richer understanding of a research topic will be gained by combining several methods together in a single piece of research or research program.

Through a pluralist approach different aspects of the development of new information infrastructures (e.g. design, participation, integration, usage, etc.) would focus on different points of view and, thus, the richness of real-world situations would be dealt with more effectively. Also, since the development of new information infrastructures is not a single event but a process that proceeds through a number of different phases which raises different issues and problems for the researchers, the concept of combining different approaches would help generate more opportunities for creatively dealing with each of those issues and problems.

For example, Fomin and Egyedi (2007) proposed a multi-method data collection approach for obtaining better insights into the design and use of new information infrastructure services. Specifically, the researchers conducted research on the actual use of mobile data services by citizens of Copenhagen, including information about bus schedules and routes delivered through voice, SMS, and mobile Internet/WAP. Because of the complexity of these information infrastructure services, the researchers drew on theories of social learning, sense-making, consumer research, and ethnographic studies, and used participant observation, statistical records on data and phone usage, interviews, personal experience, and newspaper and company publications to inform their logic and ethics. Specifically, to study the environment (i.e. technology development trends, available infrastructure services, and consumer practices) they started with statistical data and scholarly publications (e.g. on average use patterns). Then, they complemented these data with company telephone interviews, as well as practical experience with cellular mobile phones (e.g.

what type of information is available on mobile handsets). To study situation-specific mobile use behavior they started with participant observation (e.g. information available to people waiting for a bus) and then complemented these data with regression analysis of the users' immediate environment (e.g. to find the ratio of potential users of services to citizens). Through these multi-method data sets, the researchers aimed at producing results that were generalizable across settings and methodologies (i.e. aesthetics). They also aimed at contributing to an aspired long-term impact of multi-method research towards informing better design of new information systems through an improved understanding of users' needs, "an under-explored practice in the IS domain" (Fomin & Egyedi, 2007, pp.1418) (i.e. the highest good).

The above example is not meant to argue that all research studies should aim to cover all possibilities emerging in a research setting. In practice, only some will be relevant to a particular study and this will depend on contextual parameters such as, the particular research objectives, the boundaries drawn and the time and resource constraints, the researchers involved and their own competencies and commitments, and the research methods relevant to the situation. Instead, the above example is meant to argue that whatever choices researchers make should be made consciously in view of a full range of possibilities, rather than implicitly from a very limited repertoire as informed by a disciplinary tradition.

At the same time, Deetz (1996, pp.204) warns that pluralist research, while desirable, is very difficult in practice, primarily because of the underlying rationalities driving the research:

Each orientation creates a vision of social problems and tries to address them. Different orientations have developed specific ways of answering the types of questions they pose and do not work terribly well in answering the questions of others. The choice of orientation, to the extent that it can be freed from training histories and department/

discipline politics, can probably be reduced to alternative conceptions of social good and preferred ways of living. This grounds the theory and method debate in a moral debate...

Thus, to Deetz (1996), the difficulty in applying pluralist research in practice is not, and should not be due to logical incompatibilities (i.e. difficulties in combining seemingly conflicting paradigmatic assumptions), but rather because of the lack of embracing a larger set of interaction processes that can produce identifiable (plural) social discourses on ethics, aesthetics, and the highest good. Deetz (1996, pp.204) argues:

Studies need to be understood and evaluated on their own terms but should also appeal to larger social needs where both the needs and means of accomplishment are contested... let us make our claims and the relation between our claims and procedures clearer... In doing so, the ultimate point is not in arguing it out to get it right, but to reclaim the suppressed tensions and conflicts among the many contemporary stakeholders to negotiate a life together based in appreciation of different and responsive decision making.

In other words, researchers should not be aiming at pluralism for the sake of pluralism or for proving to others that they got it right. Rather, researchers should aim for their research to appeal to larger social needs. Only then can researchers begin to disrupt the historical, disciplinary rationalities that drive their research, to uncover hidden assumptions toward the highest good.

Representing Knowledge from the Research

In writing their reports on their research, whether for a conference or a journal publication, researchers often spend a considerable amount of journal space explaining their theory and methodology (i.e. their logic), at the expense of other higher ends.

This is a general problem found in social science research (Flyvberg, 2001), organizational research (Flyvberg, 2006), and IS research (Hirschheim & Klein, 2003).

Mingers (2001, pp.249) summarizes the problematic choices in the representation of knowledge emerging from IS research as follows:

...academics are increasingly under publication pressure and it is certainly much easier to sell clear-cut, well-defined, mono-method work both to funding agencies and to journals. This is particularly crucial to less senior faculty still needing to establish their reputation and tenure.

In other words, IS research–like research in other disciplinary traditions–is already implicated in specific power relations that determine the choices IS researchers make. And it is especially difficult for junior IS faculty to break free from the rationalities of action (e.g. funding and journal guidelines) that determine their choices because junior faculty have yet to establish their reputation and tenure.

Researchers can attempt to break free from the underling rationalities of action by carrying out phronetic research into new information infrastructures through a questioning of (a) how researchers represent the complex realities they wish to portray and inform (i.e. logic), (b) how extant (technical) ways of representing methods of conduct affect the ability to report deeper ethical issues (e.g. power asymmetries among participants) (i.e. ethics), (c) how knowledge from a single research study becomes generalized across research settings (i.e. aesthetics), (d) how the long-term impact of the research can be represented in ways that will be comprehendible and exploitable in future research (i.e. the highest good), and (e) how the representation of the research results is shaped by asymmetrical relations of power (e.g. funding, publication, supervisory relations, disciplinary control).

Answers to the above questions will depend on the choices researchers make around topics and ways of designing and executing their research, as discussed in the previous two sections. Assuming researchers choose a pluralist approach, while being open to different possibilities, they would be in a better position to classify their research knowledge in relation to different phenomena observed and through which perspectives. They would also be in a better position *not* to remove their ethical responsibility to report specific ethical issues which confronted the conduct of the study through "a strangely technical and creative exercise to fit the study specifics into a typical … representation" (Constantinides et al., 2012, pp.12) espoused by a given publication outlet. In other words, logical and ethical ends should not be dealt with by resorting to the technical language of a preferred theory and methodology, just to satisfy a review team.

In relation to aesthetic ends, Lee and Baskerville (2003) offer a framework for mapping out the transformation of knowledge into a more generalized form. Their framework is pluralistic in that it is "capable of reaching across diverse and contrasting scientific traditions," and it rests on two building blocks (Lee & Baskerville, 2003, pp.232). The first building block is a distinction between empirical statements (e.g. data, measurements, observations, or descriptions, about empirical phenomena) and theoretical statements (e.g. the existence of entities and relationships that cannot be directly observed, and hence can only be theorized). The second building block is the distinction between what the researcher is generalizing *from* and what the researcher is generalizing *to* (e.g. *from a* sample *to a* population, *from* a case study's findings *to a* theory). By joining the two building blocks, Lee and Baskerville (2003) propose four different ways of generalizing knowledge. Firstly, generalizing from empirical statements to other empirical statements (e.g. using individual news reports on hacker attacks on Amazon's website to generalize about customer experiences on e-commerce sites that suffered hacker attacks); secondly, generalizing from empirical statements to theoretical statements (e.g. using the set of incentives behind the participation of a group of programmers in a FOSS project to generalize a theory of motivation); thirdly, generalizing from theoretical statements to empirical statements (e.g. using the commons framework to explain empirical data and observations from a FOSS project); and fourthly, generalizing from theoretical statements to other theoretical statements (e.g. comparing and contrasting different concepts of explaining conflicts in intellectual property rights to develop new theory). These four different ways of generalizing indicate that the outputs of generalizing (the "general notions") can be either theoretical statements or empirical statements, and the inputs to generalizing (the "particular instances") can also be either theoretical statements or empirical statements (Lee & Baskerville, 2003, pp.232).

By adopting Lee and Baskerville's (2003) proposals, researchers can generate alternative and even conflicting visions of the development of new information infrastructures. For example, as discussed in Chapter 9 of this book, WikiLeaks was found to function simultaneously as a technology of freedom *and* as a technology of surveillance and control. These visions should not be minimized to a mere enabling-and-constraining argument of the role of new information infrastructures. Rather, these conflicting visions should be explored in more depth toward a revised representation of the possible highest good of the research–i.e. what are the consequences of the enabling and constraining aspects of new information infrastructures? In other words, researchers need to question their own representations of knowledge in anticipation of possible directions for future research. "Important here is to realize that our awareness of and various answers to the different ends of research inquiry will shift as we uncover new directions and possibilities for the highest good" (Constantinides et al., 2012, pp.12).

From this discussion it becomes evident that our role as phronetic researchers is never-ending; our job is not done when our research gets published. Our representation of knowledge in published texts imposes constraints upon other researchers, who will read them (Eco, 1994). That is, we are already implicated in the choices represented in our texts, which will affect how other researchers carry out further research, whether that means following in the same tradition as our own research, critiquing and re-conceptualizing our research, or ignoring it altogether. While we cannot directly influence further research, we should, at least, take an active role in indirectly contributing to a collective understanding of the development of new information infrastructures. Constantinides, Chiasson, and Introna (2012, pp.16) caution:

Important here is to realize that all IS research must be striving for a collective revealing of the highest good–otherwise we remain a fragmented group of separate and competing CoP&K [communities of practice and knowing], divided by hard answers to theory and methods. ...

Thus, the aim of IS researchers would be to recognize these conventions and, at the same time, seek to successfully disrupt them through their conscious choices.

CONCLUSION & RECOMMENDATIONS

This chapter explored the role of the researcher in new information infrastructure research. Using the pragmatic framework of Constantinides, Chiasson, and Introna (2012), the focus of the discussion was on developing a better understanding of the consequences of research choices through phronetic research–the reflective development of prudent knowledge that is continuously shaped by and imbued with situated values and interests (Flyvberg, 2001). Specifically, it was argued

that, IS researchers must recognize that research involves not just choices about *how to conduct a study* (i.e. theoretical and methodological choices), but also about *why we study what we study and who is affected by our work* (i.e. the desirable outcomes and long-term impact of our research).

It has been acknowledged that many researchers may believe that their work is completed once they publish their research. However, it was argued that researchers should at a minimum regard research as involving choices and value judgments about how to conduct their work and towards which outcomes. In becoming aware that research involves not just choices but also value judgments, the higher ends and how they affect and are affected by our choices about theory and method need specific attention.

Engaging these higher ends will make the practice of research much more difficult. However, in choosing to engage these higher ends, researchers make it their own responsibility to deal with the consequences of their research rather than leaving those to be dealt with elsewhere (e.g. in informed consent forms) and by others (e.g. research councils). By becoming more responsible of our own research we increase the possibilities of constructing "a solid ground under our feet" (Flyvbjerg, 2006, pp.375).

Given this, the chapter ends with a set of practical recommendations with which researchers can carry out phronetic research on new information infrastructures.

Practical Recommendations for Phronetic Research on New Information Infrastructures

This chapter has already made a number of recommendations on how to question established disciplinary traditions and rationalities of action to conduct phronetic research. In addition to the specific questions listed in Table 1, researchers should consider the following recommendations when conducting research in new information infrastructures: (1) break free from the problems concerning choices around theory and methodologies by building collaborative research through transparent ethical methods of conduct, and (2) reflect on the often problematic influence of underlying rationalities of action.

Building Collaborative Research through Transparent Ethical Methods of Conduct

Firstly, scholarship on the development of information infrastructures has drawn on a wide variety of research methods including abstract formal models and constructs (Byrd & Turner, 2000; Duncan, 1995), case studies (Ciborra & associates, 2001; Weill & Broadbent, 1998), historical analyses (Abbate, 1999; Bowker & Star, 1999), cross-national comparisons (Braa et al., 2004), and even field experiments (Fomin & Egyedi, 2007). This wide variety is due to the fact that the development of information infrastructures touches upon issues of relevance to the social and computer sciences, as well as the more specialized literatures on public policy and legislation, among others. Yet, despite this wide variety, the choice of methodology tends to signal one's theoretical perspective, as does the nature of methodological critique. On the one hand, those who discount qualitative methods as incapable of evaluating general relationships signal a belief in both law-like social relations and in the relative unimportance of factors such as culture, history, and individualism. On the other hand, critiques of quantitative methods often charge that they do not capture the most important aspects of social conditions.

Both critiques target theoretical assumptions as reflected in methodological choices, even though the influence of theory (including ontological and epistemological assumptions) on methodological practice cannot be assumed and should not be overstated. Theoretical changes can and do occur independently of changes in methodological

practice either due to opportunism (e.g. a special issue that targets a specific theory), influence by peers (e.g. a supervisor or a colleague) and external bodies (e.g. a research council, a partner organization), or even because of a widespread use of a particular type of theoretical approach that forces further adoption in new research studies (e.g. the recent wave of "sociomaterial" IS research). Moreover, methodological challenges (e.g. lack of data or different types of data) sometimes seem to drive theoretical arguments rather than the other way around. Despite the presence of some or all of these factors, theoretical choices are usually critiqued in relation to methodological choices and vice versa.

A way to overcome the problems concerning choices around theory and methodologies is to use multiple methods. Combinations of quantitative and qualitative methods–including the use of stakeholder involvement to validate findings–are thought to address some of the problems described above (Lee, 1999; Mingers, 2001). The use of multiple methods, however, raises questions whether the research is rigorous enough because different methods are thought to reflect different ontological and epistemological assumptions (Goles & Hirschheim, 2000). Furthermore, the conditions posited by some theories imply that the assumptions underlying different methods are violated (e.g. the problematic use of statistics to understand culture). But even if ontological and epistemological assumptions pose no barrier, practical considerations complicate methodological choice.

As mentioned earlier, interest in multiple methods demands more intensive and diversified forms of technical skill-development that are rarely mastered by individual researchers. In addition, when research demands intensive fieldwork and substantial local knowledge, unavoidably large investments in data collection present additional obstacles.

Collaborative research is a way to expand the potential for using multiple methods as it can bring scholars from multiple disciplines together on the same research team with strengths in complementary methods, increasing confidence that each method is rigorously applied. There are, though, practical challenges related to the trade-offs in research training and actual research practice, as well as professional incentives that constrain cross-method and cross-discipline research.

At a minimum, each scholar must have a solid command of at least one method, be conversant with a range of other methods and disciplines, and engage in scholarship produced from a variety of methodological and disciplinary perspectives. These minimum conditions would help to address possible problems, such as not recognizing situations when key assumptions have been violated, overlooking procedures that limit the risk of bias or fail to use diagnostics that can reveal and compensate for problems, interpreting the results in a misleading manner, or worse, inappropriately applying the method and generating misleading results. Thus, there is a need for rigorous methodological training and application to avoid such problems. There is also a need for researchers to participate in interdisciplinary projects which would expose them to multiple methods and ways of thinking about research.

However, even when researchers manage to secure their participation in interdisciplinary research and recognize complementarities among methodological approaches, they may confront powerful professional incentives to produce more specialized research. These include reliance on methodological and disciplinary assessments of research quality and the priority given to the volume and pace of publication in assessments of productivity (Bennis & O'Toole, 2005; Mingers, 2001). As suggested by Constantinides, Chiasson, and Introna (2012), the peer-review process that influences hiring, advancement, publications, and grant applications generally means review by specialists. Reviewers are more likely to approach research outside their own area of specialization with greater scepticism, especially if it combines

multiple methods or disciplines and they do not understand or accept the rationale for combining various approaches. Even if such research gets published, an emerging question is how much credit should a researcher receive for co-authored versus single-authored publications? Thus, the influence of individual, specialized research remains strong despite the recent promotion of research combining multiple methods and discipline traditions (Chiasson et al., 2009; Mingers, 2003, 2008).

Academic and practitioner (e.g. policy) communities, however, would be collectively better off if more research made use of multiple methods and integrated insights from a variety of disciplines toward the highest good of research findings. For example, in the natural sciences, much higher levels of co-authorship occur that rely on the coordinated activities of research teams. This leads to more publications, some of which may lead to breakthrough discoveries. Research in the development of new information infrastructures should learn from the research practices followed in the natural sciences toward generating more collaborative analyses and more co-authored publications that incorporate multiple methods and disciplines.

Collaborative research would benefit from the development of a research information infrastructure to share research data, protocols, and software. Within the natural sciences, it is common practice to share data, illustrated by the success of biomedical information such as the Human Genome Project. Within the IS research there are few attempts to share data and models (see AISnet website), but in practice it is difficult to get scholars to contribute. Low contribution to the provision of such shared data is stimulated by the lack of incentives as journals and funding agencies do not encourage nor do they recognize use of such data. Uniform data-sharing policies are unlikely to work well given the degree of diversity of methodological practices. However, a research information infrastructure could be established where researchers and others interested in specific topics could debate theoretical ideas, methodological practices, and empirical findings found in published IS research. These debates would help to open up the black box of review processes, by commenting on the comprehensibility and importance of the research, while identifying alternative interpretations, applied applications, and further reflection on areas for further research (Introna & Whittaker, 2004; Ramiller et al., 2008).

The challenge is to develop policies that effectively encourage collaborative research and data sharing while acknowledging differences in the form and sensitivity of data. That is, the key to building collaborative research is to establish transparent ethical methods of conduct. Transparency should cut through data access, data collection and analysis, and final representation of the findings. In other words, collaborating researchers should be able to act as reviewers to each others' research practices, from tracing the source of the data, assessing its credibility, evaluating possible surface- and deep-level ethical issues (e.g. from informed consent to power asymmetries), and reflecting on the rhetoric used to represent the findings.

Great emphasis should be placed on the anticipated (ethical) consequences of the research not just for the research team but also those communities affected by the research, whether those are research participants or other academics. Exploring the anticipated consequences of the research in advance would move the aim beyond the possibilities of whether the research will be published in a top journal, to the influence of the research on other topic areas, methodologies, and theories within the field of infrastructure research. Through such an engagement, researchers will no longer be simply concerned with their situated relationships with research subjects, but also with the way that their activities take place within a broader field of knowledge production (Constantinides et al., 2012). That is, researchers are not 'innocent seekers of the truth'; rather they

are active participants in the exercise of power toward the production of knowledge (Alvesson & Sköldberg, 2000). Thus, researchers should constantly reflect on the conditions and consequences of the formation of their research choices toward the production of knowledge (Flyvbjerg, 2001).

Reflect on Underlying Rationalities of Action

The above discussion raises sensitivity to the underlying rationalities of action that determine research choices. As discussed earlier, such rationalities include but are not limited to disciplinary traditions, funding schemes, journal and review team preferences, departmental aspirations, etc. Although it has been repeatedly argued that researchers should attempt to disrupt such rationalities and develop new programs of action, it is acknowledged that this would not always be possible or desirable. It should also be stressed that, although this chapter has argued for pluralist, post-paradigmatic research through collaborations across disciplines, it is acknowledged that not all research has the capabilities to be collaborative, interdisciplinary, or use multiple methods. Furthermore, even if research achieves such objectives, it does not mean that such research is free from underlying rationalities.

The key point here is that researchers should become aware and reflect on the choices they make throughout the evolution of a research program, and more broadly, their research careers. Granted, professional incentives for career advancement will play a big role in the choices researchers make. However, choices around research on the development of new information infrastructures should be carefully made and reflected upon because of the ubiquity of new information and communication technologies and the increased impact they can have on both work and social life.

Taking WikiLeaks as an example, research into the production, sharing, and wide distribution of sensitive information through such an information infrastructure should tread with care while ensuring a balanced protection of freedom of speech and private, corporate, and/or state interests. The same holds for research into such information infrastructures as Second Life and Facebook, where researchers should assess the trade-offs in protecting personal data versus the exploitation of data on consumer behaviour. As discussed in Chapters 8 and 9 in this book, there are powerful interests behind the development and exploitation of such information infrastructures. These interests will most likely spill over research agendas and the reporting of research findings. This does not mean that researchers should abstain from participating in such research but should rather always reflect on the possible consequences of the choices they make (and the contracts they sign) when agreeing to participate.

At the same time, reflexivity should not be glorified in the sense that researchers use it as a rhetorical device to justify knowledge claims emerging from their research. If knowledge is a product of power relations, so too is reflexivity. That is, reflexivity is a construction of communities of researchers whose work is informed by particular rationalities of action and "who use language to promote particular versions of 'truth' or claims to superior insights" (Alvesson et al., 2008, pp.498). In other words, reflexivity is a construction, which itself can–and must–be subjected to critique if it is not to become reified and glorified. As such, the construction of reflexivity and the consequences of the processes of construction warrant closer examination if we are to "articulate the operations of modern knowledge without being caught in unreflective representational webs" (Calás & Smircich, 1999, pp.652).

Reflexive researchers must be disruptive (Knights, 1992) in that they should seek different ways in understanding a phenomenon and, thus, produce different knowledge(s). Reflexive researchers also need "to decenter authors as authority figures; and to involve participants, readers and audiences in the production of re-search" (Putnam, 1996, pp.386). In doing so, the authority of the research account is undermined–it is positioned as one representation among many; the privileged power position of the researcher in relation to the research subject is reduced (Marcus, 1994) and the reader is given a more active role in the interpretation process (Eco, 1994).

More importantly, reflexive researchers need to unmask the networks, conventions, and macro-discourses in which they act and the ways in which the social institutions of academia and society shape research processes and outcomes (Deetz, 1996; Hardy et al., 2001; Putnam, 1996). In identifying the political and institutional limits of research and surveying how networks of scientists negotiate the meaning of data between themselves, reflexive researchers play an important role in constructing the meaning of reflexivity. "Thus the practices outlined here collectively construct the meaning of reflexivity and, as such, warrant closer examination" (Alvesson et al., 2008, pp.498).

In summary, researchers should take an active role in questioning the ways they construct knowledge claims about particular infrastructural phenomena, but they should also question those very knowledge claims and the ways they have been constructed as such.

REFERENCES

Abbate, J. (1999). *Inventing the internet*. Cambridge, MA: MIT Press.

Alvesson, M., Hardy, C., & Harley, B. (2008). Reflecting on reflexivity: Reflexive textual practices in organization and management theory. *Journal of Management Studies*, 45(3), 480–501. doi:10.1111/j.1467-6486.2007.00765.x

Alvesson, M., & Sköldberg, K. (2000). *Reflexive methodology: New vistas for qualitative research*. London, UK: Sage.

Apel, K.-O. (1995). *C. S. Peirce: From pragmatism to pragmaticism*. Amherst, MA: The University of Massachusetts Press.

Astley, W. G., & Zammuto, R. F. (1992). Organization science, managers, and language games. *Organization Science, 3*(4), 443–460. doi:10.1287/orsc.3.4.443

Bennis, W. G., & O'Toole, J. (2005). How business schools have lost their way. *Harvard Business Review, 83*(5), 96–104.

Bowker, G., & Star, S. L. (1999). *Sorting things out–Classification and its consequences*. Cambridge, MA: MIT Press.

Braa, J., Monteiro, E., & Sahay, S. (2004). Networks of action: Sustainable health information systems across developing countries. *Management Information Systems Quarterly, 28*(3), 337–362.

Byrd, T. A., & Turner, D. E. (2000). Measuring the flexibility of information technology infrastructure: Exploratory analysis of a construct. *Journal of Management Information Systems, 17*(1), 167–208.

Calás, M., & Smircich, L. (1999). Past postmodernism: Reflections and tentative directions. *Academy of Management Review, 24*(4), 649–671.

Chiasson, M., Germonprez, M., & Mathiassen, L. (2009). Pluralistic action research: A review of the information systems literature. *Information Systems Journal, 19*(1), 31–54. doi:10.1111/j.1365-2575.2008.00297.x

Ciborra, C. U. (ed.), & associates. (2001). *From control to drift: The dynamics of corporate information infrastructures*. Oxford, UK: Oxford University Press.

Constantinides, P., Chiasson, M., & Introna, L. (2012). The ends of information systems (IS) research. MIS Quarterly, 36(1), 1-19.

Davison, R. M., Martinsons, M. G., Lo, H. W. H., & Kam, C. S. P. (2006). Ethical values of IT professionals: Evidence from Hong Kong. *IEEE Transactions on Engineering Management, 53*(1), 48–58. doi:10.1109/TEM.2005.861817

Deetz, S. (1996). Describing differences in approach to organization science: Rethinking Burrell and Morgan and their legacy. *Organization Science, 7*(2), 191–207. doi:10.1287/orsc.7.2.191

Duncan, N. B. (1995). Capturing flexibility of information technology infrastructure: A study of resource characteristics and their measure. *Journal of Management Information Systems, 12*(2), 37–57.

Eco, U. (1994). *The limits of interpretation*. Bloomington, IN: Indiana University Press.

Elkjær, B., & Simpson, B. (2006, June 15-16). Towards a pragmatic theory of creative practice. Paper presented at *Second Organization Studies Summer Workshop Re-turn to practice: Understanding Organization as it Happens*, Mykonos, Greece.

Fitzgerald, B. (1997). The use of systems development methodologies in practice: A field study. *Information Systems Journal, 7*(3), 201–212. doi:10.1046/j.1365-2575.1997.d01-18.x

Fitzgerald, B. (2006). The transformation of open source software. *Management Information Systems Quarterly, 30*(3), 587–598.

Flyvbjerg, B. (2001). *Making social science matter: Why social inquiry fails and how it can succeed again* (Sampson, S., Trans.). Cambridge, UK: Cambridge University Press.

Flyvbjerg, B. (2004). Phronetic planning research: Theoretical and methodological reflections. *Planning Theory & Practice, 5*(3), 283–306. doi:10.1080/1464935042000250195

Flyvbjerg, B. (2006). Making organization research matter: Power, values, and phronesis. In Clegg, S. R., Hardy, C., Lawrence, T. B., & Nord, W. R. (Eds.), *The Sage handbook of organization studies* (2nd ed., pp. 370–387). Thousand Oaks, CA: Sage.

Fomin, V. V., & Egyedi, T. M. (2007). Multimethod approach to guide design and use of ICT infrastructure services. H. Österle, J. Schelp, & R. Winter (Eds.), In *Proceedings of the 15th European Conference on Information Systems*, (pp.1410-1420). St. Gallen, Switzerland: University of St. Gallen.

Giddens, A. (1984). *The constitution of society: Outline of the theory of structuration*. Berkeley, CA: University of California Press.

Goles, T., & Hirschheim, R. (2000). The paradigm is dead, the paradigm is dead... long live the paradigm: The legacy of Burrell and Morgan. *Omega, 28*(3), 249–268. doi:10.1016/S0305-0483(99)00042-0

Habermas, J. (1992). Peirce and communication. In Habermas, J. (Ed.), *Postmetaphysical thinking* (pp. 88–113). (Hohengarten, W. M., Trans.). Cambridge, UK: Polity Press.

Habermas, J. (1994). *Justification and application: Remarks on discourse ethics*. Cambridge, MA: The MIT Press.

Habermas, J. (1998). *On the pragmatics of communication*. Cambridge, MA: The MIT Press.

Hanseth, O., & Monteiro, E. (1997). Inscribing behaviour in information infrastructure standards. *Accounting, Management and Information Technology, 7*(4), 183–211. doi:10.1016/S0959-8022(97)00008-8

Hardy, C., Phillips, N., & Clegg, S. (2001). Reflexivity in social studies: A study of the production of the research subject. *Human Relations, 54*, 3–32.

Hirschheim, R., & Klein, H. (1994). Realizing emancipatory principles in information systems development: The case for ETHICS. *Management Information Systems Quarterly, 18*(1), 83–109. doi:10.2307/249611

Hirschheim, R., & Klein, H. (2003). Crisis in the IS field? A critical reflection on the state of the discipline. *Journal of the Association for Information Systems, 4*(5), 237–293.

Introna, L. D., & Whittaker, L. (2004). Journals, truth, and politics: The case of *MIS Quarterly*. In Kaplan, B., Truex, D. P. III, Wastell, D., Wood-Harper, A. T., & DeGross, J. I. (Eds.), *Information systems research: Relevant theory and informed practice* (pp. 103–120). Norwell, MA: Kluwer Academic Publishers. doi:10.1007/1-4020-8095-6_7

Knights, D. (1992). Changing spaces: The disruptive impact of a new epistemological location for the study of management. *Academy of Management Review, 17*, 514–536.

Kohlberg, L. (1981). The philosophy of moral development: *Vol. 1. Essays on moral development*. San Francisco, CA: Harper & Row.

Lee, A. (1999). Rigor and relevance in MIS research: Beyond the approach of positivism alone. *Management Information Systems Quarterly, 23*(1), 29–33. doi:10.2307/249407

Lee, A., & Baskerville, R. (2003). Generalizing generalizibility in information systems research. *Information Systems Research, 14*(3), 221–243. doi:10.1287/isre.14.3.221.16560

Liszka, J. (1978). Community is C. S. Peirce: Science as a means and as an end. *Transactions of the C.S. Peirce Society, 14*(4), 305–321.

Marcus, G. E. (1994). What comes just after "post": The case of ethnography. In Denzin, N., & Lincoln, Y. (Eds.), *Handbook of qualitative research* (pp. 563–574). Thousand Oaks, CA: Sage.

Mingers, J. (2001). Combining IS research methods: Towards a pluralist methodology. *Information Systems Research, 12*(3), 240–259. doi:10.1287/isre.12.3.240.9709

Mingers, J. (2003). The paucity of multimethod research: A review of the information systems literature. *Information Systems Journal, 13*(3), 233–249. doi:10.1046/j.1365-2575.2003.00143.x

Mingers, J. (2008). Pluralism, realism, and truth: The keys to knowledge in information systems research. *International Journal of Information Technologies and Systems Approach, 1*(1), 81–92. doi:10.4018/jitsa.2008010106

Mingers, J., & Walsham, G. (2010). Toward ethical information systems: The contribution of discourse ethics. *Management Information Systems Quarterly, 34*(4), 1–23.

Mumford, E. (2006). The story of socio-technical design: Reflections on its successes, failures and potential. *Information Systems Journal, 16*(4), 317–342. doi:10.1111/j.1365-2575.2006.00221.x

Peirce, C. S. (1958). *Collected papers of Charles Sanders Peirce* (Burks, A. W., Ed.). *Vol. VII-VIII*). Cambridge, MA: Harvard University Press.

Peirce, C. S. (1931-35). In Hartshorne, C., & Weiss, P. (Eds.), *Collected papers of Charles Sanders Peirce* (*Vol. I-VI*). Cambridge, MA: Harvard University Press.

Pettigrew, A. M. (1985). Contextualist research and the study of organizational change processes. In Mumford, E. (Ed.), *Research methods in information systems* (pp. 53–78). Amsterdam, The Netherlands: Elsevier Science.

Putnam, L. (1996). Situating the author and text. *Journal of Management Inquiry, 5*, 382–386. doi:10.1177/105649269654013

Ramiller, N. C., Swanson, E. B., & Wang, P. (2008). Research directions in information systems: Toward an institutional ecology. *Journal of the Association for Information Systems, 9*(1), 1–22.

Rynes, S. L., Bartunek, J. M., & Daft, R. L. (2001). Across the great divide: Knowledge creation and transfer between practitioners and academics. *Academy of Management Journal, 44*, 340–356. doi:10.2307/3069460

Shapiro, I. (2005). *The flight from reality in the human sciences*. Princeton, NJ: Princeton University Press.

Snell, R. S. (1996). Complementing Kohlberg: Mapping the ethical reasoning used by managers for their own dilemma cases. *Human Relations, 49*(1), 23–49. doi:10.1177/001872679604900102

Stahl, B. (2008). Discourses on information ethics: The claim to universality. *Ethics and Information Technology, 10*(2), 97–108. doi:10.1007/s10676-008-9171-9

Star, S. L., & Ruhleder, K. (1996). Steps toward an ecology of infrastructure: Design and access for large information spaces. *Information Systems Research, 7*(1), 111–134. doi:10.1287/isre.7.1.111

Starkey, K., & Madan, P. (2001). Bridging the relevance gap: Aligning stakeholders in the future of management research. *British Journal of Management, 12*, 3–26. doi:10.1111/1467-8551.12.s1.2

Walsham, G. (1993). *Interpreting information systems in organizations*. Chichester, UK: John Wiley & Sons.

Walsham, G. (1995). Interpretive case studies in IS research: Nature and method. *European Journal of Information Systems, 4*(2), 74–81. doi:10.1057/ejis.1995.9

Weill, P., & Broadbent, M. (1998). *Leveraging the new infrastructure: How market leaders capitalize on information*. Boston, MA: Harvard Business School Press.

ADDITIONAL READING

Barge, J. K. (2004). Reflexivity and managerial practice. *Communication Monographs, 71*, 70–96. doi:10.1080/03634520410001691465

Benbasat, I., & Zmud, B. (1999). Empirical research in information systems: The practice of relevance. *Management Information Systems Quarterly, 23*(1), 3–16. doi:10.2307/249403

Benbasat, I., & Zmud, R. (2003). The identity crisis within the IS discipline: Defining and communicating the discipline's core properties. *Management Information Systems Quarterly, 27*(2), 183–194.

Burrell, G., & Morgan, G. (1979). *Sociological paradigms and organizational analysis*. London, UK: Heinemann.

Collins, W. H. (1998). The meaning of data: Open and closed evidential cultures in the search for gravitational waves. *American Journal of Sociology, 1042*, 293–338. doi:10.1086/210040

Cunliffe, A. L. (2003). Reflexive inquiry in organizational research: Questions and possibilities. *Human Relations, 56*(8), 983–1003. doi:10.1177/00187267030568004

Cunliffe, A. L. (2004). On becoming a critically reflexive practitioner. *Journal of Management Education, 28*(4), 407–426. doi:10.1177/1052562904264440

Davenport, T., & Markus, M. (1999). Rigor vs. relevance revisited: Response to Benbasat and Zmud. *Management Information Systems Quarterly, 23*(1), 19–23. doi:10.2307/249405

DeSanctis, G. (2003). The social life of information systems research: A response to Benbasat and Zmud's call for returning to the IT artefact. *Journal of the Association for Information Systems, 4*(7), 360–376.

Feyerabend, P. (1978). *Against method*. London, UK: Verso.

Fournier, V., & Grey, C. (2000). At the critical moment: Conditions and prospects for critical management studies. *Human Relations, 53*(1), 7–32. doi:10.1177/0018726700531002

Gergen, M., & Gergen, K. (2000). Qualitative inquiry: Tensions and transformations. In Denzin, N., & Lincoln, Y. (Eds.), *Handbook of qualitative research* (2nd ed., pp. 1025–1046). Thousand Oaks, CA: Sage.

Gioia, D., & Pitre, E. (1990). Multiparadigm perspectives on theory building. *Academy of Management Review, 15*(4), 584–602.

Golden-Biddle, K., & Locke, K. (1993). Appealing work: An investigation of how ethnographic texts convince. *Organization Science, 4*(4), 595–617. doi:10.1287/orsc.4.4.595

Hassard, J. (1991). Multiple paradigms and organisational analysis: A case study. *Organization Studies, 12*(2), 275–299. doi:10.1177/017084069101200206

Jackson, N., & Carter, P. (1993). "Paradigm wars": A response to Hugh Willmott. *Organization Studies, 145*, 721–725. doi:10.1177/017084069301400505

Jeffcutt, P. (1994). From interpretation to representation in organizational analysis: Postmodernism, ethnography and organizational symbolism. *Organization Studies, 15*(2), 241–274. doi:10.1177/017084069401500204

Johnson, P., & Duberley, J. (2003). Reflexivity in management research. *Journal of Management Studies, 40*(5), 1279–1303. doi:10.1111/1467-6486.00380

King, J., & Lyytinen, K. (Eds.). (2006). *Information systems: The state of the field*. Chichester, UK: John Wiley & Sons.

Knorr-Cetina, K. (1999). *Epistemic cultures: How the sciences make knowledge.* Cambridge, MA: Harvard University Press.

Kuhn, T. S. (1970). *The structure of scientific revolution.* Chicago, IL: University of Chicago Press.

Lynch, M. (2000). Against reflexivity as an academic virtue and source of privileged knowledge. *Theory, Culture & Society, 17*(3), 26–54. doi:10.1177/02632760022051202

Robertson, J. (2002). Reflexivity redux: A pithy polemic on positionality. *Anthropological Quarterly, 75*(4), 785–793. doi:10.1353/anq.2002.0066

Robey, D. (1996). Diversity in information systems research: Threat, promise, and responsibility. *Information Systems Research, 7*(4), 400–408. doi:10.1287/isre.7.4.400

Robey, D., & Markus, M. L. (1998). Beyond rigor and relevance: Producing consumable research about information systems. *Information Resources Management Journal, 11*(1), 7–15.

Schultz, M., & Hatch, M. J. (1996). Living with multiple paradigms: The case of paradigm interplay in organizational culture studies. *Academy of Management Review, 212*, 529–557.

Weick, K. (2002). Real-time reflexivity: Prods to reflection. *Organization Studies, 3*, 893–899. doi:10.1177/0170840602236011

Willmott, H. (1993). Breaking the paradigm mentality. *Organization Studies, 145*, 681–719. doi:10.1177/017084069301400504

ENDNOTES

[1] The "language games" concept was introduced by Wittgenstein (1972) to describe the way in which the linguistic conventions of a domain of practice reflects its knowledge and comprehension of the world. The term 'game' is used to stress the fact that practices are performed and that individuals participating in a language game take on specific roles by following certain rules of practice.

[2] Also see a special research forum on the transfer of knowledge between academics and practitioners published in the *Academy of Management Journal* (Rynes et al., 2001), and a special issue of the *British Journal of Management* on the relevance of management research (Starkey & Madan, 2001).

[3] Other approaches to ethical IS research have been proposed in the past. One proposed approach is "ethical reasoning" (Davison et al., 2006), which focuses on ideal ethical categories such as the social contract, individual rights, and moral justice (Kolhberg, 1981). Despite its considerable merits, however, the focus on ideal ethical categories has a tendency to exclude and perhaps obscure the local and situated concerns, values, and dilemmas people may face in different and particular contexts (Snell, 1996; also see Habermas, 1994, pp.120). It has been argued that, beyond the development and use of abstract moral categories to guide ethical research practices, there is a need to consider the situated and emerging ends of IS research (Hirschheim & Klein, 2003). Habermas' work on communicative action (1992, 1998) and discourse ethics (1994) has also been proposed as an alternative approach to dealing with the situated and emerging ends of IS research. Specifically, Habermasian ideas toward ethical research have been extensively applied to ethics and IS–from Enid Mumford's ETHICS framework (e.g. Hirschheim & Klein, 1994; Mumford, 2006) to discourse ethics (e.g. Mingers & Walsham, 2010; Stahl, 2008). On the one hand, the ETHICS framework provides explicit ethical principles in order to inform moral practices, including the emancipation of human subjects involved in

the research. One the other hand, discourse ethics is grounded in a radical approach to democratic participation through communicative acts among those affected by research practice decisions and proposals. The key difference between Habermas' critical theoretical approach to understanding ethics and the approach proposed in this book is that, in the former more emphasis is placed on discourse (ex ante), whereas in the latter more emphasis is placed on evolutionary experience (ex post) (see Apel, 1995).

4   'CP' refers to *Collected Papers of Charles Sanders Peirce* (1931-58). The first number indicates the volume and the second number following the period indicates the paragraph.

Compilation of References

Abbate, J. (1999). *Inventing the Internet.* Cambridge, MA: MIT Press.

Abel-Smith, B., Calltorp, J., Dixon, M., Dunning, A., Evans, R., Holland, W., & Mossialos, E. (1994). *Report on the Greek health services.* Athens, Greece: Farmetrika.

Abernethy, C. L., & Sally, H. (2000). Experiences of some government-sponsored organisations of irrigators in Niger and Burkina Faso, West Africa. *Journal of Applied Irrigation Science, 35*(2), 177–205.

Acheson, J., & Brewer, J. (2003). Changes in the territorial system of the Maine lobster industry: Implications for management. In Dolšak, N., & Ostrom, E. (Eds.), *The commons in the new millennium: Challenges and adaptations* (pp. 37–60). Cambridge, MA: MIT Press.

Adams, J. S. (1963). Towards an understanding of inequality. *Journal of Abnormal and Normal Social Psychology, 67*, 422–436. doi:10.1037/h0040968

Addley, E., & Halliday, J. (2010, December 8). Operation payback cripples MasterCard site in revenge for WikiLeaks ban. *The Guardian.* Retrieved April, 27 2011, from http://www.guardian.co.uk/media/2010/dec/08/operation-payback-mastercard-website-wikileaks

Adler-Milstein, J., McAfee, A. P., Bates, D. W., & Jha, A. K. (2008). The state of regional health information organizations: Current activities and financing. *Health Affairs, 27*(1), 60–69. doi:10.1377/hlthaff.27.1.w60

Advisory Committee on Health Infostructure (ACHI). (2001). *Tactical plan for a pan-Canadian health infostructure, 2001 update.* Ottawa, Canada: Office of Health and the Information Highway, Health Canada.

Agerfalk, P., & Fitzgerald, B. (2008). Outsourcing to an unknown workforce: Exploring open sourcing as a global sourcing strategy. *Management Information Systems Quarterly, 32*(2), 385–410.

Agrawal, A. (1994). Rules, rule making, and rule breaking: Examining the fit between rule systems and resource use. In Ostrom, E., Gardner, R., & Walker, J. M. (Eds.), *Rules, games, and common-pool resources* (pp. 267–282). Ann Arbor, MI: University of Michigan Press.

Agrawal, A. (1999). *Greener pastures: Politics, markets, and community among a migrant pastoral people.* Durham, NC: Duke University Press.

Agrawal, A. (2008). Sustainable governance of common-pool resources: Context, method, and politics. In Bardhan, P., & Ray, I. (Eds.), *The contested commons: Conversations between economists and anthropologists* (pp. 46–65). Oxford, UK: Blackwell Publishing.

Akrich, M., & Latour, B. (1992). A summary of a convenient vocabulary for the semiotics of human and nonhuman assemblies. In W.E., Bijker, & J. Law (Eds.), *Shaping technology/building society,* (pp. 259-264). Cambridge, MA: MIT Press.

Alavi, M., & Leidner, D. (2001). Review: Knowledge management and knowledge management systems: Conceptual foundations and research issues. *Management Information Systems Quarterly, 25*(1), 107–136. doi:10.2307/3250961

Alvesson, M., Hardy, C., & Harley, B. (2008). Reflecting on reflexivity: Reflexive textual practices in organization and management theory. *Journal of Management Studies, 45*(3), 480–501. doi:10.1111/j.1467-6486.2007.00765.x

Alvesson, M., & Sköldberg, K. (2000). *Reflexive methodology: New vistas for qualitative research*. London, UK: Sage.

Anderies, J. M., Janssen, M. A., & Ostrom, E. (2004). A framework to analyze the robustness of social-ecological systems from an institutional perspective. *Ecology & Society*, *9*(1), 18–34.

Anderson, C. (2010, July). Julian Assange: Why the world needs WikiLeaks. *TED*. Retrieved May 8, 2011, from http://www.ted.com/talks/julian_assange_why_the_world_needs_wikileaks.html

Anderson, C. L., Nugent, R. E., & Locker, L. B. (2002). Microcredit, social capital, and common-pool resources. *World Development*, *30*(1), 95–105. doi:10.1016/S0305-750X(01)00096-1

Anderson, K. P., & Hoskins, M. W. (2004). Information use and abuse in the local governance of Common-Pool Forest Resources. *Forests. Trees & Livelihoods*, *14*, 295–312.

Anderson, R. (2005). Open and closed systems are equivalent (that is, in an ideal world). In Feller, J., Fitzgerald, B., Hissam, S., & Lakhani, K. (Eds.), *Perspectives on free and open source software* (pp. 127–142). Cambridge, MA: MIT Press.

Andersson, K., & Ostrom, E. (2008). Analyzing decentralized natural resource governance from a polycentric perspective. *Policy Sciences*, *41*(1), 1–23.

Apel, K.-O. (1995). *C. S. Peirce: From pragmatism to pragmaticism*. Amherst, MA: The University of Massachusetts Press.

Appadurai, A. (2001). Deep democracy. *Environment and Urbanization*, *13*(2), 23–43. doi:10.1177/095624780101300203

Armitage, D. (2005). Adaptive capacity and community-based natural resource management. *Environmental Management*, *35*(6), 703–715. doi:10.1007/s00267-004-0076-z

Armitage, D. (2008). Governance and the commons in a multi-level world. *International Journal of the Commons*, *2*(1), 7–32.

Astley, W. G., & Zammuto, R. F. (1992). Organization science, managers, and language games. *Organization Science*, *3*(4), 443–460. doi:10.1287/orsc.3.4.443

Axelrod, R. (1984). *The evolution of cooperation*. New York, NY: Basic Books.

Baiocchi, G. (2003). Participation, activism, and politics: The Pôrto Alegre experiment. In Fung, A., & Wright, E. O. (Eds.), *Deepening democracy: Institutional innovations in empowered participatory governance* (pp. 45–76). London, UK: Verso.

Bakos, J. Y., & Nault, B. R. (1997). Ownership and investment in electronic networks. *Information Systems Research*, *8*(4), 321–341. doi:10.1287/isre.8.4.321

Balland, J., & Platteau, J. (1996). *Halting degradation of natural resources: Is there a role for rural communities?* Oxford, UK: Clarendon.

Ballas, A., & Tsoukas, H. (2004). Measuring nothing: The case of the Greek national health system. *Human Relations*, *57*(6), 661–690. doi:10.1177/0018726704044951

Bangemann, M., da Fonseca, E. C., Davis, P., de Benedetti, C., Gyllenhamman, P., & Hunsel, L. …von Pierer, H. (1994). *Europe and the global information society: Bangemann report recommendations to the European council*. Brussels, Belgium: European Council.

Bannon, L. J., & Griffin, J. (2001). New technology, communities, and networking: Problems and prospects for orchestrating change. *Telematics and Informatics*, *18*(1), 35–49. doi:10.1016/S0736-5853(00)00021-6

Barnes, M., Harrison, S., Mort, M., Shardlow, P., & Wistow, G. (1999). The new management of community care: Users groups, citizenship and co-production. In Stoker, G. (Ed.), *The new management of British local governance* (pp. 112–127). Houndmills, UK: Macmillan.

Baroudi, J. J., Olson, M. H., & Ives, B. (1986). An empirical study of the impact of user involvement on system usage and information satisfaction. *Communications of the ACM*, *29*(3), 232–237. doi:10.1145/5666.5669

Barrett, M., Fryatt, B., Walsham, G., & Joshi, S. (2005). Building bridges between local and global knowledge: New ways of working at the World Health Organisation. *Knowledge Management for Development Journal*, *1*(2), 31–46.

BBC. (2010, February 12). Iceland's journalism freedom dream prompted by Wikileaks. *BBC Online*. Retrieved May 8, 2011, from http://news.bbc.co.uk/2/hi/technology/8510927.stm

Beck, U. (1992). *Risk society: Toward a new modernity*. London, UK: Sage.

Beck, U. (1999). *World risk society*. Cambridge, UK: Polity.

Beniger, J. R. (1996). Who shall control cyberspace? In Strate, L., Jacobson, R., & Gibson, S. (Eds.), *Communication and cyberspace* (pp. 49–58). Cresskill, NJ: Hampton.

Benkler, Y. (2001). Siren songs and Amish children: Information, autonomy and law. *N.Y.U. Law Review*, *76*(23), 59–77.

Benkler, Y. (2002). Coase's penguin, or Linux and the nature of the firm. *The Yale Law Journal*, *112*(3), 1–42. doi:10.2307/1562247

Benkler, Y. (2004). Sharing nicely: On shareable goods and the emergence of sharing as modality of economic production. *The Yale Law Journal*, *114*, 273–358. doi:10.2307/4135731

Benkler, Y. (2006). *The wealth of networks: How social production transforms markets and freedom*. New Haven, CT: Yale University Press.

Bennis, W. G., & O'Toole, J. (2005). How business schools have lost their way. *Harvard Business Review*, *83*(5), 96–104.

Benslimane, D., Dustdar, S., & Sheth, A. (2008). Services mashups: The new generation of Web applications. *Internet Computing, IEEE*, *12*(5), 13–15. doi:10.1109/MIC.2008.110

Berkes, F. (2006). From community-based resource management to complex systems: The scale issue and marine commons. *Ecology and Society*, *11*(11), 45–59.

Berlage, M. (1997). The role of local access networks in regional economic integration in Eastern Europe. In Roche, E., & Bakis, H. (Eds.), *Developments in telecommunications* (pp. 177–193). Aldershot, UK: Ashgate.

Beveridge, W. (1942). *Social insurance and allied services. Cm 6404*. London, UK: HMSO.

Beyer, H., & Holtzblatt, K. (1998). *Contextual design*. San Francisco: Morgan Kaufmann.

Bhowmik, S. (2003). National policy for street vendors. *Economic and Political Weekly*, *38*(16), 1543–1546.

Bijker, W. E., Hughes, T. P., & Pinch, T. (1987). *The social construction of technological systems*. Cambridge, MA: The MIT Press.

Birner, R., & Wittmer, H. (2003). Using social capital to create political capital: How do local communities gain political influence? A theoretical approach and empirical evidence from Thailand. In Dolšak, N., & Ostrom, E. (Eds.), *The commons in the new millennium: Challenges and adaptations* (pp. 291–334). Cambridge, MA: MIT Press.

Blackler, F. (2006). Chief executives and the modernization of the English National Health Service. *Leadership*, *2*(1), 5–30. doi:10.1177/1742715006060651

Blomquist, W. (1992). *Dividing the waters: Governing groundwater in southern California*. San Fransisco, CA: Institute for Contemporary Studies Press.

Blümel, W., Pethig, R., & von dem Hagen, O. (1986). The theory of public goods: A survey of recent issues. *Journal of Institutional and Theoretical Economics*, *142*(2), 241–309.

Bode, I. (2007). Co-governance within networks and the nonprofit-forprofit divide. In Pestoff, V., & Brandsen, T. (Eds.), *Co-production: The third sector and the delivery of public services* (pp. 81–98). London, UK: Routledge.

Bødker, S. (1996). Creating conditions for participation: Conflicts and resources in systems development. *Human-Computer Interaction*, *11*(3), 215–236. doi:10.1207/s15327051hci1103_2

Boehm, B., & Bell, T. (1977). Issues in computer performance evaluation: Some consensus, some divergence. *Performance Evaluation Review*, *4*(2), 4–40.

Bolin, M., Webber, M., Rha, P., Wilson, T., & Miller, R. C. (2005). Automation and customization of rendered Web pages. In *Proceedings of UIST '05 the 18th annual ACM symposium on user interface software and technology*, 163-172.

Borovits, I., & Giladi, R. (1993). Evaluating cost/utilization of organizations' information systems and users. *Information & Management, 25*(3), 273–280. doi:10.1016/0378-7206(93)90076-6

Boulos, M. N. K., Scotch, M., Cheung, K. H., & Burden, D. (2008). Web GIS in practice VI: A demo playlist of geomashups for public health neogeographers. *International Journal of Health Geographics, 7*(38), 1–16.

Bowker, G., Star, L., Turner, W. A., & Gasser, L. (Eds.). (1997). *Social science, technical systems and cooperative work: Beyond the great divide*. Mahwah, NJ: Lawrence Erlbaum Associates.

Bowker, G., & Star, S. L. (1999). *Sorting things out– Classification and its consequences*. Cambridge, MA: MIT Press.

Boyer, C. (1994). *The city of collective memory*. Cambridge, MA: MIT Press.

Boyle, J. (2003). The second enclosure movement and the construction of the public domain. *Law and Contemporary Problems, 66*(1-2), 33–75.

Braa, J., Monteiro, E., & Sahay, S. (2004). Networks of action: Sustainable health information systems across developing countries. *Management Information Systems Quarterly, 28*(3), 337–362.

Braa, J., Monteiro, E., & Sahay, S. (2004). Networks of action: Sustainable health information systems across developing countries. *Management Information Systems Quarterly, 28*(3), 337–362.

Brandsen, T., & Pestoff, V. (2006). Co-production, the third sector and the delivery of public services. *Public Management Review, 8*(4), 593–601. doi:10.1080/14719030601022874

Brennan, S. (2005). *The NHS IT project: The biggest computer programme in the world... ever!* Oxford, UK: Radcliffe Publishing.

Brennan, S. (2007). The biggest computer programme in the world ever! How's it going? *Journal of Information Technology, 22*(3), 202–211. doi:10.1057/palgrave.jit.2000104

Bricklin, D. (2006). The cornucopia of the commons: How to get volunteer labor. Retrieved April 5, 2011, from http://www.bricklin.com/cornucopia.htm

Briggs, X. (1998). Doing democracy up close: Culture, power, and communication in community building. *Journal of Planning Education and Research, 18*, 1–13. doi:10.1177/0739456X9801800101

Brin, D. (1995). The Internet as a commons. *Information Technology and Libraries, 14*(4), 240–242.

Broadbent, M., Weill, P., & St. Clair, D. (1999). The implications of information technology infrastructure for business process redesign. *Management Information Systems Quarterly, 23*(2), 159–182. doi:10.2307/249750

Brown, C. V. (1997). Examining the emergence of hybrid IS governance solutions: Evidence from a single case site. *Information Systems Research, 8*(1), 69–94. doi:10.1287/isre.8.1.69

Brown, C. V., & Magill, S. L. (1998). Reconceptualizing the context-design issue for the information systems function. *Organization Science, 9*(2), 177–195. doi:10.1287/orsc.9.2.176

Brown, S. J., & Duguid, P. (2001). Knowledge and organization: A social-practice perspective. *Organization Science, 12*(2), 198–213. doi:10.1287/orsc.12.2.198.10116

Burns, J. F., & Somaiya, R. (2010, October 23). WikiLeaks founder on the run: Trailed by notoriety. *The New York Times*. Retrieved May 8, 2011, from http://www.nytimes.com/2010/10/24/world/24assange.html

Burns, L. R. (2002). *The health care value chain: Producers, purchasers and providers*. San Francisco, CA: Jossey Bass.

Byrd, T. A., & Turner, D. E. (2000). Measuring the flexibility of information technology infrastructure: Exploratory analysis of a construct. *Journal of Management Information Systems, 17*(1), 167–208.

Calabresi, M. (2010, December 2). WikiLeaks' war on secrecy: Truth's consequences. *TIME Magazine*. Retrieved May 8, 2011, from http://www.time.com/time/world/article/0,8599,2034276-3,00.html

Calás, M., & Smircich, L. (1999). Past postmodernism: Reflections and tentative directions. *Academy of Management Review*, 24(4), 649–671.

Callon, M. (1991). Techno-economic networks and irreversibility. In Law, J. (Ed.), *A sociology of monsters: Essays on power, technology and domination* (pp. 132–161). London, UK: Routledge Press.

Carlsson, L., & Sandstrom, A. (2008). Network governance of the commons. *International Journal of the Commons*, 2(1), 33–54.

Castells, M. (2010). *The information age: Economy society and culture I: The rise of the network society* (2nd ed.). Malden, MA: Wiley-Blackwell.

CCR. (2010, December 7). CCR statement on arrest of WikiLeaks founder Julian Assange. *Center for Constitutional Rights*. Retrieved May 8, 2011, from http://ccrjustice.org/newsroom/press-releases/ccr-statement-arrest-of-wikileaks-founder-julian-assange

Centers for Medicare & Medicaid Services. (CMS). (2010). Medicare and Medicaid programs; electronic health record incentive program. Final rule. *Federal Register*, 75(144), 44313–44362.

Cerny, P. G. (1995). Globalization and the changing logic of collective action. *International Organization*, 49(4), 595–625. doi:10.1017/S0020818300028459

Chandler, J. (1982). A multiple criteria approach for evaluating information systems. *Management Information Systems Quarterly*, 6(1), 61–74. doi:10.2307/248755

Chiasson, M., Germonprez, M., & Mathiassen, L. (2009). Pluralistic action research: A review of the information systems literature. *Information Systems Journal*, 19(1), 31–54. doi:10.1111/j.1365-2575.2008.00297.x

Christiaanse, E., & Venkatraman, N. (2002). Beyond SABRE: an empirical test of expertise exploitation in electronic channels. *Management Information Systems Quarterly*, 26(1), 15–38. doi:10.2307/4132339

Chung, S. H., Rainer, K. R. Jr, & Lewis, B. R. (2003). The impact of information technology infrastructure flexibility on strategic alignment and application implementations. *Communications of the AIS*, 11(11), 191–206.

Ciborra, C. U. (Ed.), & associates (2001). *From control to drift: The dynamics of corporate information infrastructures*. Oxford, UK: Oxford University Press.

Ciborra, C. U. (2001). A critical review of the literature on the management of corporate information infrastructure. In Ciborra, C. U. (Ed.), *From control to drift: The dynamics of corporate information infrastructures* (pp. 15–40). Oxford, UK: Oxford University Press.

Ciborra, C. U. (2007). When is an Intranet? The topsy-turvy unfolding of a web-based information system. In Hanseth, O., & Ciborra, C. (Eds.), *Risk, complexity and ICT* (pp. 183–210). London, UK: Edward Elgar.

Ciborra, C. U., & Failla, A. (2001). Infrastructure as a process: The case of CRM in IBM. In Ciborra, C. U. (Ed.), *From control to drift: The dynamics of corporate information infrastructures* (pp. 105–124). Oxford, UK: Oxford University Press.

Ciborra, C. U., & Hanseth, O. (2001). Introduction. In Ciborra, C. U. (Ed.), *From control to drift: The dynamics of corporate information infrastructures* (pp. 1–14). Oxford, UK: Oxford University Press.

Clarke, D., & Bradford, M. (1998). Public and private consumption and the city. *Urban Studies (Edinburgh, Scotland)*, 35(5-6), 865–888. doi:10.1080/0042098984592

Clark, G. (1999). The retreat of the state and the rise of the pension fund capitalism. In Martin, R. (Ed.), *Money and the space economy* (pp. 241–260). London, UK: Wiley.

Clemons, E. K. (1991). Evaluation of strategic investment in information technology. *Communications of the ACM*, 34(1), 22–36. doi:10.1145/99977.99985

Close, D. H. (2002). *Greece since 1945*. London, UK: Longman.

Connecting for Health. (2004). *Business plan*. Retrieved February 20, 2011, from http://www.connectingforhealth.nhs.uk

Constantelou, N. (2001). *In search of a vision: Information society policies in peripheral and middle-income countries*. Athens, Greece: National Technical University of Athens.

Constantinides, P. (2012). (forthcoming). The development and consequences of new information infrastructures: The case of mashup platforms. *Media Culture & Society*.

Constantinides, P., & Barrett, M. (2005). Approaching information infrastructure as an ecology of ubiquitous sociotechnical relations. In Sorensen, C., Yoo, Y., Lyytinen, K., & DeGross, J. I. (Eds.), *Designing ubiquitous information environments: Sociotechnical issues and challenges* (pp. 249–260). New York, NY: Springer. doi:10.1007/0-387-28918-6_19

Constantinides, P., & Barrett, M. (2006). Negotiating ICT development and use: The case of a regional telemedicine system in Crete. *Information and Organization*, *16*(1), 27–55. doi:10.1016/j.infoandorg.2005.07.001

Constantinides, P., & Blackler, F. (2008). Co-orienting the object: An activity theoretical analysis of a public report on the UK's National Program for IT. In Barrett, M., Davidson, E., Middleton, C., & DeGross, J. (Eds.), *Information technology in the service economy: Challenges and possibilities for the 21st century* (pp. 259–270). Boston, MA: Springer. doi:10.1007/978-0-387-09768-8_18

Copeland, D., & McKenney, J. (1988, September). Airline reservations systems: Lessons from history. *Management Information Systems Quarterly*, *12*(3), 353–370. doi:10.2307/249202

Cornes, R., & Sandler, T. (1996). *The theory of externalities, public goods, and club goods*. New York, NY: Cambridge University Press.

Costanza, R., Low, B. S., Ostrom, E., & Wilson, J. (Eds.). (2001). *Institutions, ecosystems, and sustainability*. New York, NY: Lewis Publishers.

Council of the European Union. (2000). *Conclusions of the Lisbon European Council*. Lisbon, Portugal.

Coutard, O. (Ed.). (1999). *The governance of large technical systems*. London, UK: Routledge.

Coward, E. W. Jr., (Ed.). (1980). *Irrigation and agricultural development in Asia: Perspectives from the social sciences*. Ithaca, NY: Cornell University Press.

Cox, K., & Jonas, A. (1993). Urban development, collective consumption and the politics of metropolitan fragmentation. *Political Geography*, *12*(1), 8–37. doi:10.1016/0962-6298(93)90022-Y

Crawford, M., Rutter, D., & Thelwall, S. (2004). *User involvement in change management: A review of the literature*. London, UK: Imperial College.

Crotty, J. (2009). Structural causes of the global financial crisis: A critical assessment of the new financial architecture. *Cambridge Journal of Economics*, *33*(4), 563–580. doi:10.1093/cje/bep023

Cruickshank, J. (2010). *Fixing NHS IT: A plan of action for a new government*. Retrieved February 20, 2011, from http://www.2020health.org/export/sites/2020/pdf/2020itdocA4MASTERlow27-04.pdf

Cruickshank, J. (2010). *Fixing NHS IT: A plan of action for a new government*. Retrieved March 1, 2011, from http://www.2020health.org/2020health/research/nhsit.html

Culnan, M. J., McHugh, P., & Zubillaga, J. (2010). How large U.S. companies can use Twitter and other social media to gain business value. *MIS Quarterly Executive*, *9*(4), 243–259.

Currie, W. L., & Guah, M. (2007). Conflicting institutional logics: A national program for IT in the organisational field of healthcare. *Journal of Information Technology*, *22*(3), 235–247. doi:10.1057/palgrave.jit.2000102

Curtis, P. (2010, December 30). Ministers must 'wise up not clam up' after WikiLeaks disclosures. *The Guardian*. Retrieved May 8, 2011, from: http://www.guardian.co.uk/politics/2010/dec/30/wikileaks-freedom-information-ministers-government

Curwen, P. (1999). Survival of the fittest: Formation and development of international alliances in telecommunications. *Info*, *1*(2), 141–160.

Davaki, K., & Mossialos, E. (2005). *Plus ça change*: Health sector reforms in Greece. *Journal of Health Politics, Policy and Law*, *30*(1–2), 143–167. doi:10.1215/03616878-30-1-2-143

David, P. (2001). Tragedy of the public knowledge 'commons'? Global science, intellectual property and the digital technology boomerang. *MERIT-Infonomics Research Memorandum series 2001-003*.

Davison, R. M., Martinsons, M. G., Lo, H. W. H., & Kam, C. S. P. (2006). Ethical values of IT professionals: Evidence from Hong Kong. *IEEE Transactions on Engineering Management, 53*(1), 48–58. doi:10.1109/TEM.2005.861817

Dawes, R. (1980). Social dilemmas. *Annual Review of Psychology, 31*, 169–193. doi:10.1146/annurev.ps.31.020180.001125

Dawes, R. M., McTavish, J., & Shaklee, H. (1977). Behavior, communication, and assumptions about other people's behavior in a commons dilemma situation. *Journal of Personality and Social Psychology, 35*(1), 1–11. doi:10.1037/0022-3514.35.1.1

De La Merced, M. (2010, November 30). WikiLeaks' next target: Bank of America? *The New York Times.* Retrieved May 8, 2011, from http://dealbook.nytimes.com/2010/11/30/wikileaks-next-target-bank-of-america/

Dean, J., & Sharfman, M. (1996). Does decision process matter? A study of strategic decision-making effectiveness. *Academy of Management Journal, 39*(2), 368–396. doi:10.2307/256784

Dean, M. (1997). *Critical and effective histories: Foucault's methods and historical sociology.* London, UK: Routledge.

Deetz, S. (1996). Describing differences in approach to organization science: Rethinking Burrell and Morgan and their legacy. *Organization Science, 7*(2), 191–207. doi:10.1287/orsc.7.2.191

Delone, W., & McLean, E. (1992). Information systems success: The quest for the dependent variable. *Information Systems Research, 3*(1), 60–95. doi:10.1287/isre.3.1.60

Dempsey, B., Weiss, D., Jones, P., & Greenberg, J. (2002, February). Who is an open source developer? *Communications of the ACM, 45*(2), 67–72. doi:10.1145/503124.503125

Demsetz, H. (1967). Toward a theory of property rights. *The American Economic Review, 57*(2), 347–359.

Department of Health (DoH). (1997). *The new NHS: Modern, dependable. Cm 3807.* London, UK: Author.

Department of Health (DoH). (2000). *The NHS plan: A plan for investment, a plan for reform. Cm 4818-I.* London, UK: Author.

Department of Health (DoH). (2002). *Delivering 21st century IT support for the NHS–National strategic programme.* London, UK: Author.

Department of Health (DoH). (2002). *Delivering 21st century IT support for the NHS–national strategic programme.* Retrieved February 20, 2011, from http://www.connectingforhealth.nhs.uk/resources/policyandguidance/delivery_21_century_it.pdf

Department of Health (DoH). (2003). *Integrated care records service: Introduction to the output based specification.* Retrieved February 20, 2011, from http://www.dh.gov.uk/prod_consum_dh/groups/dh_digitalassets/@dh/@en/documents/digitalasset/dh_4055049.pdf

Department of Health (DoH). (2004). *National programme for IT: Initial guidance for existing system suppliers.* Retrieved February 20, 2011, from http://www.ehiprimarycare.com/img/document_library0282/NPfITsuppliersguide.pdf

Department of Health (DoH). (2010). *The future of the national programme for IT.* London, UK: Author.

DeSanctis, G., Staudenmayer, N., & Wong, S. (1999). Interdependence in virtual organizations. In Cooper, C., & Rousseau, D. M. (Eds.), *Trends in organizational behavior* (pp. 81–104). New York, NY: John Wiley & Sons.

Devaraj, S., & Kohli, R. (2003). Performance impacts of information technology: Is actual usage the missing link? *Management Science, 49*(3), 273–289. doi:10.1287/mnsc.49.3.273.12736

Dietz, T., Ostrom, E., & Stern, P. C. (2003). The struggle to govern the commons. *Science, 302*(5652), 1907–1912. doi:10.1126/science.1091015

Doctor, R. (1992). Social equity and information technologies: Moving toward information democracy. *Annual Review of Information Science & Technology, 27*, 43–96.

Dolšak, N., & Ostrom, E. (2003). The challenges of the commons. In Dolšak, N., & Ostrom, E. (Eds.), *The commons in the new millennium: Challenges and adaptations* (pp. 3–34). Cambridge, MA: MIT Press.

Doz, Y., Santos, J., & Williamson, P. (2001). *From global to metanational: How companies win in the knowledge economy.* New York, NY: Harvard Business School Press.

Dreyfus, H. L., & Rabinow, P. (1982). *Michel Foucault: Beyond structuralism and hermeneutics.* Chicago, IL: The University of Chicago Press.

Duncan, N. B. (1995). Capturing flexibility of information technology infrastructure: A study of resource characteristics and their measure. *Journal of Management Information Systems, 12*(2), 37–57.

Dunham, G. S. (2002). Carnivore, the FBI's e-mail surveillance system: Devouring criminals, not privacy. *Federal Communications Law Journal, 54*, 543–566.

Dupuy, G. (2000). A revised history of network urbanism, *Oase*, 4-29.

Dutta, S., & Jain, A. (2006). An assessment of the relative level of development of an information society in the enlarged European Union. In Dutta, S., De Meyer, A., Jain, A., & Richter, G. (Eds.), *The information society in an enlarged Europe* (pp. 7–44). Munich, Germany: Springer, Roland Berger Strategy Consultants. doi:10.1007/3-540-33156-5_2

Eco, U. (1994). *The limits of interpretation.* Bloomington, IN: Indiana University Press.

Ehn, P., & Kyng, M. (1991). Cardboard computers: Mocking-it-up of hands-on the future. In Greenbaum, J., & Kyng, M. (Eds.), *Design at work* (pp. 169–196). Hillsdale, NJ: Erlbaum.

Ehn, P., & Löwgren, J. (1997). Design for quality-in-use: Human–computer interaction meets information systems development. In Helander, M., Landauer, T. K., & Prabhu, P. (Eds.), *Handbook of human–Computer interaction* (pp. 299–313). Amsterdam, Netherlands: Elsevier.

Elkjær, B., & Simpson, B. (2006, June 15-16). Towards a pragmatic theory of creative practice. Paper presented at *Second Organization Studies Summer Workshop Re-turn to practice: Understanding Organization as it Happens,* Mykonos, Greece.

Ellingsen, G., & Monteiro, E. (2003). A patchwork planet: integration and cooperation in hospitals. *Computer Supported Cooperative Work, 12*(1), 71–95. doi:10.1023/A:1022469522932

European Commission. (1994). *Europe's way to the information society: An action plan.* Brussels, Belgium: European Commission.

European Commission. (1999). *An information society for all: eEurope action plan.* Brussels, Belgium: Council and the European Commission for the Feira European Council, European Commission.

European Commission. (2001, July 25). *European governance.* COM (2001) 428 final.

European Commission. (2003). European parliament council commission: Inter-institutional agreement on better law-making. *Official Journal of the European Union, 46*(C 321/01).

European Commission. (2008). *Commission recommendation of 2 July 2008 on cross-border interoperability of electronic health record systems.* Retrieved from http://eur-lex.europa.eu/LexUriServ/LexUriServ.do?uri=CELEX:32008H0594:EN:NOT

European Health Telematics (EHTEL). (2008). *eHealth interoperability: State of play and future perspectives.* Retrieved from http://ec.europa.eu/information_society/activities/health/docs/cip/calliope_assessment_eu_countries_questionnaire-recomm.pdf

Eurostat. (2003). *Statistics on the information society in Europe.* Luxembourg, Luxembourg: Office for Official Publications of the European Communities.

Evans, G. E. (1999). Information systems as interventions: The case for outcomes based evaluation. *Journal of Computer Information Systems, 39*(2), 69–74.

Evans, G. E., & Costa, B. A. (2003). Outcome-based systems evaluation to assess information technology impact using ARIMA methods. *Communications of the Association for Information Systems, 11*, 660–677.

Executive, N. H. S. (1998). *Information for health: An information strategy for the modern NHS 1998–2005: A national strategy for local implementation.* London, UK: Department of Health.

Ερευνητικό Ακαδημαϊκό Ινστιτούτο Τεχνολογίας Υπολογιστών (EAITY). (2001). *Επιχειρησιακό σχέδιο για την ανάπτυξη της πληροφορικής στην υγεία & πρόνοια για το επιχειρησιακό πρόγραμμα κοινωνία της πληροφορίας του Γ'ΚΠΣ: δράση 7 – τυποποίηση δεδομένων.* Υπουργείο Υγείας και Πρόνοιας, (In Greek).

Ερευνητικό Ακαδημαϊκό Ινστιτούτο Τεχνολογίας Υπολογιστών (EAITY). (2008). *Η χρήση των ΤΠΕ στον ευρύτερο δημόσιο και ιδιωτικό τομέα.* Παρατηρητήριο για την ΚτΠ, (In Greek).

Faaborg, A., & Lieberman, H. (2006). A goal-oriented Web browser. In *Proceedings of CHI '06 the SIGCHI conference on Human Factors in computing systems*, 751-760.

Fairfield, J. A. (2005). Virtual property. *Boston University Law Review. Boston University. School of Law, 85*(4), 1047–1102.

Farjoun, M., & Starbuck, W. H. (2007). Organizing at and beyond the limits. *Organization Studies, 28*(4), 541–566. doi:10.1177/0170840607076584

Feeny, D., Berkes, F., McCay, B. J., & Acheson, J. M. (1990). The tragedy of the commons: Twenty-Two years later. *Human Ecology, 18*(1), 1–19. doi:10.1007/BF00889070

Feller, J., Fitzgerald, B., Hissam, S., & Lakhani, K. (Eds.). (2005). *Perspectives on free and open source software.* Cambridge, MA: MIT Press.

Ferlander, S., & Timm, D. (2001). Local nets and social capital. *Telematics and Informatics, 18*(1), 51–65. doi:10.1016/S0736-5853(00)00018-6

Fernandopulle, R., & Patel, N. (2010). How the electronic health record did not measure up to the demands of our medical home practice. *Health Affairs, 29*(4), 622–628. doi:10.1377/hlthaff.2010.0065

Fishman, R. (1990). Metropolis unbound: The new city of the twentieth century. *Flux, 6*(1), 43–55. doi:10.3406/flux.1990.1172

Fitzgerald, B., & Kenny, T. (2003). Open source software in the trenches: Lessons from a large-scale implementation. In *Proceedings of the 24th International Conference on Information Systems* (ICIS), 316-326.

Fitzgerald, B. (1997). The use of systems development methodologies in practice: A field study. *Information Systems Journal, 7*(3), 201–212. doi:10.1046/j.1365-2575.1997.d01-18.x

Fitzgerald, B. (2006). The transformation of open source software. *Management Information Systems Quarterly, 30*(3), 587–598.

Flyvbjerg, B. (2001). *Making social science matter: Why social inquiry fails and how it can succeed again* (Sampson, S., Trans.). Cambridge, UK: Cambridge University Press.

Flyvbjerg, B. (2004). Phronetic planning research: Theoretical and methodological reflections. *Planning Theory & Practice, 5*(3), 283–306. doi:10.1080/1464935042000250195

Flyvbjerg, B. (2006). Making organization research matter: Power, values, and phronesis. In Clegg, S. R., Hardy, C., Lawrence, T. B., & Nord, W. R. (Eds.), *The Sage handbook of organization studies* (2nd ed., pp. 370–387). Thousand Oaks, CA: Sage.

Folke, C., Hahn, T., Olsson, P., & Norberg, J. (2005). Adaptive governance of social-ecological systems. *Annual Review of Environment and Resources, 30*, 441–473. doi:10.1146/annurev.energy.30.050504.144511

Fomin, V. V., & Egyedi, T. M. (2007). Multi-method approach to guide design and use of ICT infrastructure services. H. Österle, J. Schelp, & R. Winter (Eds.), In *Proceedings of the 15th European Conference on Information Systems*, (pp. 1410-1420). St. Gallen, Switzerland: University of St. Gallen.

Ford, S. (2005). Letter: Challenges to implementing NPfIT: Nothing counts except what is in front of the clinician to use. *British Medical Journal, 331*, 516. doi:10.1136/bmj.331.7515.516

Foster, I. (2002). The grid: A new infrastructure for 21st century science. *Physics Today, 55*(2), 42–47. doi:10.1063/1.1461327

Foster, I. (2003). The grid: Computing without bounds. *Scientific American, 288*(4), 78–85. doi:10.1038/scientificamerican0403-78

Foster, I., & Kesselman, C. (1999). *The grid: Blueprint for a new computing infrastructure*. San Francisco, CA: Morgan Kaufmann.

Foucault, M. (1979). The history of sexuality: *Vol. 1. An introduction* (Hurley, R., Trans.). London, UK: Allen Lane.

Foucault, M. (1982). Afterword: The subject and power. In Dreyfus, H., & Rabinow, P. (Eds.), *Michel Foucault: Beyond structuralism and hermeneutics* (pp. 208–226). Brighton, UK: Harvester.

Foucault, M. (1984). *Foucault: A reader* (Rabinow, P., Ed.). New York, NY: Pantheon.

Foucault, M. (1988). Politics and reason. In Kritzman, L. D. (Ed.), *Politics, philosophy, culture: Interviews and other writings 1977-1984*. New York, NY: Routledge.

Foucault, M. (1991). Governmentality. In Burchell, G., Gordon, C., & Miller, P. (Eds.), *The Foucault effect* (pp. 87–104). Chicago, IL: University of Chicago Press.

Foucault, M. (1993). About the beginning of the hermeneutics of the self: Two lectures at Dartmouth. *Political Theory*, *21*(2), 198–227. doi:10.1177/0090591793021002004

Foucault, M. (1995). *Discipline & punish: The birth of the prison* (2nd ed.). (Sheridan, A., Trans.). New York, NY: Vintage Books.

Friedman, M. (2010, December 15). Julian Assange: Readers' choice for TIME's Person of the Year 2010. *TIME Magazine*. Retrieved May 8, 2011, from http://newsfeed.time.com/2010/12/13/julian-assange-readers-choice-for-times-person-of-the-year-2010/

Fujima, J., Lunzer, A., Hornbaek, K., & Tanaka, Y. (2004). Clip, connect, clone: Combining application elements to build custom interfaces for information access. In *Proceedings of UIST '04 the 17th annual ACM symposium on User interface software and technology*, 175-184.

Fung, A. (2004). *Empowered participation*. Princeton, NJ: Princeton University Press.

Fung, A., & Wright, E. O. (2003). Thinking about empowered participatory governance. In Fung, A., & Wright, E. O. (Eds.), *Deepening democracy* (pp. 3–42). New York, NY: Verso.

Galant, R. (2010, July 16). WikiLeaks founder: Site getting tons of 'high caliber' disclosures. *CNN Online*. Retrieved May 8, 2011, from http://edition.cnn.com/2010/TECH/web/07/16/wikileaks.disclosures/

Garfinkel, S. (2000). *Database nation: The death of privacy in the 21st century*. Sebastopol, CA: O'Reilly.

Gaudin, S. (2011, April 26). Sony warns users of data loss from PlayStation network hack. *ComputerWorld Online*. Retrieved April 27, 2011, from http://www.computerworld.com/s/article/9216191/Sony_warns_users_of_data_loss_from_PlayStation_network_hack?source=toc

Gershuny, J. (1983). *Social innovation and the division of labour*. Oxford, UK: Oxford University Press.

Ghosh, R. A., & Glott, R. (2002). *Free/libre and open source software: Survey and study*. Retrieved March 30, 2011, from http://www.flossproject.org/index.htm

Giannopoulos, G., & Gillepsie, A. (Eds.). (1993). *Transport and communications innovations in Europe*. London, UK: Belhaven.

Giddens, A. (1984). *The constitution of society: Outline of the theory of structuration*. Berkeley, CA: University of California Press.

Goetz, A. M., & Gaventa, J. (2001). *Bringing citizen voice and client focus into service delivery*. Institute of Development Studies, Working Paper No. 138. Retrieved November 24, 2011, from http://www.ids.ac.uk/go/idspublication/bringing-citizen-voice-and-client-focus-into-service-delivery

Goles, T., & Hirschheim, R. (2000). The paradigm is dead, the paradigm is dead… long live the paradigm: The legacy of Burrell and Morgan. *Omega*, *28*(3), 249–268. doi:10.1016/S0305-0483(99)00042-0

Gómez-Ibáñez, J. A. (2003). *Regulating infrastructure: Monopoly, contracts, and discretion*. Cambridge, MA: Harvard University Press.

Goodwin, D. (2008, February 21). Wikileaks judge gets Pirate Bay treatment. *The Register*. Retrieved April 28, 2011, from http://www.theregister.co.uk/2008/02/21/wikileaks_bulletproof_hosting/

Gordon, C. (1991). Governmental rationality: An introduction. In Burchell, G., Gordon, C., & Miller, P. (Eds.), *The Foucault effect* (pp. 1–51). Chicago, IL: University of Chicago Press.

Gordon, W. J. (1993). A property right in self-expression: Equality and individualism in the natural law of intellectual property. *The Yale Law Journal, 102*, 1533–1543. doi:10.2307/796826

Graham, G. (1999). *The Internet: A philosophical inquiry.* New York, NY: Rutledge.

Graham, S., & Marvin, S. (2001). *Splintering urbanism: Networked infrastructures, technological mobilities and the urban condition.* New York, NY: Routledge. doi:10.4324/9780203452202

Greek Ministry of National Economy. (2000). *Operational program for the information society.* Athens, Greece.

Greek Observatory for Information Society. (2010). *Έρευνα για την αποτύπωση, λειτουργία και αξιολόγηση των πληροφοριακών συστημάτων και των διαδικτυακών πυλών που χρηματοδοτήθηκαν κατά το Γ' ΚΠΣ από το Ε.Π. Κοινωνία της Πληροφορίας.* Παρατηρητήριο για την ΚτΠ, (In Greek).

Greenbaum, J., & Kyng, M. (Eds.). (1991). *Design at work: Cooperative design of computer systems.* Hillsdale, NJ: Erlbaum.

Greenberg, A. (2010, November 29). An interview with WikiLeaks' Julian Assange. *Forbes.* Retrieved April 28, 2011, from http://blogs.forbes.com/andygreenberg/2010/11/29/an-interview-with-wikileaks-julian-assange/2/

Greener, I. (2005). Health management as strategic behaviour: Managing medics and performance in the NHS. *Public Management Review, 7*(1), 95–110. doi:10.1080/1471903042000339437

Greener, I. (2009). *Healthcare in the UK: Understanding continuity and change.* Bristol, UK: Policy Press.

Gripenberg, P., Skogseid, I., Botto, F., Silli, A., & Thunainen, V. K. (2004). Entering the European information society: Four rural development projects. *The Information Society, 20*(1), 3–14. doi:10.1080/01972240490269807

Gross, P. (Ed.). (1986). *Proceedings of the 15-17 October 1986 Joint Meeting of Internet Engineering and Internet Architecture Task Forces. Fourth IETF.* Menlo Park, California: Corporation for National Research Initiatives. Retrieved October 13, 2010, from http://www.ietf.org/old/2009/proceedings/prior29/IETF04.pdf

Grossman, L. (2006, December 16). Time's Person of the Year: You. *Time Magazine.* Retrieved April 20, 2011, from http://www.time.com/time/magazine/article/0,9171,1569514,00.html

Grossman, S. J., & Hart, O. D. (1986). The costs and benefits of ownership: A theory of vertical and lateral integration. *The Journal of Political Economy, 39*, 691–719. doi:10.1086/261404

Guillet, D. W. (1992). Comparative irrigation studies: The Orbigo Valley of Spain and the Colca Valley of Peru. *Poligonos, 2*, 141–150.

Gupta, A., Jukic, B., Parameswaran, M., Stahl, D. O., & Whinston, A. B. (1997). Streamlining the digital economy: How to avert a tragedy of the commons. *IEEE Internet Computing, 1*(6), 38–46. doi:10.1109/4236.643935

Guy, S., Graham, S., & Marvin, S. (1997). Splintering networks: Cities and technical networks in 1990s Britain. *Urban Studies (Edinburgh, Scotland), 34*(2), 191–216. doi:10.1080/0042098976140

Haas, T. C. (2001). Carnivore and the Fourth Amendment. *Connecticut Law Review, 34*, 261–291.

Habermas, J. (1992). Peirce and communication. In Habermas, J. (Ed.), *Postmetaphysical thinking* (pp. 88–113). (Hohengarten, W. M., Trans.). Cambridge, UK: Polity Press.

Habermas, J. (1994). *Justification and application: Remarks on discourse ethics.* Cambridge, MA: The MIT Press.

Habermas, J. (1998). *On the pragmatics of communication.* Cambridge, MA: The MIT Press.

Haliday, J. (2011, August 8). London riots: BlackBerry to help police probe Messenger looting 'role'. *The Guardian.* Retrieved November 1, 2011, from http://www.guardian.co.uk/uk/2011/aug/08/london-riots-blackberry-messenger-looting

Han, K., Kauffman, R. J., & Nault, B. R. (2004). Information exploitation and interorganizational systems ownership. *Journal of Management Information Systems*, *21*(2), 109–135.

Hanna, S., Folke, C., & Mäler, K.-G. (1996). *Rights to nature: Ecological, economic, cultural, and political principles of institutions for the environment*. Washington, DC: Island Press.

Hanseth, O. (2001). The economics of standards. In Ciborra, C. U. (Ed.), *From control to drift: The dynamics of corporate information infrastructures* (pp. 56–70). Oxford, UK: Oxford University Press.

Hanseth, O., Ciborra, C., & Braa, K. (2002). The control devolution: ERP and the side-effects of globalization. *The Data Base for Advances in Information Systems*, *32*(4), 34–46. doi:10.1145/506139.506144

Hanseth, O., Jacucci, E., Grisot, M., & Aanestad, M. (2006). Reflexive standardization: Side effects and complexity in standard making. *Management Information Systems Quarterly*, *30*, 563–581.

Hanseth, O., Jacucci, E., Grisot, M., & Aanestad, M. (2006, August). Reflexive standardization: Side effects and complexity in standard making. *Management Information Systems Quarterly*, *30*, 563–581.

Hanseth, O., & Lundberg, N. (2001). Designing work oriented infrastructures. *Computer Supported Cooperative Work*, *10*(3-4), 347–372. doi:10.1023/A:1012727708439

Hanseth, O., & Monteiro, E. (1997). Inscribing behaviour in information infrastructure standards. *Accounting. Management and Information Technology*, *7*(4), 183–211. doi:10.1016/S0959-8022(97)00008-8

Hanseth, O., Monteiro, E., & Hatling, M. (1996). Developing information infrastructure: The tension between standardisation and flexibility. *Science, Technology & Human Values*, *21*(4), 407–426. doi:10.1177/016224399602100402

Hardin, G. (1968). The tragedy of the commons. *Science*, *162*(3859), 1243–1248. doi:10.1126/science.162.3859.1243

Hardin, R. (1982). *Collective action*. Baltimore, MD: Johns Hopkins University Press.

Hardy, C., Phillips, N., & Clegg, S. (2001). Reflexivity in social studies: A study of the production of the research subject. *Human Relations*, *54*, 3–32.

Harris, N., & Fabricius, I. (1996). *Cities and structural adjustment*. London, UK: UCL Press.

Harrison, S., & Pollitt, C. (1994). *Controlling health professionals: The future of work and organization in the national health service*. Milton Keynes, UK: Open University Press.

Hart, O., & Moore, J. (1990). Property rights and the nature of the firm. *The Journal of Political Economy*, *98*(6), 1119–1158. doi:10.1086/261729

Hay, J., & Packer, J. (2004). Crossing the media(-n): Auto-mobility, the transported self, and technologies of freedom. In Couldry, N., & McCarthy, A. (Eds.), *MediaSpace: Scale and culture in a media age* (pp. 209–232). New York, NY: Routledge.

Healey, P. (1996). The communicative turn in planning theory and its implications for spatial strategy formation. *Environment and Planning. B, Planning & Design*, *23*(2), 217–234. doi:10.1068/b230217

Hecht, G., & Allen, M. T. (2001). Introduction: Authority, political machines, and technology's history. In Allen, M. T., & Hecht, G. (Eds.), *Technologies of power* (pp. 1–24). Cambridge, MA: MIT Press.

Heeks, R. (1999). The tyranny of participation in information systems: Learning from development projects. *Developing informatics: Working paper series*. Manchester, UK: Institute for Development Policy and Management, University of Manchester.

Heikkila, T., & Isett, K. R. (2004). Modeling operational decision-making in public organizations: An integration of two institutional theories. *American Review of Public Administration*, *34*(1), 3–19. doi:10.1177/0275074003260911

Hellenic Republic. (1995). *Greek strategy for the information society: A tool for employment, development and quality of life*. Athens, Greece: Author.

Hellenic Republic. (1999). *Greece in the information society: Strategy and actions*. Athens, Greece: Author.

Henderson, J. C., & Venkatraman, N. (1993). Strategic alignment: Leveraging information technology for transforming organisations. *IBM Systems Journal, 38*(2-3), 472–484. doi:10.1147/sj.382.0472

Hess, C., & Ostrom, E. (2003). Ideas, artifacts, and facilities: Information as a common-pool resource. *Law and Contemporary Problems, 66*(1-2), 111–146.

Hess, C., & Ostrom, E. (2007). *Understanding knowledge as a commons: From theory to practice*. Cambridge, MA: MIT Press.

Hirschheim, R., & Klein, H. (2003). Crisis in the IS field? A critical reflection on the state of the discipline. *Journal of the Association for Information Systems, 4*(5), 237–293.

Hirschheim, R., & Klein, H. K. (1994). Realizing emancipatory principles in information systems development: The case for ETHICS. *Management Information Systems Quarterly, 18*(1), 83–109. doi:10.2307/249611

Hirshleifer, J. (1983). From weakest-link to best-shot: The voluntary provision of public goods. *Public Choice, 41*, 371–386. doi:10.1007/BF00141070

Hirshleifer, J. (1985). From weakest-link to best-shot [Correction]. *Public Choice, 46*, 221–223. doi:10.1007/BF00179743

Hodgkinson, S. T. (1996). The role of the corporate IT function in the federal IT organization. In Earl, M. J. (Ed.), *Information management: The organizational dimension* (pp. 247–260). Oxford, UK: Oxford University Press.

Hoeksma, J. (2009, October 1). South liable for greenfield penalties. *E-Health Insider.*

Hoeksma, J. (2011, May 18). NAO says NPfIT is not value for money. *E-Health Insider.*

Holmes, P. K. (2001). FBI's Carnivore: Is the government eating away our right of privacy? *Roger Williams University Law Review, 7*, 247–272.

Holzinger, K. (2008). Treaty formation and strategic constellations: An extension of Sandler. *Illinois Law Review, 1*, 187–200.

Hopper, M. (1990, May-June). Rattling SABRE–New ways to compete on information. *Harvard Business Review*, 1–9.

House of Commons (HC). (2007). The electronic patient record. *Sixth Report of Session 2006-07, Vol III–Oral & Written Evidence*, HC 422-III. House of Commons, Health Committee. Retrieved February 20, 2011, from http://www.publications.parliament.uk/pa/cm200607/cmselect/cmhealth/422/42202.htm

House of Commons (HC). (2007a). Department of health: The national programme for IT in the NHS. *Twentieth Report of Session 2006-07*, HC 390. House of Commons, Committee of Public Accounts. Retrieved February 20, 2011, from http://www.publications.parliament.uk/pa/cm200607/cmselect/cmpubacc/390/390.pdf

House of Commons (HC). (2007a). The electronic patient record. *Sixth Report of Session 2006-07, Vol I - Written Evidence*, HC 422-I. House of Commons, Health Committee. Retrieved February 24, 2011, from http://www.publications.parliament.uk/pa/cm200607/cmselect/cmhealth/422/42202.htm

House of Commons (HC). (2007b). The electronic patient record. *Sixth Report of Session 2006-07, Vol II - Written Evidence*, HC 422-II. House of Commons, Health Committee. Retrieved February 24, 2011, from http://www.publications.parliament.uk/pa/cm200607/cmselect/cmhealth/422/42202.htm

House of Commons (HC). (2007c). The electronic patient record. *Sixth Report of Session 2006-07, Vol III–Oral & Written Evidence*, HC 422-III. House of Commons, Health Committee. Retrieved February 20, 2011, from http://www.publications.parliament.uk/pa/cm200607/cmselect/cmhealth/422/42202.htm

House of Commons (HC). (2009). The national programme for IT in the NHS: Progress since 2006. *Second Report of Session 2008-09*, HC 153. House of Commons, Committee of Public Accounts. Retrieved February 20, 2011, from http://www.publications.parliament.uk/pa/cm200809/cmselect/cmpubacc/153/15302.htm

Howcroft, D., & Light, B. (2006). Reflections on issues of power in packaged software selection. *Information Systems Journal, 16*(3), 215–235. doi:10.1111/j.1365-2575.2006.00216.x

Howcroft, D., & McDonald, R. (2007). An ethnographic study of IS investment appraisal. *International Journal of Technology and Human Interaction*, *3*(3), 69–86. doi:10.4018/jthi.2007070106

Hsiao, C.-J., Beatty, P. C., Hing, E. S., Woodwell, D. A., Rechtsteiner, E. A., & Sisk, J. E. (2009). *Electronic medical record/electronic health record use: United States, 2008 and preliminary 2009*. Atlanta, GA: National Center for Health Statistics, Center for Disease Control and Prevention.

Huberman, B. A., & Rajan, M. L. (1997). Social dilemmas and Internet congestion. *Science*, *277*(5325), 535–537. doi:10.1126/science.277.5325.535

Hughes, A., & Hughes, T. P. (2000). *Systems, experts and computers*. Cambridge, MA: MIT Press.

Hughes, T. P. (1983). *Networks of power: electrification in western society 1880-1930*. Baltimore, MD: Johns Hopkins.

Hughes, T. P. (1987). The evolution of large technological systems. In Bijker, W. E., Hughes, T. P., & Pinch, T. (Eds.), *The social construction of technological systems* (pp. 51–82). Cambridge, MA: The MIT Press.

Information Society. (2004). *Διακήρυξη έργου - «Πληροφοριακό Σύστημα Υγείας του Πε.Σ.Υ.Π. Κρήτης», Μέρος Α'*. Κοινωνία της Πληροφορίας Α.Ε., Αθήνα 24/11/2004 (In Greek).

Introna, L. D., & Whittaker, L. (2004). Journals, truth, and politics: The case of *MIS Quarterly*. In Kaplan, B., Truex, D. P. III, Wastell, D., Wood-Harper, A. T., & DeGross, J. I. (Eds.), *Information systems research: Relevant theory and informed practice* (pp. 103–120). Norwell, MA: Kluwer Academic Publishers. doi:10.1007/1-4020-8095-6_7

Introna, L., & Nissenbaum, H. (2000). Shaping the Web: Why the politics of search engines matter. *The Information Society*, *16*(3), 169–185. doi:10.1080/01972240050133634

Isaac, R. M., Mathieu, D., & Zajac, E. E. (1991). Institutional framing and perceptions of fairness. *Constitutional Political Economy*, *2*(3), 329–370. doi:10.1007/BF02393135

Isaac, R. M., Walker, J. M., & Thomas, S. (1984). Divergent evidence on free riding: an experimental examination of some possible explanations. *Public Choice*, *43*, 113–149. doi:10.1007/BF00140829

Isacsson, A., Koutis, A. D., Cedervall, M., Lindholm, L. H., Lionis, C. D., Svenninger, K., & Fioretos, M. (1992). Patient-number-based computerised medical records in Crete: A tool for planning and assessment of primary health care. *Computer Methods and Programs in Biomedicine*, *37*, 41–49. doi:10.1016/0169-2607(92)90027-5

ISO/IEC. (1995). Open distributed processing-reference model. *Part 3: architecture*. IS 10746-3/ITU-T Recommendation X.903.

Jarvenpaa, S. L., & Ives, B. (1994). The global network organization of the future: Information management opportunities and challenges. *Journal of Management Information Systems*, *10*(4), 25–57.

Jessop, R. (2000). The rise of the national spatio-temporal fix and the tendential ecological dominance of globalising capitalism. *International Journal of Urban and Regional Research*, *24*(2), 333–360. doi:10.1111/1468-2427.00251

Joshi, K. (1990). An investigation of equity as a determinant of user information satisfaction. *Decision Sciences*, *21*(4), 786–807. doi:10.1111/j.1540-5915.1990.tb01250.x

Kaijser, A. (2002). System building from below: Institutional change in Dutch water control systems. *Technology and Culture*, *43*(3), 521–548. doi:10.1353/tech.2002.0120

Karsh, B. T., Weinger, M. B., Abbott, P. A., & Wears, R. L. (2010). Health information technology: Fallacies and sober realities. *Journal of the American Medical Informatics Association*, *17*(6), 617–623. doi:10.1136/jamia.2010.005637

Katz, M. L., & Shapiro, C. (1985). Network externalities, competition, and compatibility. *The American Economic Review*, *75*(3), 424–440.

Katz, M. L., & Shapiro, C. (1994). System competition and network effects. *The Journal of Economic Perspectives*, *8*(2), 93–115. doi:10.1257/jep.8.2.93

Kaushal, R., Blumenthal, D., Poon, E. G., Jha, A. K., Franz, C., & Middleton, B. (2005). The costs of a national health information network. *Annals of Internal Medicine*, *143*(3), 165–173.

Keen, A. (2007). *The cult of the amateur: How today's internet is killing our culture*. New York, NY: Doubleday/Currency.

Keen, P. G. W. (1991). *Shaping the future: Business design through information technology*. Boston, MA: Harvard Business School Press.

Kensing, F., & Blomberg, J. (1998). Participatory design: Issues and concerns. *Computer Supported Cooperative Work, 7*(3-4), 167–185. doi:10.1023/A:1008689307411

Khan, R. E., & Cerf, V. G. (1988). An open architecture for a digital library system and a plan for its development. *The digital library project vol. 1: The world of knowbots*. Reston, VA: Corporation for National Research Initiatives. Retrieved October 13, 2010, from http://www.cnri.reston.va.us/kahn-cerf-88.pdf

Khan, R. E. (1994). The role of government in the evolution of the Internet. *Communications of the ACM, 37*(8), 15–19. doi:10.1145/179606.179729

Khatchadourian, R. (2010, June 7). No secrets. *The New Yorker*. Retrieved May 8, 2011, from http://www.newyorker.com/reporting/2010/06/07/100607fa_fact_khatchadourian?currentPage=9

King, A. (1998). Writing the transnational city: The distant spaces of the Indian city. In Dandekar, H. (Ed.), *City, space and globalization: An international perspective* (pp. 25–31). Ann Arbor, MI: University of Michigan.

Klein, R. (2000). *The new politics of the NHS*. Harlow, UK: Longman.

Knights, D. (1992). Changing spaces: The disruptive impact of a new epistemological location for the study of management. *Academy of Management Review, 17*, 514–536.

Koelliker, A. (2001). Bringing together or driving apart the union? Towards a theory of differentiated integration. *West European Politics, 24*(4), 125–151. doi:10.1080/01402380108425468

Kohlberg, L. (1981). The philosophy of moral development: *Vol. 1. Essays on moral development*. San Francisco, CA: Harper & Row.

Kosseim, P., & Brady, M. (2008). Policy by procrastination: Secondary use of electronic health records for health research purposes. *McGill Journal of Law and Health, 2*, 5–45.

Kyriopoulos, J., & Tsalikis, G. (1993). Public and private imperatives of Greek health policies. *Health Policy (Amsterdam), 26*(2), 105–117. doi:10.1016/0168-8510(93)90113-4

Lakhani, K. R., & Wolf, R. (2005). Why hackers do what they do: Understanding motivation and effort in free/open source software projects. In Feller, J., Fitzgerald, B., Hissam, S., & Lakhani, K. (Eds.), *Perspectives on free and open source software* (pp. 3–22). Cambridge, MA: MIT Press. doi:10.2139/ssrn.443040

Latour, B. (1991). Technology is society made durable. In Law, J. (Ed.), *A sociology of monsters: Essays on power, technology & domination* (pp. 103–131). London, UK: Routledge Press.

Latour, B. (1993). *We have never been modern*. London, UK: Harvester Wheatsheaf.

Lauder, S. (2010, December 7). Law experts say WikiLeaks in the clear. *The World Today*: ABC Radio. Retrieved May 8, 2011, from http://www.abc.net.au/worldtoday/content/2010/s3086781.htm

Law, J., & Callon, M. (1995). Engineering and sociology in a military aircraft project: A network analysis of technological change. In Star, S. L. (Ed.), *Ecologies of knowledge: Work and politics in science and technology* (pp. 281–301). New York, NY: State University of New York Press. doi:10.1525/sp.1988.35.3.03a00060

Laws, D., Susskind, L., Abrams, J., Anderson, J., Chapman, G., Rubenstein, E., & Vadgama, J. (2001). *Public entrepreneurship networks*. Cambridge, MA: MIT Press.

Lee, A. (1999). Rigor and relevance in MIS research: Beyond the approach of positivism alone. *Management Information Systems Quarterly, 23*(1), 29–33. doi:10.2307/249407

Lee, A., & Baskerville, R. (2003). Generalizing generalizibility in information systems research. *Information Systems Research, 14*(3), 221–243. doi:10.1287/isre.14.3.221.16560

Leigh, D., & Evans, R. (2010, October 14). WikiLeaks says funding has been blocked after government blacklisting. *The Guardian*. Retrieved May 8, 2011, from http://www.guardian.co.uk/media/2010/oct/14/wikileaks-says-funding-is-blocked

Leonard, P. (1997). *Postmodern welfare: Reconstructing an emancipatory project*. London, UK: Sage.

Lerner, J., & Tirole, J. (2001). The open source movement: Key research questions. *European Economic Review*, *45*(4-6), 819–826. doi:10.1016/S0014-2921(01)00124-6

Lerner, J., & Tirole, J. (2002). Some simple economics of open source. *The Journal of Industrial Economics*, *50*(2), 197–234. doi:10.1111/1467-6451.00174

Lessig, L. (2001). *The future of ideas: The fate of the commons in a connected world*. New York, NY: Random House.

Lessig, L. (2004). *Free culture: How big media uses technology and the law to lock down culture and control creativity*. New York, NY: The Penguin Press.

Lessig, L. (2008). *Remix: Making art and commerce in the hybrid economy*. New York, NY: The Penguin Press. doi:10.5040/9781849662505

Levi, M. (1988). *Of rule and revenue*. Berkeley, CA: University of California Press.

Levine, M. E. (1987). Airline competition in deregulated markets: Theory, firm strategy, and public policy. *Yale Journal on Regulation*, *4*(2), 393–494.

Li, T. M. (2006). Neo-liberal strategies of government through community: The social development program of the World Bank in Indonesia. *IILJ Working Paper*. Global Administrative Law Series. New York, NY: Institute for International Law and Justice, New York University School of Law.

Liszka, J. (1978). Community is C. S. Peirce: Science as a means and as an end. *Transactions of the C.S. Peirce Society*, *14*(4), 305–321.

Li, T. M. (1996). Images of community: Discourse and strategy in property relations. *Development and Change*, *27*(3), 501–527. doi:10.1111/j.1467-7660.1996.tb00601.x

Litman, J. (2001). *Digital copyright*. Amherst, NY: Prometheus Books.

Loveman, M. (1998). High-risk collective action: Defending human rights in Chile, Uruguay, and Argentine. *American Journal of Sociology*, *104*, 477–525. doi:10.1086/210045

Lyon, D. (2001). *Surveillance society: Monitoring everyday life*. Buckingham, UK: Open University Press.

MacAskill, E. (2010a, December 3). "U.S. blocks access to WikiLeaks for federal workers. *The Guardian*. Retrieved May 8, 2011, from http://www.guardian.co.uk/world/2010/dec/03/wikileaks-cables-blocks-access-federal

MacAskill, E. (2010b, December 2). WikiLeaks website pulled by Amazon after U.S. political pressure. *The Guardian*. Retrieved May 8, 2011, from http://www.guardian.co.uk/media/2010/dec/01/wikileaks-website-cables-servers-amazon

Madison, M. (2003, Fall). Reconstructing the software license. *Loyola University of Chicago Law Journal. Loyola University of Chicago. School of Law*, *35*(1), 275–340.

Mandelkern Report. (2001, November 13). *Mandelkern group on better regulation*. Retrieved February 22, 2011, from http://ec.europa.eu/governance/better_regulation/documents/mandelkern_report.pdf

Mansell, R. E., & Steinmueller, E. (2000). *Mobilizing the information society: Strategies for growth and opportunity*. New York, N.Y: Oxford University Press.

Marcus, G. E. (1994). What comes just after "post": The case of ethnography. In Denzin, N., & Lincoln, Y. (Eds.), *Handbook of qualitative research* (pp. 563–574). Thousand Oaks, CA: Sage.

Marsden, C. (2008). Beyond Europe: The Internet, regulation, and multi-stakeholder governance: Representing the consumer interest? *Journal of Consumer Policy*, *31*, 115–132. doi:10.1007/s10603-007-9056-z

Marshall, G. R. (2005). *Economics for collaborative environmental management: Renegotiating the commons*. London, UK: Earthscan Publications.

Martin, R. (1999). Selling off the state: Privatization, the equity market and the geographies of shareholder capitalism. In Martin, R. (Ed.), *Money and the space economy* (pp. 261–283). London, UK: Wiley.

Mayo, E., & Moore, H. (Eds.). (2002). *Building the mutual state: Findings from the virtual thinktank*. London, UK: New Economics Foundation/Mutuo.

McGinnis (Ed.). (1999). *Polycentric governance and development: Readings from the workshop in political theory and policy analysis*. Ann Arbor, MI: Univ. of Michigan Press.

McGowan, D. (2001). Legal implications of open source software. *University of Illinois Review, 241*(1), 241–304.

McGowan, D. (2005). Legal aspects of free and open source software. In Feller, J., Fitzgerald, B., Hissam, S., & Lakhani, K. (Eds.), *Perspectives on free and open source software* (pp. 361–392). Cambridge, MA: MIT Press.

McGowan, F. (1999). The internationalization of large technical systems: Dynamics of change and challenges to regulation in electricity and telecommunications. In Coutard, O. (Ed.), *The governance of large technical systems* (pp. 130–148). London, UK: Routledge.

McKean, M. A. (2002). Nesting institutions for complex common-pool resource systems. In J. Graham, I. Reeve, & D. Brunckhorst (Eds.), In *Proceedings of the 2nd International Symposium on Landscape Futures*. Armidale, Australia: Institute for Rural Futures, University of New England.

McKeen, J. D., Guimaraes, T., & Wetherbe, J. C. (1994). The relationship between user participation and user satisfaction: an investigation of four contingency factors. *Management Information Systems Quarterly, 18*(4), 427–449. doi:10.2307/249523

McLuhan, M. (1962). *The Gutenberg galaxy: The making of typographic man*. Toronto, Canada: University of Toronto Press.

McLuhan, M. (1994). *Understanding media: The extensions of man*. Cambridge, MA: MIT Press. (Original work published 1964)

Medb, R. (2010, December 11). Where's the democracy in hunting Wikileaks off the Net? *The Irish Independent*. Retrieved May 1, 2011, from http://www.independent.ie/opinion/columnists/medb-ruane/medb-ruane-wheres-the-democracy-in-hunting-wikileaks-off-the-net-2456960.html

Mendelson, L. (2003). Privatizing knowledge: The demise of fair use and the public university. *Albany Law Journal of Science & Technology, 13*, 593–612.

Merkel, C., Xiao, L., Farooq, U., Ganoe, U. H., Lee, R., Carroll, J. M., & Rosson, M. B. (2004). Participatory design in community computing contexts: Tales from the field. In *Proceedings of the Eighth Conference on Participatory Design: Artful Integration: Interweaving Media, Materials and Practices-Volume 1*, (pp. 1-10).

Merl, S. R. (2001). Internet communication standards for the 21st century: International terrorism must force the U.S. to adopt 'Carnivore' and new electronic surveillance standards. *Brooklyn Journal of International Law, 27*, 245–284.

Merrill, D. (2009). *Mashups: The new breed of Web app*. Retrieved April 6, 2011, from http://www.ibm.com/developerworks/xml/library/x-mashups/index.html

Mingers, J. (2001). Combining IS research methods: Towards a pluralist methodology. *Information Systems Research, 12*(3), 240–259. doi:10.1287/isre.12.3.240.9709

Mingers, J. (2003). The paucity of multimethod research: A review of the information systems literature. *Information Systems Journal, 13*(3), 233–249. doi:10.1046/j.1365-2575.2003.00143.x

Mingers, J. (2008). Pluralism, realism, and truth: The keys to knowledge in information systems research. *International Journal of Information Technologies and Systems Approach, 1*(1), 81–92. doi:10.4018/jitsa.2008010106

Mingers, J., & Walsham, G. (2010). Toward ethical information systems: The contribution of discourse ethics. *Management Information Systems Quarterly, 34*(4), 1–23.

Mirani, R., & Lederer, A. L. (1998). An instrument for assessing the organizational benefits of IS projects. *Decision Sciences, 29*(4), 803–838. doi:10.1111/j.1540-5915.1998.tb00878.x

Monteiro, E. (1998). Scaling information infrastructure: The case of the next generation IP in Internet. *The Information Society, 14*(3), 229–245. doi:10.1080/019722498128845

Monteiro, E. (2001). Actor-network theory and information infrastructure. In Ciborra, C. U. (Ed.), *From control to drift: The dynamics of corporate information infrastructures* (pp. 71–83). Oxford, UK: Oxford University Press.

Monteiro, E., & Hepsø, V. (2002). Purity and danger of an information infrastructure. *Systemic Practice and Action Research, 15*(2), 145–167. doi:10.1023/A:1015292508667

Morrisett, L. (2003). Technologies of freedom? In Jenkins, H., & Thorburn, D. (Eds.), *Democracy and new media* (pp. 21–31). Cambridge, MA: MIT Press.

Muller, M. J. (2002). Participatory design: The third space in HCI. In Jacko, J. A., & Sears, A. (Eds.), *The human computer interaction handbook: Fundamentals, evolving technologies and emerging applications* (pp. 1051–1068). Mahwah, NJ: Lawrence Erlbaum.

Mumford, E. (1983). *Designing Human Systems–The ETHICS Method*. Manchester, UK: Manchester Business School.

Mumford, E. (1995). *Effective systems design and requirements analysis: The ETHICS approach*. London, UK: Macmillan.

Mumford, E. (2006). The story of socio-technical design: Reflections on its successes, failures and potential. *Information Systems Journal, 16*(4), 317–342. doi:10.1111/j.1365-2575.2006.00221.x

Musgrave, R. A. (1959). *The theory of public finance: A study in public economy*. New York, NY: McGraw-Hill.

Nambisan, S., & Baron, R. (2009). Virtual customer environments: Testing a model of voluntary participation in value co-creation activities. *Journal of Product Innovation Management, 26*(4), 388–406. doi:10.1111/j.1540-5885.2009.00667.x

NAO. (2006). *Department of health: The national programme for IT in the NHS. Report by the Comptroller and Auditor General: Session HC 1173*. London, UK: NAO.

NAO. (2011). *The national programme for IT in the NHS: An update on the delivery of detailed care records systems. Report by the Comptroller and Auditor General: Sesion HC 888*. London, UK: NAO.

National Audit Office (NAO). (2004, November 5). Improving IT procurement. *Report by the Comptroller and Auditor General, Session 2003–4*, HC 877. London, UK: The Stationery Office Limited.

National Committee on Vital and Health Statistics (NCVHS). (2001). *Information for health: A strategy for building the national health information infrastructure*. Washington, DC: U.S. Department of Health and Human Services.

National Health Information Management Advisory Council (NHIMAC). (2001). *Health online: A health information action plan for Australia* (2nd ed.). Australian Institute of Health and Welfare.

National Health Service (NHS). (2004, October 4). *National program for IT: Initial guidance for existing system suppliers*.

National Health Service (NHS). (n.d.). *Foundation trust directory*. Retrieved on January 13, 2011, from http://www.monitor-nhsft.gov.uk/home/about-nhs-foundation-trusts/nhs-foundation-trust-

National Library of Australia (NLA). (n.d.). *Social Media Policy*. Retrieved November 01, 2011, from http://www.nla.gov.au/policy-and-planning/social-media

National Research Council. (2002). *The drama of the commons* (Ostrom, E., Dietz, T., Dolsak, N., Stern, P., Stonich, S., & Weber, E., Eds.). Washington, DC: National Academy Press.

National Telecommunications and Information Administration (NTIA). (1993). *The national information infrastructure: Agenda for action*. Washington, DC: U.S. Department of Commerce.

NCVHS. (2001). *Information for health: A strategy for building the national health information infrastructure*. Washington, DC: US Dept of Health and Human Services.

Nebehey, S. (2010, November 4). WikiLeaks founder says may seek Swiss asylum. *Reuters*. Retrieved May 1, 2011, from http://www.reuters.com/article/2010/11/04/us-usa-wikileaks-idUSTRE6A369920101104

Neumann, P. G. (2005). Attaining robust open source software. In Feller, J., Fitzgerald, B., Hissam, S., & Lakhani, K. (Eds.), *Perspectives on free and open source software* (pp. 123–136). Cambridge, MA: MIT Press.

Noble, D. W. (1984). *Forces of production: A social history of industrial automation.* New York, NY: Alfred A. Knopf.

Nordstrom, L. (2010, December 10). Former WikiLeaks worker: Rival site under way. *The Washington Times.* Retrieved May 1, 2011, from http://www.washingtontimes. com/news/2010/dec/10/former-wikileaks-worker-rival-site-under-way/

Nutting, P. A., Miller, W. L., Crabtree, B. F., Jaen, C. R., Stewart, E. E., & Stange, K. C. (2009). Initial lessons from the first national demonstration project on practice transformation to a patient-centered medical home. *Annals of Family Medicine, 7*(3), 254–260. doi:10.1370/afm.1002

O'Mahony, S. (2005). Non-profit foundations and their role in community-firm software collaboration. In Feller, J., Fitzgerald, B., Hissam, S., & Lakhani, K. (Eds.), *Perspectives on free and open source software* (pp. 393–414). Cambridge, MA: MIT Press.

O'Reilly, T. (2005, September 30). What is Web 2.0: Design patterns and business models for the next generation of software, *O'Reilly Network Online*. Retrieved May 8, 2011, from http://www.oreillynet.com/pub/a/oreilly/tim/news/2005/09/30/what-is-web-20.html

O'Reilly, T. (2005b). *What is Web 2.0: Design patterns and business models for the next generation of software.* Retrieved May 8, 2011, from http://www.oreillynet.com/pub/a/oreilly/tim/news/2005/09/30/what-is-web-20.html

O'Reilly, T. (2005a). The open source paradigm shift. In Feller, J., Fitzgerald, B., Hissam, S., & Lakhani, K. (Eds.), *Perspectives on free and open source software* (pp. 461–482). Cambridge, MA: MIT Press.

OECD. (2001). *Regulatory reform in Greece.* Paris, France: Author.

Offner, J.-M. (1999). Are there such things as small networks? In Coutard, O. (Ed.), *The governance of large technical systems* (pp. 217–238). London, UK: Routledge.

Offner, J.-M. (2000). Territorial deregulation: Local authorities at risk from technical networks. *International Journal of Urban and Regional Research, 24*(1), 165–182. doi:10.1111/1468-2427.00241

Ogborn, M. (1999). *Spaces of modernity: London's geographies 1680-1780.* New York, NY: Guildford.

Olson, M. (1965). *The logic of collective action: Public goods and the theory of groups.* Cambridge, MA: Harvard University Press.

Ondrejka, C. (2007). Second Life: Collapsing geography. *Innovations: Technology, Governance, Globalization, 2*(3), 27–55. doi:10.1162/itgg.2007.2.3.27

Open Source Initiative. (n.d.). *Open source licenses.* Retrieved from http://www.opensource.org/licenses

Osborne, D., & Gaebler, T. (1992). *Reinventing government: How the entrepreneurial spirit is transforming the public sector.* Reading, MA: Addision-Wesley.

Osei-Joehene, D., & Ciborra, C. U. (2007). The duality of risk and the evolution of danger in global ICT integration. In Hanseth, O., & Ciborra, C. (Eds.), *Risk, complexity and ICT* (pp. 154–182). London, UK: Edward Elgar.

Ostrom, E. (2009, December 8). Beyond markets and states: Polycentric governance of complex economic systems. *The Sveriges Riksbank Prize in Economic Sciences in Memory of Alfred Nobel 2009.* Lecture conducted from Stockholm University, Aula Magna.

Ostrom, E., & Hess, C. (2001, November). Artifacts, facilities, and content: Information as a common-pool resource. In *Proceedings of the Conference on the Public Domain, Duke Law School, Durham, NC.*

Ostrom, E. (1990). *Governing the commons: The evolution of institutions for collective action.* New York, NY: Cambridge University Press.

Ostrom, E. (1996). Crossing the great divide: Coproduction, synergy and development. *World Development, 24*(6), 1073–1087. doi:10.1016/0305-750X(96)00023-X

Ostrom, E. (1999). Coping with tragedies of the commons. *Annual Review of Political Science, 2,* 493–535. doi:10.1146/annurev.polisci.2.1.493

Ostrom, E. (2003). How types of goods and property rights jointly affect collective action. *Journal of Theoretical Politics*, *15*(3), 239–270. doi:10.1177/0951692803015003002

Ostrom, E., & Ahn, T. K. (Eds.). (2003). *Foundations of social capital*. Cheltenham, UK: Edward Elgar Publishers.

Ostrom, E., Gardner, R., & Walker, J. (1994). *Rules, games, and common-pool resources*. Ann Arbor, MI: University of Michigan Press.

Ostrom, E., & Hess, C. (2007). A framework for analyzing the knowledge commons. In Hess, C., & Ostrom, E. (Eds.), *Understanding knowledge as a commons: From theory to practice* (pp. 41–81). Cambridge, MA: MIT Press.

Ostrom, E., Schroeder, L., & Wynne, S. (1993). *Institutional incentives and sustainable development: Infrastructure policies in perspective*. Boulder, CO: Westview Press.

Ostrom, E., Walker, J., & Gardner, R. (1992). Covenants with and without a sword: Self-governance is possible. *The American Political Science Review*, *86*(2), 404–417. doi:10.2307/1964229

Ostrom, V., & Ostrom, E. (1977). Public goods and public choices. In Savas, E. S. (Ed.), *Alternatives for delivering public services: Toward improved performance* (pp. 7–49). Boulder, CO: Westview Press.

Pain, D., Owen, J., Franklin, I., & Green, E. (1993). Human-centred systems design: A review of trends within the broader systems development context. In Green, E., Owen, J., & Pain, D. (Eds.), *Gendered by design? Information technology and office systems*. London, UK: Taylor & Francis.

Palmer, E. (2010, December 2). WikiLeaks backup plan could drop diplomatic bomb. *CBS Online*. Retrieved May 8, 2011, from http://www.cbsnews.com/stories/2010/12/02/eveningnews/main7111845.shtml

Patel, S., d'Cruz, C., & Burra, S. (2002). Beyond evictions in a global city: People-managed resettlement in Mumbai. *Environment and Urbanization*, *14*(1), 159–172. doi:10.1177/095624780201400113

Pawley, M. (1997). *Terminal architecture*. London, UK: Reaktion Books.

Peck, F. (1996). Regional development and the production of space: The role of infrastructure in the attraction of new inward investment. *Regional Studies*, *28*, 327–339.

Peckham, S., Exworthy, M., Greener, I., & Powell, M. (2005). Decentralizing health services: More local accountability or just more central control? *Public Money and Management*, *25*(4), 221–228. doi:10.1111/j.1467-9302.2005.00477.x

Peirce, C. S. (1931-35). In Hartshorne, C., & Weiss, P. (Eds.), *Collected papers of Charles Sanders Peirce* (*Vol. I-VI*). Cambridge, MA: Harvard University Press.

Peirce, C. S. (1958). *Collected papers of Charles Sanders Peirce* (Burks, A. W., Ed.). *Vol. VII-VIII*). Cambridge, MA: Harvard University Press.

Penney, T. M. (2005). Letter: Challenges to implementing NPfIT: Clinicians are becoming increasingly more influential. *British Medical Journal*, *331*, 516. doi:10.1136/bmj.331.7515.516-a

Perrons, D. (2004). *Globalisation and social change: People and places in a divided world*. New York, NY: Routledge.

Perrow, C. (1999). *Normal accidents: Living with high risk technologies*. Princeton, NJ: Princeton University Press.

Perry, D. (1995). *Building the public city: The politics, governance and finance of public infrastructure*. London, UK: Sage.

Persaud, B. (1992). Foreward. In Christopher, A., Cavendish, W., & Mistry, P. S. (Eds.), *Adjusting privatization: Case studies from developing countries*. London, UK: James Currey.

Pettigrew, A. M. (1985). Contextualist research and the study of organizational change processes. In Mumford, E. (Ed.), *Research methods in information systems* (pp. 53–78). Amsterdam, The Netherlands: Elsevier Science.

Pillay, N. (2010, December 9). UN High Commissioner for human rights Navi Pillay voices concern at reports of pressure being exerted on private companies to halt financial or internet services for WikiLeaks. *UN TV*. Retrieved May 8, 2011, from http://www.unmultimedia.org/tv/unifeed/d/16541.html

Piven, B. (2010, December 17). Copycat WikiLeaks sites make waves. *Al Jazeera English.* Retrieved May 8, 2011, from http://english.aljazeera.net/indepth/featur es/2010/12/20101216194828514847.html

Platt, C. (2000). Re-energizer. *Wired,* 114-30.

Polski, M. (2003). *The invisible hands of U.S. commercial banking reform: Private action and public guarantees.* Boston, MA: Kluwer Academic. doi:10.1007/978-1-4615-0441-2

Pool, I. (1983). *Technologies of freedom.* Cambridge, MA: Harvard University Press.

Poundstone, W. (1992). *Prisoner's dilemma.* New York, NY: Doubleday.

Power, M. (1999). *The audit society: Rituals of verification.* Oxford, UK: Oxford University Press.

Puri, S. K., & Sahay, S. (2003). Participation through communicative action: A case study of GIS for addressing land/water development in India. *Information Technology for Development, 10,* 179–199. doi:10.1002/itdj.1590100305

Putnam, L. (1996). Situating the author and text. *Journal of Management Inquiry, 5,* 382–386. doi:10.1177/105649269654013

Putnam, R. D. (1993). *Making democracy work.* Princeton, NJ: Princeton University Press.

Quarmby, B. (2009). Pirates among the Second Life islands–Why you should monitor the misuse of your intellectual property in online virtual worlds. *Cardozo Arts & Entertainment Law Journal, 26,* 667–694.

Ramiller, N. C., Swanson, E. B., & Wang, P. (2008). Research directions in information systems: Toward an institutional ecology. *Journal of the Association for Information Systems, 9*(1), 1–22.

Randall, D., & Cooper, C. (2010, December 5). WikiLeaks hit by new online onslaught. *The Independent.* Retrieved May 8, 2011, from http://www.independent. co.uk/news/world/politics/wikileaks-hit-by-new-online-onslaught-2151570.html

Raymond, E. S. (2001). *The cathedral and the bazaar: Musings on Linux and open source by an accidental revolutionary.* Sebastopol, CA: O'Reilly.

Reich, R. (1992). *The work of nations.* New York, NY: Simon & Schuster.

Rheingold, H. (1993). *The virtual community: Homesteading on the electric frontier.* New York, NY: Addison-Wesley.

Ribot, J. C. (2002). *Democratic decentralization of natural resources: Institutionalizing popular Participation.* Washington, DC: World Resources Institute.

Rider, G. (1999, April 30). Watershed. *Utility Week,* 16-18.

Ritter, T. (2010, February 10). Fujitsu settlement of NPfIT dispute unlikely in next year, says Cerner. *Computer Weekly.com.* Retrieved February 18, 2011, from http://www.computerweekly.com/blogs/public-sector/2010/02/fujitsu-settlement-of-npfit-di.html

Robinson, W. (2001). Social theory and globalization: The rise of a transnational state. *Theory and Society, 30*(2), 157–200. doi:10.1023/A:1011077330455

Rodrigues, M. J. (2002). Introduction for a European strategy at the turn of the century. In Rodrigues, M. J. (Ed.), *The new knowledge economy in Europe* (pp. 1–27). Cheltenham, UK: Edward Elgar.

Rolland, K. H., & Monteiro, E. (2002). Balancing the local and the global in infrastructural information systems. *The Information Society, 18*(2), 87–100. doi:10.1080/01972240290075020

Rolland, K. H., & Monteiro, E. (2007). When 'perfect' integration leads to increasing risks: The case of an integrated information system in a global company. In Hanseth, O., & Ciborra, C. (Eds.), *Risk, complexity and ICT* (pp. 97–117). London, UK: Edward Elgar.

Rose, M. (1995). *Cities of lights and heat: Domesticating gas and electricity in urban America.* University Park, PA: University of Pennsylvania Press.

Roth, G. (1987). *The private provision of public services in developing countries.* New York, NY: Oxford University Press.

Rusovan, S., Lawford, M., & Parnas, D. L. (2005). Open source software development: Future or fad? In Feller, J., Fitzgerald, B., Hissam, S., & Lakhani, K. (Eds.), *Perspectives on free and open source software* (pp. 107–122). Cambridge, MA: MIT Press.

Rybczynski, W. (1983). *Taming the tiger: The struggle to control technology*. New York, NY: Penguin.

Rynes, S. L., Bartunek, J. M., & Daft, R. L. (2001). Across the great divide: Knowledge creation and transfer between practitioners and academics. *Academy of Management Journal, 44*, 340–356. doi:10.2307/3069460

Safran, C., Bloomrosen, M., Hammond, M., Labkoff, S., Markel-Fox, S., Tang, P., & Detmer, D. (2007). Toward a national framework for the secondary use of health data: An American Medical Informatics Association white paper. *Journal of the American Medical Informatics Association, 14*(1), 1–9. doi:10.1197/jamia.M2273

Sahay, S., Monteiro, E., & Aanestad, M. (2009). Configurable politics and asymmetric integration: Health e-infrastructures in India. *Journal of the Association for Information Systems, 10*(5), 399–414.

Sambamurthy, V., & Zmud, R. (1999). Arrangements for information technology governance: A theory of multiple contingencies. *Management Information Systems Quarterly, 23*(2), 261–290. doi:10.2307/249754

Samuelson, P. (2003). Digital rights management {and, or, vs.} the law. *Communications of the ACM, 46*(4), 41–55. doi:10.1145/641205.641229

Samuelson, P. A. (1954). The pure theory of public expenditure. *The Review of Economics and Statistics, 36*(4), 387–389. doi:10.2307/1925895

Sancho, D. (2002). European national platforms for the development of the information society. In Jordana, J. (Ed.), *Governing telecommunications and the information society in Europe* (pp. 202–227). Cheltenham, UK: Edward Elgar.

Sandler, T. (2008). Treaties: Strategic considerations. *Illinois Law Review, 1*, 155–180.

Sassen, S. (2000). Spatialities and temporalities of the global: Elements for a theorization. *Public Culture, 12*(1), 215–232. doi:10.1215/08992363-12-1-215

Sassen, S. (2001). *The global city* (2nd ed.). Princeton, NJ: Princeton University Press.

Satter, R. G., & Svensson, P. (2010, December 3). WikiLeaks fights to stay online amid attacks. *Associated Press*. Retrieved May 8, 2011, from http://www.businessweek.com/ap/financialnews/D9JSHKUG0.htm

Saunders, C. S., & Jones, J. W. (1992). Measuring performance of the information systems function. *Journal of Management Information Systems, 8*(4), 63–82.

Savage, C. (2010, December 1). U.S. weighs prosecution of WikiLeaks founder, but legal scholars warn of steep hurdles. *The New York Times*. Retrieved April 28, 2011, from http://www.nytimes.com/2010/12/02/world/02legal.html

Schachter, H. L., & Aliaga, M. (2003). Educating administrators to interact with citizens: A research note. *Public Organization Review, 3*(2), 191–200. doi:10.1023/A:1024292931120

Schlager, E., & Ostrom, E. (1992). Property rights regimes and natural resources: A conceptual analysis. *Land Economics, 68*(3), 249–262. doi:10.2307/3146375

Schneider, G., & Aspinwall, M. (Eds.). (2001). *The rules of integration: The institutionalist approach to the study of Europe*. Manchester, UK: European Policy Research Unit Series, Manchester University Press.

Schroth, C., & Christ, O. (2007). Brave new Web: Emerging design principles and technologies as enablers of a global SOA. In *Proceedings of the IEEE International Conference on Services Computing, (SCC 2007)*, 597-604.

Schuler, D., & Namioka, A. (Eds.). (1993). *Participatory design: Principles and practices*. Hillsdale, NJ: Erlbaum.

Schweik, C. M. (2005, June). An institutional analysis approach to studying libre software commons. *Ugrade: The European Journal for the Informatics Professional*, 17-27.

Schweik, C. M., & Semenov, A. (2003). The institutional design of open source programming. *First Monday, 8*(1). Retrieved September 11, 2011, from www.firstmonday.org.

Schweik, C. M. (2007). Free/open-source software as a framework for establishing commons in science. In Hess, C., & Ostrom, E. (Eds.), *Understanding knowledge as a commons: From theory to practice* (pp. 277–310). Cambridge, MA: MIT Press.

Scott, J. (1998). *Seeing like a state: How certain schemes to improve the human condition have failed.* New Haven, CT: Yale University Press.

Shaikh, M., & Cornford, T. (2003). Version management tools: CVS to BK in the Linux kernel. In J. Feller, B. Fitzgerald, S. Hissam, & Lakhani, K. (Eds.), In *Proceedings of ICSE'03 International Conference on Software Engineering.*

Shapiro, C., & Varian, H. R. (1999). *Information rules: A strategic guide to the network economy.* Boston, MA: Harvard Business School Press.

Shapiro, I. (2005). *The flight from reality in the human sciences.* Princeton, NJ: Princeton University Press.

Sheth, A. P., Gomadam, K., & Lathem, J. (2007). SA-REST: Semantically interoperable and easier-to-use services and mashups. *IEEE Internet Computing, 11*(6), 91–94. doi:10.1109/MIC.2007.133

Sigurgrimsdottir, H. (2009, August 4). Iceland court lifts gag order after public outrage. *The Seattle Times.* Retrieved May 1, 2011, from http://seattletimes.nwsource.com/html/nationworld/2009597317_apeuicelandbankoutrage.html

Singer, J. W. (2006). The ownership society and takings of property: Castles, investments, and just obligations. *The Harvard Environmental Law Review, 30,* 309–338.

Singh, P.D. (2006). Slum population in Mumbai. *ENVIS Bulletin, 3*(1).

Sissouras, A., & Souliotis, K. (Eds.). (2002). *Health, health care and welfare in Greece.* Greek Ministry of Health and Welfare and the Athens Office of the European Observatory on Health Care Systems.

Siy, R. Y. Jr. (1982). *Community resource management.* Quezon City, Philippines: University of the Philippines Press.

Skalkidis, P. (1998). Implementation of a hospital information system in a Greek university hospital. In Iakovidis, I. (Eds.), *User acceptance of health telematics applications* (pp. 62–68). Amsterdam, Netherlands: IOS Press.

Sleeman, J. (1953). *British public utilities.* London, UK: Pitman.

Snell, R. S. (1996). Complementing Kohlberg: Mapping the ethical reasoning used by managers for their own dilemma cases. *Human Relations, 49*(1), 23–49. doi:10.1177/001872679604900102

Snyder, W., & Briggs, X. (2003). *Communities of practice: A new tool for government managers.* Washington, DC: IBM Center for the Business of Government.

Somaiya, R. (2010, December 5). Hundreds of WikiLeaks mirror sites appear. *The New York Times.* Retrieved May 1, 2011, from http://www.nytimes.com/2010/12/06/world/europe/06wiki.html

Sotiriou, A. (1998). Towards user acceptance of telemedicine services. In Iakovidis, I. (Eds.), *User acceptance of health telematics applications* (pp. 177–181). Amsterdam, Netherlands: IOS Press.

Spohrer, J., & Riecken, D. (2006). Services science. *Communications of the ACM, 49*(7), 31–32.

Stahl, B. (2008). Discourses on information ethics: The claim to universality. *Ethics and Information Technology, 10*(2), 97–108. doi:10.1007/s10676-008-9171-9

Stallman, R. (1999). The GNU operating system and the free software movement. In DiBona, C., Ockman, S., & Stone, M. (Eds.), *Open sources: Voices from the open source revolution.* Sebastopol, CA: O'Reilly. doi:10.1109/ICSM.2006.68

Stansfield, S., Orobaton, N., Lubinski, D., Uggowitzer, S., & Mwanyika, H. (2008). The case for a national health information system architecture: A missing link to guiding national development and implementation. Paper presented at the *Making the ehealth connection,* Bellagio, Italy, July 13–August 8, 2008.

Starkey, K., & Madan, P. (2001). Bridging the relevance gap: Aligning stakeholders in the future of management research. *British Journal of Management, 12,* 3–26. doi:10.1111/1467-8551.12.s1.2

Star, R. L., & Bowker, G. (2002). How to infrastructure. In Lievrouw, L. A., & Livingstone, S. (Eds.), *Handbook of new media: Social shaping and consequences of ICTs* (pp. 151–162). London, UK: Sage.

Star, S. L. (1995). Introduction. In Star, S. L. (Ed.), *Ecologies of knowledge: Work and politics in science and technology* (pp. 1–35). New York, NY: State University of New York Press.

Star, S. L. (1999). The ethnography of infrastructure. *The American Behavioral Scientist, 43*(3), 377–391. doi:10.1177/00027649921955326

Star, S. L. (2002). Infrastructure and ethnographic practice: Working on the fringes. *Scandinavian Journal of Information Systems, 14*(2), 107–122.

Star, S. L., & Griesemer, J. R. (1989). Institutional ecology, 'translations' and boundary objects: Amateurs and professionals in Berkeley's museum of vertebrate zoology, 1907-39. *Social Studies of Science, 19*(3), 387–420. doi:10.1177/030631289019003001

Star, S. L., & Ruhleder, K. (1996). Steps toward an ecology of infrastructure: Design and access for large information spaces. *Information Systems Research, 7*(1), 111–134. doi:10.1287/isre.7.1.111

Star, S.-L. (1999). The ethnography of infrastructure. *The American Behavioral Scientist, 43*(3), 377–391. doi:10.1177/00027649921955326

Strauss, A. Y. (2002). A constitutional crisis in the digital age: Why the FBI's 'Carnivore' does not defy the Fourth Amendment. *Cardozo Arts and Entertainment Law Journal, 20*, 231–258.

Suarez-Villa, L., & Walrod, W. (1999). Losses from the Northridge earthquake: Disruptions to high-technology industries in the Los Angeles basin. *Disasters, 21*(1), 19–44. doi:10.1111/1467-7717.00103

Suggs, R. E. (1989). *Minorities and privatization: Economic mobility at risk.* Washington, DC: Joint Center for Political Studies.

Summerton, J. (1999). Power plays: The politics of interlinking systems. In Coutard, O. (Ed.), *The governance of large technical systems* (pp. 93–113). London, UK: Routledge.

Summerton, J. (Ed.). (1994). *Changing large technical systems.* Boulder, CO: Westview Press.

Sunstein, C. R. (2002). *Republic.com.* Princeton, NJ: Princeton University Press.

Susskind, L., & Hoben, M. (2004). Making regional policy dialogues work: A credo for metro-scale consensus building. *Temple Environmental Law Journal, 22*(2), 123–140.

Swyngedouw, E. (1997). Neither global nor local: "Glocalisation" and the politics of scale. In K. Cox (Ed.), *Spaces of globalization: Reasserting the power of the local.* New York, NY: Guilford/Longman.

Swyngedouw, E. (1992). Glocalization, interspatial competition and the monetary order: The construction of new scales. In Dunford, M., & Kafkalas, G. (Eds.), *Cities and regions in the New Europe.* London, UK: Belhaven Press.

Tapscott, D., & Williams, A. (2008). *Wikinomics: How mass collaboration changes everything.* London, UK: Atlantic Books.

Tarr, J., & Dupuy, G. (Eds.), *Technology and the rise of the networked city in Europe and North America.* Philadelphia, PA: Temple University Press.

Tauxe, C. (1995). Marginalizing public participation in planning. *Journal of the American Planning Association. American Planning Association, 61*(4), 471–482. doi:10.1080/01944369508975658

Taylor, M. (2003). *Public policy in the community.* Houndmills, UK: Palgrave Macmillan.

Taylor, P. (1994). The state as container: Territoriality in the modern world-system. *Progress in Human Geography, 18*(2), 151–162. doi:10.1177/030913259401800202

Taylor, S. (1987). *The possibility of cooperation.* Cambridge, UK: Cambridge University Press.

Theodorou, M., Sarris, M., & Soulis, S. (1995). *Health systems and the Greek reality.* Athens, Greece: Papazizis. (in Greek)

Thompson, T. G., & Brailer, D. J. (2004). *The decade of health information technology: Delivering consumer-centric and information-rich health care: Framework for strategic action.* Washington, DC: U.S. Department of Health and Human Services.

Thrift, N. (2000). Performing cultures in the new economy. *Annals of the Association of American Geographers. Association of American Geographers, 4*, 674–692. doi:10.1111/0004-5608.00217

Tountas, S. W. (2003). Carnivore: Is the regulation of wireless technology a legally viable option to curtail the growth of cybercrime? *Washington University Journal of Law and Policy*, *11*, 351–377.

Tountas, Y., Karnaki, P., & Pavi, E. (2002). Reforming the reform: The Greek national health system in transition. *Health Policy (Amsterdam)*, *62*(1), 15–29. doi:10.1016/S0168-8510(01)00217-2

Traynor, M. (1996). A literary approach to managerial discourse after the NHS Reforms. *Sociology of Health & Illness*, *18*(3), 315–340. doi:10.1111/1467-9566.ep10934667

Tsoukas, H. (2005). *Complex knowledge: Studies in organizational epistemology*. Oxford, UK: Oxford University Press.

Tully, J. (1993). Governing conduct: Locke on the reform of thought and behavior. In Tully, J. (Ed.), *An approach to political philosophy* (pp. 179–241). Cambridge, UK: Cambridge University Press. doi:10.1017/CBO9780511607882.007

Turkle, S. (1995). *Life on the screen: Identity in the age of the Internet*. New York, NY: Simon and Schuster.

Turkle, S. (2005). *The second self: Computers and the human spirit*. Cambridge, MA: MIT Press.

Turkle, S. (2006). Always-on/always-on-you: The tethered self. In Katz, J. E. (Ed.), *Handbook of mobile communication studies* (pp. 121–138). Cambridge, MA: MIT Press.

Turner, W., Bowker, G., Gasser, L., & Zackland, M. (2006). Information infrastructures for distributed collective practices. *Computer Supported Cooperative Work*, *15*(2-3), 1–18. doi:10.1007/s10606-006-9014-3

U.S. Congress. (2010). Patient protection and affordable care act. *111th Congress United States, Federal Statute*, HR 3590. Retrieved November 20, 2012, from http://burgess.house.gov/UploadedFiles/hr3590_health_care_law_2010.pdf

U.S. Department of Health and Human Services (US DHHS). (2005). *Summary of nationwide health information network (NHIN) request for information (RFI) responses*. Washington, DC: U.S. Department of Health and Human Services Office of the National Coordinator for Health Information Technology.

Ungerleider, N. (2011, February 16). Leaked emails: Anti-WikiLeaks security firm targeted journalists. *Fast Company*. Retrieved May 9, 2011, from http://www.fastcompany.com/1728259/leaked-emails-anti-wikileaks-security-firm-targeted-journalists

Van House. N. A. (2003). Science and technology studies and information studies. In B. Cronin (Ed.), *Annual review of information science and technology 38,* (pp. 3-86). Medford, NJ: Information Today.

Vargo, S. L., & Lusch, R. E. (2004). Evolving to a new dominant logic for marketing. *Journal of Marketing*, *68*(1), 1–17. doi:10.1509/jmkg.68.1.1.24036

Ventura, H., Mitchell, M., & Deflem, M. (2005). Governmentality and the war on terror: FBI project Carnivore and the diffusion of disciplinary power. *Critical Criminology*, *13*(1), 55–70. doi:10.1007/s10612-004-6167-6

Vickery, G., & Wunsch-Vincent, S. (2007). *Participative web and user-created content: Web 2.0, wikis and social networking*. Paris, France: OECD Publishing.

Von Simson, E. M. (1990, July-August). The centrally decentralized IS organization. *Harvard Business Review*, 158–162.

Wade, R. (1994). *Village republics: Economic conditions for collective action in South India*. Oakland, CA: ICS Press.

Waldron, J. (1993). From authors to copiers: Individual rights and social values in intellectual property. *Chicago-Kent Law Review*, *68*, 841–850.

Walsham, G. (1993). *Interpreting information systems in organizations*. Chichester, UK: John Wiley & Sons.

Walsham, G. (1995). Interpretive case studies in IS research: Nature and method. *European Journal of Information Systems*, *4*(2), 74–81. doi:10.1057/ejis.1995.9

Walsham, G. (2001). Knowledge management: The benefits and limitations of computer systems. *European Management Journal*, *19*(6), 599–608. doi:10.1016/S0263-2373(01)00085-8

Wang, P., & Ramiller, N. C. (2009). Community learning in IT innovation. *Management Information Systems Quarterly*, *33*(4), 709–734.

Ward, V. (2010, December 3). WikiLeaks website disconnected as U.S. company withdraws support. *The Daily Telegraph*. Retrieved May 8, 2011, from http://www.telegraph.co.uk/news/worldnews/wikileaks/8178457/WikiLeaks-website-disconnected-as-US-company-withdraws-support.html

Weber, S. (2004). *The success of open source*. Cambridge, MA: Harvard University Press.

Webster, S. C. (2010, December 7). MasterCard, Visa shut down electronic donations to WikiLeaks. *The Raw Story*. Retrieved May 8, 2011, from http://www.rawstory.com/rs/2010/12/07/mastercard-shuts-donations-wikileaks-calling-site-illegal/

Weill, P. (1992). The relationship between investment in information technology and firm performance: A study of the valve manufacturing sector. *Information Systems Research*, *3*(4), 307–333. doi:10.1287/isre.3.4.307

Weill, P., & Broadbent, M. (1998). *Leveraging the new infrastructure: How market leaders capitalize on information*. Boston, MA: Harvard Business School Press.

Weill, P., & Ross, J. (2004). *IT governance: How top performers manage IT decision rights for superior results*. Boston, MA: Harvard Business School Press.

Weinstock, C. B., & Hissam, S. A. (2005). Making lightning strike twice. In Feller, J., Fitzgerald, B., Hissam, S., & Lakhani, K. (Eds.), *Perspectives on free and open source software* (pp. 143–160). Cambridge, MA: MIT Press.

Whiteman, J. (1990). Responding to Fritz: On disarming words and pictures in the telling of teleological stories. In Angeli, M. (Ed.), *On architecture, the city and technology* (pp. 26–32). Washington, DC: Butterworth.

WikiLeaks website (2008, April 19). *WikiLeaks' submissions page*. (archived from the original). Retrieved May 8, 2011, from http://classic-web.archive.org/web/20080419013425/http:/www.wikileaks.org/wiki/Wikileaks:Submissions

WikiLeaks website (2011). *WikiLeaks' main page*. Retrieved May 8, 2011, from http://www.wikileaks.ch/

Willcocks, L. P., & Lester, S. (1999). *Beyond the IT productivity paradox: Assessment issues*. Chichester, UK: John Wiley & Sons.

Williamson, A., & Fung, A. (2005). Public deliberation: Where are we? Where can we go? *National Civic Review*, *93*(4), 3–15. doi:10.1002/ncr.66

Williamson, O. E. (2002). The theory of the firm as governance structure: From choice to contract. *The Journal of Economic Perspectives*, *16*(3), 171–195. doi:10.1257/089533002760278776

Wilson, J. A., Acheson, J., Metcalfe, M., & Kleban, P. (1994). Chaos, complexity, and community management of fisheries. *Marine Policy*, *18*, 291–305. doi:10.1016/0308-597X(94)90044-2

Winner, L. (1980). Do artifacts have politics? *Daedalus*, *109*(1), 121–136.

Winner, L. (1993). Upon opening the black box and finding it empty: Social constructivism and the philosophy of technology. *Science, Technology & Human Values*, *18*(3), 362–378. doi:10.1177/016224399301800306

Winsbury, R. (1997). How grand are the grand alliances? *Intermedia*, *25*(3), 26–31.

Womack, J. P., Jones, D. T., & Roos, D. (1991). *The machine that changed the world: The story of lean production*. New York, NY: HarperCollins.

Young, O. R. (2002). Institutional interplay: The environmental consequences of cross-scale interactions. In Ostrom, E., Dietz, T., Dolšak, N., Stern, P. C., Stonich, S., & Weber, E. U. (Eds.), *The drama of the commons* (pp. 263–291). Washington, DC: National Academy Press.

Yu, J., Benatallah, B., Casati, F., & Daniel, F. (2008, September-October). Understanding mashup development. *IEEE Internet Computing*, *13*(5), 44–52. doi:10.1109/MIC.2008.114

About the Author

Panos Constantinides is Assistant Professor of Management Information Systems at Frederick University`s Business School. Before joining Frederick University, Panos held positions at Lancaster University`s Management School and the Judge Business School at the University of Cambridge, where he also earned his Ph.D. Panos has previously worked on research projects on the development and implementation of healthcare-related IT, in association with IBM (UK), BT Health (UK), Synbiotix (UK & Cyprus), and the Institute of Computer Science at the Foundation for Research and Technology Hellas (Greece). He is interested in the negotiation of collective action problems around the development of information infrastructures such as public and corporate IT networks, as well as Web 2.0 technologies. He is also interested in professional and research ethics. Panos has recently joined a group of researchers from different disciplines to initiate a new model of open innovation through an online platform (www.idea-talk.org). Building on the commons perspective discussed in this book, IdeaTalk offers an online commons whereby different individuals can communicate directly with each other and with commercial organizations to research, develop, and fund the projects they are interested in.

Index